Dante Gabriel Rossetti Revisited

Twayne's English Authors Series

Herbert Sussman, Editor

Northeastern University

TEAS 495

DANTE GABRIEL ROSSETTI
Self Portrait, 1861
Photographed by the City of Birmingham Museum & Art Gallery
Reproduced by permission of Birmingham City Council, Museum & Art Gallery

Dante Gabriel Rossetti Revisited

David G. Riede

Ohio State University

Twayne Publishers • New York
Maxwell Macmillan Canada • Toronto
Maxwell Macmillan International • New York Oxford Singapore Sydney

Dante Gabriel Rossetti Revisited
David G. Riede

Twayne Publishers   Maxwell Macmillan Canada, Inc.
Macmillan Publishing Company   1200 Eglinton Avenue East
866 Third Avenue   Suite 200
New York, New York 10022   Don Mills, Ontario M3C 3N1

Macmillan Publishing Company is part of the Maxwell Communication Group
of Companies.

Library of Congress Cataloging-in-Publication Data

Riede, David G.
    Dante Gabriel Rossetti revisited / by David G. Riede.
        p.   cm.—(Twayne's English authors series)
    Includes bibliographical references and index.
    ISBN 0-8057-7027-5 :
    1. Rossetti, Dante Gabriel, 1828–1882—Criticism and
interpretation. I. Title. II. Series.
    PR5247.R5   1992
    821'.8—dc20   92-8848
                                             CIP

The paper used in this publication meets the minimum requirements
of American National Standard for Information Sciences—Permanence
of Paper for Printed Library Materials. ANSI Z3948-1984. ∞™

10 9 8 7 6 5 4 3 2 1

Printed in the United States of America

Contents

Illustrations

Preface

In recent years Dante Gabriel Rossetti has come to be increasingly highly regarded as a painter by art historians, by collectors (at least if the prices fetched by his work are any guide), and by the general public—posters and postcards of his paintings abound, and reproductions of his pictures even adorn one of the sound stages of the popular television show "Saturday Night Live." As a poet he has not fared as well. Though he retains his place as a "canonical" writer of the Victorian age, he is generally accorded only a few pages in modern anthologies, and is recognized as a distinctly minor poet compared to some of his contemporaries, especially Tennyson, Robert Browning, Arnold and, increasingly, Christina Rossetti and Elizabeth Barrett Browning. Yet in the late nineteenth century he was considered a painter of importance, and even more emphatically, as a poet of the highest order. Some of his most illustrious contemporaries regarded him as nothing less than their "master," a sublimely inspired genius, an example of the highest kind of artistic aspiration and achievement. He was, in short, a legend in his own time.

My intention in this study is both to present a general introduction to Rossetti's works as poet and painter, and to offer a reappraisal of his achievement. I will not argue that he ought to be more highly regarded today than he is, but rather will examine his poetry and painting in its historical setting and explore the ways in which the Rossetti legend grew and the reasons why his work had such extraordinary appeal to the other artists and critics of his time. In general, I will argue that the Rossetti legend involved an extreme idealization of the artistic or imaginative "genius," and of the devotion of the artist to his art as a kind of high spiritual vocation. Both in his works and in his own contributions to and cultivation of the cult of his own genius, Rossetti helped to establish a new belief in the autonomy of art and the necessary isolation of the artist from his society. Ironically, it is when he is judged by the dubious standards of a pure or transcendent art that his poetry is often found inadequate—or, at any rate, relatively minor. What I hope to show is that placing Rossetti's painting and poetry back in the social context from which he assiduously attempted to divorce it results in a fuller, more compelling understanding of his achievement, and of his significance as a kind of representative Victorian *malgré lui,* than we can achieve by simply accepting and assessing him on his own terms, the terms of a romantic idealization of art and the artist that he helped to propagate.

Acknowledgments

I am grateful to the Birmingham City Council Museums and Art Gallery for permission to reproduce the Rossetti *Self Portrait,* and to the Tate Gallery for permission to reproduce *Ecce Ancilla Domini!, The Girlhood of Mary Virgin, Beata Beatrix, The Passover in the Holy Family: Gathering Bitter Herbs,* and *The Beloved.* I would also like to thank Herbert Sussman for his helpful comments on the manuscript, and Colleen Romick Hammers for invaluable research and editorial assistance.

Chronology

1828   Born 12 May, at No. 38, Charlotte Street, Portland Place, London, to Gabriele and Frances Polidori Rossetti.

1836   Begins school at Mr. Paul's day school, Portland Place.

1837–1842   Attends King's College School.

1842–1846   Attends Cary's Academy of Art.

1846–1847   Attends Royal Academy Antique School.

1847   Begins brief apprenticeship and lifelong friendship with Ford Madox Brown.

1848   Joins with William Holman Hunt, John Everett Millais, James Collinson, Thomas Woolner, Frederic Stephens, and William Rossetti to form the Pre-Raphaelite Brotherhood.

1849   First exhibited picture, *The Girlhood of Mary Virgin,* at the Free Exhibition in London.

1850   Exhibits *Ecce Ancilla Domini!* (later renamed *The Annunciation*) at the National Institution.

1857   Joins with William Morris, Edward Jones (later Burne-Jones), and others to paint murals in the Oxford Union. Meets Jane Burden (later Jane Morris) and Algernon Swinburne at Oxford.

1860   Marries Elizabeth Siddall.

1861   Publishes *The Early Italian Poets.*

1862   Death of Elizabeth Siddall from an overdose of laudanum. Rossetti buries his manuscript poems in her coffin.

1869   Exhumes the poems in preparation to publish a volume of verse.

1870   Publishes *Poems.*

1871   Severely criticized on moral grounds in Robert Buchanan's "The Fleshly School of Poetry: Mr. D. G. Rossetti," and responds with "The Stealthy School of Criticism."

1872 Suffers a mental and physical breakdown following publication of Buchanan's attack in an enlarged pamphlet form.

1874 Republishes *The Early Italian Poets* as *Dante and His Circle*.

1881 Publishes *Ballads and Sonnets*.

1882 Dies at Birchington, Kent, 9 April.

Chapter One

Rossetti and the Rossetti Legend

Dante Gabriel Rossetti has been variously characterized as an Italian Englishman, a painter-poet, a Pre-Raphaelite Victorian, and a Victorian romantic. The labels, though somewhat self-contradictory, suggest that the critical tradition has managed to pin him down, to define the quintessential Rossetti. The generally accepted quintessence of Rossetti was distilled early in the critical tradition, and is perhaps best described in an appreciative essay by another "Victorian romantic," Walter Pater. According to Pater, Rossetti's distinctive achievement, his most significant contribution to the art of his day, was the careful and minute recording of his own inner self, his own soul. As Pater put it, Rossetti's "characteristic, his really revealing work, lay in the adding to poetry of fresh poetic material, of a new order of phenomena, in the creation of a new ideal," the extraordinarily accurate transcription of "certain wonderful things he really felt and saw."[1] The themes and subjects of Rossetti's work, however, these "wonderful things," are not found so much in the world without as in the world within: "His own meaning was always personal and even recondite" (229), and the representation of his intensely personal moments was always "the just transcript of that peculiar phase of soul which he alone knew, precisely as he knew it" (230). For Pater and for the long critical tradition that has followed, Rossetti's greatness as an artist was his ability to transcribe with extraordinary sincerity and precision his own soul, but the source of his greatness was that soul itself, the soul of a man of genius who lived life intensely, and drew on the experiences of a life lived as "a crisis at every moment" (235).

Rossetti's own versions of his achievement, though appropriately modest, give ample warrant for Pater's. All his life he was particularly concerned that his work be recognized as original and sincere—as he once recorded in a notebook, "I was one of those whose little is their own."[2] And as we shall see, his poetry and, less directly, his painting are overtly and repeatedly concerned with issues of self-expression, of

I

the artistic endeavor to record an intensely personal dream. Indeed, so true is this that commentators have repeatedly, and with some justice, cited the words of a speaker from a prose sketch of a never completed poem entitled "The Orchard Pit" as though they were Rossetti's own: "Men tell me that sleep has many dreams; but all my life I have dreamt one dream alone" (*Works*, 607). Not surprisingly, most critics of Rossetti's work have attempted to elucidate that dream, usually by reference to the biographical facts of Rossetti's life, but this critical process has scarcely done justice to the diversity of Rossetti's work, or the complexity of his relations with his age. A fuller understanding of both the poetry and the painting can be achieved by recognizing that the traditional critical formulations rest upon a number of romantic assumptions about art and the artist, and by examining the ways in which these assumptions and other mid-Victorian beliefs and circumstances affected Rossetti's practices as both poet and painter.

The notions of originality, of genius, even of artistic sincerity that prevailed in Rossetti's day led him to conceptualize his artistic career and even his personal identity in certain ways. As an aspiring poet and painter nurtured on the writings of, among others, Byron, Shelley, Keats, Coleridge, Blake, Poe, and the young Robert Browning, Rossetti inherited an idea of the artistic sensibility as somehow living apart from society, drawing upon its own resources for aesthetic sustenance. The poet was a special order of being, and his one duty was to be true to his own inner vision—like the Poet of Shelley's *Alastor*, or like Keats's Endymion, or the lover of Browning's *Pauline*, and indeed, like the protagonist of Rossetti's own early prose tale, "Hand and Soul." Yet Rossetti was well aware that, as the example of Shelley's Poet makes especially clear, the pursuit of a too intensely personal vision may lead to narcissism, solipsism, and ruin. His poetry and painting alike tend to conflate the Shelleyan ideal of the soul within the soul with visionary beauty but also with death, and a notebook entry records his awareness of the danger of exclusively introspective vision: "Seek thine ideal anywhere except in thyself. Once fix it there, and the ways of thy real self will matter nothing to thee, whose eyes can rest on the ideal already perfected" (*Works*, 607). Still, the danger adds a kind of tragic luster to the visionary quest, a kind of morbid attraction, as it makes the figure of the artist more distinctively singled out from society than ever—even if, like Coleridge's Ancient Mariner, he is a tragic figure, singled out more by a curse than a blessing.

Rossetti was actually far more than the introspective, brooding dreamer of the critical tradition. His early work, especially, represents diverse approaches and dramatic perspectives, and many of the ballads written throughout his career were, if anything, *too* objective, *too* impersonal. Nevertheless, he did develop a characteristic style and characteristic themes in both arts, and the persistence of his introspective focus on the subjects of beauty, love, and death supplies abundant material for the critical emphasis on his "one dream." Many of his most distinctive works involved the narcissistic brooding of the self upon the soul, and further, as we shall see, he conceived not only of his protagonists, but at times even of himself, as a version of the introspective romantic visionary. He formulated and propagated a distinctive personal and poetic idea of himself, an idea that involved the peculiar kind of inner vision described by Pater, a strange access to mysterious regions of the soul.

Inevitably the forms of this supposed intensely personal vision were dictated in very large measure by the tastes and conditions of the age, but for Rossetti, despite his unpretentious and robust geniality as a young man, unquestioned romantic assumptions about individual creative genius led to an oddly exaggerated differentiation of himself from others, and for both his contemporaries and subsequent commentators, it led to the construction of a kind of Rossetti legend based on romantic interpretations of both his works and his life. The Rossetti legend, a tale of innate genius not quite at home in a mundane world, was promoted in Rossetti's own lifetime by himself and by the many fellow writers and painters who admired his works and were drawn to his powerful personality. Comments by such contemporaries as John Ruskin, William Morris, Edward Burne-Jones, Algernon Swinburne, and George Meredith promoted the idea of Rossetti's uniquely individual genius. A seemingly absurd comment by the blind poet Philip Bourke Marston in 1873 fairly accurately described the feelings of most of Rossetti's associates: "What a supreme man is Rossetti! Why is he not some great exiled king, that we might give our lives in trying to restore him to his kingdom?"[3] But it was the posthumous accounts, the glut of biographical and anecdotal material following his death in 1882, that consolidated the legend of the alienated and tortured man of genius, the unworldly dreamer seeking to materialize in words and colors his one dream alone.

The persistence into the twentieth century of this way of looking at Rossetti becomes obvious from a glance at some of the most influential studies. Critics refer to the external facts of Rossetti's life as "merely incidental accompaniments of his spiritual career,"[4] insist that he was "inspired entirely by his own imagination and hardly at all by outer influences,"[5] and that his "art was not a transformation of an external but of his own internal reality. The reality of his soul was his domain as an artist, his goal was to faithfully portray what was to him: 'The soul's sphere of infinite images.'"[6] Ironically, however, despite the critical insistence that the mere external events of Rossetti's life are relatively insignificant, the overwhelming critical desire to elucidate the inner life, the vision or dream, has resulted in a mass of biographical criticism. Rossetti's poetry and painting have been understood in relation to his life as a man of genius, and his life has been understood by interpreting his works as the "sincere" self-expressive outpourings of imagination.[7]

But as critics have only very recently begun to point out, the emphasis on the artist's life and creativity reinforces the romantic notion that art is spontaneously generated in the crucible of genius, that it is created apart from the influences of its age, and independently of the material conditions of history. Griselda Pollock, speaking of the copious biographical contributions made by Rossetti's brother William, has described some of the effects of romantic accounts of artists: such books secure "an image of the artist as a creative individual who is both amenable to understanding and yet fascinatingly different. The narration of the life is interspersed with those details of the 'difference' of artistic life—sudden deaths, obsessive pursuits, erratic business activities and social hours, unusual dwellings, special languages, coteries and friendships, drugs—which consolidate and distinguish the artistic temperament and life-style."[8] The understanding of aesthetic production in terms of such "difference" exalts the artist for his genius, but at the same time makes him at least faintly ridiculous in his eccentricity, and diminishes the import of work produced in what might either be called splendid isolation from society or, less flatteringly, pointless irrelevance to society. It also obscures the real achievement of the artist, veiling the careful craftsmanship of the poet or painter behind the notion that the finished product is somehow a direct transcript of the soul, not a construct laboriously wrought from the materials at hand.

The result might seem at first to be a removal of the work of art from the mundane, vulgar world of commodity production, but in fact the confusion of the artist's art with his soul ends by making the artist himself a commodity—a Rossetti, for example, does not simply produce paintings, but produces "Rossettis." This critical process is shown very clearly in a characteristic assessment of Rossetti's accomplishment by Arthur C. Benson, who maintained that his art was "the climax of personality; and moreover it was freely recognised by all who knew him best, that his was not a nature which had slowly made the best of and matured one species of excellence, but that his work was only a faint expression of an inner force, and streamed from him like light from the sun" (226). But this praise both discounts Rossetti's craft, and exalts his personality at the expense of his achievement: "those who knew him best always held that the man was infinitely greater than his work, which carelessly and inevitably radiated from him, hurled out from an inner restlessness. The medium in which he worked, whether words or colours, was a hindrance rather than a help to him" (203). Benson also romanticizes Rossetti's specialized production of an artistic commodity, the Rossetti "type," explaining that "It is not that he seems to have narrowed his output deliberately, to have recognised that to work effectively in a world of specialists it is necessary to be a specialist too. One rather feels that this opulent nature is becoming the tool of circumstance; that by deliberately excluding from his life so many wholesome human influences, the character, instead of opening freely like a flower in the free air, is growing like an exotic in the corner of a hothouse" (227).

As William Fredeman has pointed out, emphasis on the personality of the artist rather than on the poems and paintings has too often led to conclusions such as that reached in a recent reassessment, that Rossetti was a "genius whose personality seems somehow greater than his work"—a conclusion that "merely echoes the frustrations of dozens of commentators who, mired in the anecdotal and biographical tradition of the past, take refuge in a view of Rossetti that reduces him to what Waugh calls a 'melancholy old fraud,' a 'mediocrity' of the first order."[9] Paradoxically, a more just estimate of Rossetti can be arrived at by dispensing with the legend of Rossetti as a magnificent genius generating obscurely personal visions from the depths of his soul, and assessing the ways in which his work impressed his contemporaries precisely because it spoke powerfully within the idiom of its time to the concerns of its time.

Yet a brief review of the facts of his life makes it clear why Rossetti's critics have relentlessly pursued the biographical impulse. All the "differences" described by Pollock are manifested, along with a few others. William Rossetti somewhat disingenuously remarked that Rossetti's life was "outwardly uneventful," and it is true enough that for most of his life he lived in quiet artistic retirement. Yet the few major events of his life are almost luridly melodramatic. Even his origins contribute to the romantic cast of his biography. His father, Gabriele Rossetti, was an Italian political refugee, a poet whose verses had forced him into political exile, and subsequently a commentator on the poetry of Dante with a gift for finding (or inventing) arcane and subversive meanings wherever he looked. His mother was the daughter of an Italian expatriate father and an English mother, and, perhaps more to the purposes of the romantic story, the sister of John William Polidori, author of *The Vampyre* and physician to Byron, who once described him as "a young man more likely to contract diseases than to cure them" (Angeli, 11).

The second of four children, Rossetti was born on 12 May 1828 and christened Gabriel Charles Dante (his decision at some point in his late teens to adopt the professional name of Dante Gabriel Rossetti reflects his attempt to define himself, to shape the contours of a personal as well as a professional identity). From childhood, apparently, he was determined to become an artist of some sort—a poet or a painter—and he evidently spent a good deal of time engaged in juvenile artistic pursuits with his talented older sister Maria, his solidly intelligent younger brother William, and his brilliant younger sister, the poet Christina. Despite later legends of his precocity, however, none of Rossetti's surviving juvenile efforts suggest any unusual degree of talent— as he himself once noted with some mortification. Nevertheless, from 1842 to 1846 he attended Cary's Academy of Art, where he seems to have been at best a dilatory student, though apparently his inventiveness won him a small following among his fellow students. From there he went on to the Royal Academy Antique School, where he showed little interest in formal studies and apparently made little progress in what were, evidently, rather tedious exercises.

Although the Antique School did not seem to have much to offer Rossetti in terms of its curriculum, it did offer him companionship with other aspiring artists, including William Holman Hunt and John Everett Millais. In 1848 Rossetti joined with Hunt, Millais, and four lesser talents (including his brother William) to form what they called the Pre-Raphaelite Brotherhood, a band of aspiring artists with the revolutionary desire to overthrow the principles of the current regime at the Royal Academy, but with no very clear principles of their own beyond a rather vague idea of painting with "truth to nature" rather than in slavish adherence to rules of painting derived from the works of Raphael. Though Rossetti contributed a great deal to the Pre-Raphaelite interest in "literary" painting and symbolism, and probably a great deal also to the characteristically linear and angular style of Pre-Raphaelite drawing, he was far less technically proficient as a painter than Hunt and Millais, and it may be argued that his early fame came more as a result of his association with his more advanced brethren than of his own artistic achievements. It was the paintings of Hunt and Millais that were seen at the Royal Academy (Rossetti's only two oil paintings of this period were shown at far less conspicuous exhibitions, and received only moderate attention), and it was the paintings of Hunt and Millais that were reviewed, reviled, eventually championed by Ruskin, and finally praised in a controversy that made a success of Pre-Raphaelitism, the unlikely revolution of exceedingly young artists. It is not surprising that Hunt and Millais resented the notion, widespread by the mid-1850s, that Rossetti was the leader or chief of the Pre-Raphaelite Brotherhood, but whether he strictly merited the title or not, he was, by his midtwenties, recognized as the leader of an influential national movement in painting—though he himself had still not mastered the technical difficulties of painting in oils.

Though Pre-Raphaelitism was, for the most part, a movement in painting, it also, through Rossetti's undisputed leadership, had a strong literary element. The brotherhood not only painted pictures from literary themes, but even produced a short-lived journal entitled the *Germ* that consisted, as its subtitle put it, of *Thoughts towards Nature in Poetry, Literature, and Art.* In what sense the thoughts were "towards Nature" is scarcely clear in most of the contributions, but though it expired after only four issues, the *Germ* did launch Rossetti's career as a writer in 1850 with the publication of "Hand and Soul" in its first issue, and early versions of some of his best-known poems in subsequent issues. Publication of versions of "The Blessed Damozel," "My Sister's Sleep," and some other poems in 1850 may not quite justify the claim that Rossetti had "established himself among the great English poets" by the age of 21 (Mégroz, 96), but it provided some grounds for the legend that he was a prodigy, an untutored genius, and it also was to help him gather around himself a second group of aspiring artists, a group for whom he was the unquestioned leader.

In the early 1850s Rossetti's growing fame attracted the attention of two undergraduates at Oxford, William Morris and Edward Jones (later Burne-Jones), both of whom aspired after a kind of beauty and significance that the modern age seemed to lack. Morris and Jones immersed themselves in the writings of Malory, toured the gothic ca-

thedrals of France, longed vaguely to form a kind of monastic brotherhood of art, and actually did form a group known as the Oxford
Brotherhood. Not surprisingly, they recognized in the Pre-Raphaelite
Brotherhood a model for their own aspirations. They admired the
works of Hunt and Millais in the Royal Academy exhibitions of 1854
and 1855, but they were especially attracted to the works of Rossetti
that they chanced to encounter: the watercolor, *Dante Drawing an Angel*, the illustration of the *Maids of Elfinmere* in William Allingham's
Night and Day Songs, and the writings in the *Germ*. Morris and Jones
sought out Rossetti as their acknowledged master, began a literary
magazine entitled the *Oxford and Cambridge Magazine*, which published
a number of Rossetti's works including "The Burden of Nineveh,"
"The Staff and the Scrip," and a new version of "The Blessed Damozel,"
and in effect became artists at least in part in response to Rossetti's
enthusiastic encouragement.

In 1857, in the famous "jovial campaign," Rossetti, Morris, Jones,
and other artists undertook the project of decorating the Oxford Union
with frescoes—a project that failed utterly in its avowed purpose, since
the artists, oblivious to the technical demands of fresco painting, produced works that soon flaked off the unprepared walls. But in another
sense the project was a sort of success, if only because it brought together a rising group of artists that included not only Rossetti, Morris,
and Jones, but also the young poet Algernon Swinburne, who had
come to watch the excitingly bohemian artists in action, and had remained to become yet another of Rossetti's enthusiastic disciples. This
group of friends came to be regarded as a second wave of Pre-Raphaelites, though they had no connection to the original brotherhood except through Rossetti. The significant point is that by the late 1850s
the term "Pre-Raphaelite" had almost come to mean, simply, "Rossettian," a fact that emphatically illustrates Rossetti's centrality in the
world of Victorian painting and poetry. Certainly, the lavish praise
bestowed upon him by Jones, Morris, and Swinburne went a long way
to establishing his reputation not only as a genius in his own right,
but as a cause of genius in others. As a later member of the Rossetti
circle, poet and novelist George Meredith, was eventually to put it,
"You are our Master, of all of us."[10]

Rossetti's leadership among the rising generation of Victorian artists
is both a historical fact and a key ingredient of that part of the Rossetti
legend that sees him as a "genius whose personality seems somehow
greater than his work," but a more fundamental part of the legend

involves his relations with the various women in his life. The first and in many ways most important of these women was Elizabeth Eleanor Siddall (Rossetti for some reason chose to spell her name "Siddal," as have nearly all subsequent commentators), whom he met in 1850. She served as a model to various painters in the original Pre-Raphaelite group before becoming more and more exclusively Rossetti's model, his lover, and, after seemingly endless vicissitudes and delays, his wife in 1860. As has only recently been pointed out by Griselda Pollock, the real Elizabeth Siddall has traditionally been effaced in the Rossetti legend by "Siddal," also known as "Guggums," "the Sid," "Ida," and by a variety of other nicknames. Her name, her age, her social class, her very identity were displaced by Rossetti, and subsequently by commentators, by her role as model, or more emphatically, as inspiration, for the painter-poet. She was to be the soul within his soul, the Beatrice to his Dante. As I will discuss in a later chapter, a version of her face did become for several years the dominant image in Rossetti's art: "One face looks out from all his canvasses," wrote Christina Rossetti, though she added, "Not as she is, but as she fills his dream."[11]

Given this dynamic in their relationship, it is hardly surprising that Rossetti and Siddall failed to understand one another on merely human terms, or even that from the late 1850s Rossetti sought more sensual fulfillment elsewhere, in a relationship with another model, Fanny Cornforth. In any case, his marriage to Siddall ended tragically. She had long been subject to depression and mysterious undiagnosed illnesses, and became more distressed than ever after giving birth to a stillborn child in May 1861. Quite possibly she was additionally distressed by suspicions of Rossetti's affair with Cornforth. Whether deliberately or accidentally, she took an overdose of laudanum on 10 February 1862 and died the next morning without regaining consciousness. Dark rumors about what Rossetti might have said or done to drive her to her death, about a mysteriously destroyed suicide note, and about suppressed evidence inevitably supplied materials for the already growing Rossetti legend, but the most melodramatic material was supplied by Rossetti himself, who made the grand romantic gesture of burying the only copies of his yet unpublished poems in his wife's coffin. He was later to add the crowning touch to the story by changing his mind: in 1869 he had his wife's grave opened so that his poems could be retrieved.

Shortly after the death of his wife Rossetti moved into an old mansion at 16 Cheyne Walk in Chelsea, where he would spend the rest of his life in ever-increasing seclusion—and where, as Oswald Doughty has said, even as early as the 1860s, "the sinister but useful legend of Tudor House was taking shape" (Doughty, 337). For a time, however, the life Rossetti lived at Cheyne Walk was less sinister than bohemian. His housemates—full and part-time—included Swinburne, George Meredith, his brother William, and a menagerie consisting of peacocks, a wombat, raccoons, an armadillo, and for a short time a zebu. The stories of Rossetti's artistic eccentricity take on a certain lurid coloring by association with the antics of Swinburne, the "demoniac youth," who was periodically deposited in a drunken heap on the doorstep, and was said to romp about the house naked. Rossetti, himself fairly conservative in his life-style, tactfully evicted Swinburne in 1863, and lived more or less alone from that point on. He seemed to embody a kind of splendid artistic isolation, withdrawn within his own world, avoiding the contamination of vulgar society, and refusing to compromise his artistic integrity even by exhibiting his pictures.

In the late 1860s, however, his poetic ambitions were revived, perhaps as a result of a renewed love for Jane Morris, whom he had first known and been attracted to in 1857, before his own marriage, and before her marriage to Morris. He finally arranged to publish his first volume of original poems in 1870, and his elaborate preparations for that event seem hardly to reflect indifference to the opinion of the vulgar world. He prepared the volume with extraordinary care, not only constantly revising and rearranging the poems, but worrying about the type font, the paper, the cover, and, above all, the reviews. He arranged in advance to be reviewed in the major publications by his friends, and was consequently greeted in 1870 by a chorus of praise that celebrated him as one of the great poets of the age, if not of the ages. Rossetti had, quite obviously, set the terms of his own legendary stature.

To cap his triumph, he was at this time settled in an unconventional version of domestic bliss with Jane Morris at Kelmscott, a country house that he coleased with Morris. This love affair has provided yet another romantic element in the Rossetti story: as Elizabeth Siddall had seemed the very embodiment of Rossetti's soul in the early years, so Jane Morris seemed in the later years. But Florence Boos has made a compelling point about this element of the legend: "Rossetti and Jane Morris's brief period of apparent happiness and (presumably) sexual liaison has attracted biographers by its supposed romantic unconventionality. It might be more sympathetic as well as realistic to keep in mind the situation's infirmities and constraints: Rossetti's obesity, addiction, hydrocele, bad eyesight, and growing anxieties; and Jane Morris's ever-present children, neuralgia, and bad back."[12]

His triumph and happiness, such as they were, were short lived. In October 1871 Robert Buchanan, a mediocre poet with a grudge against the Rossetti coterie, pseudonymously published an extraordinarily virulent, and still more extraordinarily fatuous, attack on Rossetti's poems, accusing him of grossly immoral sensuality, of "fleshliness." Rossetti seemed able at first to shrug off Buchanan's absurd attack, but when it was reissued in 1872 in expanded pamphlet form as *The Fleshly School of Poetry and Other Phenomena of the Day,* it contributed to a nervous breakdown from which he never fully recovered. His weakened mental health can undoubtedly be attributed to other causes as well, particularly to feelings of guilt about infidelities to his wife and about his exhumation of her body, to anxieties about involving Jane Morris in scandal, to a long-standing problem with insomnia, and to abuse of the opiate chloral and of alcohol. But Buchanan's attack evidently confirmed him in the paranoid delusion that a vast conspiracy existed to defame him. After an apparent attempt to kill himself, as his wife had done, with an overdose of laudanum, Rossetti eventually recovered to a certain extent, but the last decade of his life was spent in ill health, increasing seclusion even from old friends, and somewhat gloomy defenses of his work from charges that his idiosyncracies and addictions were making his works, his "Rossettis," too excessively peculiar for the general taste. After a last brief burst of poetic energy that resulted in the publication of a second volume of poems in 1881, Rossetti subsided into ever-worsening health, and died on 9 April 1882.

Rossetti's charismatic leadership among younger artists, his unconventional relations with women, his involvement in Elizabeth Siddall's death and exhumation, his entanglement in the "Fleshly School" controversy, his addictions, and his psychoses supply abundant materials for the legend of the gifted genius, the man either blessed or cursed by his difference. But emphases on this supposed difference to explain his art as the effusions of mysterious genius are exceedingly misleading. In the first place, a focus on the manifestations of artistic "difference" tends to obscure the artist's often very mundane connections to the world around him and to veil the historical and material conditions of his work. As I will discuss more fully in the next chapter, Rossetti's early works, for example, were not the spontaneous outpourings of inherent genius: they were attempts to formulate an artistic style and identity out of his experiences with the works of other painters and poets; out of the social, intellectual, and religious issues of his day; and out of his own limited training and technical proficiency. Perhaps the best way to make the point that Rossetti's work was not, as Pater would have it, the transcription of his soul, but rather the representation of a carefully formulated romantic idea of the artistic soul, is to look with some care at the early prose works that were specifically concerned with the romantic ideal of self-expression: "Hand and Soul" and "Saint Agnes of Intercession."

According to Rossetti, "Hand and Soul" was written in one night to meet a deadline for inclusion in the first number of the *Germ*. The work has been regarded by most critics as a Pre-Raphaelite manifesto, and apparently on the authority of Rossetti himself it has been described as "an artistic *confessio fidei*."[13] It is the story of a thirteenth-century Italian painter (a *genuine* Pre-Raphaelite) named Chiaro dell' Erma, who seeks the true path in art, a path that will satisfy the "extreme longing after a visible embodiment of his thoughts."[14] At age 19 he seeks out the tutelage of the most famous painter in Italy, Giunta of Pisano, but upon seeing the famous painter's "lifeless and incomplete" works, "a sudden exultation possessed him as he said within himself, 'I am the master of this man'" (*Germ*, 24). Since Chiaro has apparently yet to produce any notable work, his assumption of mastery is evidently based not on his proven abilities, but rather on a recognition of his superior genius, his superior soul—yet to manifest this superiority to others, he will need to "work out thoroughly some one of his thoughts, and let the world know him" (*Germ*, 25).

At first, Chiaro paints "for the race of fame" (*Germ*, 27), but once he achieves fame he remains unsatisfied. He comes to realize that even though he has always painted with a "feeling of worship and service," yet "that reverence which he had mistaken for faith had been no more than the worship of beauty" (*Germ*, 27), and so he enters upon a second phase of his art. From this point his work will present only "some moral greatness that should impress the beholder: and, in doing this, he did not choose for his medium the action and passion of human life, but cold symbolism and abstract impersonation" (*Germ*, 28). Yet this art fails also, as Chiaro is forced to recognize when the feuding factions in his town of Pisa engage in battle in a church porch decorated with frescoes he had painted to present "a moral allegory of Peace": "there was so much blood cast up the walls on a sudden, that it ran in long streams down Chiaro's paintings" (*Germ*, 29). But at this point, after "Fame failed [him]; faith failed [him]" (*Germ*, 30), and ambition to preach moral virtue failed him, Chiaro is finally vouchsafed a vision of the true function of art in the form of a woman who suddenly appears before him, declaring "I am an image, Chiaro, of thine own soul within thee. See me, and know me as I am. Thou sayest that fame has failed thee, and faith failed thee; but because at least thou hast not laid thy life unto riches, therefore, though thus late, I am suffered to come into thy knowledge" (*Germ*, 31).

The woman's message is exceedingly simple: look into your soul and paint what you find there. The injunction is to produce a self-expressive art without care of consequences, to paint from the soul—and not only to paint from the soul, but to paint the soul itself. Of course, this feat is made somewhat easier when the woman presents herself for a sitting: "Chiaro, servant of God, take now thine Art unto thee, and paint me thus, as I am, to know me: . . . Do this; so shall thy soul stand before thee always, and perplex thee no more" (*Germ*, 33). As an "artistic *confessio fidei*" the point of the work is quite clear: genius resides in the soul of the artist, and its direct and faithful transcription is the artist's sole duty. As commentators have long pointed out, it seems to forecast Rossetti's own future career, painting female heads to express his own inmost feelings, and transcribing the phases of his soul in the just phrases of his verse.

A moment's reflection, however, suggests the obvious point that the story's supernatural symbolism obscures the actual difficulties involved in the romantic creed of self-expressive art. Rossetti's soul never did present itself for a sitting, and the idea of painting the portrait of a woman as though it were one's own soul is, to say the least, fraught with difficulties. To begin with, the attempt to paint one's own soul, in any form, leads to the danger of falling into a morbid narcissistic solipsism, a danger perhaps hinted at by the soul's remark that "Not till thou lean over the water shalt thou see thine image therein: stand erect, and it shall slope from thy feet and be lost" (*Germ*, 33). But if one fails to stand erect, the rest of the world is lost. The implication is that the artist is entirely sufficient unto himself, that his art draws on nothing but his own inner self. Yet the story "Hand and Soul" also shows how manifestly absurd such a notion is, for the story itself draws heavily on Rossetti's reading of Dante, on Poe's stories about mysterious doubles, and on romantic—especially Shelleyan—notions about the soul within the soul, the "epipsyche" that appears as a vision of a beautiful woman. The very idea that the soul would appear as a woman comes not from Rossetti's introspection, but from a long tradition that sees women as the passive sources of inspiration that generate active creative power on the part of the male artist. The representation by a male artist of a female finally will have less to do with "inspiration" than with the dominant assumptions about women in his age. Speaking of Rossetti's drawings of Elizabeth Siddall, for example, Pollock notes that he is not only not representing his own soul, but further, he is not even representing his model. Rather, the drawings

operate within an emergent regime of representation of woman in the 1850s. They signify in the ideological process of a redefinition of woman *as image,* and as *visibly* different. They appropriate "woman," as an explicitly visual image—seen to be seen—as a signifier in a displaced and repressed discourse on masculinity. The drawings do not record an individual man's personal fantasies or romantic obsessions. They are rather symptoms of and sites for the renegotiation and redefinition of femininity and sexuality within the complex of social and gender relations of the 1850s. (Pollock, 113)

The larger point is that Rossetti's representation of how art works, a representation that has traditionally been accepted more or less at face value, glosses over the complex interrelationships between artistic production, the prevailing assumptions about art, and the prevailing views of the age.

One function of the story "Hand and Soul" was to produce an idealized image of the artist and of artistic production that would seem, as an "artistic *confessio fidei,*" actually to describe Rossetti himself. In so doing, it represents him (and other true artists) not only as removed from the vulgar assumptions and beliefs of the common people, but as peculiarly lofty souls, ambitious perhaps for fame ("That last infirmity of noble mind") but certainly above any vulgar desire for gain—Chiaro, at least, has "not laid [his] life unto riches" (*Germ,* 31). Yet as we shall see, the market conditions of the mid-Victorian world had a vast amount to do with Rossetti's own productions, especially in painting but also, to an extent, in poetry. My point, here and throughout, is not that Rossetti was a hypocrite, but that he himself believed in the romantic idealization of the artist and tried to live up to it, yet it is an impossible ideal, and he had in the end to live in the "real" world. The problem was, as Jerome McGann has recently argued, the central one in Rossetti's life, and further, "It is a problem without a solution because it is a problem framed within its own rooted misunderstanding about the nature of art and imagination: that these are transcendental forms standing free of the sublunary orders of human things."[15]

The difficulty appears clearly, as McGann has pointed out, in "Saint Agnes of Intercession," another parable about art that draws heavily on Rossetti's own experiences and aspirations. Though the story involves some supernatural machinery akin to that of "Hand and Soul," it is set in the modern age and in its representation of the practical difficulties besetting the artist in the mid–nineteenth century it exhibits what could be described as a Pre-Raphaelite truth to nature. But the artist-narrator's account of his painting makes it clear that the use of modern subjects and of truth to nature will still in some way involve painting the soul itself:

I now set to work with all the energy of which I was capable, upon a picture of some labour, involving various aspects of study. The subject was a modern one, and indeed it has often seemed to me that all work, to be truly worthy, should be wrought out of the age itself, as well as out of the soul of its producer, which must needs be a soul of the age. At this picture I laboured constantly and unweariedly, my days and my nights; and Mary [his fiancée] sat to me for the principal female figure. (*Works*, 558)

As the story proceeds, it becomes clear that though the narrator had painted Mary with "uncompromising adherence to nature" (*Works*, 561), he had also reproduced a painting by a fifteenth-century Italian painter: the "Saint Agnes" of a certain Bucciuolo Angiolieri.

The coincidence, it seems at first, can be rationally explained: the narrator had seen and loved a reproduction of the "Saint Agnes" in childhood, had fallen in love with a modern woman who resembled this image of his early dreams, and had reproduced her on canvas. But investigating the coincidence more fully, the narrator discovers that not only was his fiancée the exact image of Bucciuolo's, but he himself was the exact image of Bucciuolo, as represented in the earlier artist's self-portrait. The conclusive evidence of the supernatural cannot be avoided: "That it *was* my portrait,—that the St. Agnes was the portrait of Mary,—and that both had been painted by myself four hundred years ago,—this now rose up distinctly before me as the one and only solution of so startling a mystery" (*Works*, 566). Rossetti never finished the tale, but it is evident that just as Bucciuolo's fiancée had died while sitting for her portrait, so eventually would the narrator's Mary die as history repeated itself and the lovers played out their destiny. The implications of this tale are in some ways akin to those of "Hand and Soul." The painter is born with a certain genius (though in this case not exactly his own) and his art, the representation of his soul, has a mysterious transcendent power.

But the problems involved in this self-expressive credo are more evident in "Saint Agnes of Intercession" than in the earlier tale. In the first place, the difficulties of "transcribing" the soul are made obvious. The young artist describes his early technical training, as well as the study and labor that go into the making of a picture—he does not, like Chiaro, effortlessly pour forth his soul in pigments. But further, the nature of the "self" that is to be expressed is unclear. The aspiring artist evidently has a certain vision within him that he must make manifest, but what that vision may be is difficult to determine: "What was then the precise shape of the cloud within my tabernacle, I could scarcely say now; or whether through so thick a veil I could be sure of its presence there at all" (*Works*, 557). In addition, the soul of the artist is not presented as inborn genius, independent of its surroundings, but as "a soul of its age," and his "vision" is not brought from some transcendent realm, but from exposure to the works of other artists. Indeed, the tale expresses considerable reservations about the extent to which the artist can call his soul his own even before it becomes clear that the narrator's soul had in fact lived before. The difficulties are obvious—clearly the tale casts doubt on the romantic idea of unique individual genius, but it hardly presents a coherent view of what constitutes the soul, or artistic vision. How can the narrator's soul be a "soul of the age" if it is also the soul of the fifteenth-century?

Perhaps because it was never completed, perhaps because Rossetti never declared it an "artistic *confessio fidei*," or perhaps because it lacks the focused coherence of the other tale, "Saint Agnes of Intercession" has not generally been seen, like "Hand and Soul," as a way to explain Rossetti's early career. Yet in its very uncertainties and incoherences, it would seem to reflect the young artist's doubts about the precise shape of the cloud within his tabernacle. On a more or less lofty metaphysical plane, the tale expresses anxieties about the possibility and meaning of artistic integrity, of achieving and maintaining a "vision" uniquely one's own. But the tale also describes the mundane material anxieties of a young nineteenth-century artist struggling to forge a successful career. The young artist of the story must not only labor at his craft, but must send off his work to be judged, worry about whether it will be accepted at the Royal Academy, and if so, whether it will be hung prominently enough to be noticed, and if noticed, whether it will garner praise or blame. Wondering how well his picture has been hung, the young artist is explicit about these concerns:

On that now depended its success; on its success the fulfilment of my most cherished hopes might almost be said to depend. That is not the least curious feature of life as evolved in society—which, where the average strength and the average mind are equal, as in this world, becomes to each life another name for destiny,—when a man, having endured labour, gives its fruits into the hands of other men, that they may do their work between him and mankind; confiding it to them, unknown, without seeking knowledge of them; to them, who have probably done in likewise before him, without appeal to the sympathy of kindred experience: submitting to them his naked soul, himself, blind and unseen. (*Works,* 558–59)

As McGann has pointed out, what is at issue in this passage is "the public and commercial 'success' of the work, as opposed to its 'artistic achievement' or 'intrinsic value.' Or rather, the passage shows how the sensibility of a man who is committed to the 'intrinsic values' of art suffers a crucifixion of the imagination when he feels compelled to operate in and through the mediations 'evolved in society'" (McGann, 340). What is at issue is the way in which the romantic artist, prizing the individuality of his genius, must accommodate himself to the rest of society, must live by the judgments of others.

Rossetti's own early career as an artist was, inevitably, much more akin to that of the narrator of "Saint Agnes of Intercession" than to the independent and self-assured endeavors of Chiaro dell' Erma. To the extent that his early works as both poet and painter express his own soul, they express a soul formed by its early cultural experiences and "a soul of the age." His efforts in poetry overtly reflect his reading of Dante and the early Italians, and still more so of Coleridge, Keats, Poe, Browning, and other nineteenth-century writers, and his aesthetic concerns plainly reflect current public issues, particularly the Tractarian, or High Church, movement in religion. Moreover, he was not averse to seeking advice and direction from others. Just as his Chiaro dell' Erma sought out the advice of Giunta of Pisano, Rossetti sought out the advice of Ford Madox Brown, and if he thought to himself that he was the "master of this man," it was not before he had been heavily influenced by Brown's interest in the art of a German school of religious painters known as the Nazarenes. Similarly he wrote for advice to the poet-painter William Bell Scott, and to Leigh Hunt, poet, critic, journalist, and former friend of Keats and Shelley. To Hunt he sent a selection of his poems and inquired whether he would be best advised to follow a career in painting or in poetry. Hunt responded with practical, commonsense counsel: "If you paint as well as you write, you may be a rich man; or at all events, if you do not care to be rich, may get leisure enough to cultivate your writing. But I hardly need tell you that poetry, even the very best—nay, the best, in this respect, is apt to be the worst—is not a thing for a man to live upon while he is in the flesh" (Fredeman, xxii). Hunt was unarguably right, and Rossetti made painting his vocation, poetry his avocation.

Inevitably, the material conditions of art in his day had much to do with his attitudes toward the two arts—especially in later life, as he became more prosperous, painting became for him a business, tainted by practical concerns and consequently looked upon with some contempt, while poetry, aloof from mere money-making concerns, seemed to him his true calling. As he wrote in 1870, "My own belief is that I am a poet (within the limit of my powers) primarily, and that it is my poetic tendencies that chiefly give value to my pictures: only painting being—what poetry is not—a livelihood—I have put my poetry chiefly in that form. On the other hand, the bread-and-cheese question has led to a good deal of my painting being pot-boiling and no more— whereas my verse, being unprofitable, has remained (as much as I have found time for) unprostituted."[16] The simultaneous necessity and reluctance to view artistic endeavor as commodity production could hardly be clearer.

But from the point of view of the "bread-and-cheese question," Rossetti could not have come of age as a painter at a better time. For a variety of reasons, shifts in the patronage of the arts were occurring at midcentury, so that art collectors were no longer buying old masters, but were spending their money on the works of living British artists. One reason for this involved a change in the social class of art patrons. In earlier times painting had been patronized primarily by the aristocratic classes, but with the effects of the Industrial Revolution, and the redistribution of wealth to the manufacturing classes, patronage of the arts shifted also: "By 1849 there could be no doubt as to the identity of the new collecting class. In the August number of the *Art-Journal* of that year, the writer roundly proclaimed: 'it is the middle classes chiefly by whom our school is patronised: many of these are gathering round them galleries of Art which, at some future day, will rank as high as any of past times, and in monetary value will be as marketable.'"[17]

These new buyers had no standing collections of old masters to augment, no loyalty to tradition, and no strong predisposition to favor what was old over what was new. Modern works, representing modern subjects, were simply more likely to appeal to these new buyers, since they were more easily understood and appreciated by the untutored eye. Further, buyers were being warned away from the purchase of old masters by the art journals of the day because a thriving trade in counterfeits had made speculation in such works dangerous. At the same time, a vigorous national discussion of the arts in an era of extreme national pride in all things British was inflating the value of works by contemporary artists. For all of these reasons, as Jeremy Maas has pointed out, the "great manufacturers of Manchester, Liverpool, and Birmingham were in due course to make it a point of honour to buy pictures by living artists" (Maas, 16–17).[18] And finally, not only were the new patrons buying contemporary art, but they were buying more art than ever before. Maas points out that the number of print sellers and picture dealers more than doubled between 1840 and 1855 (Maas, 43).

Clearly the market was inviting for British artists in general, but it was especially so for a young artist like Rossetti, who conspicuously lacked the technical finish that would have made his pictures appeal to a previous generation of buyers. Indeed, for the Pre-Raphaelites generally the new buyers were particularly useful because they lacked the discrimination—or prejudice—to see that by conventional standards the pictures were lamentably faulty in composition and color. Rossetti was plainly alert to the opportunity the market afforded. According to Holman Hunt, Rossetti maintained that there were "hundreds of young aristocrats and millionaires growing up who would be only too glad to get due direction how to make the country as glorious as Greece and Italy had been."[19] In fact, by 1860 one art critic, Tom Taylor, was noting that the manufacturing class was "now doing for art in England what the same class did in earlier times in Florence, Genoa, and Venice, for the art of Italy; in Bruges, Antwerp, and Amsterdam for that of the Low Countries and Holland" (Maas, 18). But though this would seem to represent a chance to create a new school in art, the situation, as Taylor recognized, also had its dangers for art. Possibly the artists might create the taste of their age, but just as possibly they might pander to the uneducated tastes already formed. Rossetti himself seemed at times more than willing to make whatever compromise might be necessary to bridge the gap between his artistic genius and the vulgar taste. In 1848 he was perusing a book he "had long wished to see, called *An Exposition of the False Medium and Barriers precluding Men of Genius from the Public*" (*Letters*, 1:40).

In the later stages of his career, certainly, Rossetti's art does seem to have been damaged by a too great willingness to give his patrons what they wanted, even when this meant simply making replicas of prior works. Whether his work was compromised by such concerns in his early years is less clear, but there can be no doubt that his success, like that of his Pre-Raphaelite brethren, was not wholly due to a spontaneous public recognition of his unique genius. As Rowland Elzea has recently noted, the Pre-Raphaelites did not attract patronage because they painted their souls, but because "they were men of their times. Their subject matter dealt with contemporary topics. They used the latest marketing tools—the dealers, the alternative exhibition schemes and art journalism—and they directed their efforts towards a new audience and new money with a newly formed appetite for art collecting."[20] Indeed, the extent to which they used the media to influence the public reception of their works is striking. Not only were they in danger of being laughed into oblivion until they recruited Ruskin to defend them prominently in the *Times,* but very early in the movement two of the original seven members of the Pre-Raphaelite Brotherhood became art critics—and thereby propagandists for their brethren—in influential journals. William Rossetti became art critic for the *Spectator,* and F. G. Stephens for the *Athenaeum.* In fact, though Rossetti always maintained that at least his poetry was untainted by such manipulation, the use of influence in high journalistic places for his painting was rather precisely duplicated by his efforts in 1870 to manipulate public opinion of his poetry.

Finally, Rossetti's "soul," like everyone else's, was inescapably "a soul of its age," subject to the same influences, inclined to the same beliefs and assumptions, troubled by the same doubts, and constrained by the same material needs as others. I have stressed the disparity between the claims for his unique genius and the actualities of his career not to discredit his achievement, but rather to emphasize the difficulties that resulted from his—and his age's—idea of romantic genius. If Rossetti's accommodations to the demands of his age disturb us, it is in part because we continue to believe in the romantic ideal, and in part also because Rossetti's own emotional adherence to that ideal made his inevitable breaks with it all the more conspicuous. In the following chapters I will examine the ways in which Rossetti's ambitions and achievements reflect the aspirations, attainments, and, of course, also the limitations of the age in which he lived.

Chapter Two
Art-Catholicism, Pre-Raphaelitism, and Beyond

The legend of Rossetti's astonishing precocity seems to be confirmed by a glance at his prolific and prodigious achievements from the mid-1840s through 1852. The table of contents in his brother's edition of the poetical works, for example, lists 15 "Principal Poems," of which 8 are said to have been written, at least in an early form, by 1852, and a 9th by 1854. Even *The House of Life*, though mostly written much later, is listed as originating in 1847, the date of the earliest sonnets included in the sequence. In addition, roughly half of the 120 or so "Miscellaneous Poems" are dated 1853 or earlier—and this does not include another substantial group of poems indexed under the title "Juvenilia and Grotesques." In addition, according to William's dating, the brilliant translations of Dante's *Vita Nuova* and of hundreds of lyrics by Dante and his contemporaries were mostly done from 1845 to 1849, though they were not published until 1861, as *The Early Italian Poets*. In the same period, of course, Rossetti was also beginning his career as a painter, training (however lackadaisically) in the Academy schools, pursuing instruction from Ford Madox Brown and from Holman Hunt, and producing scores of drawings as well as two of his most famous pictures, *The Girlhood of Mary Virgin* (1849), and *Ecce Ancilla Domini!* (1850). And finally, also at this time, he was helping to originate a minor revolution in art with the formation of the Pre-Raphaelite Brotherhood, and was establishing what has occasionally been called the first British journal of the avant-garde, the *Germ*.

His achievements at an extremely young age and in an extremely short period of time are, indeed, extraordinarily impressive, though the legend of his precocity must be qualified in some respects. As I have shown at length elsewhere, most of the work of this period was hasty and unfinished, and those poems that have lasted, and have provided the grounds for Rossetti's reputation for precocity, were extensively rewritten in later years before publication in their most widely known forms.[1] In fact, Rossetti's real achievement is somewhat obscured when he is praised as a precocious and fully formed genius by the age of 21. Such praise not only comes at the expense of presenting his subsequent career as an anticlimax, if not an absolute decline, but it also misrepresents what Rossetti was actually doing at various periods in his life, and consequently obscures the close relation of his work and thought to very precise historical moments. Certainly, his work at this time does not show a settled purpose, does not reflect the transcription of a fully developed, fully realized artistic "soul." Rather it is quite excitingly the reverse: the work shows a young poet and painter seeking the "precise shape of the cloud in [his] tabernacle," experimenting in a number of different directions, responding to the diverse influences of other writers and painters, and reacting to currents of thought and feeling in the world around him.

Some of the more obvious influences can be briefly listed, though it should be noted that Rossetti was no more derivative or imitative than any other artist. He strove for originality, and has been celebrated precisely for achieving it, but no writer or painter can achieve a uniquely characteristic style from thin air. Even the most startlingly original style is formed as a response to, synthesis of, and struggle with the multitudinous influences—both artistic and historical—on the individual. Not surprisingly, Rossetti was profoundly affected by the influence of Dante and the early Italian poets. Through his father's studies, after all, the atmosphere of his early life had been saturated with Dante. Moreover, his own diligent labors as a translator helped form his aesthetic sensibility and his craftsmanship as a poet. He was also deeply influenced by gothic tales of the supernatural and especially by recent and contemporary English poetry; these influences are easily spotted in his writings and in the subjects of his paintings. His drawings dabble in the supernatural, representing scenes from Poe, from Goethe's *Faust,* and from such lesser works as Meinhold's *Sidonia the Sorceress,* and despite his often expressed desire to avoid any echoes of other writers, his poems manifestly reflect his reading.

In many cases the effects of others on his early efforts are trivial, and suggest only the inevitable and temporary dependence of a young poet on established models, but one important and enduring influence was that of Browning's dramatic monologues. Some of Rossetti's most ambitious poems of this period, particularly "Jenny" (the earliest version dates from 1847 or 1848) and "A Last Confession," are representations of the speech of dramatic characters in imagined settings, and many

others, including "The Bride's Prelude," and even "The Blessed Damozel," consist largely of the speeches of dramatic characters. Indeed,
the prevalence of dramatic utterances in Rossetti's early work suggests
the inadequacy of the Paterian tradition of criticism that sees him as
an exclusively self-expressive artist. In fact, Rossetti was later to insist,
only somewhat disingenuously, that his poems *generally* assumed a perspective not the author's own, that they were written from an "*inner*
standing-point," as explorations of the consciousness of others, and not
as simple self-expression (*Works,* 619). But Rossetti was, as we have
seen, drawn also toward the self-expressive aesthetic of the romantic
tradition generally and more particularly of Shelley and the Browning
of *Pauline.* Partly from these sources he developed the idea of the visionary seeking a feminine ideal of the self, and from both the early
Italians and from Keats, Shelley, and Browning he took not only the
theme of spiritually uplifting sexual love, but also his characteristic
imagery of reflecting pools and mirrors, mystic woods, and personifications of love. From both the early Italians and from Coleridge, Keats,
and Tennyson he took medieval settings and a tendency to employ
archaic language. And from Coleridge and Poe he learned to use the
supernatural to explore vague and indefinable psychic states.

As an aspiring painter, the young Rossetti was influenced by trends
in painting as well as those in literature. Though along with his fellow
Pre-Raphaelite brethren he is celebrated as something of a revolutionary in painting, his early works are strongly influenced in theme by
his readings, and in manner by the prevalent styles of the day as well
as by the influence of Brown (and the German "early Christian" painters admired by Brown) and of Holman Hunt and his dogma of fidelity
to nature. And finally, in both arts Rossetti was responding to the
dominant social issues of his time. Though he never became an overtly
political writer—though in fact he is a very model of the artist who
turns with ostentatious indifference from the age to cultivate his own
sensibilities—Rossetti could not help but be influenced by, for example, the wave of revolutionary sentiment that swept Europe in 1848.
His response is recorded in the somewhat inconsequential forms of a
sonnet entitled "At the Sun-Rise in 1848," in which he rather crypti-
cally celebrated the overthrow of kings, and of a doggerel poem entitled "The English Revolution of 1848," in which he satirized the
lower-class pretensions of English agitators for reform. But, as we shall
see, the more important effect of the revolutionary atmosphere was in
breeding the attitude that contributed to the Pre-Raphaelite reaction

against established authority in art. A more obvious sociohistorical influence on Rossetti's art was the Tractarian, or Anglo-Catholic, movement taking place at this time, a movement that clearly contributed to his "early Christian" tendencies in both poetry and painting. At the same time, the intellectual climate of the age helped shape his ultimate skepticism in religious matters and lead him beyond Christian art, and finally, though he was notoriously the most unscientific of poets, the empirical tendencies of his time contributed to the Pre-Raphaelite, and at times his own, practice of recording the modern world around him with scrupulous fidelity, recording, for example, the experience of a train journey, or the features seen on a corpse in the Paris morgue.

In his youthfully enthusiastic and energetic response to this multiplicity of influences, Rossetti inevitably produced a body of works conspicuous not for its narrowly focused concern with his own inner being, but for its diversity in style and theme. But as Rossetti ranged in both arts from medieval to modern concerns, from soulful outpourings to dramatic monologues, from early Christianity to modern train journeys, his most consistent concern was with identifying his own role as an artist. His poems of this period were often directly or indirectly about poets, and still more often about painters or painting, and his drawings frequently represented other artists at work, or even painters painting poets (*Giotto Painting the Portrait of Dante*) and, in one of his most famous designs, a poet engaged in drawing (*Dante Drawing an Angel*). At times, the relation of the artist to his world is shown to be quite simple, as in an 1849 epitaph on Blake:

> All beauty to pourtray,
> Therein his duty lay,
> And still through toilsome strife
> Duty to him was life—
> Most thankful still that duty
> Lay in the paths of beauty.
>
>   (*Works*, 176)

But more often, for Rossetti as for other Victorian artists, the relation between beauty and duty was less clear.

The complications are most evident in "Hand and Soul" and "Saint Agnes of Intercession," but are apparent in other works as well. As Joan Rees has pointed out, for example, in *Dante Drawing an Angel* the thematic concern is plainly about the relation between the visionary

artist and the vulgar herd: "The whole drawing is a very striking representation of the disruption, even the desecration, of a private vision
and moment of communion by an unsympathetic, uncomprehending,
invading, outer world."[2] The same concern is explored in the long
poem "Dante at Verona," which Rossetti regarded highly enough that
he at one time planned to use it as the title poem of a volume. "Dante
at Verona" is not an entirely successful poem since the episodic nature
of the narrative leads to both diffuseness and rather flat descriptions of
various incidents, but its main thematic concern is obvious. Dante is
portrayed not only as a political exile from his beloved Florence, but
also as a kind of spiritual exile from the world around him. The "twofold life he led / In chainless thought and fettered will" epitomizes the
life of any visionary artist whose spiritual existence transcends earthly
bounds, but whose corporeal existence is subject to earthly constraint.
The poet is shown as a being apart, blessed by a difference that exalts
him, but cursed by the same difference that subjects him to a hostile
world:

> Therefore, the loftier rose the song
>   To touch the secret things of God,
>   The deeper pierced the hate that trod
> On base men's track who wrought the wrong;
>   Till the soul's effluence came to be
>   Its own exceeding agony.
>
>   (*Works*, 6, 7)

    In practical terms, Rossetti's attempts at this time to define the
specific imaginative qualities and the precise social—or asocial—role
of the artist took the form of attempting to define himself as an artist,
and the attempt at self-definition, in its simplest manifestation, took
the form of self-naming, or of labeling himself as a certain kind of
artistic commodity. The two names that he chose to characterize and
label his work were "Art-Catholic" and "Pre-Raphaelite." The labels
do not adequately describe the diversity of Rossetti's early effort, but
they do provide convenient headings under which to examine his self-
representation as an artist and to study some of his most important
works. Rossetti coined the term "Art-Catholic" in 1847 to describe
himself in his title for the manuscript poems he sent to Leigh Hunt
and to William Bell Scott, *Songs of the Art-Catholic*. These songs evidently included "Mater Pulchrae Delectionis" (later revised to become

"Ave"), early versions of "My Sister's Sleep" and "The Blessed Damozel," and others, but the label "Art-Catholic" may also be applied to Rossetti's translations of the early Italians, to the slightly later paintings (and accompanying sonnets), *The Girlhood of Mary Virgin* and *Ecce Ancilla Domini!*, and even to considerably later paintings with religious themes, such as *The Passover in the Holy Family* (1855–56), *Mary Nazarene* (1857), *Mary in the House of St. John* (1858), *The Annunciation* (1861), and *The Seed of David* (1858–64).

All of these works are anticipated in some measure in "Mater Pulchrae Delectionis," a verse prayer to the Virgin. The poem is ostentatiously Catholic in its Mariolatry, its listing of various traditional names for the Virgin, its emphasis on her power to intercede for sinners, and its interest in such typological symbolism as that describing Mary:

> a woman-Trinity—
> Being the dear daughter of God,
> Mother of Christ from stall to rood,
> And wife unto the Holy Ghost.
>
> (*Works*, 661)

The Catholicism of the poem owes a great deal to the then-current High Church, or Anglo-Catholic, movement in the Anglican church, a movement begun a generation earlier at Oxford under the influence of Pusey, Keble, Newman, and others, and becoming increasingly widespread in the 1840s. Rossetti himself had certainly been thoroughly exposed to the movement. D.M.R. Bentley, who has discussed the Anglo-Catholic contexts of Rossetti's early work in some detail, has pointed out that "since 1843 Rossetti, together with most of his family, had been attending Christ Church, Albany Street, which was becoming renowned at this time for its High Church ritual and Catholic appearance," and further that even in the early 1850s Rossetti and his Pre-Raphaelite associates Millais and Collins (though closely associated with the Pre-Raphaelites, Collins was never actually a brother) attended St. Andrew's, also "renowned for its High Church character."[3] Bentley concludes that Rossetti's Art-Catholic works were genuine expressions of religious devotion, that "Mater Pulchrae Delectionis," or "Ave," should be regarded as "an orthodox, devotional hymn to the Blessed Virgin" (35), but such a conclusion seems unwarranted in light of Rossetti's apparent lack of interest in religious issues unrelated to his artistic purposes, and in light of the testimony of his brother William, who remarked that by 1847 Rossetti "was more than vague in point of religious faith." According to William, the emphasis in the phrase "Art-Catholic" must fall on the first word, and by "Art" his brother "meant to suggest that the poems embodied conceptions and a point of view related to pictorial art—also that this art was, in sentiment though not necessarily in dogma, Catholic—medieval and unmodern" (*Works*, 661). William's statements may be said to reflect his own atheism and the agnosticism avowed by his brother in later life, but the poem itself supplies abundant evidence of Rossetti's emphasis on "pictorial art." The opening lines seem to describe a painting rather than a saint:

> Mother of the fair delight,
> From the azure standing white
> And looking golden in the light. . . .
>
> (*Works*, 661)

And later in the poem pictorial art is invoked directly:

> And thy face looks from thy veil
> Sweetly and solemnly and well,
> Like to a thought of Raphäel.
>
> (*Works*, 662)

In addition, the Catholic source of these poems is not to be confined to the Anglo-Catholicism of the day, or to pictorial art, but surely also includes the influence of Dante and the early Italians—Leigh Hunt responded to the *Songs of the Art-Catholic* with a reference to the "Dantesque heavens" that are as evident in "Mater Pulchrae Delectionis" as in "The Blessed Damozel."

Rossetti's Art-Catholicism unquestionably drew both on his own idiosyncratic intellectual background and on the currents of thought and feeling in the age, but it did so in complex ways. Art-Catholicism represents, in effect, an aestheticizing of religion, an attempt to gain for art some of the emotional tone of a religion that was becoming outmoded. In an increasingly scientific and skeptical age, the artist drew on obviously archaic forms and beliefs to give depth and resonance to his work. A small but telling example of this method is Rossetti's deliberate alteration, in his 1844 translation of "Lenore," of the

line "pray to our Heavenly Father" to "utter an Ave Marie." Both lines
express a religious sentiment, but the second is deliberately archaic,
quaintly medieval, and vaguely "aesthetic." Quite likely Rossetti was
emulating two of his favorite poems, Keats's "The Eve of St.
Agnes" and Coleridge's "Christabel," in an essentially atmospheric use of medieval Catholicism, to give the coloring if not the conviction of spirituality to his verse. In fact, by using religion as a resource for art,
Rossetti reflected not the faith of his times, but its doubt, and he
situated himself within a tradition that was gradually replacing religion with art as a source of spiritual value. Certainly, at least, this is
the way Rossetti's "Art-Catholicism" was viewed in his own age by
others who saw art as virtually the new religion. According to Swinburne, "The influence which plainly has passed over the writer's mind,
attracting it as by charm of sound or vision, by spell of colour or of
dream, towards the Christian forms and images, is in the main an
influence from the mythologic side of the creed. It is from the sand-
banks of tradition and poetry that the sacred sirens have sung to this
seafarer."[4] Rossetti had "felt and given the mere physical charm of
Christianity, with no admixture of doctrine or of doubt" (15:24).

Like William Rossetti, however, Swinburne was writing after Rossetti had become increasingly agnostic and somewhat embarrassed by
the appearance of naive Christian faith represented in his early works.
But a much earlier, more disinterested critic, David Masson, ably
pointed out the attractions and the limitations of the artistic uses of
medieval Christianity in an 1852 essay on Pre-Raphaelitism. Masson
astutely observed that the Pre-Raphaelite use of Christian tradition
aimed

at rescuing Art from the degraded position of being a mere minister to sensuous gratification, and elevating it into an agency of high spiritual education.
That Art should be pervaded with the Christian spirit,—that it should convey
and illustrate the highest truths relating to man's being, is a maxim of the
Pre-Raphaelites for which, and for their endeavours to carry it out, they ought
to be held in honour. But it is easier to hold by such a maxim theoretically,
than to devise the appropriate artistic means for giving effect to it, in an age
when the human intellect has torn up and huddled together, as a mere heap
of relics, much that the feet of the ancients walked on as solid pavement, that
the eyes of the ancients gazed on as indestructible walls, and that the artists
who worked for the ancients had nothing to do but assume, and be in everlasting relation with, and everlastingly and obdurately point to.[5]

Masson had in mind (among other things) Rossetti's contributions to the *Germ,* and particularly the "archaic quaintness" of his "Dantesque" mode (Masson, 80). A much more recent critic has similarly noted that Rossetti used Christian symbols "because Dante uses them and gives them the full weight of grave conviction" (Rees, 138), but for Rossetti they can carry only "poetic conviction"—not "intellectual conviction."

Indeed, it may be doubted whether the Catholic trappings carry any conviction at all in the early versions of Rossetti's most famous "Art-Catholic" poem, "The Blessed Damozel," a poem about the heaven-ascended soul of a deceased maiden. The opening stanzas of the poem are filled with apparently mystic symbolism, but, as in "Mater Pulchrae Delectionis," the real inspiration seems to come from "pictorial art":

> The blessed Damozel leaned out
>   From the gold bar of Heaven:
> Her blue grave eyes were deeper much
>   Than a deep water, even.
> She had three lilies in her hand,
>   And the stars in her hair were seven.
>
> Her robe, ungirt from clasp to hem,
>   No wrought flowers did adorn,
> But a white rose of Mary's gift
>   On the neck meetly worn;
> And her hair, lying down her back,
>   Was yellow like ripe corn.
>
>   (*Germ,* 90)

The "three lilies," the "seven stars," and the "white rose" are all symbols belonging to the iconographic tradition surrounding the Blessed Virgin, but here they seem merely decorative adjuncts to the more striking descriptions of the Damozel's blue eyes and yellow hair. Indeed, throughout the poem what is most striking is that the mystic, occult furnishings of these "Dantesque heavens" are quite secondary to the representation of what we might reasonably expect to be a disembodied spirit as a thoroughly corporeal presence:

> And still she bowed herself, and stooped
>   Into the vast waste calm;

> Till her bosom's pressure must have made
> The bar she leaned on warm,
> And the lilies lay as if asleep
> Along her bended arm.
>
> (*Germ*, 91)

According to Pater, this refusal to distinguish between matter and spirit was not only quintessentially Rossettian, but was also character-istic of the medieval Christianity that inspired Rossetti: "Practically, the church of the Middle Age by its aesthetic worship, its sacramen-talism, its real faith in the resurrection of the flesh, had set itself against that Manichean opposition of spirit and matter, and its results in men's way of taking life; and in this, Dante is the central represen-tative of its spirit," ("Rossetti," 236). Dante was surely one of the sources for Rossetti's portrayal of the heavenly lady, but Pater, like Rossetti, unjustifiably sensualized Dante's religion. Rossetti's Damozel and Dante's Beatrice are worlds apart: Beatrice called Dante to the life of the spirit and the joy of heavenly bliss, but the Damozel is not at home in heaven, and weeps for her lost lover. In fact, Rossetti's poem is not about spiritual salvation, or even about heaven, so much as it is about the separation of earthly lovers. It is no wonder that Rossetti's pious sister Christina felt that the poem fell "short of expressing the highest view."[6] Like Tennyson's "Mariana," it is about a lonely woman awaiting her lover: "'I wish that he were come to me, / For he will come,' she said" (*Germ,* 91).

According to Rossetti, the poem was not so much inspired by Dante as by Poe's "The Raven." Though he acknowledged that the poem was "written in a kind of Gothic manner which I suppose [Leigh Hunt] is pleased to think belongs to the school of Dante" (*Works,* 647), he re-marked elsewhere that it had in fact been written in response to "The Raven"—where Poe had given the feeling of loss from the point of view of the male lover left on earth, Rossetti would give it from that of the maiden removed to heaven. Actually the poem achieves its finest effects by giving *both* points of view, focusing on the Damozel's, but also presenting the bereaved lover's thoughts in parenthetic interpola-tions of grief: "Alas for lonely Heaven! Alas / For life wrung out alone!" (*Germ,* 92). But it is not only in the emphasis on separation and loss rather than on spiritual consolation that Rossetti's poem is distin-guished from the medieval Catholic tradition it seems to emulate. The

cosmology, for all its medieval trappings and despite Rossetti's avowed
ignorance of the Copernican universe, is finally very much a product
of the nineteenth century, partly in its implication of the extreme re-
moteness of heaven, but more significantly in its treatment of time and
space. From the barrier of heaven the Damozel "could scarce see the
sun":

> It lies from Heaven across the flood
>   Of ether, as a bridge.
> Beneath, the tides of day and night
>   With flame and blackness ridge
> The void, as low as where this earth
>   Spins like a fretful midge.

(Germ, 90)

The image of earth as a "fretful midge," and the later reference to time
as a fierce "pulse" shaking "Through all the worlds," hardly represents
either the geocentric medieval view of the cosmos or the medieval sense
of time as an agent of Providence. However antipathetic to science
Rossetti may have been, the sense of the insignificance of the earth
within the vast tracts of time and space seems to reflect a modern
sensibility formed within an age acutely conscious that human existence and human history are evidently not at the center of a providen-
tial plan, but are a paltry late addition to the cosmic scheme. Despite
the hopefulness of the Damozel that "he will come," the space between
the lovers seems unbridgeable, and the emphasis in the poem is on
loss, not salvation. The result is that the poem has seemed to some
readers somewhat at odds with itself, since the Art-Catholic imagery,
though quaintly attractive in its own right, and though probably the
source of the poem's great popularity, is not entirely compatible with
the theme of earthly love and separation.

"The Blessed Damozel" is best understood, of course, not as a medieval and Catholic poem, but as a medievalist and "Art-Catholic"
poem, as an expression of nineteenth-century nostalgia for an age of
faith rather than of an actual faith. In this respect it is very obviously
a product of its times, consistent not only with the more religiously
serious impulses that had moved the Tractarian originators of Anglo-
Catholicism, but more fundamentally with the medievalizing of
Coleridge, Keats, and Scott in an earlier generation, and of Tennyson,
Carlyle, and Ruskin in the early Victorian age. Though Rossetti's Art-

Catholicism cannot be taken at face value as even a version of Catholicism, it nevertheless represents a serious endeavor to explore in art the psychological need for religion that was particularly acute for an age just learning to do without it. In the early version of "The Blessed Damozel" the Catholic trappings do offer a kind of consolation, or at least distraction from the grief of separation. However fancifully, the Damozel can be imagined in a kind of mystic heaven, and can be imagined to remain faithful to her earthly love. Despite the great gulf set between heaven and earth, heaven does offer the solace of an afterlife where the earthly lovers will be reunited:

> "To have more blessing than on earth
>   In nowise; but to be
> As then we were,—being as then
>   At peace. Yea, verily.
>
> "Yea, verily; when he is come
>   We will do thus and thus:
> Till this my vigil seem quite strange
>   And almost fabulous;
> We two will live at once, one life;
>   And peace shall be with us."

(Germ, 93)

Clearly this represents no traditional Christian consolation, and indeed its inadequacy is made manifest when the Damozel is shown weeping over the "golden barriers" in the poem's final stanza.

Rossetti has often been criticized for the superficiality of his Art-Catholic imagery, for separating the symbolism of the religious tradition from its meaning. There is a measure of justice in this charge as applied to the early version of "The Blessed Damozel." In this version it is very difficult to know quite what to make of the religious imagery, since heaven is presented both as a consolatory afterlife and as a poor and lonely alternative to earthly love. In later versions of the poem Rossetti's revisions reduced the possibility of reunion in heaven to mere wishful thinking: stanzas envisioning the reunited lovers in heaven are deleted, and the earth-bound lover is given lines expressing his doubt about the possibility of reunion. In the late versions the Christian symbolism is assuredly not merely decorative—the inadequacy of the Christian consolation is juxtaposed with the grief of the lovers to *subvert* traditional faith.

In fact, the poem in its indirect way thus reflects an important development in nineteenth-century intellectual history: the attempt to substitute human love for the lost comfort of divine love. As McGann has said, "Rossetti is doing . . . what many other nineteenth-century artists did (witness *Tristan and Isolde*): he is replacing Love as agapé with Love as eros."[7] Numerous other analogues might be mentioned, but perhaps the best is *Wuthering Heights,* a book Rossetti greatly admired. In that novel Emily Brontë established the passionate erotic love of Cathy and Heathcliff precisely by setting it against the comparatively tame reward of the Christian heaven—when Cathy dreams that she is in heaven, she weeps until the angels toss her out. Similarly, though the Blessed Damozel has in effect become an angel, she is not quite at home in heaven. From this perspective, indeed, it becomes clear that Rossetti's use of the heavenly setting and Christian symbolism, like Brontë's, quite deliberately exploits conventional Christian ideals to emphasize the romantic love that surpasses them. Rossetti's later revisions of the poem, which considerably darken its tone and deepen its melancholy, make it clear that the Christian symbolism is in fact being subverted—not only is heaven an inadequate consolation for earthly loss, but it is contrary to the spirit of earthly love. And from a slightly different perspective, the poem can be regarded as a reflection of the dehumanizing Victorian characterization of the woman as an angel, an attitude that tended to idealize women out of earthly existence altogether, and that certainly contributed to the spate of paintings and literary evocations of dead and dying women.

A somewhat different exploration of Victorian and Christian thought is apparent in the early and later versions of "My Sister's Sleep," another of Rossetti's Art-Catholic poems. "My Sister's Sleep," forgoing "Dantesque heavens," is set instead in a highly particularized Victorian domestic interior. It is a dramatic lyric in which a brother describes the quiet sleep and subsequent death of his sister on Christmas Eve. The Christmas setting, of course, provides a conspicuously religious context. In stanzas later excised, presumably as too Art-Catholic, the brother established the religious mood:

> Silence was speaking at my side
>   With an exceedingly clear voice:
>   I knew the calm as of a choice
> Made in God for me, to abide.

> I said, "Full knowledge does not grieve:
>   This which upon my spirit dwells
>   Perhaps would have been sorrow else:
> But I am glad 'tis Christmas Eve."

When midnight strikes, the mother piously notes the moment:

> "Glory unto the Newly Born!"
>   So, as said angels, she did say;
>   Because we were in Christmas-day,
> Though it would still be long till dawn.

And when she discovers that her daughter has died, the coincidence of her death with the celebration of Christ's birth provides consolation:

> Then kneeling, upon Christmas morn
>   A little after twelve o'clock
>   We said, ere the first quarter struck,
> "Christ's blessing on the newly born!"
>
> (*Germ,* 21–23)

Much more clearly than "The Blessed Damozel," this poem juxtaposes mundane reality with the hope of heaven. The speaker notes his mother's care to work quietly, to prevent her work-light from disturbing the sleeping girl; he describes with care the particular tone of the light in the room, notes the silence and every slight sound that disturbs it: the clicking of his mother's needles, the settling of her silken gown, the "pushing back of chairs" in the room above. The closely observed details have sometimes, perversely, been regarded as a blemish on the poem because of their apparent irrelevance to the Christian theme, but in fact, as McGann (1969) has noted, they are the primary index of the poem's most fundamental concern. The poem is not about the truth or falseness of Christian symbolism, but about the states of mind of the brother and mother during their deathbed vigil. The sharply rendered details suggest the hyperconsciousness of one engaged in such a vigil in the dead of night. And, of course, once the poem is recognized as a dramatic lyric, an exploration of a certain psychological state, the Christian setting can be regarded not as Art-Catholic decoration, but as essential to the poem's interest in the psychology of grief within a traditional Christian society.

Nevertheless, because the poem was written, as William Rossetti noted, "with an air of truth-telling," readers in Rossetti's day often thought it recorded an actual death in his family, and even later readers, aware that it has "no relation to actual fact," have read it as a reflection of Rossetti's own sensibility. Such responses are interesting as an indication of the strong biographical bias of Rossetti criticism, but what is still more interesting is that in later life Rossetti himself found the poem "very distasteful" and revised it to "eliminate the religious element altogether" (*Letters,* 2:731). The revisions leave the mother's faith intact, but remove four stanzas (including the two quoted above beginning "Silence was speaking . . .") in which the brother reflects on his own faith and quasi-mystical experience. The clear implication is that Rossetti expected readers to identify him with the brother in this "rather spoony affair" (*Letters,* 2:722), or at least with the brother's point of view—and perhaps that he had so identified himself in the past. In any case, the revisions, like those made to "The Blessed Damozel," indicate a clear dissatisfaction with the "religious element" in his early works, and a clear effort to develop and heighten the psychological examination of Christian faith that had been at least latent in those works.

Rossetti's Art-Catholic works included paintings as well as poems— indeed, his Art-Catholicism can only be fully understood if his poems and paintings of this period are studied as complementary attempts to explore traditional symbolism. Though the term was used to designate a group of poems, it was also, as William said, to suggest a "point of view related to pictorial art" and "Ave," as Rossetti later said, was "originally written as a prologue to a series of designs" (*Works,* 661). The most famous of these designs were *The Girlhood of Mary Virgin* (Figure 1) and *Ecce Ancilla Domini!* (Figure 2), the only two oil paintings he completed in his Art-Catholic and Pre-Raphaelite phase. These paintings reflect Rossetti's interest in the Anglo-Catholic movement and in the iconography of the Catholic tradition as he knew it from Dante and the other early Italians, but they resulted still more directly from a contemporary trend in painting. As A. I. Grieve has pointed out, early Italian art was newly fashionable in the late 1840s—in fact, Lord Lindsay's *History of Christian Art,* published in 1847, "had urged young artists to study the Early Italians in whose work he found 'a holy purity, an innocent naiveté, a child-like grace and simplicity, a freshness, a fearlessness, an utter freedom from affectation, a yearning after all things truthful, lovely and of good report.'"[8] In modern painting,

Fig. 1 The Girlhood of Mary Virgin
Reproduced by permission of The Tate Gallery, London

Fig. 2 Ecce Ancilla Domini! (The Annunciation)
Reproduced by permission of The Tate Gallery, London

a precedent for returning to the early Italians (the *real* Pre-Raphaelites) had been set by a group of German painters known as the Nazarenes, or the "Evangelists of Saint Luke." The influence of these painters on Rossetti was indirect but significant—Ford Madox Brown, at least theoretically Rossetti's teacher at this time, had visited the studios of the Nazarene leaders, Cornelius and Overbeck, and had admired both their aims and their pictorial techniques. And finally, at one of the founding meetings of the Pre-Raphaelite Brotherhood, at Millais's house, the assembled brethren had admired Lasinio's engravings after the early Italian Ghiberti. Indeed, given Rossetti's prior interest in the Tractarian movement and in early Italian literature, it was almost inevitable that he would adopt some version of an "early Christian" style in his painting.

The first of his Art-Catholic paintings, the first of his Pre-Raphaelite paintings, and indeed the first of his oil paintings, was *The Girlhood of Mary Virgin*. The picture represents the young Virgin Mary and her mother, Saint Anne, embroidering as her father, Saint Joachim, prunes a vine in the background. The design is dense with symbolic details, most obviously a haloed dove representing the Holy Ghost, a child angel, a lily, a rose, a seven-thorned briar, seven palm fronds, and six books representing all but one of the traditional virtues (justice is missing). Clearly, the painting must be appreciated within the Ruskinian and generally Victorian aesthetic that pictures be not only viewed, but *read,* and the viewer/reader must read not only the most obvious symbols, but every detail. The red cloth hanging over the balustrade, for example, represents the robe of Christ, the vine is a traditional symbol for Christ, and the cruciform trellis upon which part of the vine grows plainly suggests the Crucifixion. And, of course, the painting must be read in a quite literal sense, since it includes a surprising number of painted words. The books are labeled with the Latin names of the virtues, *"Fortitudo," "Temperantia," "Prudentia," "Spes," "Fides,"* and *"Caritas."* In addition, a scroll in the foreground is inscribed *"Tot dolores tot gaudia,"* a portable organ behind the Virgin is inscribed *"O sis, Laus deo,"* and the halos around the heads of the figures are labeled with their names: *"S. Maria S.V.," "S. Anna,"* and *"S. Ioachimus."*

Finally, the viewer/reader is expected to read beyond the painted surface to a pair of sonnets affixed to the frame. The second sonnet spells out some of the symbolism:

> These are the symbols. On that cloth of red
> I' the centre is the Tripoint—perfect each,

Except the second of its points, to teach
That Christ is not yet born. The books—whose head
Is golden Charity, as Paul hath said—
    Those virtues are wherein the soul is rich:
    Therefore on them the lily standeth, which
Is Innocence, being interpreted.

The seven-thorn'd briar and the palm seven-leaved
    Are her great sorrows and her great reward.
    Until the end be full, the Holy One
Abides without. She soon shall have achieved
    Her perfect purity: yea, God the Lord
    Shall soon vouchsafe His Son to be her Son.

                                        (*Works,* 173)

The sonnet provides a "reading" of the picture, though an incomplete
one. In addition, viewers might have noticed Tractarian influences that
went beyond the use of Catholic iconography. Bentley suggests that
"the balustrade at the rear of the painting, with the trellis-work cross
at its center, closely resembles an altar constructed of stone and decorated in the Catholic manner, with flowers (the rose in a glass jar),
lights (the adjacent lamp), and a frontal (the 'cloth of red' embroidered
with a 'Tripoint'" (34). And as David Todd Heffner has suggested, the
theological subtlety of the work is revealed by the absence of a book
entitled "*Justitia*" since, as Emile Mâle points out, according to Saint
Ambrose, "each of the four ages of man also corresponds to a virtue.
The first age, from Abel to Noah, is that of Prudence; the second,
from Abraham to Jacob, that of Chastity; the third, from Moses to the
prophets, that of Fortitude; the fourth, which begins with Jesus, is
that of Justice." Consequently, Hefner points out, Justice may be missing simply because the scene "pre-dates Jesus' coming. Thus, the omis-
sion of *Justitia* is another of the lack-of-completion motifs in the
painting, the others being the incomplete Tripoint, the embroi-
dery, the unfolding curtain, and the dove waiting outside."[9] Yet it
would seem unlikely that Rossetti was especially interested in preach-
ing subtle doctrinal points to his contemporaries. Rather, he seems
to have been taking part in the general revival of interest in the
moral earnestness of early painting, and to have found in Tractarian
thought, with its insistence on the spiritual significance of material
things, a convenient way to introduce a clearly legible symbolism in
painting.

But *The Girlhood of Mary Virgin* was much more than an arid study in symbol making. The return to early Christian art involved adopting a specific style and technique. The technique, derived from the Nazarenes via Brown, involved a departure from the methods for oil painting currently taught in the Royal Academy schools (a method regarded as "sloshy" by the Pre-Raphaelite brethren) and the adoption of a more naive style of coloring. According to Grieve, Rossetti's method was imitative of the primitives as described by current authorities. The technique was described by William Bell Scott, who had seen him at work on the picture: "He was painting in oils with water-colour brushes, as thinly as in water-colour, on canvas which he had primed with white till the surface was as smooth as cardboard, and every tint remained transparent."[10] As a result, the brightness of the picture was somewhat exceptional for the mid-Victorian period, though no more so than the paintings of Brown that it emulated, and though it does not quite rival contemporary paintings by Holman Hunt and Millais, who were experimenting with painting on a wet white ground. The design, pushing the principal figures into the foreground, breaking the picture into separate, manageable units, and altogether foregoing perspective, also reflects a deliberately archaic, or primitive style. The final result was a picture that, for all its arcane symbolism, was meant to suggest a kind of naive sincerity, an honesty unmediated by merely academic training.[11]

But like the Art-Catholic poems, the painting expresses at least as much interest in the psychology of religion as in the symbolic adjuncts. The focus of the picture is on the realistically portrayed facial expressions of the Virgin and her mother, modeled by Rossetti's sister Christina and his mother; without the halos and angel, the picture might almost be taken as a representation of Victorian domesticity, a variation on the motif of the angel in the house. In fact, Rossetti seemed eager to make this point in an 1852 letter to F. G. Stephens: "That picture of mine was a symbol of female excellence. The Virgin being taken as its highest type. It was not her *Childhood* but *Girlhood*" (Grieve 1973, 8).

Rossetti's next important picture, *Ecce Ancilla Domini!*, was in effect a sequel to *The Girlhood of Mary Virgin*. It represents the fulfillment of Mary's girlhood as the angel of the Annunciation appears to her, and it represents also the fulfillment of the first picture: the angel now is full grown, the lily plucked, the embroidered cloth completed, and the dove has entered the room. But despite the symbolism—the halos, the flaming feet of the angel, and so on—the painting is even more clearly a kind of psychological study than was its predecessor, the focus still more clearly on the posture and facial expression of the Virgin. The subject of the picture was announced in the first of the two sonnets appended to the frame of *The Girlhood:*

> This is that blessed Mary, pre-elect
> God's Virgin. Gone is a great while, and she
> Was young in Nazareth of Galilee.
> Her kin she cherished with devout respect:
> Her gifts were simpleness of intellect
> And supreme patience. From her mother's knee
> Faithful and hopeful; wise in charity;
> Strong in grave peace; in duty circumspect.
>
> So held she through her girlhood; as it were
> An angel-watered lily, that near God
> Grows, and is quiet. Till one dawn, at home,
> She woke in her white bed, and had no fear
> At all,—yet wept till sunshine, and felt awed;
> Because the fulness of the time was come. [12]

Unlike the other sonnet, this one is only passingly interested in the symbolism—the emphasis is squarely on the ordinary humanity of the Virgin, her attributes and her emotional response to the awesome presence of God. In the painting itself, the angel, the lily, and the dove are important primarily to clarify the occasion: the emotional center of the picture is the cowering, awe-struck Virgin modeled by Christina.

The realism of the principal figures within these heavily symbolic paintings suggests the juxtaposition of the Art-Catholic or "early Christian" emphasis that Rossetti had brought to the Pre-Raphaelite Brotherhood with the insistence on "truth to nature" of Hunt and Millais. Both works were painted under the direct supervision of Hunt, who deplored the "Overbeckian" qualities of the work, and in both Rossetti stretched his still limited technical capabilities to the utmost in order to copy accurately from his models. He evidently reduced a series of children to tears as he struggled to reproduce their features for the child-angel of *The Girlhood* and he rubbed out the heads of a series of models for the full-grown angel of the second picture before he got the expression he wanted. Even the flames around the angel's feet were painted "from nature"—or at least from a flaming concoction of wine and spirits. The juxtaposition of the doctrines of the Pre-Raphaelite Brotherhood with those of the "Brotherhood of Saint Luke," of "truth to nature" with archaic symbolism, is best understood by reference to Rossetti's sonnet of 1849, "St. Luke the Painter":

> Give honour unto Luke Evangelist;
>   It was this Luke (the aged legends say)
>   Who first taught Art to fold her hands and pray.
> Scarcely at once she dared to rend the mist
> Of devious symbols: but soon having wist
>   How sky-breadth and field-silence and this day
>   Are symbols also in some deeper way,
> She looked through these to God and was God's priest.
>
> And if, past noon, her toil began to irk,
>   And she sought nostrums, and had turned in vain
>   To soulless self-reflections of man's skill,—
>   Yet now, in this the twilight, she might still
>   Kneel in the latter grass to pray again,
> Ere the night cometh and she may not work. [13]

Clearly, the Marian pictures depend to a great extent on "devious symbols," but their impact finally depends still more on the faithful representation of the principal figures. They "are symbols also in some deeper way," Pre-Raphaelite symbols that gain their significance in the way suggested by Robert Browning's Pre-Raphaelite Fra Lippo Lippi, who exhorts artists to paint from nature, to paint "God's works—paint any one, and count it crime / To let a truth slip" ("Fra Lippo Lippi," ll. 295–96).

Among all the symbols and writings that the public was expected to read in the canvas of *The Girlhood,* perhaps the most important was the inscription following Rossetti's signature, the then-mysterious letters "PRB." Because Rossetti chose to exhibit his picture at the so-called Free Exhibition of the Society of Artists prior to the Royal Academy Exhibition where Hunt and Millais were sending their pictures, *The Girlhood* was the first Pre-Raphaelite painting shown to the public. And though Hunt and Millais came to feel that Rossetti's works led to a misguided public association of Pre-Raphaelitism with papist beliefs, *The Girlhood,* in its combination of high moral purpose with realism of detail, was in many respects a fitting herald for the movement. As Hunt said, *The Girlhood* was excessively "Overbeckian," and in its imitation of an early Christian mode already in practice on the Continent and in English paintings by Brown as well as "Herbert, Dyce, Maclise, and others," it was hardly revolutionary. Still, it was "completed and realised with that Pre-Raphaelite thoroughness which Brown's medieval supervision would not have instilled, so it appeared with our monogram, P.R.B." (Hunt, 1:120). In fact, both of Rossetti's early paintings epitomize what has been called the "shared style" of the PRB: "severe outline, mannered gestures, intense exchange of glance, controversial subjects in disguise."[14]

Nevertheless, Hunt and Millais were no doubt justified in being distressed by the effects of Rossetti's work on the public perception of their own works. When the first Pre-Raphaelite paintings were exhibited in 1849 they attracted little critical notice, and that little was generally favorable. But in the following year, when the meaning of the initials "PRB" had leaked out (through Rossetti), and when Rossetti's painting had once again been exhibited prior to those of his brethren at the Royal Academy, the art critics of the day were primed to respond to an apparently revolutionary attack on established values in painting—and more, to a revolution that smacked of papacy. The outcry was mostly directed against Millais and Hunt, and there is no need to dwell here on the critical absurdities uttered in defense of the academic status quo. But a few comments may be offered on the state of the market for contemporary painting, and its effects on Rossetti's art. When Rossetti presented himself to the public as a Pre-Raphaelite and an Art-Catholic, he was working within contemporary movements in both religious thought and pictorial art. He had every reason to suppose that his approach might be professionally rewarding and, indeed, he may even have been aiming for the patronage of the woman who in fact bought *The Girlhood*, the dowager marchioness of Bath, an Anglo-Catholic with whom he had a family connection. But in 1850, after various attacks were mounted on the papist tendencies of Pre-Raphaelite painting, and of his own *Ecce Ancilla Domini!*, and when his Art-Catholic painting looked for a time like an unsaleable commodity, Rossetti began to move away from the "early Christian" line.

Still, though all of the Pre-Raphaelite brothers were angered and embarrassed by the outraged reception they received in 1850, they got more or less what they asked for, and it made them famous. In fact, the PRB, having its origins in 1848, the great year of European revolutions, drew its impetus from vaguely revolutionary sentiments. Debate about the brotherhood has usually taken the form of disputing who was its most influential leader, and what were its most important artistic beliefs, but in fact the PRB had no single leader and no single set of beliefs: what held it together for the short time it lasted was youthful exuberance and a desire to rebel against the teachings of the Academy schools. Rossetti himself was no political revolutionary, and it might even be argued that his most revolutionary sentiment in art was that it should have nothing to do with current movements in society, yet his quasi-autobiographical portrait of the artist in "Saint Agnes of Intercession" includes the inspiring effect of the exiled father's patriotic songs of revolution on the young artist's developing sensibility. But the revolutionary motive was more clearly apparent in Hunt, who acknowledged in later life that "Like most young men, I was stirred by the spirit of freedom of the passing revolutionary time," (1:81), and who characterized his ideas as "irreverent, heretical, and revolutionary," and as a calculated and daring revolt against the authority of his elders (1:57). The point, however, is not that the Pre-Raphaelites were politically revolutionary, but that as in an earlier romantic generation, the spirit of political rebellion against inherited authority went hand in hand with a spirit of aesthetic rebellion that, seen from another angle, was one and the same with a desire to be assertively *original*. As Hunt put it, the young artist has not "the faintest chance of developing his art into living power, unless he investigates the dogmas of his elders with critical mind, and dares to face the idea of revolt from their authority" (1:57).

Finally, the most significant element in the somewhat confused Pre-Raphaelite program may have been the insistence on revolutionary originality. As Herbert Sussman has argued, the most important single fact about Pre-Raphaelitism may well be that in forming a coterie devoted to newness above all, the PRB may represent the origins of the concept of the avant-garde in art:

Certainly the creation of all art involves some innovation, some divergence from earlier models, but the work of the Brotherhood sets the modernist model for Victorian art in that the central strategy is to achieve freshness of response through radical innovation. Furthermore, this innovation or rejection of the forms offered by the culture is programmatic, here involving the formation of a society to oppose the academy and the publication of a manifesto in *The Germ;* and this posture of opposition is overt, rather than covert as in the work of Tennyson, Browning and Arnold. [15]

But, of course, the programmatic effort to be continuously revolutionary and countercultural is not easily maintained, and indeed the counterculture tends rapidly to be assimilated to the main culture. In the case of Pre-Raphaelitism, the notoriety of the brothers was soon converted to fame, largely through the intervention of Ruskin, and their revolutionary defiance ended up making their fortunes. Still, nothing could be more characteristic of Rossetti's career than the desire to be programmatically separated from society, and at the same time accepted and admired by society.

The contents of the *Germ*, consisting mostly of poetry, stories, and literary criticism, reveal that if only through Rossetti's influence, Pre-Raphaelitism soon came to be a literary effort as well as a movement in painting. The Pre-Raphaelite program in literature, however, was still less focused than the program in art. The *Germ* included Rossetti's Art-Catholic poems, and some quaint and dreamy medievalizing by others, but it hardly seems to have included any literary "return to nature." Yet according to William Rossetti, a genuine Pre-Raphaelite poetry ought to include a purely objective fidelity to facts and, indeed, he himself attempted such a poem in "Mrs. Holmes Gray," a versified but otherwise ludicrously prosaic rendition of a coroner's inquest. But a more impressive kind of fidelity to nature is evident in D. G. Rossetti's verse journal written during a brief trip to the Continent with Holman Hunt.

Most of the journal was written off the cuff, and Rossetti plainly regarded it lightly, but it is interesting nevertheless as demonstrating a road not taken—or at least not taken seriously. Much of the verse consists of a kind of accurate Pre-Raphaelite recording of things seen, as in the opening description of the rail journey from London to Folkestone:

> A constant keeping-past of shaken trees,
> And a bewildered glitter of loose road;
> Banks of bright growth, with single blades atop
> Against a white sky; and wires—a constant chain—
> That seem to draw the clouds along with them
>
> (*Works*, 176)

The lines are particularly interesting both as an early response to the new sense of speed inspired by railway travel, and because they hint at the limits of Pre-Raphaelite truth to nature. The various items in the landscape are given with as much fidelity as possible, and with minimal commentary, so that the poetry is akin to twentieth-century imagism. But the description clearly differs from anything that might be offered in a Pre-Raphaelite painting. In painting, the close attention to detail inevitably forced the artist to record everything in stasis, not as the eye perceives the scene, but as the patient brush records all that the eye might dwell upon *if* it could focus on everything at once and *if* the world would only stand still. Rossetti's verse records not nature, but perception, and reflects an impressionistic rather than a purely mimetic art—in verse, at least, he was closer to Turner than to Holman Hunt.[16] Rossetti's casual verse also shows an attention to kinds of detail that are conspicuously lacking in his more serious artistic efforts, as in his description of the swollen face of a drowned man at the Paris morgue: "all the flesh / Had furred, and broken into a green mould" (*Works*, 182). The verse epistle records experience in a more or less raw state, not attempting to gloss over its vulgarity, or to find beauty and mystery in matters of fact. One further example, a description of a pause during a night train journey, will make the point:

> Some time 'twixt sleep and wake. A dead pause then,
> With giddy humming silence in the ears.
> It is a Station. Eyes are opening now,
> And mouths collecting their propriety.
> From one of our two windows, now drawn up,
> A lady leans, hawks a clear throat, and spits.
>
> (*Works*, 183)

No one would argue that Rossetti's art needed more such spitting images of nature, but his casual verse does have a vigor and a kind of realism that might have infused more life into the typically unworldly quest for beauty in most of his more serious art. Indeed, by their very difference from his usual efforts, the playful verses written on his continental excursion reveal how far Rossetti generally was from attempting anything like fidelity to nature or common experience, how completely he detached art from the common life around him. The few poems he wrote on modern and deliberately coarse subjects, such as "Jenny" and "A Last Confession," reveal that he could, when he chose, produce vivid works based on these materials, but these works were much more aesthetically mediated; their craftsmanship as dramatic monologues, their careful control of imagery, their reflectiveness frame and interpret the rawness of experience.

Not surprisingly, the only verses from his journal that Rossetti took seriously enough to publish were interpolated sonnets, most of which were not about the life around him, but about the art around him, the paintings he saw at various museums. The six of these sonnets on paintings that were published in the *Germ* obviously suggest not an art based on a return to nature, but an art based on art, and consequently they point not toward realism or even imagism, but toward aestheticism and symbolism. The first two sonnets, on religious paintings by Hans Memling, seem at first to be consistent with Rossetti's Art-Catholicism. The very first, on "A Virgin and Child, by Hans Memmeling; in the Academy of Bruges," in some ways resembles the sonnet "On Mary's Girlhood"—and anticipates Yeats's "Leda and the Swan"— in its wonder at the confrontation of human weakness and fragility with divine knowledge and power, but finally instead of providing a key to the symbols of the painting, a "reading" consistent with Christian theology, its emphasis falls on the significant word with which it begins: "Mystery." The second sonnet, on "A Marriage of St. Katharine, by the Same; in the Hospital of St. John at Bruges," similarly begins with the word "Mystery," and similarly seeks to deepen the sense of mystery evoked rather than to explicate the devious symbols and interpret the painting. In fact, the sonnet closes with an image that simply returns the viewer to the painted surface: "Whereon soe'er thou look, / The light is starred in gems, and the gold burns" (*Germ,* 199). The point would seem to be that pictorial truth cannot be reduced to words, a point made emphatically in a note to the third sonnet, on "A Dance of Nymphs, by Andrea Mantegna; in the Louvre": "It is necessary to mention, that this picture would appear to have been in the artist's mind an allegory, which the modern spectator may seek vainly to interpret." Once again, as in the sonnets on Memling, and indeed, as in the sonnets on his *Girlhood of Mary Virgin,* the picture remains somehow deeper, more significant, than any verbal interpretation:

> Its meaning filleth it,
> A portion of most secret life: to wit:—
> Each human pulse shall keep the sense it had
> With all, though the mind's labour run to nought.

> (*Germ,* 200)

The poem makes the Keatsian point that the highest truth and beauty must be felt along the pulses. It is not that the symbols have no meaning, but that their meaning eludes the intellect—there is no longer a transcendental key, as in the Art-Catholic works, to unlock the meaning.

The most famous of these sonnets, "A Venetian Pastoral, by Giorgione; in the Louvre," takes a similar stance against interpretation. After simply describing the scene, the two men and the nude woman, the poem concludes with a deepened sense of inexplicable, indescribable mystery:

> the green shadowed grass
> Is cool against her naked flesh. Let be:
> Do not now speak unto her lest she weep,—
> Nor name this ever. Be it as it was:—
> Silence of heat, and solemn poetry.
>
> (*Germ*, 200)

Like the others, this sonnet is somewhat akin to the verse descriptions of Rossetti's journal-letter in its insistence that description of the image is sufficient. But its distance from the verse epistle is also obvious— the focus is on an image already solemnized by art, and the attempt is to deepen our sense of awe and wonder. Rossetti later revised the last line, insisting that "'Solemn poetry' belongs to the class of phrases absolutely forbidden I think *in* poetry. It is intellectually incestuous,— poetry seeking to beget its emotional offspring on its own identity" (*Letters*, 2:726–27). But the sonnets on pictures are perhaps aptly described as intellectual incest—the emotion Rossetti sought was precisely a kind of vague appreciation of the mysteriously poetic. The effect, of course, is an art removed as far as possible from the ordinary affairs of life.

The sonnet on Giorgione is representative of the other sonnets, and of much of Rossetti's other work, in another important respect. The sense of strangeness, of mysterious otherness, is evoked not so much by the direct reference to "solemn poetry" as by the presence of the woman. In all six sonnets, the sense of mystery is evoked by reference to women—to the Virgin, to Saint Katharine, to the dancing nymphs, to the nude figure in Giorgione's pastoral, and, in the final two sonnets, to the naked figure of "'Angelica Rescued from the Sea-monster,' by Ingres; in the Luxembourg." The last sonnet in the series, in fact, follows a series of questions not with an answer, but with the naked image of the naked woman:

> He turns to her: and she
> Cast from the jaws of Death, remains there, bound,
> Again a woman in her nakedness.
>
> *(Germ,* 201)

In their attempt to unite the sister arts of painting and poetry, to evoke a sense of the solemnity of art, to separate art from mundane reality, and to ponder what Rossetti saw as the mysterious otherness of women, these sonnets are finally more suggestive of the central concerns of Rossetti's art than any of his programmatic works of Art-Catholicism or Pre-Raphaelitism. In fact, the sense of wonder and mystery evoked for Rossetti by women is apparent in numerous diverse works of this period, works that certainly cannot be filed away under either of his two artistic labels. Clearly, the theme of "Woman as other" is an important element in the Marian pictures, in the prose tales, and in "The Blessed Damozel," but it is also a central concern of "Jenny," in which a rather philosophic young man ponders the mystery of a sleeping prostitute, of "A Last Confession," in which a man is driven to murder by a young woman he cannot fully comprehend, of "Sister Helen," in which a forsaken woman exercises a fatal and mysterious power over her lover, and of "On Mary's Portrait," in which the portrait of a dead woman seems almost to come to life. Certainly, these interests suggest the direction Rossetti's art would take in the following years. Rossetti was never fully committed to Pre-Raphaelite realism, and was too skeptical to continue long with Art-Catholicism, but he *was* deeply interested in cultivating the mysterious and beautiful in art, so it is not surprisingly that after his early years of experimentation he began to work in forms that brought together the two most potent sources of mysterious and beautiful otherness he could imagine: art itself, and women. And as we shall see in the next chapter, though Rossetti's art was deliberately removed from the mundane and vulgar world, it also was shaped by, and helped in turn to shape, Victorian attitudes toward both art and women.

Chapter Three

Medievalism, Aestheticism, Eroticism

The short-lived Pre-Raphaelite Brotherhood began to break up early in the 1850s as the major figures drifted in different directions. Hunt, determined to paint religious pictures with absolute fidelity to nature, departed in 1854 for the Holy Land to paint from the geographically and atmospherically correct nature, and Millais in 1853 left the avant-garde behind and crossed over to the art establishment when he accepted an invitation to join the Royal Academy. Rossetti, still experimenting with different themes and styles in art, moved further and further away from the Pre-Raphaelite principle of transcription from nature. Moreover, partly because of the critical reaction against the supposed papist tendencies of the PRB, and partly because he lacked genuine Christian faith, he less often drew upon explicit Christian symbolism and moved toward a more vaguely suggestive secular symbolism. In general, he was gradually moving from the morally earnest art of the PRB to a more sensual art, and toward aestheticism. In addition, he was drifting away from such boyish camaraderie as the brotherhood offered, and was coming under different influences. He had met Elizabeth Siddall in 1850, had become increasingly involved with her, eventually engaged to her, and still more eventually, in 1861, he married her. In 1853 he became involved in a complicated friendship with John Ruskin that had serious consequences for his career and his art, and throughout the central years of the decade he became the focal figure in a newly emergent group of young artists who in effect constituted a second avant-garde.

The long affair and engagement with Elizabeth Siddall was biographically, and perhaps artistically, the most important relationship of this period. Though their initially idealistic love affair had considerably soured by the time they were married, Rossetti regarded Siddall not only as a "stunner," in the Pre-Raphaelite slang, but also as a genius, an artist in her own right who would develop under his guidance. His rather complex personal and artistic relations with Siddall reflect both his desire to live an unconventional, more or less bohemian life and, more significantly, his attempt to see all things in the terms of his art. What might be called his shaping vision as an artist took the form of producing a personal vision of her in art and, Pygmalion-like, of transforming the subject of his art into his lover, and finally into a reflection of himself as an artist. But this "shaping vision" might also be called a distorting vision, and Rossetti's relations with his model/lover are extremely revealing concerning even the most apparently "advanced" Victorian assumptions about both art and women.

According to Ford Madox Brown, Rossetti had a "monomania" for drawing Siddall ("Guggums")—"Drawing wonderful and lovely Guggums one after another, each one a fresh charm, each one stamped with immortality."[1] These very delicate, very beautiful drawings have inevitably been romanticized as the apotheosis of the artist-model relationship: the artist, inspired by love, reproduces that love, his own soul, in the portrait. Variations on the theme were told by Rossetti himself, even before he met Siddall, in both "Hand and Soul" and an early version of "The Portrait." But such an idea glorifies romantic love and art in a thoroughly one-sided, gender-biased way: the man is the active agent as both artist and lover while the woman is merely a passive object to be appreciated and recorded. Rossetti's drawings of Siddall clearly reflect one way in which artistic representation draws on and contributes to the cultural production of a particular social conception of "woman." His idealized Siddall is invariably shown to be quiet, passive, demure, with downcast eyes, soft, loose hair, and slightly beseeching upturned lips. As Christina Rossetti's sonnet states, the model is not represented "as she is, but as she fills his dream" ("In an Artist's Studio").

She is, moreover, fragile and sickly, well within the tradition of such nineteenth-century dying beauties as Camille and the Lady of Shalott. Indeed, though no doctor was ever able to diagnose any specific disease, the historical Siddall was always mysteriously ill in a way that, at least for the sake of the romantic story, only enhanced her beauty. According to William Rossetti, "All this fine development, and this brilliancy of hue, were only too consistent with a consumptive taint in the constitution." Pollock, who quotes this passage, notes that "In patriarchal discourses on woman feminine beauty is transitory; in the case of Elizabeth Siddall it appears to have been fatal" (103). Certainly, it was not by chance that Millais painted her as the dying Ophelia, or that Rossetti cast her frequently in the role of the fated Beatrice.

The drawings reproduce not only Victorian ideas about female passivity and weakness, but also romantic ideas about masculine creativity and control. In fact, since the artist is actually recording his own idealized version of her (his "vision," or his "soul"), the model becomes only the occasion for the artist's celebration of his own imagination. It is for this reason that, as Pollock has said, "'Siddal' functions as a sign. More than the name of an historical personage it does not simply refer to a woman, or even Woman. Its signified is masculine creativity" (95). Pollock has forcefully spelled out the implications:

In patriarchal ideologies of art the role ascribed to the feminine position is either as art's object, the model, or as its muse by virtue of a romantic affiliation with an artist. In Pre-Raphaelite literature "Siddal" functions as both. Recognition of woman's active part in culture as producer is thus eroded. The notion that art is made from that "natural" condition of men looking at lovely women effaces from art history consideration of how art is socially produced. Instead it offers merely the hagiography of individual male artists, the celebration of masculine creativity and its collateral, the aesthetic autonomy of art. (96)

Rossetti should not be seen as the patriarchal villain in all this. His insistence on Siddall's own creative powers reveals that he was not in fact satisfied with the traditional role of the beautiful woman as passive inspiration. But he was inevitably a product of his age, and his drawings of Siddall reveal both prevalent attitudes toward women and, perhaps more interestingly, toward the increasing autonomy of art and the artist. Further, as the terms of Pollock's argument imply, the drawings reflect some of the origins of the Rossetti legend in the "celebration of masculine creativity."

While Rossetti's relationship with Siddall reveals the complications arising between artist and model as well as artist and lover, his friendship with John Ruskin reveals those arising between artist and patron, and between artist and critic. Ruskin had almost single-handedly rescued the Pre-Raphaelites from attacks in the press with his letters to the *Times* in 1851, but those letters had been concerned only with the works he had seen at the Royal Academy—works by Millais, Hunt, and Charles Collins. He did not know Rossetti's work until 1853, when he saw three of his drawings exhibited at the Winter Exhibition of Sketches and Drawings, and when, shortly after, he agreed to assess *Ecce Ancilla Domini!* (now called simply *The Annunciation,* to avoid charges of Romanism) for its purchaser. By Rossetti's account, Ruskin's enthusiasm was extreme, and promised to be profitable:

R goes into raptures about the colour and grouping which he says are superior to anything in modern art—which I believe is almost as absurd as certain absurd objections which he makes to them. However, as he is only half informed about art, anything he says in favour of one's work is of course sure to prove invaluable in a professional way, and I only hope, for the sale of my rubbish, that he may have the honesty to say publicly in his new book what he has said privately—but I doubt this. (*Letters*, 1:133–34)

Ruskin did "have the honesty" to praise Rossetti publicly, even to the extent of establishing his reputation as the clear leader of the Pre-Raphaelite movement, and his praise and patronage had an immense effect on Rossetti's career. Ruskin soon established himself as a friend and adviser to Rossetti, and even as a steady purchaser of the works now being done by Elizabeth Siddall, but his most significant effect on the artist's life was, that by establishing his reputation and helping him to make a market for his works, he enabled Rossetti to avoid further exhibitions, to live in mysterious seclusion as a famous but isolated and inaccessible artist. Indeed, this status as a leading painter of the age, whose paintings could not be seen, went a long way toward establishing the Rossetti legend. But the results were, perhaps, not wholly positive.

Though Rossetti has frequently been described as an unusually shrewd man of business, manipulating his patrons to pay high prices for his creative works, it seems likely that his withdrawal from the world of exhibitions and dealers, while it preserved a semblance of high artistic integrity, may have had two seriously adverse results. In the first place, the decision probably hurt him financially—despite Ruskin's help, he struggled to make a decent living in these years, and might have done far better if he had marketed his pictures through the exhibitions and through such newly established dealers as Ernest Gambart.[2] But more importantly, by avoiding public scrutiny and critical discussion of his work, he may have damaged his art in two seemingly contradictory ways. First, he was able to withdraw more and more deeply into his own idiosyncratic artistic idiom, and thus to develop even his worst excesses without interference. And second, as he eventually became more and more dependent on fewer and fewer patrons, he became locked into the style and themes that had pleased them in the first place. In short, his means of marketing himself, made possible in large measure by Ruskin's assistance, eventually restricted his range of experimentation, narrowed his scope, and encouraged his excesses.

A third important development in Rossetti's life and career during the 1850s was his role in the formation of an extremely important mid-Victorian artistic coterie. The somewhat misleadingly named Pre-Raphaelite circle that formed around Rossetti in the mid- to late 1850s, including William Morris, Edward Burne-Jones, and Algernon Swinburne, had even less of a specific aesthetic agenda than their predecessors, but ultimately had a far greater effect on Victorian culture. As Sussman has pointed out, the avant-garde strategies of the first group were repeated by the second (8): they set themselves in opposition to prevailing tastes and standards, and they even established a journal, the *Oxford and Cambridge Magazine,* to express their views and display their works. But their challenge to Victorian culture was more extreme than that of their predecessors. They set conventional morality at defiance, exalted beauty above duty, and used often medieval subject matter specifically as a sensually liberated and liberating antidote to Victorian prudery, earnestness, and high seriousness. The influence of this group in painting through Burne-Jones and Rossetti, in poetry through Swinburne, Morris, and Rossetti, and in the arts of design through Morris, Burne-Jones, and Rossetti, was to transform Victorian culture by establishing a new idea of "advanced" culture as, in a sense, countercultural—always in advance of, or opposed to, conventional thought. As the acknowledged leader of this group, Rossetti was consequently at the center of a movement that went a long way toward establishing the modern relation of the arts to the larger society.

Though in the course of the 1850s Rossetti developed a unique, highly idiosyncratic personal style, his artistic production in both painting and poetry was still experimental and diverse. His primary artistic efforts were in painting, mainly because, as he often noted, painting was a living, and poetry was not, but also because, as he frequently remarked, the long tradition of English poetry had seemed to exhaust the possibilities for the modern poet. Plenty of scope remained for the painter, but in poetry "it has all been said and sung."[3] By 1856 Rossetti claimed, not quite accurately, that he had "given up poetry as a pursuit of my own" (*Letters,* 1:279). But in painting he was following a number of different lines. He by no means abandoned the themes and style of his PRB and Art-Catholic years, but even as he pursued—or attempted to pursue—these established modes, he increasingly branched off in other directions. In the early and mid-1850s he concentrated mainly on sketches, book illustrations, and small watercolors (partly because he was able to produce and sell them quickly), and developed a remarkably luminous style of coloring. His subject matter ranged from literary themes drawn from Poe, Browning, Tennyson, and Shakespeare to such imaginative designs as his well-known *How They Met Themselves,* a drawing of two lovers meeting their spectral doubles in a mysterious wood. But the most characteristic works of the period fall into four categories: drawings of Elizabeth Siddall, carryovers from his PRB and Art-Catholic days, watercolors after subjects from Dante, and small, brightly colored watercolors of Arthurian and generally chivalric themes.

The single project that most occupied Rossetti in these years was an attempt at Pre-Raphaelite realism in oils. The painting *Found,* begun under the principles and influence of Hunt's realism, was meant to be a representation of modern life painted direct from nature. The painting, possibly begun as early as 1851, occupied Rossetti's time and attention at least from 1853 to 1855, and indeed from time to time throughout his life, but was never completed. It was meant to be, as he said, "a great modern work" (*Letters,* 1:142), and was to deal with *the* great modern problem: prostitution. Rossetti described the picture in an 1855 letter to Hunt:

The picture represents a London street at dawn, with the lamps still lighted along a bridge which forms the distant background. A drover has left his cart standing in the middle of the road (in which, *i.e.,* the cart, stands baa-ing a calf tied on its way to market), and has run a little way after a girl who has passed him, wandering in the streets. He had just come up with her and she, recognizing him, has sunk under her shame upon her knees, against the wall of a raised churchyard in the foreground, while he stands holding her hands as he seized them, half in bewilderment and half guarding her from doing herself a hurt. (Quoted in Surtees, 1:28)

The easily readable symbolism and the moral point would be characteristic of the art of the PRB, but the most significant element of the picture was to be its "truth to nature." Rossetti laboriously painted the calf, hair by hair, and searched diligently for the appropriate wall to paint brick by brick.

His failure to finish the picture suggests just how far he was from Hunt's version of Pre-Raphaelitism, but at the same time, his persistent returns to the painting suggest its importance to him. Even late in his life, he labored to finish it if only to prove that he was capable of accurate mimetic representation, to refute "the charge that a painter adopts the poetic style simply because he cannot deal with what is real and human"—to demonstrate that "my preference of the ideal does not depend on incapacity to deal with simple nature" (*Letters*, 4:1635). Yet he was *not* capable of Hunt's kind of realism, and many of his artistic choices were the consequence, at least in part, of his inadequate training. One reason why he never finished *Found* seems to have been that he could not figure out a way to paint the middle ground of the picture, to make the transition from the figures in the foreground to the city in the background. *Found* was important to him, however, not only as an exercise in realism, but also as an exploration of one of his favorite themes in art. Rossetti's interest in the subject of prostitution reflects, for him, a somewhat unusually direct concern with a current social problem, but, as in "Jenny," his real interest seems to lie in the bafflement of a man confronting the problem of female sexuality, and this interest would become a dominant one in his later art.

Still, what Rossetti's failure with *Found* shows most clearly is his general shift away from a kind of realism that he lacked the technical expertise to achieve, and that did not, in any case, appeal to his artistic desire for imaginative self-expression. In fact, his letters from this period reveal a somewhat whimsical attitude toward Huntian realism. Or at least one hopes that an inquiry he made in 1852 is to be taken as a whimsically ghoulish commentary on Pre-Raphaelite excesses: "Are there any opportunities at the Hospital of seeing such a thing as a dying boy? Consequent emotions in bystanders desirable—mother especially so—If you have any youth in such position, and he is accessible, I wish you would let me know before the looks are entirely vacant" (*Letters*, 1:106). Another jesting comment, in an account of an early version of his poem "The Card Dealer," rather more seriously makes a point about the limitations of a purely objective aesthetic stance. One stanza of the poem was "intended to indicate that state before death when the forms of things may be supposed to be lost, while their colours throb, as it were, against the half-closed eyelids, making them to ache with confused lights. I suppose it is dangerous for a man who has not the advantage of dying to attempt a description of death, and afterwards unfortunately there are obstacles in the way" (*Letters*, 1:46).

Rossetti was hardly likely to endorse painting with the eyes closed as an alternative to Pre-Raphaelite realism, but the letter does suggest an interest in speculative and subjective modes of expression, the eyes half-closed, in effect, and the artistic vision combining the world without with the world within the mind. Such subjectivity, a kind of willfully exaggerated impressionism, is also apparent in an epistolary account of a seascape: "Sometimes through the summer mists the sea and sky are one; and, if you half shut your eyes, as of course you do, there is no swearing to the distant sail as boat or bird, while just under one's feet the near boats stand together immovable, as if their shadows clogged them and they would not come in after all, but loved to see the land. So one may lie and symbolize till one goes to sleep, and that be a symbol too perhaps" (*Letters*, 1:201). Such casual comments in a letter hardly amount to an artistic manifesto, but they do reflect the direction in which Rossetti's art was moving—away from mimetic representation and toward a kind of dreamy personal symbolism.

He was also, however, still working throughout the 1850s with the combination of realism and theological symbolism that had characterized his early Art-Catholic works. Among his major works in this mode were *The Passover in the Holy Family* (1855–56), *Mary Magdalene Leaving the House of Feasting* (1857), *Mary Nazarene* (1857), *The Seed of David* (1858–64), *Mary in the House of St. John* (1858), *Mary Magdalene at the Door of Simon the Pharisee* (1858), and another version of *The Annunciation* (1861). Some of these were carried out for purely professional purposes—*The Seed of David,* a triptych, was commissioned as an altarpiece for the Llandaff Cathedral, and *The Annunciation* was designed for a pulpit in St. Martin's Church, Scarborough. And the Mary Magdalene pictures probably had more to do with Rossetti's interest in the theme of the fallen woman than with any Art-Catholic motive.

The most interesting and important of these pictures, however, not only represent important continuations of the Pre-Raphaelite and Art-Catholic programs, but contributed to Rossetti's reputation as the *leader* of the PRB. Though painted in watercolors rather than in oil, *The Passover in the Holy Family* (Figure 3) and *Mary in the House of St. John* were both continuations of the earlier manner in their combination of realism and symbolism. *The Passover* was commissioned by Ruskin, but never finished because Ruskin, annoyed by Rossetti's continued alterations of it, eventually took it away unfinished rather than see it further tampered with. Even in its incomplete state, the painting is in some respects more impressive than the earlier oils, if only because Rossetti had better control of his medium. The coloring is more impressive, and, as Grieve has pointed out, the painting effec-

Fig. 3 The Passover in the Holy Family
Reproduced by permission of The Tate Gallery, London

tively suggests the textures and "qualities of different materials—
brick, thatch, wattle, foliage, flesh" (Bowness et al., 274).

The historical realism of the picture is the result of Pre-Raphaelite
fidelity to nature and the homely domestic details that Rossetti drew
from the description in Exodus (12: 1–13) of the preparations in the
Jewish family for Passover. Rossetti himself later described the work
in a note for a sonnet written to accompany and explain it: "The scene
is the house-porch, where Christ holds a bowl of blood from which
Zacharias is sprinkling the posts and lintel. Joseph has brought the
lamb and Elizabeth lights the pyre. The shoes which John fastens and
the bitter herbs which Mary is gathering form part of the ritual"
(*Works*, 210). Ruskin was so impressed by the realism of the work that

he denied it any symbolic function at all: "I call that Passover plain prosy Fact. No Symbolism at all" (Rossetti 1899, 140). But Ruskin was being either obtuse or disingenuous, for the quite obvious symbolism, like all Christian typology, resides in the inherence of spiritual significance in material forms. The scene inevitably prefigures Christian revelation, if only because Christian readings of the Old Testament see the Passover itself as prefiguring Christian revelation, and Rossetti's details make the pictorial symbolism difficult to miss. A cross-shaped water-drawing apparatus at the well prefigures the Crucifixion; bread and wine within the house symbolize the Eucharist; a vine represents Christ as the true vine; and most obviously the lamb's blood held in a bowl by Christ and smeared on the lintel by Zachary prefigures the blood of the Lamb of God.

Rossetti's sonnet, written in 1867, spelled out some of the symbolism:

> Here meet together the prefiguring day
>   And day prefigured. "Eating, thou shalt stand,
>   Feet shod, loins girt, thy road-staff in thine hand,
> With blood-stained door and lintel,"—did God say
> By Moses' mouth in ages passed away.
>   And now, where this poor household doth comprise
>   At Paschal-Feast two kindred families,—
> Lo! the slain lamb confronts the Lamb to slay.
>
> The pyre is piled. What agony's crown attained,
>   What shadow of Death the Boy's fair brow subdues
> Who holds that blood wherewith the porch is stained
>   By Zachary the priest? John binds the shoes
>   He deemed himself not worthy to unloose;
> And Mary culls the bitter herbs ordained.
>
>   (*Works,* 210)

Characteristically, the sonnet both describes the symbolism and, with its unanswered questions, attempts to deepen the sense of mystery presented in the picture. As in the early Art-Catholic works, the theological symbolism is abundantly clear, but the confrontation of human knowledge with divine truth and power remains mysterious and awesome.

Even more obviously than *The Passover, Mary in the House of St. John* was a continuation of Rossetti's early interest in Marian themes. In-

deed, the work was apparently conceived as early as 1849, and seems
to have been anticipated in the 1849 poem "Ave":

> Mind'st thou not (when the twilight gone
> Left darkness in the house of John,)
> Between the naked window-bars
> That spacious vigil of the stars?—
>
> *(Works,* 168)

Like the others, this picture combines typological symbolism, historical realism, and a sense of awed mystery. After Rossetti's death, it was
this work that Ruskin singled out to substantiate his claim that Rossetti was the true leader of the PRB and, by implication, the greatest
religious painter of his age: "Rossetti's great poetical genius justified
my claiming for him total, and, I believe, earliest, originality in the
sternly materialistic, though deeply reverent, veracity, with which
alone, of all schools of painters, this brotherhood of Englishmen has
conceived the circumstances of the life of Christ. And if I had to choose
one picture which represented in purity and completeness this manner
of their thought, it would be Rossetti's 'Virgin in the House of St.
John.'"[4] But at the same time, Ruskin realized that Rossetti's primary
interests were not religious at all, but literary, that to him "the Old
and New Testaments were only the greatest poems he knew; and he
painted scenes from them with no more actual belief in their relation
to the present life and business of men than he gave also to the Morte
d'Arthur and the Vita Nuova" (Ruskin, 7–8).

In fact, by the time he painted *The Passover* and the still later *Mary
in the House of St. John,* Rossetti had long since been devoting himself
primarily to medieval topics from Dante and from Arthurian legend,
had been moving further and further from realism toward a highly
stylized personal idiom, had for the most part abandoned religious
symbolism for a vaguely "poetic" kind of symbolism, and had moved
from ascetic chasteness to aesthetic sensuality. Themes from Dante had
interested him from very early in his career, and went hand in hand
with his translations of the *Vita Nuova* and other works. Though Dante
was a profoundly religious poet, Rossetti seems to have had little interest in exploring Dante's version of Christian thought. Rather, Dante
interested him as an artist separated from his society, and as the lover
of a quite unallegorical Beatrice, a man perplexed by the mystery of
female beauty.

Both the very early drawings of *The First Anniversary of the Death of Beatrice (Dante Drawing an Angel)* in 1849 and the later watercolor version of 1853 clearly suggest not religious interests, but a concern with the role of the artist within a society that interferes with his visions and his work, and the relations between literary and graphic arts. Similarly, an 1852 picture of *Giotto Painting the Portrait of Dante* is a complex study of the relations between the arts, and their sources of inspiration: Giotto paints the poet Dante as Dante gazes upon his source of inspiration, Beatrice. For the most part, the other works based on Dante, such as *Beatrice Meeting Dante at a Wedding Feast, Denies Him Her Salutation* (1851) and *Dante's Dream at the Time of the Death of Beatrice* (1856) represent the convergence of love and art as Dante (in the first work actually leaning against a painting) stares raptly at his beloved. And still other works, such as *Dante's Vision of Mathilda Gathering Flowers* (1855), *Dante's Vision of Rachel and Leah* (1855), and various versions of *Paolo and Francesca da Rimini* (1849–55) are all studies of female beauty or passionate love. None of these pictures demonstrate any interest in Dante's faith, but instead use his works to give a kind of literary legitimation to Rossetti's "poetic" watercolors of medieval subjects and a safely medievalized courtly love.

Perhaps the best of the Dantean watercolors, and the one most suggestive of Rossetti's stylistic innovations at this time, is the 1853 version of the *First Anniversary of the Death of Beatrice*. The picture is in some respects susceptible to the same kind of "reading" as earlier Pre-Raphaelite pictures, but in other ways it baffles such reading. The room in which Dante is surprised by his visitors is filled with objects of apparent symbolic significance—a picture of the Madonna and Child in the background, a conspicuous mirror, a lute, an hourglass, lilies, a frieze of angel heads—but they do not add up to a coherent meaning. Rather the objects are, like the picture itself, essentially decorative, yet vaguely suggestive of hidden depths of significance. The success of the work results not from any thematic or symbolic coherence, but rather from the suggestiveness of the symbols and from the intricately controlled design, its contrasts of direct and indirect lighting, and its carefully modulated color harmonies—from the dazzling blues and greens seen through the doorway and window to the more muted colors within the room.

The design is characteristic of Rossetti's best work throughout the 1850s in its presentation of a crowded interior, a group of intense, awkwardly postured figures, a glut of quasi-symbolic objects, and openings suggesting a world beyond or behind the painted surface. In this last respect, the picture is particularly interesting, for in addition to the open doorway and window, which show a vividly "real" landscape, the painting on the back wall functions as almost a false window, opening onto another realm of being altogether, and the prominent mirror is yet another false window, suggesting another false depth. Combined with an absence of any attempt at perspective, the total effect is to call attention to the picture as an elaborately ornamented surface. The major significance of the painting is the painting itself, a carefully worked and mysteriously suggestive work of art.

Rossetti's extremely self-conscious artifice is still more obvious in his generally medievalist, often Arthurian, watercolors, where the resonance of Dantean texts no longer troubles the brightly colored surfaces. These works, inspired by medieval illuminations and stained glass, were small (the average size would be about 12″ × 14″) and rapidly produced for sale to such friends as Ruskin and Morris, but though they were, in a sense, "potboilers," they are now often regarded as Rossetti's best and most innovative works. The best-known include *Arthur's Tomb* (1855—though dated 1854), *Fra Pace* (1856), *The Blue Closet* (1857), *The Damsel of the Sanct Grael* (1857), *The Tune of Seven Towers* (1857), *The Wedding of St. George and the Princess Sabra* (1857), *Chapel before the Lists* (1857), *Before the Battle* (1858), and *Sir Galahad at the Ruined Chapel* (1859). The first of these, *Arthur's Tomb*, representative of the rest in theme and style, depicts a meeting of Lancelot and Guinevere quite literally over Arthur's dead body. Lancelot leans over the effigy of Arthur on his tomb to kiss the kneeling Guinevere, who interposes a hand to keep him away. Obvious symbolism in the picture includes a snake and an apple in the lower left corner, and two paintings on the tomb—one showing Lancelot being knighted by Arthur and Guinevere, and the other showing the knights of the Round Table seeing the Holy Grail. But the emotional force of the picture is conveyed less in its symbolism than in its design. The work has been well described by T. Earle Welby:

Into those few inches . . . Rossetti has forced the crouching and menacing figure of Lancelot, the uncloistered, drawn and recoiling figure of Guinevere, the horizontal sculptured figure of Arthur, making the tacit commentary which the dead make on the acts of the living; and then, with a magnificent stroke of designer's genius, he has crushed them down with the stiff, incumbent, stark bough of the tree. The picture is, as it was resolutely intended to be, without relief. The eye yearns for the consolation of the perpendicular, and in vain.

The picture avoids any problems with perspective simply by filling the foreground so completely that no background exists—the figures are all pressed onto one pictorial plane. The effect is extraordinarily claustrophobic and the figures, crushed between the tomb and the trees, seem oddly contorted, but the result, as Welby has said, was to convey "the emotional tension through tension of design."[5] Ruskin, who bought the painting, admired it in spite of its ostentatious indifference to "truth to nature," but he seemed almost unable to account for his admiration, calling it "imperfect," and adding that "the Launcelot is so funnily bent under his shield, and Arthur points his toes so over the tomb, that I dare not show it to Anti-Pre-Raphaelites, but I value it intensely myself" (Surtees, 1:35). Ruskin's praises at this time of the stylization and brilliant colors of medieval manuscript illuminations indicate that it was these qualities that he admired in Rossetti's watercolors. Indeed, he later eulogized Rossetti for just these characteristics in his work: "I believe his name should be placed first on the list of men, within my own range of knowledge, who have raised and changed the spirit of modern Art: raised, in absolute attainment; changed, in direction of temper. Rossetti added to the before accepted systems of colour in painting, one based on the principles of manuscript illumination, which permits his design to rival the most beautiful qualities of painted glass, without losing either the mystery or the dignity of light and shade" (5).

At the same time, the emphasis on purely decorative qualities was so utterly counter to Ruskin's most fundamental teachings about the accurate representation of nature, and so utterly indifferent to his emphasis on the moral function of art, that the great critic was bound to be somewhat ambivalent:

The specialty of colour-method which I have signalized in Rossetti, as founded on missal painting, is in exactly that degree conventional and unreal. Its light is not the light of sunshine itself, but of sunshine diffused through coloured glass. And in object-painting he not only refused, partly through idleness, partly in the absolute want of opportunity for the study of nature involved in his choice of abode in a garret at Blackfriars,—refused, I say, the natural aid of pure landscape and sky, but wilfully perverted and lacerated his powers of conception with Chinese puzzles and Japanese monsters, until his foliage looked generally fit for nothing but a fire-screen, and his landscape distances like the furniture of a Noah's Ark from the nearest toy-shop. (9)

I quote Ruskin at some length partly because his comments suggest the troubled relationship between Rossetti and his dogmatic patron, partly because his praise reflects Rossetti's achievement in these years, and partly because his disparagement indicates how rapidly and how far Rossetti had distanced himself from the original ideas of Pre-Raphaelitism. The PRB had defined itself in opposition to all conventions and artifice and had prided itself on a return to nature, but by the mid-1850s Rossetti was consciously returning to artifice, and was deliberately producing an art that defined itself as precisely what was *not* to be found in nature. In short, his medieval watercolors were contributing to the origin of an art separated from nature, separated from mimetic constraints, and tending toward purely decorative purposes. His medievalism was leading the way toward aestheticism.

The other medievalist watercolors of the period produce the same effects as *Arthur's Tomb*. *The Tune of Seven Towers,* for example, is another brilliantly colored, claustrophobic presentation of a pair of awkwardly postured lovers. Here a man leans toward a seated maiden playing on a stringed instrument while a lady in waiting gazes over her shoulder and another, leaning into the picture from a mysterious aperture in the back wall, places an orange branch on a bed. Myriad objects, including the branch, the instrument, a pennon, bells, and a dove, provide possible symbolism, but as in the other medievalist works, the symbols do not provide a coherent, readable commentary for the picture. Once again the apparent symbols offer only a vague sense of the mysteriously poetic, of unapprehended possibilities of meaning. And again the impact of the design results from the claustrophobic intensity of the design and the brilliance of the colors. Not only are the rich blues, greens, and reds of the medieval costumes balanced against one another, but everything in the picture is elaborately patterned, from the wallpaper to the pennon to the richly ornamented furniture—finally the figures themselves seem almost a part of the pattern.

The same effects are seen in a still more exaggerated form in *The Wedding of St. George and the Princess Sabra,* in which once again an awkwardly postured pair of lovers occupies the center of the composition, and once again a mysterious aperture in the back wall reveals attendant damsels, and once again a musical motif is provided, this time by the playing of bells. The quasi-symbolic adjuncts and elaborate patterns are more obvious than ever. In this case the bells, the head of the slain dragon, a rose hedge, and various heraldic devices provide the vague symbolic resonance, but once again the effect of the picture depends primarily on the brilliance of color and on the sense of a claustrophobic, elaborately ornamented surface. The often-quoted description by James Smetham gives the contemporary response to the picture so well that it is worth quoting yet again. It was, he said, "one of the grandest things, like a golden dim dream. Love 'credulous all gold,' gold armour, a sense of secret enclosure in 'palace chambers far apart'; but quaint chambers in quaint palaces where angels creep in through sliding panel doors, and stand behind rows of flowers, drumming on golden bells, with wings crimson and green." The picture had, for Smetham, both the powerful appeal and the mystery of dream. As he put it, the dragon's head seemed to ask, "Do you believe in St. George and the Dragon? If you do, I don't. But do you think we mean *nothing*, the man in gold and I? Either way I pity you, my friend" (Surtees, 1:55).

The full significance of Rossetti's medievalist watercolors is indirectly suggested by another contemporary comment, this one from a review of some works shown at the Pre-Raphaelite Exhibition of 1857. The critic suggested that "there is no other artist living who demands so much mental and moral culture for his appreciation, or who appeals so little to the passive senses, by which alone ninety-nine spectators out of a hundred are to be won." The works were, he felt, too mysterious to be appreciated by the masses, and indeed it seemed to him doubtful "whether the strange delight which these works must afford to all imaginative minds is capable of being explained to the understanding" (quoted in Doughty, 217). Such criticism, quite clearly, reflects the separation of art from the common concerns of society, the cultivation of art for elite sensibilities. Indeed, the example of Rossetti's works and of their reception may suggest some reasons for the withdrawal of art from a larger public discourse in the mid–nineteenth century. The vague and personal nature of the symbolism that made the watercolors "unreadable" may reflect the loss of a common symbolic language—if the symbols allude to no commonly recognized source of meaning, such as Christianity, how were they to be understood? In addition, the artist, himself withdrawn from society, conspicuously looks to another age for his sources of inspiration, and cultivates his sensibility not *with* but *against* the temper of his own times.

Further, the purpose of art is no longer—as it clearly had been even for the PRB—to perform a moral duty for society, to find and preach some form of truth, but was to represent the imaginative and the beautiful. At most, the function of art within the larger society would be to present beautiful alternatives to drab contemporary reality, to provide brief escape from what Arnold called the "strange disease of modern life" into an aesthetic realm of the timelessly beautiful. It is no wonder that Hunt deplored Rossetti's adoption of a "kind of art devised only for the initiated" and indifferent to the needs of the "vulgar" (1:104), but it is also not surprising that Morris, Burne-Jones, and others, bitterly disillusioned by the ugliness of mid-Victorian life, were attracted to Rossetti's medievalism, and made him the master of a countercultural coterie devoted to all things unmodern.

But the turn to medieval subject matter was, in itself, a profoundly Victorian strategy for coping with the difficulties of modern life. In an age in which scientific and critical advances were eroding the foundations of Christian faith, in which industrial and technological changes were fundamentally altering the traditional social structure, and in which political changes were uprooting traditional loyalties, the Middle Ages—or at least a romanticized view of them—had the immense attraction of representing a coherent society, unified by faith in God and devotion to established law. Newman and his companions in the Oxford Movement had looked to the Middle Ages to support their faith, and so, in a very different way, had Ruskin. Carlyle and Pugin had contrasted the wholesome integrity of medieval society with the malaise of modern life, and Tennyson, in the *Idylls of the King,* was soon to associate the loss of the Round Table with the fall of modern civilization.

But the immense difference between the medievalizing of Rossetti and his circle and that of their contemporaries was that for Ruskin, Carlyle, and Tennyson the ideals of the Middle Ages were precisely the ideals, however unrealized, of middle-class Victorian culture. Their men of the Middle Ages were idealized Victorians in fancy dress, pointing the way for their nineteenth-century contemporaries. Indeed, Tennyson's King Arthur was, as Gladstone admiringly noted, the very image of the perfect Victorian gentleman. But for Rossetti, Morris, Swinburne, and others, the Middle Ages were valued precisely as the antithesis of modern values. In Morris's "The Defence of Guenevere," for example, the adultery of Lancelot and Guenevere that had, for Tennyson, been enough to bring down all the ideals of medieval civilization is justified for its passion, for the grace and beauty of Guenevere, and for the chivalric valor of Lancelot. For all the poets and painters of this circle, indeed, the passionate and headstrong lovers of the Middle Ages were celebrated at the expense of Christian virtues—as Pater saw it, such works were faithfully echoing the sentiments of the Middle Ages. For Pater, both the poetry of the Middle Ages and the "aesthetic poetry" of his own age were characterized by "the strange suggestion of a deliberate choice between Christ and a rival lover." The best and most profound medieval poets wrote both within and against their Christian faith: "Coloured through and through with Christian sentiment, they are rebels against it."[6]

Certainly it was a rebelliousness of this sort that characterized Rossetti and his companions: it was not the exercise of Christian virtue in the Middle Ages that appealed to them, but the defiance of conventional standards of morality, of humdrum, unimpassioned life. The real point of their work was not to represent medieval rebellion, but to present an alternative to Victorian decorum. The "aesthetic" or Pre-Raphaelite countertradition of medievalism was at least as radically unmedieval, as utterly modern, as the moralizing tradition of Carlyle, Ruskin, and Tennyson. The very fact that Pater immediately identified the Pre-Raphaelite uses of the past as "aesthetic" indicates that from the start it was not a backward-looking art, like that of the German Nazarenes, perhaps, but a thoroughly modern, even avant-garde art, challenging current assumptions about the relation of art to conventional morality and to society at large. In fact, in its attempt to separate art from modern society, in its initiation of the "aesthetic" movement, this mode of Pre-Raphaelitism went a long way to establish the modern predicament of art on the fringes of society. In this separation, Pre-Raphaelite medievalism ironically reveals not the cohesion of medieval society, but the fragmentation of modern society.

The artist, of course, cannot escape his own age, and even Rossetti's mysterious watercolors represent a longing within the Victorian period for a greater intensity of passion, a more vivid coloring to life. Unfortunately, they could only provide that intensity and coloring in the form of wall decorations. Like the ornaments and patterns within them, the pictures were mysteriously, symbolically suggestive of a lost dream of romance, and they provoked only aesthetic reverie, an imaginative withdrawal from the contemporary world and an implicit critique of it, but no real challenge to contemporary beliefs. Ironically, they appealed very directly to the tastes of the emerging age—precisely those industrialist entrepreneurs who were contributing to the ugliness of modern cities were buying Pre-Raphaelite paintings to decorate the walls of the country homes to which they themselves escaped. Though Pre-Raphaelitism was, as has been said, "in part a protest against towns like Liverpool, yet it was gladly welcomed by them" (Hough, 40). In fact, since the collections of the early patrons of the Pre-Raphaelites ended up in local museums, the great industrial cities of Liverpool, Manchester, and Birmingham now testify to the tastes of the Industrial Revolution, for their museums are filled with Pre-Raphaelite medievalist fantasies.

Though Rossetti wrote and published relatively little poetry during the 1850s and early 1860s, what he did write is both intrinsically interesting and significant for the light it sheds on his other artistic concerns of the period. Perhaps the most important and illuminating of these poems is "The Burden of Nineveh," a work that Rossetti himself regarded as likely to be popular, but uncharacteristic of him since he preferred "the more emotional order of subject" (*Letters*, 2:760). "The Burden of Nineveh" may have been written in some form as early as 1850, but it was not published until 1856, in the *Oxford and Cambridge Magazine*. The 1856 version of the poem, later revised to be in tune with the more "emotional order" of subjects for the *Poems* of 1870, is characterized by a jocular irony at the expense of religion. The poem describes the entry into the British Museum of an ancient sculpture found in the recently discovered ruins of the ancient city of Nineveh:

> I have no taste for polyglot:
> At the Museum 'twas my lot,
> Just once, to jot and blot and rot
> In Babel for I know not what.
>   I went at two, I left at three.
> Round those still floors I tramp'd to win
> By the great porch the dirt and din;
> And as I made the last door spin
> And issued, they were hoisting in
>   A wingèd beast from Nineveh.[7]

But the jocular tone cannot conceal a serious point: the "wingèd beast," once a god, has now been reduced to a cultural artifact to be gazed upon by the vulgar and uncomprehending:

Here cold-pinched clerks on yellow days
Shall stop and peer; and in sun-haze
Small clergy crimp their eyes to gaze;
And misses titter in their stays,
    Just fresh from "Layard's Nineveh."

Here, while the Antique-students lunch,
Shall Art be slang'd o'er cheese and hunch,
Whether the great R.A.'s a bunch
Of gods or dogs, and whether Punch
    Is right about the P.R.B.
Here school-foundations in the act
Of holiday, three files compact,
Shall learn to view thee as a fact
Connected with that zealous tract,
    "Rome: Babylon and Nineveh."

                                              (p. 514)

These lines not only reflect the lively sense of humor that Rossetti too
rarely allowed to penetrate the rather solemn world of his art and poetry, but they also imply several important points. First, they reflect
his usual attitude toward the public reception of works of art, his good-
natured contempt for the vulgar herd. Second, they reflect both England's cultural imperialism and its eventual demise. Nineveh's god has
now been appropriated by triumphant British culture, but that
triumph will be short lived—the next item in the zealous tract that
tells of the rise and fall of great powers will, of course, be "London."
And third, they imply that gods, like civilizations, come and go. Not
only will London go the way of past civilizations, but Christianity will,
by implication, go the way of past religions. Later in the poem the
point is made explicitly as the speaker envisions a distant future in
which some Australian archaeologist will find the "wingèd beast" in
the ruins of London and will

            hold us for some race
        That walk'd not in Christ's lowly ways,
    But bow'd its pride and vow'd its praise
        Unto the god of Nineveh.

                                              (p. 516)

    The poem is of particular significance for an understanding of Ros-
setti's thought because its ironies clearly indicate a much more sophis-

ticated historicism than he is usually credited with. The poem almost programmatically demonstrates his understanding that religious and artistic symbols removed from their social and historical context are emptied of their meaning. If the lessons of "The Burden of Nineveh" are applied to Rossetti's own artistic production, the clear implications are that as he moved from Art-Catholicism to Dantean and Arthurian themes, from figural symbolism to a presentation of quasi-symbolic objects, he was representing the stripping away of real spiritual significance that inevitably attends the reduction of sacred images to artifacts. It is presumably for this reason that the myriad objects and artifacts in his medievalist watercolors are presented without any coherent symbolic meaning.

A similar awareness of the ways in which once forceful symbols lose their significance is apparent in some of Rossetti's briefer poems of the mid-1850s. "The Landmark," a sonnet written in 1854 and later included in *The House of Life,* hints at traditional Christian symbolism only to show that it no longer presents clear guidance in modern life:

> Was *that* the landmark? What,—the foolish well
>   Whose wave, low down, I did not stoop to drink,
>   But sat and flung the pebbles from its brink
> In sport to send its imaged skies pell-mell,
> (And mine own image, had I noted well!)—
>   Was that my point of turning?—I had thought
>   The stations of my course should rise unsought,
> As altar-stone or ensigned citadel.
>
> But lo! the path is missed, I must go back,
>   And thirst to drink when next I reach the spring
> Which once I stained, which since may have grown black.
>   Yet though no light be left nor bird now sing
>   As here I turn, I'll thank God, hastening,
> That the same goal is still on the same track.
>
> (*Works,* 97)

Evidently the speaker has not wholly lost faith in God, or in the possibility of finding his true path, but just as evidently the traditional symbols are no longer available to guide him. The absence of clearly marked "stations of [his] course"—a pun on the "stations of the cross"—implies a general absence of clear spiritual guidance in modern life. And further, the use of the well and its reflecting waters as the landmark suggests that the remaining source of guidance is one's own reflection.

Though the speaker thanks God, the implication of the sonnet is that the modern wayfarer has only himself upon which to rely, and further, that the path is to be found not through symbols charged with divine significance, but through self-examination, through introspection. The lack of divine meaning in nature is even more evident in "The Woodspurge," written in 1856. Here the speaker describes a state of "perfect grief" in which, having purposely wandered and aimlessly seated himself in the grass, he had confronted an apparent symbol:

> My eyes, wide open, had the run
> Of some ten weeds to fix upon;
> Among those few, out of the sun,
> The woodspurge flowered, three cups in one.
>
> (*Works*, 205)

The "three cups in one" might well suggest the Holy Trinity, or perhaps some other association with the mystical number three, but in fact it suggests no meaning beyond itself, and teaches no lesson but a purely botanical one:

> From perfect grief there need not be
> Wisdom or even memory:
> One thing then learnt remains to me,—
> The woodspurge has a cup of three.
>
> (*Works*, 205)

"The Woodspurge" perfectly illustrates Rossetti's tendency in the mid-1850s simultaneously to hint at spiritual symbolism *and* to empty his imagery of symbolic meaning. The poem is not about the meaning to be found in nature: it is about the psychology of grief in a world without a divinely invested meaning. Yet though objects do not point in a clear symbolic way to any generally recognizable body of truths, they are invested in Rossetti's work with a personal resonance: the well and the woodspurge become significant at least as psychological landmarks for the speakers of the poems. The same is true in the brief lyric "Sudden Light," where a scene of no general symbolic significance is freighted with personal meaning through the speaker's sense of déjà vu:

I have been here before,
    But when or how I cannot tell:
I know the grass beyond the door,
    The sweet, keen smell,
The sighing sound, the lights around the shore.

                                                    (*Works*, 200)

"Meaning" has become intensely subjective and personal—external reality has symbolic significance only to the extent that it calls forth or resonates with the psychological states of the perceiver.

The use of an idiosyncratic symbolism to suggest individual psychological states and of an increasingly introspective poetic mode would eventually come to be regarded, by Pater and others, as quintessentially Rossettian, and would characterize the great majority of the sonnets in *The House of Life* and such closely allied works as "The Stream's Secret." The images of the reflecting well, the singing or silent birds, and the oddly familiar landscape would all be frequently reverted to in later works. In the mid-1850s the most ambitious attempt to evoke a landscape resonant with personal symbolic meaning was "Love's Nocturn." Written in 1854 but much revised before publication in 1870, "Love's Nocturn" is a reverie addressed to the "Master of the murmuring courts / Where the shapes of sleep convene!" (*Works*, 70). The speaker, requesting a dream to send to his beloved, describes "dreamworld" at length:

Vaporous, unaccountable,
    Dreamworld lies forlorn of light,
Hollow like a breathing shell.
    Ah! that from all dreams I might
    Choose one dream and guide its flight!
        I know well
    What her sleep should tell to-night.

                                                    (*Works*, 70)

The furniture of "dreamworld" consists of "Poets' fancies," particularly including the kind of doppelgängers that Rossetti was familiar with in the works of Poe and Shelley, and that he had previously used in the early version of "The Portrait" and in his drawing *How They Met Themselves*.

The symbolism in the poem is, for the most part, vaporous and unaccountable, though the dark coverts, spectral doubles, reflections, and echoes are characteristic of Rossetti's tendency to use vague supernaturalism to suggest states of mind. What is most important about the poem, however, is simply the attempt to evoke a kind of dream symbolism, to find a symbolic language for the unconscious. Consequently, it offers an interesting parallel to the medievalist watercolors, to their evocation of a "golden dim dream" and their use of vaguely symbolic accoutrements. But "Love's Nocturn" is entirely too dreamy—it lacks the almost startlingly brilliant clarity of the watercolors, and its vaporous "Poets' fancies" lack the force of the starkly realized images of "The Landmark," "The Woodspurge," and "Sudden Light." Much of Rossetti's most characteristic work attempts to evoke an almost dreamlike sense of psychological depths, but as "Love's Nocturn" seems to illustrate by negative example, he was most effective when he found a specific, concrete image to suggest a specific, if undefinable, emotional state.

Not all of Rossetti's poems of this period were explicitly concerned with the development of a personal symbolism. Some, like "Stratton Water," "The Staff and Scrip," and "Dennis Shand," were explorations in the various medievalist modes of the second Pre-Raphaelite group. "Stratton Water" was an imitation of old ballads that, according to Swinburne, was "too close to be no closer" (15:29). But in this case, at least, the imitation of an archaic form seems to have been less than wholly in earnest. The most serious divergence from the old ballads is a description of a fat priest attempting to climb through a church window: "There's never a saint but Christopher / Might hale such buttocks through!" (*Works,* 204). The ballad is important primarily as an illustration of the Pre-Raphaelite sense of humor about medievalist topics that is all too rarely evident in their works. Like "The Burden of Nineveh," "Stratton Water" indicates that Rossetti was capable of considerable ironic detachment from his uses of the past. But "The Staff and Scrip" and "Dennis Shand" seem to reflect a notion that simply evoking a past mode might be a sufficient end for poetry. Both poems admirably and effectively tell old tales in an old idiom, but they lack any engagement with current concerns. As Swinburne said of "The Staff and Scrip," it has "passages that search and sound pure depths of sentiment . . . but the air of the poem is too remote and refined for any passionate interest" (Swinburne, 15:29).

In other works, however, Rossetti managed to make the old forms
and settings resonate with modern concerns. In "The Bride's Prelude,"
for example, he combined a Keatsian sensuality and richness of language with a medieval story of passionate and betrayed love to explore
the conflict of erotic desire with an ascetic code of conduct. The combination of sensuality, a gothic setting, and archaic diction is obvious:

> Against the haloed lattice-panes
>   The bridesmaid sunned her breast;
> Then to the glass turned tall and free,
> And braced and shifted daintily
> Her loin-belt through her côte-hardie.
>
> *(Works,* 17)

But also as in Keats, the poem involves much more than the evocation
of a lush, medieval atmosphere. The religious constraints of the Middle
Ages are shown to be unnatural and destructive. Aloÿse, the heroine
of the poem, has been raised in a convent with

> "but preachings of the rood
> And Aves told in solitude
>
> To spend my heart on."
>
> *(Works,* 20)

Her ascetic training is not only a "lifelong theft / Of life," but it also
leaves her unprepared to cope with her natural passion, for she is seduced and impregnated.

The details of her narrative are relatively unimportant, especially
since Rossetti never finished the poem or resolved the plot: what matters is the exploration of the heroine's state of mind. Aloÿse's Christian
training and her passionate love effectively set God against a rival lover,
and produce not a resolution, but doubt and introspection. Pregnant,
abandoned by her lover, racked by fear and guilt, rejected by her father
and brothers, she even begins to doubt the existence of God: "'Is there
a God,' she said, 'at all'?" (*Works,* 25). The emotional state described
is less that of any medieval damsel in distress than of a medievalized
Victorian woman, still living under the strictures of a medieval moral
code in the modern world, and trapped within an enforced passivity
that denies her every vital impulse. Even Aloÿse's sister Amelotte,

trapped by the tale and the stifling bridal chamber, is, like Tennyson's
Mariana, the very embodiment of pent-up emotion:

> Her fingers felt her temples beat;
> Then came that brain-sickness
> Which thinks to scream, and murmureth;
> And pent between her hands, the breath
> Was damp against her face like death.
>
> (*Works*, 25)

She has become utterly self-enclosed, registering only her own bodily
sensations,—even her voice and breath cannot escape. The poem thus
evokes a sense of solipsistic stagnation that, as in many of Rossetti's
other works, fails to find any significant meaning outside the confines
of the morbidly introspective self.

The gap between Aloÿse's inner life and the life around her is so
extreme that when the priest condemns sexually fallen women, she can
only recognize herself in the description by a curious detachment:

> "Yet I grew curious of my shame,
> And sometimes in the church,
> On hearing such a sin rebuked,
> Have held my girdle-glass unhooked
> To see how such a woman looked."
>
> (*Works*, 28)

The characterization of Aloÿse demonstrates Rossetti's thoroughly unmedieval recognition that human individuality is defined not in accor-
dance with social prescription, but in alienation from prescribed rules.
It is precisely her "shame" that makes Aloÿse curious and self-reflec-
tive; it is her fall that makes her an individual; and it is the depth of
her suffering that generates the depths of her consciousness.

"The Bride's Prelude" is an intriguing poem not only because it
effectively uses a medieval idiom to gain perspective on a modern form
of consciousness, but also because it focuses on the figure of the fallen
woman to do so. Rossetti's interest in the fallen woman was in many
ways characteristic of an age that sentimentalized the "weaker" sex,
but at the same time was obsessed with the supposed dangers of moral
pollution that the sexually fallen woman presented to her society. Pure
women had to be protected at all costs from sexual contamination, and

society in general had to be protected from the already sexually contaminated women. The resultant denial of any sexual impulse at all in the pure woman made her into a powerful force for moral good, while the presence of sexual appetite in the fallen woman made her deformed and monstrous, a deadly fiend. The most thoughtful Victorians, of course, did not accept this preposterous polarization of women into angels and fiends, but even they were powerfully influenced by the extreme fear of female sexuality that lay behind it.

Female sexuality, then, developed an extraordinarily exaggerated importance in the Victorian mind. It epitomized the power of women for good or evil: sexual desire was a mysterious force from which men must protect their women, and at the same time it was the force in women from which men must protect themselves. And, of course, since men desired female sexuality at least as much as they feared it, these attitudes led to an extraordinary ambivalence toward women generally, and especially toward the erotic appeal of beauty in women. Further, since the presence or absence of sexual appetite could not necessarily be read on the countenance of women like Aloÿse, every woman became, in effect, a mystery. All of these conflicting ideas about female sexuality are explored in Rossetti's painting and poetry. He repeatedly defined women as a kind of sacred or demonic mystery, and he consistently represented women's beauty as fatally dangerous, either for themselves or, more often, for the men they ensnared. But for Rossetti, as for the other poets and painters of the Pre-Raphaelite or aesthetic movement, the fatal attraction of female sexuality took on an added dimension. She was the embodiment of beauty, and therefore both the subject matter for art and, in a curious way, analogous to art—for the artist who saw himself as "countercultural," the dangerous effect of the fallen woman on society was closely akin to the effect art should have. She was also, in a sense, analogous to the artist: both were separated from society and therefore forced to develop their own individuality as a result of their alienation.

The best known of Rossetti's early poetic treatments of fatal female sexuality is "Sister Helen," apparently written in 1852, and published in 1854. The ballad presents a seduced and abandoned woman who exercises a demonic power by burning a waxen effigy of her lover, and so killing him and sending his unredeemed soul to the eternal fires of hell. The poem is far more complex than the traditional ballad—each stanza offers a dialogic exchange between Helen and her brother and concludes with a kind of chorus (it is not really a ballad refrain, since it varies from stanza to stanza). The complex construction enables some limited development of Helen's character, though she remains essentially a type of the fatal woman, and even affords room for some bitter wit. After the lover's father begs for his son's life, the following exchange occurs:

> "Oh he prays you, as his heart would rive,
>   Sister Helen,
> To save his dear son's soul alive."
> "Fire cannot slay it, it shall thrive,
>   Little brother!"
> (*O Mother, Mary Mother,*
> *Alas, alas, between Hell and Heaven!*)
>
> (*Works,* 67)

But his soul shall thrive, of course, in hellfire. "Sister Helen" is of particular interest because it combines Rossetti's enthusiasm for archaic forms, his use of the medieval machinery of magic and of heaven and hell, and his fascination with the seductive and fatal power of female sexuality. This combination of interests, fusing eroticism and medievalism with modern concerns about the dangerous appeal of beauty, almost seems to define the "aesthetic" as it would later be characterized by Pater and others.

By the close of the 1850s the experimental diversity of Rossetti's work in both arts was coming to a close as he came to focus more and more narrowly on the mystery and fatality of female beauty, and on the sensual and quasi-spiritual nature of sexual love. "The Song of the Bower," written in 1860, reveals the increased sensuality of his work at this time:

> What were my prize, could I enter thy bower,
>   This day, to-morrow, at eve or at morn?
> Large lovely arms and a neck like a tower,
>   Bosom then heaving that now lies forlorn.
> Kindled with love-breath, (the sun's kiss is colder!)
>   Thy sweetness all near me, so distant to-day;
> My hand round thy neck and thy hand on my shoulder,
>   My mouth to thy mouth as the world melts away.
>
> (*Works,* 207)

The growing sensuality of his art is generally attributed to biographical causes: his disappointment in love with Elizabeth Siddall and his affair with Fanny Cornforth, the large-armed beauty of "The Song of the Bower." But however much or little biographical events contributed, the increased eroticism seems to have been an inevitable part of the development of a Victorian countercultural art, of aestheticism as a devotion to beauty in defiance of conventional duty. In any case, Rossetti's more and less frank portrayals of sexuality were to bring him into direct confrontation with the more extreme forms of Victorian moral convention. When he finally published his first volume of original poems in 1870, his heaving bosoms and hot kisses were to set off a controversy about the moral function and moral limits of art that would go a long way toward defining the modern relation of the arts to society.

On the other hand, however, countercultural art invariably owes more to dominant cultural assumptions than artists seeking originality would care to admit, and Rossetti's art, certainly, in many ways unambivalently reflects his society's values, its assumptions about women and about beauty in art. Starting in 1859, with a painting of Fanny Cornforth as *Bocca Baciata,* Rossetti developed a rich, sensual style in oil paintings devoted to female beauty, and from that point his work consists almost entirely of what William Rossetti called "beautiful women with floral adjuncts."[8] If Holman Hunt's reaction is considered, the painting would seem to have been an offense against Victorian decency: "it impresses me as very remarkable in power of execution— but still more remarkable for gross sensuality of a revolting kind, peculiar to foreign prints, that would scarcely pass our English Custom house from France" (Surtees, 1:69). Ruskin, like Hunt, responded to this new development in Rossetti's art with a mixture of admiration for the technique and a horror at the new "coarseness" that was making his work, "compared to what it used to be—what Fannie's face is to Lizzie's" (Angeli, 92). *Bocca Baciata* was, in fact, unambiguously a study in what his admiring and hostile critics alike called "fleshliness" (Swinburne, 15:13),[9] and what Rossetti called "body's beauty" as opposed to "soul's beauty." Still, many of Rossetti's contemporaries, and most conspicuously, his patrons, were more than willing to accept "body's beauty" as within the proper domain of art. In establishing two distinct types of female beauty, a "body's beauty" related to Fanny Cornforth, and a "soul's beauty" related to Elizabeth Siddall, Rossetti was reflecting and contributing to his age's polarization of women into fatal seductresses and beautiful angels.

The shift in Rossetti's style seems to have been at least in part a response to market conditions. Ruskin had largely supported Rossetti by creating (and being) a market for his watercolors, but as he himself told Rossetti in 1855, "you must consider market value in all things, and a painful and sad-coloured subject never fetches so much, on the average, as a pleasant and gay one. . . . remember in *market*, oil fetches always about six or seven times as much as water-colour. Very foolish it is, but so it is" (Rossetti, 60). Rossetti, in fact, found a ready market and high prices for his paintings of "body's beauty," including variations of Fanny Cornforth from *Bocca Baciata,* to *Fair Rosamund* (1861), *Fazio's Mistress* (1863), *The Blue Bower* (1865), and culminating in *Lady Lilith* (1868), the painting Rossetti specifically alluded to as "Body's Beauty." Not all of the "fleshly" pictures were painted from Fanny Cornforth (in fact, her head was painted over in "Lady Lilith," replaced by that of another model), but all of them are characterized by what Rossetti saw as a Venetian richness of coloring, a bright and sensual treatment of flesh tones, and exotic, richly colored "adjuncts"—flowers, costumes, jewelry.

Most conspicuously, as F. G. Stephens said of *The Blue Bower,* they are characterized by "the marvelous fleshiness of the flesh; the fascinating sensuousness of the expression," and simultaneously by a "cunning combination and variety of the colour [that] will delight the student and those who are content to receive a picture in the spirit which is proper to the highest form of Art" (quoted in Henderson, 94). The pictures, in short, make "fleshliness" respectable through virtuosity: dangerous female seductiveness is made safe through art, and can be brought into the Victorian home as wall decoration. Rossetti's correspondence with his various patrons clearly illustrates how well his art was adapted to Philistine pretensions to high art. Attempting to sell *Monna Vanna* in 1866, for example, Rossetti wrote to a potential buyer not only that it represented "the Venetian ideal of female beauty," but also, perhaps more to the point, that it was "one of my best I believe, and probably the most effective as a room decoration which I have ever painted" (*Letters,* 2:606). As Virginia Allen has said, "Rossetti worked first and last, in his painting, in accord with the demands of the marketplace,"—and more, "he shared, first and last, his audience's social prejudices."[10]

The "fleshly" paintings, as Allen has argued, appealed to Rossetti's contemporaries not only as "room decorations" but as representations of women—or rather, of Woman. For precisely this reason they provide, according to Pollock, a "symptomatic site for the study of a new regime of representation of woman on the axis of bourgeois realism and erotic fantasy" (124). The nature of the erotic fantasy is abundantly evident in Arthur Hughes's comment that the purchaser of *Bocca Baciata* "will I expect kiss the dear thing's lips away" (quoted in Pollock, 129), but the relation of Rossetti's paintings to the structure of Victorian desire is more complicated than Hughes suggests. The important issues can best be suggested, perhaps, by a brief consideration of *Lady Lilith* which, according to Allen, "incorporates the fears and fascination of Rossetti and his generation," particularly the fears of emancipated women, no longer submissive to male control (286). Lilith, after all, was the serpent-woman of Eden, prior to Eve, and prior to any notion of male dominance. Rossetti's description of the picture emphasizes her autonomy: she "represents a *Modern Lilith* combing out her abundant golden hair and gazing on herself with that self-absorption by whose strange fascination such natures draw others within their own circle." Both the picture and the sonnet Rossetti wrote to accompany it are intended to suggest the same "essential notion"—that "of the perilous principle in the world being female from the first" (*Letters,* 2:850).

In the sonnet she is "subtly of herself contemplative" and so "Draws men to watch the bright web she can weave, / Till heart and body and life are in its hold." She is the fatal woman, dangerous yet enticing, and her representation in art reproduces the frisson without the actual danger. Early in the century Hannah More had advised men never to take into their homes a woman who displayed evident vanity—unlike a picture that would stay on the wall where it was placed, she argued, the woman was likely to gad about and make trouble. Rossetti supplied the picture that would both entice and stay put. F. G. Stephens's account of the picture, too long to quote in its entirety, epitomizes the way in which the seductiveness of the woman is transfigured into the safe and acceptable form of art. The description modulates from the voluptuousness of the woman "reckless how much or how little of her bosom and shoulders is displayed" to the "delicious harmony of colour" in the painting (quoted in Surtees, 1:116–17). As the displacement of the word "delicious" from the sexual to the aesthetic realm implies, the dangerous image is tamed and made accessible in art.

Rossetti's highly stylized representations of female beauty, however, do not merely reflect a displacement of Victorian sexual desire to artistic representation: they also contribute to the construction of a new ideal of "woman." As Pollock has pointed out, Rossetti's paintings were never portraits, never about the model or about any actual woman, but were instead masculine constructions of a highly artificial model of female beauty. Pollock makes this point by comparing the anatomical impossibilities of Rossetti's stylized beauties with the stylization of female beauty in cosmetic advertisements, so that all women aspire to one unreal "type" of beauty. Both were characterized by "systematic disproportions of the faces, the absence of volume and of the remotest suggestion of three-dimensional bone-structure" so that they are "not faces . . . but fantasies." As Pollock points out, the "myth of woman is that she is simply revealed by the genius of the artist," but the actual works, with their "heavily laboured surfaces belie that myth with evidence of the work required to manufacture it" (121–22). Rossetti's paintings are not "Siddalls," or "Cornforths," or "Morrises," but "Rossettis," and their trademark is a new type not of female beauty, but of fantasy.

The stylization can be seen in all of Rossetti's paintings, but is perhaps most obvious from a glance at one of his most beautiful, *The Beloved* (1865–66) (Figure 4). The painting, conceived as a *Beatrice,* perhaps because it came out more "fleshly" than "spiritual," was later more or less arbitrarily declared to represent the bride from Solomon's song—perhaps simply because, as Rossetti put it, "I have got my model's bright complexion, which was irresistible, & Beatrice was pale" (quoted in Surtees, 1:105). The painting represents the bride as she unveils herself, surrounded by four bridesmaids and a black page or attendant. The whole is brilliantly colored and meant to draw the eye to the central figure with her neck like a tower, her full, smooth expanse of cheek, and high-set eyes. But as T. Earle Welby noted, the artificiality of this image is startlingly contrasted with the superbly painted figure of the black attendant: "the realism of that head makes war on the almost uncontoured, vaguely poetic face of the bride herself. . . . if anyone thinks that Rossetti could not paint the human animal with understanding alike of osseous structure and of the pathos of the soul unconscious of its cage, let him look at that negro child and learn the enormity of his error" (73). The contrast illustrates very clearly just how deliberate Rossetti's stylization was—as deliberate as the elaborate makeup and airbrushing that removes "osseous structure" from the models in cosmetic advertisements.

The point is not that Rossetti was an incompetent artist, but just the contrary: he fashioned a new type of beauty that spoke powerfully to the needs and desires of his time. Even in pictures of "Body's Beauty" he did not, after all, aim at portraiture, but at what he

Fig. 4 The Beloved ("The Bride")
Reproduced by permission of The Tate Gallery, London

thought of as an ideal of beauty, even a vague mysticism. The idealization is even more evident in pictures such as *Sibylla Palmifera* that were meant to represent "Soul's Beauty":

> Under the arch of Life, where love and death,
> Terror and mystery, guard her shrine, I saw
> Beauty enthroned.

(Works, 100)

The attempt to create an idealized, even a mystic, kind of beauty is most abundantly evident, however, in the remarkable *Beata Beatrix* (1864) (Figure 5), a painting in which Elizabeth Siddall is transfigured as Beatrice. The painting, developed from drawings done before his wife's death, had a particular significance for Rossetti, but even beyond the personal meaning, the subject, drawn from Dante, brought into focus all of his thought and feeling about the spiritual or mystic significance of love and of female beauty.

The portrayal of Beatrice in a trance, "suddenly rapt from earth to heaven," and accompanied by various mystical Dantean symbols, has always been regarded as a masterpiece. Even the usually reserved and even caustic Evelyn Waugh has described it as "a painting of consummate delicacy and beauty, unsurpassed in his own age and comparable with the greatest creations of the past. . . . the most purely spiritual and devotional work of European Art since the fall of the Byzantine Empire."[11] Flesh is certainly toned down in this picture, and the pale Beatrice, her hair illuminated as by a halo, is manifestly spiritual, more heavenly than earthly. As Rossetti himself described it to a patron when selling a replica, the painting represents a "sudden spiritual transfiguration" (quoted in Surtees, 1:96). At the same time, however, the loosened hair, the yearning expression, the half-closed eyes and half-opened mouth, are not without sensuous appeal. The painting embodies, or at least was meant to embody, Rossetti's highest ideal in art, the meeting point of flesh and spirit, death and life, in the most exalted love.

In the terms of Rossetti's poem "The Portrait," the painting becomes a "shrine" to love and beauty. F. W. H. Myers no doubt had this picture in mind, among others, when he wrote shortly after Rossetti's death of the "new and haunting beauty" of Rossetti's paintings: "they may be called (and none the less so for their shortcomings) the sacred pictures of a new religion; forms and faces which bear the same relation to that mystical worship of Beauty . . . as the forms and faces of a Francia or a Leonardo bear to the medieval mysteries of the worship of Mary or of Christ."[12] The cult combines Rossetti's passionate idealizations of both love and art—the "spiritual transfiguration" of the flesh occurs not when it is drawn up to heaven, but when it is translated by the painter's genius into is own shrine, the work of art.

From a modern perspective, it is not difficult to see that Rossetti's transfigurations of female beauty reflect the general tendency of the age to translate threatening female otherness into manageable terms.

Fig. 5 Beata Beatrix
Reproduced by permission of The Tate Gallery, London

The cult of beauty enshrines, finally, the artist's vision, not the model's soul. The expression of personal vision is generally regarded within the myth of artistic autonomy—genius raises itself and its subject matter above the sordid concerns of its age. But Rossetti was painting precisely what his patrons wanted, and his "vision," however personal, evidently reflected (and probably contributed to) the Victorian desire to make female attraction somehow more spiritual than carnal. Rossetti wanted to see himself as making shrines, but he was also well aware that he was producing a commodity to meet a certain demand. Indeed, he was not above making replicas even of the *Beata Beatrix* when money was short—and it always was. Further, when Rossetti sold his paintings to his various patrons, he was often at pains to point out that the presence in them of "the ideal" gave them an added value as commodities.[13]

Despite his undoubtedly sincere belief in his artistic "vision," Rossetti could not help feeling himself at the mercy of the market, and he quite explicitly felt himself cheapened as a painter by the need to paint for money. By 1870 he came to see himself as somehow compromised by his commercialization of painting, which is one reason why he was eager to establish himself as a poet by the long-delayed publication of his *Poems*. His poetry, precisely because unprofitable, was a pure, an autonomous art: "my verse, being unprofitable, has remained (as much as I have found time for) unprostituted" (*Letters*, 2:850). As it would turn out, the issue was not quite so simple, and unlike the paintings, which could be seen only by a small circle of friends and patrons, the verse would be subjected to the scrutiny and censure of Victorian society at large. The ideal of autonomy in art was to be far more severely tested by the poetry than by the painting.

Chapter Four
Poems, 1870

By 1870, Rossetti had established himself as a successful painter and as the acknowledged leader of an increasingly important circle of painters and poets, but since he refused to exhibit his paintings publicly, and since little of his original poetry had been published outside the coterie magazines, his work had received little public recognition. Further, though he was the oldest and most respected member of his circle, his various friends and associates had begun to outstrip him in what Chiaro dell' Erma called the race of fame—in painting, Hunt and Millais had received far more public attention than Rossetti, and in poetry, his sister Christina, Morris, and Swinburne had all produced significant and widely read volumes. It was clearly time for Rossetti to substantiate his claim to genius, and he intended to do so with the publication of *Poems,* a volume that would include revised versions of his early poems plus a substantial number of poems written during a period of renewed interest in poetry starting in 1868. The vindication of his "genius," moreover, would have to be in poetry rather than in painting precisely because he had been commercially successful as a painter—painting was his career, almost less an art than a business, and he felt it sullied by the marketplace. Even in his best pictures, Rossetti felt, his essential genius took the form of poetry: "My own belief is that I am a poet (within the limit of my powers) primarily, and that it is my poetic tendencies that chiefly give value to my pictures: only painting being—what poetry is not—a livelihood—I have put my poetry chiefly in that form" (*Letters,* 2:849). His poetry was tarnished by no "trade associations" (*Letters,* 1:377). In poetry, as he put it, he had "done no pot-boiling at any rate" (*Letters,* 2:729). His poetry, buffered from sordid worldly concerns, could be the crucible of his genius, could be the expression of the quintessential Rossetti.

Not surprisingly, since Rossetti saw this volume as the first and fullest presentation of his highest art to the public, he took extraordinary care with it, revising the early poems to conform to the later ones, ordering the contents for the best effect, even taking pains to make sure that the quality of the type, the paper, and the covers was of the highest order. And not content to do all he could to ensure the high quality of the volume, he went a step further to ensure the high quality of the reviews. He packed the critical jury, arranging for his friends and admirers to place reviews in the most prominent journals. The result was a burst of acclaim that saluted Rossetti as one of the great poets of the age—even of the ages. But as Jerome McGann has noted, though Rossetti regarded *Poems* as entirely unsoiled by connections with the world of getting and spending, as a pure embodiment of the transcendentally "aesthetic," the care he took in packaging and, in a rather underhanded way, *advertising* it in the reviews, only highlighted its status as a commodity (1988, 348). It was, in part, this internal contradiction that generated a furor when the book was attacked in the following year by Robert Buchanan in the pseudonymous and scurrilous essay, "The Fleshly School of Poetry." Buchanan's attack was most obviously focused on the erotic subject matter of much of the volume, but, as we shall see, the real significance of the article was in its attack on the attempted separation of the "aesthetic" from the everyday concerns of society. As Buchanan saw it, the "aesthetic" was a "morbid deviation from healthy forms of life"—the supposed preference for "expression" over "thought" implied a groveling sensuality in which the "body" is presumed "greater than the soul."[1] The great significance of *Poems,* finally, is that in form and content it manifested the difficulties of art and the artist in the modern marketplace—attempting simultaneously to transcend conventional thought, morality, and taste, and to win public approval.

Rossetti had originally intended to publish a book of original verse shortly after his volume of translations, *The Early Italian Poets,* appeared in 1861—in fact, that volume had included an announcement of a forthcoming book to be called *Dante at Verona and Other Poems.* But after Elizabeth Siddall's death in 1862, he sacrificed his poetic ambitions with the melodramatically romantic gesture of burying the only manuscript of his poems in her coffin. In the subsequent years he devoted himself almost exclusively to painting, but in 1868 he once again began writing poetry, much of it love poetry inspired by an increased intimacy with Jane Morris, the wife of William Morris and for many years Rossetti's favorite model, his ideal of female beauty. Eventually his own ambitions as a poet, combined with the exhortation of his friends, led him to contemplate publishing—and for that purpose to retrieve the manuscript from his wife's grave. The episode has, of course, fueled the Rossetti legend—especially in a ghoulish and thoroughly fictionalized depiction in Ken Russell's film biography of Rossetti—and it is, in truth, ghoulish enough even in the subdued version of actuality. Rossetti went through the official steps, had the body legally exhumed, and waited fretfully at a friend's house. The manuscripts, less immortal than the pure spirit of poetry, were rank, decaying, and worm-eaten, but still mostly legible.

Perhaps of greater significance than what Keats would call the "wormy circumstance" was Rossetti's justification for his action. As he wrote to Swinburne, "no one so much as herself would have approved of my doing this. Art was the only thing for which she felt very seriously. Had it been possible to her, I should have found the book on my pillow the night she was buried; and could she have opened the grave, no other hand would have been needed" (*Letters,* 2:761). The important point, spelled out in Swinburne's reply, is that no consideration should be allowed to interfere with the august demands of the highest good that can be imagined—that is, of art:

no strength of words can seem too strong, can even seem adequate, to render my inmost and sincerest sense of the importance of the question whether we are all to be the richer or the poorer by one more treasure of art: of art which always was and is to me the highest, deepest, most precious and serious pleasure to be got out of life. I do think it is matter even more of justice than of humanity to see that men living who feel this, and men to come who will, should not be defrauded of anything of that noble delight which nothing can replace or repurchase. . . . We have a right to the good gifts and growths of nature, to all the light and strength and lasting joy and glory which she gives best in her highest form—art.[2]

However conveniently the duty to art may justify Rossetti's act, there is no reason to doubt his or Swinburne's sincerity in invoking it. Their language fairly reflects their genuine commitment to an exalted idea of art, and on Swinburne's part, at any rate, to the belief that Rossetti's work would indeed be a timeless and transcendent gift to humanity.

Once committed to the idea of publication, Rossetti began revising and arranging the poems to form a coherent volume. As he put it, the book was to be presented as "studied work, where unity is specially kept in view" (*Letters,* 2:823). The most important revisions were designed to eliminate traces of Art-Catholicism from the book, and to emphasize his taste for "strong savours, in art, in literature, and in life." He revised the early poems to replace suggestions of Christian faith and medieval asceticism with an emphasis on the aesthetic worship of beauty and on passion. He included "Ave" in the volume only after some hesitation, and after considering a note that would emphasize its status as art, not religion: "Art still identifies herself with all faiths for her own purposes: and the emotional influence here employed demands above all an inner standing-point" (*Works*, 661). He altered "The Blessed Damozel" to make the heavens still less "Dantesque" and to emphasize the importance of human love, and changed "My Sister's Sleep" to minimize the religious element and to delete the "spooniness."

An important change to "A Last Confession" is emblematic of the alterations. In the early version of the poem, the speaker had presented the girl he loved fraternally and later passionately with

> A little image of great Jesus Christ
> Whom yet she knew but dimly. I had not
> Yet told her all the wondrous things of Faith
> For in our life of deadly haste, the child
> Might ill be taught that God and Truth were sure.[3]

But revising out such Christian certainty, and changing the tone of the poem's, and the book's, imagery, Rossetti substituted a quite different gift in the published version:

> A little image of a flying Love
> Made of our coloured glass-ware, in his hands
> A dart of gilded metal and a torch.
> And him she kissed and me, and fain would know
> Why were his poor eyes blindfold, why the wings
> And why the arrow. What I knew I told
> Of Venus and of Cupid,—strange old tales.
>
> (*Works*, 46)

The displacements of "great Jesus Christ" by a "flying Love" and of "God and Truth" by "strange old tales" must be understood within the terms of the dramatic monologue, of course, yet they are in fact representative of the general shift in Rossetti's work signaled by the *Poems* of 1870.

The order of the poems was also designed to contribute to the studied unity of the book. As his letters show, Rossetti struggled to order the poems so that the early Art-Catholic impulse would be subordinated to the later interests, and so that each poem would be read in the context that would best illuminate it. He broke the volume into three sections, "Poems," "Sonnets and Songs: Towards a Work to Be Called 'The House of Life,'" and "Sonnets for Pictures, and Other Sonnets." The opening section included his longer poems and ballads and introduced the dominant themes in his work; the second section narrowed and intensified the thematic and formal focus in the sonnets that Rossetti was increasingly coming to regard as the particularly "Rossettian" mode; and the final section emphasized both the sonnet form and Rossetti's special status as a painter-poet, a master in two arts. All three sections culminate in poems that highlight the poet's skeptical outlook. The first ends in a series of six translations, three from François Villon, two from Old French ballads, and one from Sappho (though this last is an adaptation, not a translation—Rossetti's Greek was minimal). The translations were no doubt lumped together at the end of the section to segregate them from the original work, but they also function to emphasize the erudition and aesthetic background of the poet—to remind readers of the long tradition in which the present poems are to be read. The last original poem in the first section, "Aspecta Medusa," epitomizes the aesthetic viewpoint of the book:

> Andromeda, by Perseus saved and wed,
> Hankered each day to see the Gorgon's head:
> Till o'er a fount he held it, bade her lean,
> And mirrored in the wave was safely seen
> That death she lived by.
>
>   Let not thine eyes know
> Any forbidden thing itself, although
> It once should save as well as kill: but be
> Its shadow upon life enough for thee.
>
>   (*Works,* 209)

The poem was originally intended to accompany a painting, but the patron who ordered it absurdly canceled his order when he realized it was to include the severed head of the Medusa—even though, as Rossetti said, the severed head would be treated as "a pure ideal," aesthetically distanced (*Letters,* 2:643). The comment on the proposed painting serves as a gloss on the poem, which is precisely about aesthetic distance. The poem invokes the classical tradition to justify its "strong savour" of death, forbidden knowledge, and the fatal appeal of female sexuality, and suggests that such things are best known indirectly. The implication is that art is the mirror that provides a safe way to view the forbidden: "be / Its shadow upon life enough for thee," but also that direct knowledge of ultimate things is not possible except in death.

The poem ending the second section, "The Sea-limits," also makes the point, though somewhat obscurely, that full knowledge is not available to mankind. The poem describes the limits of human vision and comprehension, and closes with an enigmatic image of human limitation:

> Gather a shell from the strown beach
>   And listen at its lips: they sigh
>   The same desire and mystery,
> The echo of the whole sea's speech.
>   And all mankind is thus at heart
>   Not anything but what thou art:
> And Earth, Sea, Man, are all in each.

> (*Works*, 191)

The poem hints at an apprehension of mystic unity between mankind and some transcendent reality in nature, but finally affirms only that human perception is limited to knowledge of one's own sensations—the shell echoes the listener's own pulsing blood. Rather than a mystic union of mankind and nature, the poem affirms that for each individual "Earth, Sea, Man" are reduced to "what thou art." The last poem in the third section is equally skeptical about the possibilities of human knowledge. "The Monochord," rather like "The Landmark," suggests that the signs made available on life's pilgrimage are unreadable: the poem consists entirely of four unanswerable questions about the meaning of individual experience, about life and death.

Rossetti enforced the skeptical outlook of the volume by his careful arrangements within sections—and particularly within section 1, which included the most diverse group of poems. He began the volume with "The Blessed Damozel," but immediately followed that now-chastened version of Dantesque heavens with "Love's Nocturn," a poem that explicitly equates love with erotic longing, and displaces faith with dreams. The erotic tenor of the volume is then increased with the ballad "Troy Town," about the pagan power of Venus and the fatal power of female love, and this, in turn, is followed by "The Burden of

Nineveh," which establishes the perspective of historical relativism through which all faiths—including both Christianity and paganism—are called into question. This in turn is followed by another erotic ballad about destructive female passion, "Eden Bower," and then by the most Art-Catholic of the poems, "Ave." By this point, of course, the note declaring all faiths equally available to depiction from the "inner standing-point" of art is unnecessary—the arrangement of poems, and particularly the strategic placement of "The Burden of Nineveh," has already made the point.

Ironically, however, though the idea of an "inner standing-point" suggests a kind of Keatsian "negative capability" in which the poet can know various faiths and attitudes from within the mind of the speaker, the emphasis on the subjectivity of perception constantly reemphasizes the impossibility of knowing anything for certain, and the emphasis on the lingering forms and traditions of faith hints that only artistic representation, not faith, survives through the ages. In a way, Rossetti is presenting a version of Matthew Arnold's notion that the best part of any religion, ultimately, is its poetry—but whereas for Arnold the poetry of religion immortalized its moral strength, its underlying idea, for Rossetti it immortalized the unchanging (as he thought) sensual and psychological needs of mankind in all ages. Even "The Blessed Damozel," in its revised form, shows the ironic disjunction between faith and longing. As Stephen Spector has pointed out, the "vision of heaven inhabited by a warm-breasted damozel is properly understood as a wish-fulfilling dream in the mind of the earthly lover. The heart of the poem is the ironic conflict between the speaker's very earthly bodily desire, which he unconsciously reveals, and the tradition that heaven is a place of heavenly, disembodied souls, a tradition which is ironically emphasized by the speaker's religious language."[4] From another perspective, the poem might be described as an aesthetic vision of heaven, or a vision of an aesthetic heaven, in which the highest beauty and truth is embodied in the form of a beautiful and passionate woman.

The conflation of former faiths, aesthetic representation, and female beauty is most explicit in the ballads "Troy Town" and "Eden Bower." Like "Sister Helen," these ballads are about the destructive power of female beauty and sexuality, though now without the theme of male betrayal. Both poems reflect an idea that was becoming central to Rossetti's painting and poetry, the idea, as he described it in a letter, of "the perilous principle in the world being female from the first" (*Let-*

ters, 2:850). Rossetti was, of course, a worshipper of beauty in all its forms, and especially in the form of beautiful women, but his aesthetic appreciation was tinged with an element of fear at the supposed mysterious otherness of women, the strange sexual power they exercised over men. But though "Troy Town" and "Eden Bower" both reflect a characteristically Victorian fear of sexually potent women, they do so with extraordinary gusto, seeming to relish the "strong savours" of sin, sex, and destruction. As Florence Boos has said, "These concentrated ballad narratives of sexual vengeance constitute Rossetti's most unusual achievement; there is nothing quite so cheerfully or aggressively horrible in Victorian literature. Sex emerges from its romanticized disguises, not to render mankind happy but to extinguish totally the human ego."[5]

I would argue, however, that some of Swinburne's *Poems and Ballads,* published just two years before Rossetti wrote his ballads, are at least as exuberantly horrible on the same subjects, and that Rossetti, like Swinburne, was attempting to extend the range and deepen the passionate intensity of poetic subject matter in the Victorian age. He was certainly not merely out to shock. Both poems, like "The Burden of Nineveh," are concerned with religious faiths of bygone days. "Troy Town" represents Helen of Troy making an offer at "Venus' shrine" (*Works,* 214), and "Eden Bower" is based on a Hebraic tale about Lilith, a snake-woman temptress in the Garden of Eden. The classical and Hebraic settings give a kind of respectability to the subject matter, but what is most interesting is that the poems, taken together and with the other poems in the volume, attempt to make the point that while religions and myths come and go, certain underlying truths are permanent—and the fundamental unchanging truth seems to be that the "perilous principle in the world [was] female from the first." Creeds, myths, legends are in effect reduced to the poetic representation of truths upon which Rossetti's verse now draws. As a result, his poems represent religious views as historically relative, but they represent their aesthetic embodiment as the undying function of art, and further, they represent certain emphatically Victorian assumptions about women and about the relations of the sexes as the eternal truths underlying the greatest art. Drawing on eternal truths and their enduring mythic representations, the poems are presented as timeless artifacts, already above the merely local and temporary concerns of the present. Despite Rossetti's historical relativism in other matters, his poems operate on the assumption that art transcends its age.

The issues are particularly clear in "Troy Town," the simplest of the two poems. The subject is drawn from the most respectable possible repository of high cultural sources, Greek myth and legend—like Swinburne and others, Rossetti saw that even pagan eroticism could be acceptable to Victorian society if associated with the ancient classics that remained the educational staple of educated Englishmen. The poem describes Helen at the shrine of Venus, asking for the love of Paris in exchange for the gift of a carven cup. Venus, foreseeing the carnage of the Trojan War, accepts the gift and grants the boon:

> Venus looked in Helen's face,
> *(O Troy Town!)*
> Knew far off an hour and place,
> And fire lit from the heart's desire;
> Laughed and said, "Thy gift hath grace!"
> *(O Troy's down,*
> *Tall Troy's on fire!)*
>
> (*Works,* 216)

The refrain, repeated in each of the 14 stanzas, has struck many readers as annoying and monotonous, but it is an integral part of the poem's formal and thematic effect. Thematically, the refrain suggests the inevitable fatality, on a vast scale, of passionate female love. Formally, it reflects the poem's careful aesthetic control of its outbursts of passion and it even provides what Evelyn Waugh has called "a certain liturgical solemnity" (157). The sense of ritual, almost of prayer, transfers the religious solemnity of Helen's prayer to the poem itself—not, perhaps, as naive pagan worship of Venus, but as awed recognition of the eternal "perilous principle." Helen's description of her breasts both deepens the erotic nature of the poem, and further suggests that the source of the destructive power in the world has been "female from the first":

> Each twin breast is an apple sweet.
> *(O Troy Town!)*
> Once an apple stirred the beat
> Of thy heart with the heart's desire:—
> Say, who brought it then to thy feet?
> *(O Troy's down,*
> *Tall Troy's on fire!)*
>
> (*Works,* 215)

Helen is referring to the Apple of Discord, awarded by Paris to Venus in a divine beauty contest among Venus, Pallas Athena, and Hera, and the reference is yet another reminder of the link between the fatal destiny of Troy and the fatal power of female beauty and passion. But the apple, which will reappear as a symbol of temptation in Rossetti's poetry in "Eden Bower" and later in the fragment "The Orchard Pit," also unavoidably conjures the Garden of Eden, where again female vanity and willfulness led to disaster.

The combination of the religious, the erotic, and the aesthetic in the poem is especially clear in the gift that Helen offers to Venus, a carven cup molded in the shape of her breast:

> It was moulded like my breast;
> (*O Troy Town!*)
> He that sees it may not rest,
> Rest at all for his heart's desire.

> > (*Works,* 215)

The cup is a far cry from the "altar-cup" referred to in the early version of "My Sister's Sleep," or from the Grail represented in many of Rossetti's medievalist watercolors, but it perfectly represents an art that now translates female beauty and seductiveness into the acceptable form of art in the service of an almost religious awe. Nevertheless, though the poem is evidently intended to suggest the timelessness of the destructive female principle, and to control this principle within its formal structure, the erotic content does not, finally, seem to be entirely contained within the bounds of the mythic stories. In fact, the poem seems to fetishize Helen's breasts, which are dwelt upon to an almost absurd degree, as when she combines the mythologizing imagery with a more pure eroticism: "Mine are apples meet for his mouth" (*Works,* 215). The opening stanza is sufficient to make the point:

> Heavenborn Helen, Sparta's queen,
> (*O Troy Town!*)
> Had two breasts of heavenly sheen,
> The sun and moon of the heart's desire:
> All Love's lordship lay between.
> (*O Troy's down,*
> *Tall Troy's on fire!*)

> > (*Works,* 214)

Rossetti altered the stanza several times, and was evidently never quite happy with it, perhaps because of Swinburne's smirking observation that "to call a woman's breasts 'the sun and moon of the heart's desire' sounds as if there were a difference between them, much in favour of one. It is a burlesque notion, I know, but would, I fear, occur to others" (Swinburne, 1959–62, 2:73). It *is* a burlesque notion, and for just that reason it suggests how close Rossetti's attempt at "liturgical solemnity" comes to burlesque. My point is not to accuse Rossetti and Swinburne of a kind of high-brow snickering, but to note that the line between Victorian high culture and Victorian prurience was at times a very narrow one, and that Rossetti's poetry (and painting) tended to straddle it. The legend of the cup molded upon Helen's breast provided Rossetti with a perfect classical precedent for an art that seeks to give permanent form to the transiently erotic, but his use of classical sources to enshrine and legitimate erotic subject matter was characteristically Victorian.

"Eden Bower" draws on ancient Hebraic legend to present a still more erotically charged content. According to legend, Lilith, once the "fairest snake in Eden," was transformed to human shape to become the first wife of Adam:

> It was Lilith the wife of Adam:
> (*Sing Eden Bower!*)
> Not a drop of her blood was human,
> But she was made like a soft sweet woman.
>
> > (*Works,* 109)

Except for the first two-and-a-half stanzas, and the refrain, the poem consists of Lilith, still in human form, seducing the serpent so that she may take his shape, tempt Eve, and lead mankind to fall into sin and suffering. Though she is not human, she perfectly embodies female seductiveness and danger—indeed, the nonhuman character of female power suggests just how extreme the Victorian sense of female "otherness" could be. Lilith is manifestly the "perilous principle" and in a Manichaean universe it is she, not the male Satan, who rivals God, her "fell foe" (*Works,* 110).

The female passions of love and hate are quite evidently a serious challenge to God's power: "Is not the foe-God weak as the foeman / When love grows hate in the heart of a woman?" (*Works,* 110). The poem attempts to control the "strong savours" of its subject matter partly by remaining within established tradition, and partly by presenting itself as an artistic tour de force in which every stanza ends with a couplet in feminine rhyme. Such rhymes, however, seem better

suited to comic verse (as in Byron's *Don Juan*), so with apparently ac-
cidental irony, rhymes like "foeman" and "woman" draw this poem,
like "Troy Town," perilously close to burlesque. A number of other
rhymes could be cited to demonstrate the point, but Lilith's description of the fall of Adam and Eve will suffice: "And then they both shall
know they are naked, / And their hearts ache as my heart hath achèd"
(*Works*, 111). Perhaps more than anything else, it is these rhymes that
make the poem "cheerfully" and "aggressively horrible," and make it
akin to Swinburne's "Faustine" and "Dolores," exuberantly erotic
poems about the female "perilous principle." And like Swinburne's
poems, "Eden Bower" seemed, at least to some Victorians, to have
crossed the line from culture to titillation, from art to pornography,
especially in Lilith's graphic descriptions of sexual embrace: "What
more prize than love to impel thee? / Grip and lip my limbs as I tell
thee!" (*Works*, 113). Rossetti's defense of these lines indicates, in a
peculiar way, how difficult the line between prurience and art might
be to define. The passage, he pointed out, does not describe a human
sexual act, but rather the embrace "of a fabled snake-woman and a
snake" (*Works*, 619). The defense ignores the point that the "fabled
snake-woman" is in the shape of a "soft sweet woman," and so glosses
over the rather graphic depiction of bestiality. The crucial word seems
to be "fabled," a word that was apparently intended to remove the
poem from the sphere of sordid flesh into the higher realm of art.

Rossetti defended his subject matter rather more effectively, however, with the general argument that art has always depicted the ex-
tremes of human passion:

not even Shakespeare himself could desire more arduous human tragedy for
development in Art than belongs to the themes I venture to embody, however
incalculably higher might be his power of dealing with them. What more
inspiring for poetic effort than the terrible Love turned to Hate,—perhaps the
deadliest of all passion-woven complexities,—which is the theme of *Sister Helen,* and, in a more fantastic form, of *Eden Bower*—the surroundings of both
poems being the mere machinery of a central universal meaning? What, again,
more so than the savage penalty exacted for a lost ideal, as expressed in the
Last Confession . . . ?

(*Works*, 620)

The capitalization of "Art" and the distinction between "mere machinery" and "universal meaning" emphasize Rossetti's assumption that art,

dealing with eternal truths in enduring form, transcends the merely incidental and passing forms of moral restriction in the interest of a higher morality. Rossetti was clearly not backing away from any direct confrontation with Victorian moral outrage, but at the same time he was, like Swinburne, attempting to expand the range of what was permissible in art. Rossetti's depictions of female passion in his ballads share in the general Victorian mystification of female sexuality, and share too in the misogynistic tendency to blame the fallen human consciousness on the perilous female principle. Because they are shaped to a certain extent by sensibilities that now seem to us absurd, they do, I think, verge on the burlesque. Nevertheless, Rossetti's attempt to extend the range of art, to open the mysteries of sexuality and "passion-woven complexities" to serious inspection, ought to be recognized as a step taken against the oppressive and limiting Victorian sexual ideology.

For modern readers, "A Last Confession," a dramatic monologue after the fashion of Browning, is likely to seem a much more impressive study of "passion-woven complexities" than the ballads. The poem consists of the confession of a dying Italian freedom fighter who had raised a young girl from early childhood, fallen in love with her as she matured, and murdered her when she lost her youthful purity and coarsely laughed at him. The speaker, deranged by grief, guilt, and the pain of his wounds, and haunted, as he thinks, by the ghost of the slain girl, struggles to describe to the priest the "passion-woven complexities" that drove him to exact a "savage penalty" for his "lost ideal." As in many of Browning's dramatic monologues, the speaker's psychological state is reflected in his incoherence, in the significant but not wholly logical leaps of his thinking. As he himself vaguely realizes, his confession is not merely the description of a transgression, but the display of his entire life and being:

> I think
> I have been speaking to you of some matters
> There was no need to speak of, have I not?
> You do not know how clearly those things stood
> Within my mind, which I have spoken of,
> Nor how they strove for utterance. Life all past
> Is like the sky when the sun sets in it,
> Clearest where furthest off.
>
> (*Works*, 46)

He senses that the confession cannot win him absolution unless the priest can know his whole mind and judge it, yet he is aware that the priest cannot possibly know his whole mind:

> O Father, if you knew all this
> You cannot know, then you would know too, Father,
> And only then, if God can pardon me.
>
> (*Works*, 44)

A central concern of the monologue, then, is the isolation of the individual within his own mind, the impossibility of ever fully communicating one's consciousness to another. Indeed, the speaker has some doubts whether even God can fully comprehend his life's experience and all the mitigating circumstances of his act: "Will God remember all?" (*Works*, 45).

Both consciously and unconsciously, the speaker repeatedly reveals his frustration at the inability of one mind to know another. Love ought to be the perfect meeting of minds, but he is painfully aware that his love had not fully communicated itself to the girl, and still more painfully aware that he could not comprehend her, let alone contain her in his heart:

>   the face
> Which long had made a day in my life's night
> Was night in day to me; as all men's eyes
> Turned on her beauty, and she seemed to tread
> Beyond my heart to the world made for her.
>
> (*Works*, 51)

Far from bringing about the union of mind and spirit, the awakening of sexual love brings about confusion and uncertainty. The speaker's account of his gift to the girl of a "flying love," quoted above, suggests the beginnings of a sexual awakening and initiation, particularly when the gift falls and breaks:

> And as it fell she screamed, for in her hand
> The dart had entered deeply and drawn blood.
> And so her laughter turned to tears: and "Oh!"
> I said, the while I bandaged the small hand,—
> "That I should be the first to make you bleed,

Who love and love and love you!"—kissing still
The fingers till I got her safe to bed.

(*Works*, 47)

But the speaker only becomes aware of the changed nature of his love
some time later, when the kiss of the child is suddenly no longer a
childish kiss:

> She was still
> A child; and yet that kiss was on my lips
> So hot all day where the smoke shut us in.
>
> For now, being always with her, the first love
> I had—the father's, brother's love—was changed,
> I think, in somewise; like a holy thought
> Which is a prayer before one knows of it.

(*Works*, 47)

The startling simile offers an extraordinary revelation of the workings
of the speaker's mind. Living a life of action and violence, he had
idealized the girl as a kind of holy sanctuary to return to—originally
as a daughter or a sister, and now as a prospective lover, she has been
the angel in the house, the ideal to be fought for and preserved.

Indeed, his understanding of her from the first was based not on her
intrinsic qualities, but on his own consciousness, formed by exposure
to religion, and especially to religious art. When he first saw her, she
seemed like one who

> might have served a painter to pourtray
> That heavenly child which in the latter days
> Shall walk between the lion and the lamb.

(*Works*, 45)

And later, when she was grown, he likened her to the idealized version
of Italian womanhood represented by a marble sculpture of the Virgin:

> They seemed two kindred forms whereby our land
> (Whose work still serves the world for miracle)
> Made manifest herself in womanhood.

(*Works*, 51)

She was for him, in short, an ideal formed from his patriotism and his religion—and formed, significantly, along the lines of artistic representation of patriotism and religion. It is, in fact, quite remarkable how often the speaker refers to religious art, and it becomes clear that his consciousness and his ideals are based on that art. His image of heaven, like that in "The Blessed Damozel," is based on "painted images" of women he has seen (*Works*, 46), and for that matter his image of hell is also based on pictures:

> I have seen pictures where
> Souls burned with Latin shriekings in their mouths:
> Shall my end be as theirs?
>
> (*Works*, 52)

Ideals are not only formed by works of art, but further, taste in art reveals the individual's ideals and loyalties. The speaker becomes aware of the girl's failure to meet his ideal when she abandons her Italian marble Virgin for "some new Madonna gaily decked, / Tinselled and gewgawed, a slight German toy" (*Works*, 51).

Clearly, a consciousness formed on artistic representations of spiritual and patriotic ideals is not sufficiently able to cope with the complexities of human passion. The notion that his "holy thought" has deepened into a "prayer" reveals the speaker's failure to understand that the brotherly or fatherly love consistent with the idealizations of religion is wholly different from erotic love with its powerful and disruptive passions. In its very different way, "A Last Confession," like "The Blessed Damozel," displaces agapé with eros, but it goes further to suggest the inadequacy of a religious art to account for the true nature of human emotions. In effect, "A Last Confession," despite its Italian Catholic setting, represents a refutation of the too simple idealism of Catholic art or, at the very least, of the Art-Catholic. In a far more sophisticated way than "Troy Town" or "Eden Bower," it suggests a rationale for artistic treatment of "passion-woven complexities": any art that ignores the passions of love and hatred leads to a naive and ultimately destructive idealism. The speaker of "A Last Confession," we recall, is led to murder and madness by a "lost ideal," and the poem strongly implies that it was a false ideal to begin with.

But "A Last Confession" is about more than naive idealism in art and life. It is also about the impossibility of securing full knowledge of another, or even of attaining full self-knowledge. The implication that a false consciousness is formed by representations of religion and patriotism hints at the difficulty of finding an essential, core self, and the speaker's lack of coherence in his attempt at self-justification and self-expression may hint at the absence of a coherent self to justify or express. The speaker, however, is less tormented by his lack of self-knowledge than by his inability to comprehend the girl. At the same time, however, her mysteriousness is the source of her sexual allure:

> She had a mouth
> Made to bring death to life,—the underlip
> Sucked in, as if it strove to kiss itself.
> Her face was pearly pale, as when one stoops
> Over wan water.
>
> (Works, 48)

The description suggests a complete self-absorption, and even a complete narcissism. It calls to mind Rossetti's description of his painting *Lady Lilith,* in which the perilous female principle is described in terms of a "self-absorption by whose strange fascination such natures draw others within their own circle" (*Letters,* 2:850). The speaker's deranged fascination with the girl is akin to Rossetti's own fascination with female temptresses, with the mystery of female beauty—and such fascination is shown, as usual in Rossetti's works, to be exceedingly perilous. The women who fascinate men are those who seem not to need them, those who are wholly self-absorbed and apparently self-sufficient. In other words, women who are not confined within Victorian domestic ideology, who are not dependent on men and comprehensible as passively angelic, represent a dangerous threat to conventional ideals. At the same time, however, they offer a sense of mystery and danger that not only provides "strong savours" to life and art, but offers scope for speculation that might pass beyond the bounds of conventional thought. The speaker in this poem represents a polarizing view of women as either sweetly innocent or dangerously corrupt, but the dynamics of the poem at least hint at the limitations of such a vision.

The same issues are raised, still more strongly, in "Jenny," the interior monologue of a young man contemplating a sleeping prostitute. As her occupation and her sleeping state both indicate, Jenny is independent of men (in the sense that she is a sort of entrepreneur, or at least a "working girl") and is sufficiently self-absorbed to be indifferent to the man in her room. In her alienation from the acceptable Victorian ideal and in her self-containment, she represents a mystery to be pondered. Further, as in "A Last Confession," in their very inadequacy the broodings of the protagonist hint at the failure of artistic representation to make such women as Jenny comprehensible to men. As McGann has put it, "More than recording a failed quest for sympathetic engagement, the poem judges this to be the failure of poetry (or art) itself. This judgment is an extremely critical one, in the nineteenth century, because poetry and art were then generally regarded as the ultimate depositories, and even the creators, of spiritual and human values" (McGann 1988, 350). Certainly, the protagonist's art, his poeticizing, and his drawing on stock artistic images leads him very far from any real understanding of Jenny. Daniel Harris has made the point that in his "linguistic fondling" he "assigns her an extraordinary variety of poses. Caught in his self-pleasing alliteration, 'lazy laughing languid Jenny' is not so much observed as stereotyped." The young man's "outrageous parody . . . demonstrates his linguistic power to change the object of his imagination at will."[6]

The transformative power of language is evident in the opening description of Jenny,

> Whose eyes are as blue skies, whose hair
> Is countless gold incomparable;
> Fresh flower, scarce touched with signs that tell
> Of Love's exuberant hotbed:—Nay,
> Poor flower left torn since yesterday
> Until to-morrow leave you bare;
> Poor handful of bright spring-water
> Flung in the whirlpool's shrieking face;
> Poor shameful Jenny, full of grace.
>
> (*Works,* 36)

The metaphors metamorphose Jenny, who is seemingly everything but human. But the profusion and confusion of metaphors reveal that the language cannot satisfactorily pin Jenny down. The description begins by suggesting an association with the natural purity of "blue skies," and next an association with the gold that signals her status as a sexual commodity. The clichéd image of the flower suggests first an innocent growth of nature and next an artificial hothouse flower. The contradictions culminate in the wicked parody of "Hail Mary, full of grace"—if it is a parody. Jenny is "full of grace," at least of physical grace, yet she is also manifestly "shameful." The allusion to the Virgin, moreover, introduces the religious point of view from which conventional judgments of Jenny are made, but its failure to lead to a satisfactory judgment suggests the inadequacy, even for the protagonist, of conventional standards. Jenny remains a mystery.

Further, she is a mystery who cannot be solved by reference to the teachings of art, for though she is anything but saintly, she could well be the model for a Christian icon:

> Fair shines the gilded aureole
> In which our highest painters place
> Some living woman's simple face.
> And the stilled features thus descried
> As Jenny's long throat droops aside,—
> The shadows where the cheeks are thin,
> And pure wide curve from ear to chin,—
> With Raffael's, Leonardo's hand
> To show them to men's souls, might stand,
> Whole ages long, the whole world through,
> For preachings of what God can do.
>
> (*Works,* 40)

But such paintings do not in the least help the speaker to understand Jenny, who was evidently made by God but deformed by man: "What has man done here?":

> All dark. No sign on earth
> What measure of God's rest endows
> The many mansions of his house.
>
> (*Works,* 40)

Though the young man at times smugly declares that he can, in fact, fully comprehend Jenny, though he even declares that "yes, we know your dreams" (*Works,* 42), and compares her to a book to be read and understood, it is more often obvious even to him that she is a shut book or, more accurately, an unreadable sign. In fact, however, the young man does not even seriously try to read the book—despite his claim to "wonder what you're thinking of," he never takes the obvious step of asking her, or even of speaking aloud to her and giving her a chance to respond. Rather, he justifies *not* speaking to her by the assumption that the pages of her brain are blank, and will take no imprint anyway:

> For is there hue or shape defin'd
> In Jenny's desecrated mind,
> Where all contagious currents meet,
> A Lethe of the middle street?
> Nay, it reflects not any face,
> Nor sound is in its sluggish pace,
> But as they coil those eddies clot,
> And night and day remember not.

(*Works*, 39)

The contempt that lurks beneath the thoughtful young man's supposed compassion prevents him from making any genuine attempt to understand or help Jenny, and further, it enables him merely to observe and accept the status quo as an inevitability. But further, since Jenny's mysteriousness is precisely what makes her alluring and intriguing, his willful failure to "solve" that mystery enables him to continue to enjoy the prostitute after his own somewhat academic fashion—by means of "linguistic fondling." The implications for art are indeed disturbing, if we take the protagonist seriously as a sort of poet—his verbal pyrotechnics, his learning, his wit, are all narcissistic exercises that actively *avoid* genuine understanding or communication, and *avoid* disturbing conventionalities.

The protagonist employs a complex web of strategies to keep the mysterious woman mysterious, to retain her as an alluring enigma. Since she neither speaks nor is spoken to, she is allowed no part in the young man's discourse about her, no part in the official definition of "what thing" she is (*Works*, 37). In addition, she is excommunicated from women's discourse as well as from men's—she is, for pure women, a forbidden topic: "Like a rose shut in a book / In which pure women may not look" (*Works*, 40). Further, she is reduced from a woman to a commodity, and even as a commodity, as Harris has pointed out, she has no official existence but is only among the "things" that are "bought and sold" even though they are "not yet enroll'd / In market lists" (Harris, 203). As Harris and Robin Sheets have both recently emphasized, the young man's musings consistently tend to generalize Jenny out of existence as an actual human being (Harris, 206).[7] The process, indeed, is explicit within the poem:

> Yet, Jenny, looking long at you,
> The woman almost fades from view.
> A cipher of man's changeless sum
> Of lust, past, present, and to come,
> Is left. A riddle that one shrinks
> To challenge from the scornful sphinx.
>
> (*Works,* 41)

She is reduced first to a figure in the eternal account book, no longer a woman but merely a measure of *man's* lust, and next to an unreadable riddle, a dangerous enigma. But this is exactly where the protagonist wants to keep her.

Even her seeming likeness to other women only suggests her enigmatic difference:

> Just as another woman sleeps!
> Enough to throw one's thoughts in heaps
> Of doubt and horror.
>
> (*Works,* 39)

It is almost as though she were, like Lilith, a lamia, a monster who had usurped the shape of "soft sweet woman." To establish her difference from a proper woman, the young man contrasts her with his ideal of womanhood, his cousin Nell:

> My cousin Nell is fond of fun,
> And fond of dress, and change, and praise,
> So mere a woman in her ways:
> And if her sweet eyes rich in youth
> Are like her lips that tell the truth,
> My cousin Nell is fond of love.
> And she's the girl I'm proudest of.
>
> (*Works,* 39)

Significantly, the description of Nell at first seems to liken her to Jenny rather than to distinguish her: she is a "mere" woman, vain, changeable, and even "fond of love." The implication may be that all women are dangerously susceptible to falling into "dishonour," in which case, of course, it is all the more imperative that Jenny and Nell be sharply distinguished. Nell's frailties are just sufficient to make her interesting in youth—as she matures her little vanities will be subdued within her proper domestic sphere:

> The love of change, in cousin Nell,
> Shall find the best and hold it dear:
> The unconquered mirth turn quieter
> Not through her own, through others' woe:
> The conscious pride of beauty glow
> Beside another's pride in her,
> One little part of all they share.
>
> (*Works*, 39)

Unlike Jenny, Nell will present no mysteries, but will quietly uphold and reflect the "best" in her world.

What is most striking about Nell is that the speaker must descend to sentimental bathos in order to describe her. Even more than Jenny, Nell may well strike the reader as a "cipher," this time of the "changeless sum" of man's will for mastery. The "ideal" of Victorian womanhood is *safe* for the man, but is utterly unexciting. Consequently, it is not wholly surprising that though the speaker is "fondest of" Nell, he has spent the night with Jenny. And more, since his idealization of pure womanhood has resulted in an all-too-easily comprehended—because too dogmatically defined—version of woman, it is not surprising that he seeks to keep Jenny seemingly mysterious and slightly threatening. The various musings about the ahistorical nature of lust "living through all centuries" (*Works*, 41) represent the current attitudes about women and about the relations between the sexes as eternal truths, but for modern readers, at least, the dynamics of the poem reflect the complex dynamics underlying the Victorian polarization of women into either domestic angels or threatening, but fascinating, demons.

As is often noted, however, the "most difficult interpretational problem" with the poem "is to determine to what extent the speaker is being presented ironically" (Spector, 435). To what extent, that is, was Rossetti offering a critique of prevailing attitudes by presenting the limited notions of his protagonist, or to what extent was he attempting to offer a thoughtful analysis of the problem of prostitution through the young man's thoughtful musings? According to Harris, Rossetti was in complete ironic control, and the interior monologue deliberately demonstrates "The social repressions behind the protagonist's failure to speak" in contrast with "Rossetti's own forthright breaking of taboo to scrutinize prostitution and men's responses to it" (201). From this point of view, "Jenny" is a "radical" work, a "cultural criticism of depersonation that treats the protagonist's modes of discourse as inseparable from his sexual, psychological, and economic quandaries" (Harris, 198). I am inclined, however, to agree with Sheets, who points out that "Nothing in the circumstances of Rossetti's life would prove that he stood far enough outside [his] culture to fully understand the connection between a social system which subjugates women in prostitution and an aesthetic system which objectifies them in art" (334). In either case, the poem demonstrates for modern readers the ways in which Victorian thought "depersonized" women, but if Sheets is right, Rossetti's art was not a criticism so much as it was a part of the process, and the reduction of women to aesthetic objects for contemplation and admiration was characteristic not only of his protagonist's musings, but of Rossetti's own art. And from this point of view it makes sense to note, as Sheets does, that once again Rossetti's art is uncomfortably situated on or over the line (if such a line can be said to exist) separating art from pornography. The poem does, after all, embody a point of view that like pornography "purports to be ahistorical in order to obscure its status as ideology," and also as in pornography "Women are present only to be silenced, objectified, treated as screens on which a man projects his fantasies" (Sheets, 318). On the other hand, even though Rossetti's poem, by today's standards, may well seem disconcertingly sexist, it was plainly a serious attempt to cope with an important subject in art—any temptation to call the poem "pornography" ought to serve as a reminder that such name-calling, with its implied desire for censorship, tends to curtail not only artistic expression, but even the attempt to increase the range of human understanding and sympathy. For all its ideological limitations, "Jenny" did go well beyond the sanctimonious position that would forbid discourse about prostitutes ("pornography" in the etymological sense) altogether.

Consequently, Sheets's position must be carefully distinguished from that taken by the egregious Robert Buchanan, who regarded "Jenny," and most of the other poems in Rossetti's volume, as outright pornography, and insisted that Rossetti was consistently indistinguishable from his speakers:

Mr. Rossetti is never dramatic, never impersonal—always attitudinising, posturing, and describing his own exquisite emotions. He is the "Blessed Damozel," leaning over the "gold bar of heaven," . . . he is "heaven-born Helen, Sparta's queen" whose "each twin breast is an apple sweet"; he is Lilith, the first wife of Adam; he is the rosy Virgin of the poem called "Ave," and the Queen in the "Staff and Scrip"; he is "Sister Helen" melting her waxen man; he is all these, just as surely as he is Mr. Rossetti soliloquising over Jenny in her London lodging, or the very nuptial person writing erotic sonnets to his wife. (38–39)

This is clearly preposterous, and Rossetti quite reasonably responded to it by declaring that he *was* dramatic, particularly in "Jenny," where he had conscientiously deliberated omitting the possibly offensive situation, but had determined that

the motive powers of art reverse the requirement of science, and demand first of all an *inner* standing-point. The heart of such a mystery as this must be plucked from the very world in which it beats or bleeds; and the beauty and pity, the self-questionings and all-questionings which it brings with it, can come with full force only from the mouth of one alive to its whole appeal, such as the speaker put forward in the poem,—that is, of a young and thoughtful man of the world. To such a speaker, many half-cynical revulsions of feeling and reverie, and a recurrent presence of the impressions of beauty (however artificial) which first brought him within such a circle of influence, would be inevitable features of the dramatic relations portrayed. (*Works*, 619)

Quite clearly the poem does, as Rossetti affirmed, present a dramatic situation. Further, it seems to represent an attempt not to titillate but seriously to examine the "heart of the mystery."

On the other hand, nothing in Rossetti's explanation suggests any ironic distance from the "young and thoughtful man of the world." In adopting his viewpoint, indeed, Rossetti seems to have been adopting his views as well—or, to put it differently, to have made the young man the mouthpiece for his own thoughts, or himself the mouthpiece for the young man's thoughts. The point is not to chastize Rossetti for sharing the sexist views of his protagonist, but to suggest that he was himself very much a product of his own culture even when he attempted to probe that culture's assumptions. For all his limitations, after all, the young man of the poem does go well beyond the mere revolted condemnation of the prostitute that the more conventional views of the age would require. In adopting the "*inner* standing-point" of the young man, Rossetti remained within the standing-point of his time. Indeed, as McGann has pointed out, the situation here is emblematic of the way in which the values of Victorian culture are reproduced throughout the entire volume: "Assuming the inner standing point throughout, the book dramatizes Rossetti's enslavement to the commercial culture he despises. That culture thereby grows again in Rossetti's book, like some terrible virus in a laboratory dish" (McGann 1988, 358).

In "Jenny" as, to a lesser extent, in "A Last Confession," the formation of the speaker's consciousness by aesthetic contemplation results in a merging of the "*inner* standing-point" with the countertendency in the book, the attempt to gain perspective on life by withdrawal to an aesthetic distance, to a realm of transcendent values in art. Other poems in the book, less obviously dramatic than "Jenny" or "A Last Confession," present themselves within a romantic mode of self-expressiveness, but these poems also fail to transcend or even to explain or contain life through art. In fact, the most apparently personal poems in the book, "The Portrait," "The Stream's Secret," and the sonnets "Towards a Work to Be Called 'The House of Life,'" do tend to separate the aesthetic realm from actual experience, but only at the expense of associating aesthetic observation and control with alienation and, ultimately, with death. Although these poems do not justify Buchanan's remark that Rossetti was "never dramatic, never impersonal," they do indicate that Rossetti's work was often based on personal experience and aimed at subjective self-expression. It is such works as these—especially the sonnets of *The House of Life* (to be examined in the next chapter)—that provide the grounds for the traditional reading of Rossetti, following Pater, as a sensitive explorer and accurate recorder of the precise movements of his own soul, of the depths of the interior self. As recent readings have suggested, however, these poems do not so much record the subtleties of the soul in art, as display an alienation of the artist from his own experience, a gap between experience and artistic representation.

"The Portrait" has almost invariably been read as an autobiographical poem about Rossetti and Elizabeth Siddall, though as William Rossetti pointed out, the poem was originally written "as early as 1847" (*Works*, 663), long before Rossetti had met Siddall. The early version, "On Mary's Portrait, Which I Painted Six Years Ago," was indeed "purely imaginary," and was presented as a dramatic monologue after the fashion of Browning, and plainly inspired by "My Last Duchess." But like most of the early poems published in 1870, "The Portrait" was so thoroughly revised as to become an entirely different poem, and the revisions, drawing heavily on Rossetti's own experience of love, loss, grief and, perhaps, artistic frustration, transformed the poem from a purely dramatic monologue to a self-expressive romantic lyric. The revised version, however, retains interesting echoes of "My Last Duchess," particularly the sense of wonder evoked by a portrait that seems to present the living image of the woman who has died: "This is her picture as she was: / It seems a thing to wonder on" (*Works*, 169). And echoing the Duke of Ferrara's observation that "There she stands / As if alive," the speaker remarks that "there she stands / As in that wood that day" (*Works*, 169). The echoes of the sinister duke are disturbing, for the duke has happily substituted the work of art for the living woman, replacing a somewhat too changeable aesthetic object with a perfectly still one.

The speaker of "The Portrait," however, recognizes the inadequacy of art as a substitute for life:

> 'Tis she: though of herself, alas!
> Less than her shadow on the grass
> Or than her image in the stream.
>
> (*Works*, 169)

Nevertheless, though the portrait cannot replace the living image, it gains a strange power from its association with the woman's death. As in "St. Agnes of Intercession," it is as if the painting of the portrait has a fatal effect, as if the soul of the woman passes into the work of art. In fact, in the rather puzzling last stanza, the speaker seems to suggest that at the Resurrection it will be the portrait that comes to life:

> Here with her face doth memory sit
>   Meanwhile, and wait the day's decline,
> Till other eyes shall look from it,
>   Eyes of the spirit's Palestine,
> Even than the old gaze tenderer:
> While hopes and aims long lost with her
>   Stand round her image side by side,
>   Like tombs of pilgrims that have died
> About the Holy Sepulchre.
>
> (*Works*, 170)

The poem is consistent with Rossetti's general tendency to displace religion with art, and holy icons with images of aesthetic beauty. Significantly, the portrait becomes a shrine to both art and female beauty: "In painting her I shrined her face" (*Works,* 169). But if this is a religion of beauty, it is a melancholy and unsatisfactory one—the work of art can only, at best, memorialize past moments:

> Next day the memories of these things,
> > Like leaves through which a bird has flown,
> Still vibrated with Love's warm wings;
> > Till I must make them all my own
> And paint this picture.
>
> (Works, 170)

The painter's ambition is strangely possessive, and reveals a desire not wholly unlike the duke's to possess a stilled and unchanging memorial of the living woman. The work of art is a shrine, but it is also, like the closing images in the poem, a kind of a tomb or "Holy Sepulchre." For this reason, as John McGowan has suggested, "'The Portrait' implies that life and art are inimical, that the living thing is never art, that art only holds images of the dead."[8]

The alienation of the artist from life is suggested in rather different ways in "The Stream's Secret," another poem that has been universally understood as an expression of Rossetti's own sensibility. In this somewhat obscure and tortuous poem, the speaker leans over a murmuring stream, hoping to hear the message that he supposes has been whispered by Love into the stream's source:

> Say, hath not Love leaned low
> This hour beside thy far well-head,
> And there through jealous hollowed fingers said
> The thing that most I long to know,—
> Murmuring with curls all dabbled in thy flow
> And washed lips rosy red?
>
> (Works, 114)

For most modern readers, I would suppose, the most conspicuous feature of the poem is likely to be the extreme artificiality of this far-fetched conceit and of the personification of Love. And indeed the extremity of the artifice hints at the distance of artistic representation from any ideal of unmediated expression of emotion or consciousness. Not surprisingly, the speaker gets no satisfactory message from the stream, whose murmurs only seem to echo his own thoughts, his own memories of past hours:

> What whisperest thou? Nay, why
> Name the dead hours? I mind them well:
> Their ghosts in many darkened doorways dwell
> With desolate eyes to know them by.
>
> (*Works*, 114)

Evidently, the literary conceit has not enabled the speaker to gain deeper knowledge or understanding of life or love, but has only returned him to his own thoughts and memories. The stream, like the portrait, and like the present poem, can only memorialize the "dead hours" retained in the speaker's memory.

The romantic attempt to communicate with nature, already undercut by the conceit that not nature but love is the source of any possible message, leads only to a deepened sense of isolation and entrapment within the self. McGowan makes the excellent point that "The poet, immersed in Dante and the Romantics, goes to nature to find an intimation (a symbol) of the larger significances which give experience meaning, and only finds dead material things which resist his prayer, remain silent, and refuse incorporation into art" (McGowan, 47). As in Shelley's *Alastor,* searching the stream for signs of the beloved culminates in a narcissistic and solipsistic brooding, and can lead only to a forlorn hope of union with the beloved after death:

> Ah! by a colder wave
> On deathlier airs the hour must come
> Which to thy heart, my love, shall call me home.
> Between the lips of the low cave
> Against that night the lapping waters lave,
> And the dark lips are dumb.
>
> (*Works*, 118)

Once again, the work of art is able only to memorialize isolated and incoherent memories of the past, and to anticipate death. Disconcertingly, death, not art, may give meaning to life—and to the extent that art attempts prematurely to elucidate the meaning of life, it is associated with death.

Buchanan's notorious attack on *Poems* had insisted most obviously on their "naughtiness" (36), on their licentiousness of form and content, and had thus reopened a debate about propriety in art that had been inspired four years earlier by Swinburne's *Poems and Ballads*. To a certain extent, despite Rossetti's vehement denials, it must be said that Buchanan was right in seeing that "fleshliness" often triumphs over spirituality in the book. Rossetti was certainly not seeking merely to shock or titillate his audience, but the poems repeatedly imply that finally it is not divine love or love of the divine that motivates human behavior, but erotic love. As we will see more clearly in the next chapter, Rossetti insistently maintained that the erotic was subservient to the spiritual in his poems, but many of the poems do imply, perhaps despite Rossetti's intentions, that the consciousness formed by lofty art and spiritual aspirations is self-deceived. The poems, indeed, draw heavily on the artistic tradition to imply that although art has been at the center of modern moral consciousness, it has not been true to the difficulties and complexities of modern life—that art too far separated from sensuality has contributed to the alienation from a presumed fundamental human "nature" and its passions characteristic of the speakers of "A Last Confession" and "Jenny."

Consequently, though Buchanan's attack on Rossetti's supposed "naughtiness" could be easily dismissed, the underlying charges that his art was too purely "aesthetic," too divorced from the presumed moral purpose of art and from the realities of human experience, had a strangely ironic force. The poems were too far from acceptable Victorian morality in their eroticism, but too far from impassioned human "nature" in their continuing attempt to remain within the spiritualizing framework of the artistic tradition and of Victorian morality. In his deepest insights, Rossetti seems to have seen that the aestheticizing of experience involved an alienation from that experience, yet his fundamental loyalty remained with the "aesthetic." Since "aestheticism," by the late nineteenth century, had come to suggest medievalist posturings and the substitution of a self-conscious literary symbolism for experience, it is almost possible, after all, to sympathize with some of Buchanan's lamentations about the occasional distance of Rossetti's poetry from modern concerns: "On the whole, one feels disheartened and amazed at the poet who, in the nineteenth century, talks about 'damozels,' 'citherns,' and 'citoles,' and addresses the mother of Christ as the 'Lady Mary'" (41).

If Buchanan and others had regarded Rossetti's poetry as merely naughty, the volume would have posed no threat to Victorian morality, and could have been dismissed without comment, but a serious danger seemed to be presented when artists were disposed to "lend actual genius to worthless subjects, and thereby produce veritable monsters" (Buchanan, 38). The debate, finally, was about the use of genius, and unlike Pater, Buchanan certainly did not see the appropriate use of genius in the poet's "describing his own exquisite emotions" (38). Perhaps it was fortunate for Rossetti that the ultimate force of Buchanan's argument was intermingled with the most egregious of his absurdities: "the fleshly gentlemen have bound themselves by solemn league and covenant to extol fleshliness as the distinct and supreme end of poetic and pictorial art; to aver that poetic expression is greater than poetic thought, and by inference that the body is greater than the soul, and sound superior to sense; and that the poet, properly to develop his poetic faculty, must be an intellectual hermaphrodite, to whom the very facts of day and night are lost in a whirl of aesthetic terminology" (32). The charge that was to stick, despite Rossetti's angry denial that he had anything in common with the "aesthetic school," was that of aestheticism, and in fact Rossetti's poems did strike more intelligent contemporaries than Buchanan as both "fleshly" and "aesthetic"— Swinburne, for example, praised the sonnets of *The House of Life* for (among other things) their "fleshly form" (1925–27, 15:13). A less partisan and less enthusiastic admirer, John Morley, noted the "certain charm" of the poems that recalled "old ideals of beauty and simplicity" and saw in Rossetti's work a "combination of sadness with full joy of the senses" that was "perhaps wholesome by way of reaction against the wordy optimism which has made Tennyson so popular in the sentimental middle class." He was, he said, "particularly grateful for anything that helps me in any way to break up the hideous clerico-bourgeois amalgam that rules at present."

Very obviously, for Morley the virtue of Rossetti's poems was that they set themselves against the dominant Victorian ideology, that they were, in effect, countercultural in their aestheticism. But in the long run, Morley's qualifications are more significant than his praise: "It is true that you will never have high creative art, so long as one is content to admire work on the ground of its being effectively solvent!" Indeed, as Morley put it, "Nobody, I suppose, believes that [*Poems*] contains many elements of permanent quality, or that it can ever attract more than a few esoteric souls" (quoted in Doughty, 440–41). The problem with Rossetti's poetry, evidently, was the problem for late Victorian art: aestheticism, defining itself as separate from and above the life of its time, as opposed to the reigning religious and moral thought of its age, was condemned to appeal only to a certain elect artistic coterie, "a few esoteric souls." Art was coming to be defined as separated from the life of its times, even to the extent that the artist's merit was judged in relation to the countercultural force of his work. As Lord Lytton caustically put it, in response to Morley's comments, the poet is, "Of course . . . to upset a something that has gone before, he is to be an advanced Liberal, in the way of upsetting; and the more he goes the whole hog and rejects pearls for the last new hogwash, the more he is declared to have the divine something in the afflatus of his grunt" (quoted in Doughty, 441). For Rossetti, the problem was rather more difficult. He recognized that "the greater proportion of my poetry is suited only to distinctly poetic readers" (*Letters,* 2:760), but he had no desire to shock or outrage or even differ from acceptable Victorian standards. His poetry is torn by his conflicting desires to be self-expressive yet to remain within the "standing-point" of Victorian values, to be avant-garde and yet not too much at odds with his age, to be transcendently "aesthetic" and yet not too far from the "passion-woven complexities" of actual experience. The resultant tensions in his poetry are especially evident in his most ambitious work, the work most specifically "suited only to distinctly poetic readers," *The House of Life.*

Chapter Five
The House of Life

Among "distinctly poetic readers," at least, *The House of Life* has generally been regarded as Rossetti's masterpiece, and certainly it is his major work in terms of size and scope. The work, subtitled "A Sonnet-Sequence," consists of 102 sonnets (103 if one includes "Nuptial Sleep," which Rossetti suppressed in response to Buchanan's charge of fleshliness) written over the entire span of Rossetti's poetic career, from 1847 to 1881. The poem has been praised for Rossetti's masterful control of the sonnet form and for its expression of the ultimate spirituality of sexual love, but as has been characteristic of Rossetti criticism, it has been especially praised as the transcription of exact phases of the poet's soul precisely as he knew them. According to William Michael Rossetti, the sonnets constituted "a sort of record of his feelings and experiences, his reading of the problems of life—an inscribed tablet of his mind,"[1] and Rossetti's friend William Sharp described the sonnets as "the revelations of the inner life of a great genius" and "the heritage of a great artist" (408). The critical tradition has followed this lead, seeing the poem as the reflection of "a consistent and closely knit personality"[2] and as the "story of the poet's own experience . . . a complete revelation of his heart, its joy and its suffering."[3] Inevitably, biographical critics, entering what William Fredeman has called "the back door to the poem," have read it as an autobiographical record of his loves for Elizabeth Siddall, Fanny Cornforth, and Jane Morris,[4] but even the critics who do not regard the work as a "biographical record" have tended to see it as "an interpretation of a life."[5] Such readings are, indeed, fully justified by Rossetti's own repeated statements within the sequence and elsewhere that the highest poetry is self-expressive:

> By thine own tears thy song must tears beget,
>   O Singer! Magic mirror thou hast none
>   Except thy manifest heart; and save thine own
> Anguish or ardour, else no amulet.
>
> (61, "The Song-Throe, *Works* 95)

As Rossetti says in the introductory sonnet, the sonnet comes from the depths of the soul, and is a "Memorial from the Soul's eternity" (*Works,* 74).

Attempts to read the poem as simultaneously reflective of personal experience *and* as transcending *merely* personal experience by appealing to the universal truths of the innermost soul have occasionally led to critical difficulties. Benson, for example, remarked that "Of course it is transcendental, spun of light and dew," but at the same time blamed Rossetti's supposedly Italianate nature for a lack of manly British reserve, "which makes him appear at times as if overmastered by a kind of sensuous hysteria" (135).[6] The problem emerges in part from a perceived need to rescue the poem from the early charges of "fleshliness" by asserting that its actual domain is in the realm of spirit—it is not the individual sensual life, but the spiritualizing life of the innermost soul that gives value to the poetry. The critical response thus echoes the central theme, and the central problem, of *The House of Life.* The poem evidently described intensely personal experiences of love and loss, and consequently left Rossetti open to Buchanan's charge (faintly echoed in Benson's comments) that the poet was indecently "wheeling his nuptial couch out into the public streets" (ix), but at the same time separated itself from personal experience in an attempt to universalize this experience in art.

To the extent that Rossetti succeeded, as Pater claimed, in overcoming the false duality of matter and spirit, the poem has been praised as transcending fleshliness in the pursuit of a higher beauty. According to Bowra, for example, for Rossetti the flesh "somehow . . . was the visible image of the soul" (201), and though "Rossetti knew that there is one beauty of the flesh and another beauty of the spirit, . . . he believed that in the end both are united in a single harmony and that each fulfils and glorifies the other" (212). From this perspective, the success of the work is dependent upon Rossetti's ability to transcendentalize the flesh, but putting the matter in these terms raises some further problems. First, his very success in aestheticizing experience to provide an "interpretation of life" suggests a distancing from life, a degree of alienation. Consequently, though Buchanan's moral charge of fleshliness can be readily dismissed, the critical charge of excessively self-conscious artistry retains some force. Fleshliness is displaced by aestheticism, or as Paull Franklin Baum has put it, the "hothouse atmosphere" of the work is the result not of immorality, but of "excess of artistry" (34). But second, to the extent that Rossetti does *not* succeed in unifying body and soul, flesh and spirit, experience and art, the poem reflects not a "consistent and closely knit personality" (Bowra, 203), but a fragmented and incoherent self.

The unity of the poem, as has often been noted, "is the unity of Rossetti's life" (Baum, 46), but if that life was not unified, the poem will reflect the fissures between experience and aspiration, flesh and spirit, life and art. And indeed the poem does reflect and even overtly describe such fragmentation of the self, as it moves relentlessly from "the static, sheltered world of unity and love to the changing, exposed world of disunity and death" (Spector, 448)—and the disunity is not only between the lover and his various beloveds, but between the various and incompatible selves of the poet's past and present. Most significantly, the attempt to translate personal experience into the transcendent realm of art is itself in part the cause of the disintegration of the self that the poem describes, since it is, as Richard Stein has said, "an experiment in translating the widest range of personal experience into the terms of a formal, relatively static aesthetic scheme,"[7] but the formality of art—especially of Rossetti's rigorously controlled Petrarchan sonnets—can only be achieved at a considerable "aesthetic distance" from the messiness of circumstantial actualities. The poet-speaker of the series is distanced from the experiencing persona, so to the extent that they are both "Rossetti," it is necessarily a self-divided Rossetti. Further, the poem was bound from the start to reflect the incoherences consequent on its origins in the self-contradictory notions that art is expressive of the unique creative genius of the individual soul *and* that it is simultaneously independent of merely personal experience, that it is autonomous, transcendent, and universal. As a result, as McGann has said, "*The House of Life* is more than a mere presentation, or case history, of personality dismemberment. It is that, of course, but it is also part of a project—an execution—of such dismemberment, an active agent in the destructive project it is unfolding. . . . The history unfolds through a set of losses and disintegrations which culminate as the loss of identity" (1988, 351–52).

Rossetti, who maintained that *The House of Life* was to be regarded as a single poem with sonnets for stanzas, obviously did not intend for his magnum opus to lack unity, and he clearly worked hard to order the poems in a coherent way. But whatever unity he achieved was imposed retrospectively upon sonnets written over a period of more than

30 years. In fact, in this respect *The House of Life* can be compared to the *Poems* of 1870, in which Rossetti's revisions and careful arrangement were also intended to convey the sense of a unified, coherent poetic career. The various versions of *The House of Life* consist of a series of 16 sonnets published in the *Fortnightly* in 1869 under the title "Of Life, Love, and Death," a selection of 50 sonnets and 11 "songs" published in *Poems* (1870) under the title "Sonnets and Songs: Towards a Work to Be Called 'The House of Life,'" and the final version of 102 sonnets included in *Ballads and Sonnets* (1881). The final version attempted to combine the sonnets into a meaningful sequence, but in its attempt at inclusiveness, it is perhaps the least unified of the various groupings. The work was presented in two parts, "Youth and Change" (sonnets 1–59) and "Change and Fate" (sonnets 60–101), and the first of these, which consists overwhelmingly of sonnets written over a relatively brief span from 1868 to 1872, is by far the more coherent. It is in this part of the poem that a consistently personified Love is represented as capable of spiritualizing life, though even within part 1 the hopefulness of the early sonnets gives way to an increasing tone of melancholy and despair. Part 2, which contains a great many sonnets written earlier and later than these dates, is something of a farrago of themes—Love no longer dominates—and it both formally and thematically reflects a sense of alienation and fragmentation of the self.

It is part 1, then, that lends the work its reputation as an exploration and even a celebration of the spiritualizing power of love, and that has even led some critics to insist that the poem is properly a "House, not of Life, but of Love" (Sharp, 408). As is implied in "Stillborn Love" near the end of part 1, however, *The House of Life* is definitively not merely a House of Love, for it lacks the harmonious union that successful love would ideally bring about, and sings instead (or at least, also) of barren hours without love, hours that stand "mute before / The house of Love" and only hear "through the echoing door / His hours elect in choral consonancy" (55, "Stillborn Love," *Works*, 93). Another sonnet explicitly contrasts the beautiful coherence of the life harmonized by love with the painful clash of hours in a life lived without love. The "soul's sphere of infinite images" may consist either of

> The rose-winged hours that flutter in the van
> Of Love's unquestioning unrevealèd span,—
> Visions of golden futures: or that last

Wild pageant of the accumulated past
That clangs and flashes for a drowning man.
        (62, "The Soul's Sphere," *Works*, 95)

Significantly, the harmonious life of love is presented as a visionary
hope, while the clashing incoherence of the dying man's past is presented as an actuality. And finally it is this incoherence that *The House
of Life*, as opposed to a hypothetical House of Love, will emphatically
present.

Nevertheless, a large number of the early sonnets suggest the possibility of blissful union in love, emphasizing both the union of lover
and beloved, and the union of flesh and spirit. Ideally, love enables the
self to escape its own imprisoning boundaries and merge with another,
as in "Love's Testament" (3), in which the beloved "dost work deliv-
erance, as thine eyes / Draw up my prisoned spirit to thy soul!" (*Works*,
75). The union of lover and beloved in these poems is often expressed
in images of perfect reciprocity, of a blurring of the boundaries between
self and other that become, in effect, "debateable borders" (14,
"Youth's Spring-Tribute," *Works*, 79). Perhaps the clearest and certainly one of the most beautiful examples of these celebratory love sonnets is sonnet 12, "The Lover's Walk":

> Sweet twining hedgeflowers wind-stirred in no wise
>   On this June day; and hand that clings in hand:—
>   Still glades; and meeting faces scarcely fann'd:—
> An osier-odoured stream that draws the skies
> Deep to its heart; and mirrored eyes in eyes:—
>   Fresh hourly wonder o'er the Summer land
>   Of light and cloud; and two souls softly spann'd
> With one o'erarching heaven of smiles and sighs:—
>
> Even such their path, whose bodies lean unto
>   Each other's visible sweetness amorously,—
>   Whose passionate hearts lean by Love's high decree
> Together on his heart for ever true,
>   As the cloud-foaming firmamental blue
>   Rests on the blue line of a foamless sea.
>
>   (*Works*, 78)

The sonnet draws all of nature and the human lovers into perfect union.
The "twining hedgeflowers" correspond to clinging hands, and the

sky-reflecting water to mirroring eyes as the poem's imagery moves subtly from nature to flesh to spirit, with the octave culminating in the union of "two souls" beneath one heaven. The sestet intensifies the union, carrying it beyond the realm of sense partly through one of Rossetti's favorite images, the final image of the horizon line in which sea and sky are fused, and partly through the synaesthetic image of "visible sweetness," which fuses two senses and consequently invokes an ideal beyond any actual sensual apprehension. Similar effects are achieved in other celebratory sonnets throughout the series, as in sonnet 19, "Silent Noon," where the union of nature and the human lovers is sensed in the synaesthetic image of "visible silence," and "silence" is paradoxically exalted into "the song of love."

The beautiful if somewhat sentimental idealization of love in these sonnets could hardly have invoked the moral indignation even of a Buchanan, but in other sonnets Rossetti made bolder attempts to describe and yoke fully sensual and fully (for lack of a better word) mystical ideas of love. The clearest examples are "The Kiss" and the later suppressed "Nuptial Sleep." "The Kiss" expresses Rossetti's idealization of love at its most extreme:

> What smouldering senses in death's sick delay
>   Or seizure of malign vicissitude
>   Can rob this body of honour, or denude
> This soul of wedding-raiment worn to-day?
> For lo! even now my lady's lips did play
>   With these my lips such consonant interlude
>   As laurelled Orpheus longed for when he wooed
> The half-drawn hungering face with that last lay.
>
> I was a child beneath her touch,—a man
>   When breast to breast we clung, even I and she,—
>   A spirit when her spirit looked through me,—
> A god when all our life-breath met to fan
> Our life-blood, till love's emulous ardours ran,
>   Fire within fire, desire in deity.
>
> (*Works,* 76)

The opening quatrain powerfully describes the forces against which love must contend, the seeming inevitabilities of change and death, but only to negate them in the following quatrain. Orpheus had not quite succeeded in redeeming Eurydice from death, but the lovers here achieve what Orpheus could only long for. They are raised above the threat of death and change, and their kiss is by implication of greater efficacy than even the divine song of Orpheus. The sestet, which aroused Buchanan's ire with its clinging breasts, may be Rossetti's most explicit statement that the highest reaches of sensual love ultimately transcend the senses (except, perhaps, the remarkable statement in "Secret Parting" [45] that "as she kissed, her mouth became her soul" [*Works,* 89]). The speaker is not only drawn into union with the beloved, but his past self and present self are merged, as are his flesh and spirit. The self is not only unified, but deified, in love—or more specifically, in aroused sexual desire for the loved one. As "Nuptial Sleep" makes clear, however, the deification persists beyond desire and through fulfillment:

> At length their long kiss severed, with sweet smart:
>   And as the last slow sudden drops are shed
>   From sparkling eaves when all the storm has fled,
> So singly flagged the pulses of each heart.
> Their bosoms sundered, with the opening start
>   Of married flowers to either side outspread
>   From the knit stem; yet still their mouths, burnt red,
> Fawned on each other where they lay apart.
>
> Sleep sank them lower than the tide of dreams,
>   And their dreams watched them sink, and slid away.
> Slowly their souls swam up again, through gleams
>   Of watered light and dull drowned waifs of day;
> Till from some wonder of new woods and streams
> He woke, and wondered more: for there she lay.
>
>   (*Works,* 76)

It is hardly surprising that the sonnet offended Buchanan and made even more sympathetic readers wish Rossetti had exercised more "manly" British reserve, but the point is less in the fawning mouths than in the imagery of the sestet, which draws on the reference to Orpheus made in the preceding sonnet. Once again, love is characterized as redemptive: these redeemed souls succeed in swimming up from the depths where Orpheus and Eurydice (or at least Eurydice) had failed. Further, unafraid to mix his mythologies, Rossetti also suggests the creative power of love by invoking the creation of Eve: Adam awakens from sleep to find the newly created Eve. The image is probably indebted both to Milton's description of the incident and to Keats's Miltonic allusion in his illustration of "the holiness of the Heart's affections and the truth of Imagination": "The Imagination may be compared to Adam's dream—he awoke and found it truth."[8] Love, like imagination—and like poetry—is a transcendentally creative power that rises above death and change to overcome the painful vicissitudes of mere circumstantial existence.

Not surprisingly, it was this spiritualizing power of love that Rossetti chose to emphasize when responding to Buchanan's attack, though rather surprisingly he did not choose to defend "Nuptial Sleep" itself beyond saying that it was only a "single stanza" in the poem and could not be said to embody the author's "own representative view of the subject of love" (*Works*, 617). Instead he pointed to the sonnet "Love-Sweetness" (21) to note that the merely physical attributes of the beloved were subordinated to

> the thing
> In lacking which all these would lose their sweet:—
> The confident heart's still fervour: the swift beat
> And soft subsidence of the spirit's wing.
>
> (*Works*, 81)

The sonnet proved, he affirmed, that far from asserting that "the body is greater than the soul," his sonnets showed that "all the passionate and just delights of the body are declared—somewhat figuratively, it is true, but unmistakably—to be as naught if not ennobled by the concurrence of the soul at all times" (*Works*, 618).

Rossetti's defense, more clearly than Buchanan's attack, reveals the source of discontent in the sequence that finally leads to the representation of an overwhelming sense of loss and self-alienation. Despite Pater's claim that Rossetti denied the duality of matter and spirit, Rossetti's defense very clearly maintains this traditional distinction and, moreover, the traditional hierarchy upon which ascetic morality is based: the soul is superior to the sense. One reason why Rossetti was unable to shake off Buchanan's attack was, no doubt, that despite his moderately advanced views about the "just delights of the body," he remained very much within the same moral framework as his more prudish contemporaries. But the problem was as much an aesthetic one as a moral one. Rossetti was always at his best when using concrete, physical imagery—imagery drawn from what Wordsworth called "nature and the language of the sense"—but when he attempted to describe the soul, his language became not just "somewhat figurative," but highly artificial and ultimately unconvincing. Even Rossetti's celebratory sonnets of love abstract the soul from the body and expose a fundamental fissure in the self precisely by trying to deny it. And further, the most important part of the self, the soul, is accessible to description not through love, but only through the transcendental power of art—in practice, the soul is described by and identified with the most self-consciously stylized elements of Rossetti's poetry. The soul is, in effect, identified with art, and because the soul is divorced from the body, art is therefore divorced from human actualities.

Ideally, love and art both give meaningful coherence to life and enable perfect communion between lover and beloved. The perfect union of love, in fact, is often described in terms of poetry or song. The "consonant interlude" of the kiss is implicitly compared to the song of "laurelled Orpheus," and elsewhere "twofold silence" is "the song of love" (19, "Silent Noon," *Works*, 81), or Love breathes "Through two blent souls one rapturous undersong" (13, "Youth's Antiphony," *Works*, 79), or the two "answering spirits" of lover and beloved "chime one roundelay" (22, "Heart's Haven," *Works*, 82). But the aesthetic distance that seeks to ennoble love and life in the sacred monuments of art inevitably generates a separation between the lover/persona described in the poems, and the poet/persona describing him. This is scarcely surprising, since despite the romantic notion held by Rossetti and the Paterian tradition of criticism, experience can never be directly and unproblematically transcribed in language. Still, the extreme artificiality of Rossetti's verse highlights the distance between the immediacy of "life" and its interpretation or memorialization in art. Even in "The Kiss" and "Nuptial Sleep," as McGann has pointed out, the fragmentation between the experiencing self and the recording self is more or less explicitly at issue: the "I" of "The Kiss" is distanced from himself in "Nuptial Sleep" where a switch to third-person narration renders him as "he." And, of course, the "he" of the sonnet is also distanced, or "severed," from the beloved. The sonnet emphasizes love's redemptive power, but it also dramatizes the aesthetic detachment of the lover: "Lover observes beloved much as the young man in 'Jenny' observes, lovingly, the sleeping prostitute; and the perspective is here explicitly revealed as the perspective of art and poetry" (McGann 1988, 353).

Rossetti's description of his intentions in *The House of Life* indicates his aspirations, but also foreshadows his difficulties: "I should wish to deal in poetry chiefly with personified emotions; and in carrying out my scheme of the *'House of Life'* (if ever I do so) shall try to put in action a complete *dramatis personae* of the soul" (*Letters,* 2:850). The plan not only involved a quite self-conscious aestheticizing of the soul, but in its casting of dramatis personae it forecasts not a unified soul, but a psychomachia—the soul represented would consist not of one being, but of multiple characters. The result is evident in the first sonnet of the sequence, "Love Enthroned":

> I marked all kindred Powers the heart finds fair:—
>> Truth, with awed lips; and Hope, with eyes upcast;
>> And Fame, whose loud wings fan the ashen Past
> To signal-fires, Oblivion's flight to scare;
> And Youth, with still some single golden hair
>> Unto his shoulder clinging, since the last
>> Embrace wherein two sweet arms held him fast;
> And Life, still wreathing flowers for Death to wear.
>
> Love's throne was not with these; but far above
>> All passionate wind of welcome and farewell
> He sat in breathless bowers they dream not of;
>> Though Truth foreknow Love's heart, and Hope foretell,
>> And Fame be for Love's sake desirable,
> And Youth be dear, and Life be sweet to Love.
>
> (*Works,* 74)

The glut of personified Powers results in a somewhat overpopulated sonnet and generates some confusion, especially since the Powers are of a very diverse kind—Truth, Hope, and Fame seem compatible enough, but the Past, for example, is of a very different order, and is in fact only personified by being capitalized. Similarly Youth is presumably personified, but the sense would be unchanged if it were simply understood in its literal, uncapitalized sense. The difficulty is that abstractions and actualities are meeting on the same plane, perhaps in an attempt to draw them into a complex unity corresponding to the desired unity of matter and spirit, but the result is a sense of confused multitudinousness, not profound union. One problem with the tendency in *The House of Life* to elevate abstractions and emotions into human form is accidentally illustrated in a later sonnet, which seems almost to parody the technique in its description of "Sleep, waved back by Joy and Ruth" (39, "Sleepless Dreams," *Works,* 87). If the personification is taken seriously, if Joy and Ruth are genuinely seen as waving women, the stylization collapses into absurdity. Many readers are likely to agree with Robert Browning: "I cannot enjoy the personifications,—Love as a youth, encircling you with his arms and wings, gives me a turn" (quoted in Angeli, 168).

Other, more subtle, difficulties are also implicit in "Love Enthroned." First, if the sonnet sequence achieves its unity, as Bowra and others have argued, by reflecting a "consistent and closely knit personality" and showing "its progress along a clearly marked path" (Bowra, 203), that unity is only discovered—or imposed—by the retrospective illumination of the poet's Fame. Later sonnets in the sequence, particularly "The Landmark" (67) and "The Hill Summit" (70), more explicitly make the point that if there is a clear path lending continuity and meaning to life, it is only perceived by means of retrospective aesthetic reordering of experience. In addition, though the sonnet is plainly a celebration of the lofty place of Love in Life, it actually elevates Love entirely out of Life. The description of "Love's throne" "far above / All passionate wind of welcome and farewell" in "breathless bowers" echoes Keats's description of the lovers on the Grecian Urn, who were also "far above" "all breathing human passion." The crucial point about Keats's lovers, however, is not that they are "above" life, but that they are totally *removed* from life. Stilled in art, they cannot know human passion at all. Rossetti's sonnet also lifts love out of life into the higher realm of art, enthroning it in the sonnet form itself, and assuring its immortality, in conventional sonnet style, by linking it to the poet's fame. It is not clear, however, that Rossetti shared Keats's qualms about the displacement of life by art—instead, the sonnet seems straightforwardly to project the aim of the sequence, to enthrone love and art and assert their dominion over life. Yet in doing so it forecasts the central problem as well—making love and art transcendent is intended to draw life into unity, but instead, and inevitably, it dramatizes the separation of human actualities from human aspirations, of art and love from life, of spirit from matter.

Wherever possible, Rossetti had carefully purged God from his poetry and replaced divine love with human love, but in lifting human love to a heavenly throne, he had only replaced, not removed, the traditional moral hierarchy of body and soul. Excessive worship of the beloved woman robs her of her humanity, for in its impossible idealizations it makes her a substitute for God:

> Sometimes thou seem'st not as thyself alone,
>   But as the meaning of all things that are;
>   A breathless wonder, shadowing forth afar
> Some heavenly solstice hushed and halcyon;
> Whose unstirred lips are music's visible tone;
>   Whose eyes the sun-gate of the soul unbar,
>   Being of its furthest fires oracular;—
> The evident heart of all life sown and mown.
>   (27, "Heart's Compass" *Works*, 83)

Such utterances can be explained away as the conventional hyperbole of love poetry—but the worship of love asks to be taken seriously in this poem, and indeed, it traditionally has been. As Bowra has put it, "Rossetti's pursuit of the ideal" within the early Italian "cult of ideal love" was "his metaphysics, his gospel, his scheme of life, and his hope of salvation" (201). As his defense of *The House of Life* by reference to "Love-Sweetness" made explicit, he remained very much within the moral perspective that sees the life of the body as meaningless unless all is brought into harmony by the soul. But the obvious difficulties of drawing one's metaphysics from a medieval "cult of love" have been spelled out by Rees:

The intense mystic significance attached to love and to the woman comes to Rossetti directly from Dante and the poets of his circle whom Rossetti translated but in the new setting the idea is subjected to immense pressure. The eternity of God dominates the medieval experience but, to the nineteenth-century Rossetti, the all-pervasive element of experience is temporal change. In time, old love changes to new, joy changes to frustration, youth changes to middle-age, hope changes to disillusion, pride of youth changes to the guilt of lost days and the bitterness of "might-have-been." (163)

Even though *The House of Life* never included a traditional place for God, its use of a system from which God has been excised recapitulates the sense, widespread in the nineteenth century, that with the removal of God from the world life becomes confused, chaotic, meaningless. The same consequence follows upon the removal of a spiritualized ideal of love. The point is made in a number of sonnets, as in the octave of "Parted Love" (46):

What shall be said of this embattled day
  And armèd occupation of this night
  By all thy foes beleaguered,—now when sight
Nor sound denotes the loved one far away?
Of these thy vanquished hours what shalt thou say,—
  As every sense to which she dealt delight
  Now labours lonely o'er the stark noon-height
To reach the sunset's desolate disarray?

                                                  (*Works,* 90)

Without love—as without God—the self is fragmented into separate, lonely senses, all laboring toward an end which, itself, is only "disarray." Without love there is, for Rossetti, no soul, and without soul, there is only fragmentation and emptiness. In "Love-Sweetness," the beloved's hair, hands, mouth, "cheeks and neck and eyelids" would be, without the "spirit's wing," mere body parts. For that matter, the lover himself would consist only of dead, dismembered body parts if he did not find his vivifying soul in the beloved:

Not in thy body is thy life at all,
  But in this lady's lips and hands and eyes;
  Through these she yields thee life that vivifies
What else were sorrow's servant and death's thrall.
                              (36, "Life-in-Love," *Works,* 86)

Without love, in "Parted Love," the self is not only fragmented, but at war with itself: "thy heart rends thee, and thy body endures" (*Works,* 90). Even the address in second person of the poet/speaker to the lover/persona indicates a divided self.

Since the spiritualizing power of love is so important in *The House of Life,* it is scarcely surprising that in sonnet after sonnet attempts are made to suggest a fusion of self and other, and of body and spirit. But despite the often brilliant images of communion and reciprocity, and of the dissolving borders of the self, evoked in such sonnets as "The Lover's Walk" and "Silent Noon," Rossetti was, not surprisingly, unable consistently and convincingly to break down the fundamental duality inherent in Western thought. As we have seen, he was in many respects still committed to that duality even as he attempted to unify flesh and spirit within the self. One of the most troubling results of this project, however, was that in the conceptualization of love as union not only of male lover and female beloved, but of body and soul, the male speaker, still in the flesh, is often represented in the attempt to appropriate what amounts not only to a disembodied female spirit, but to a ghostly vision of male aspirations. As in "Hand and Soul," that is, the female is conceived as the male soul, the vision that he must appropriate and incorporate in order to be made whole. The sexist bias and ultimate narcissism implicit in this characteristically romantic quest are hinted at quite early in the sequence, in "Lovesight" (4):

> When do I see thee most, beloved one?
>   When in the light the spirits of mine eyes
>   Before thy face, their altar, solemnize
> The worship of that Love through thee made known?
> Or when in the dusk hours, (we two alone,)
>   Close-kissed and eloquent of still replies
>   Thy twilight-hidden glimmering visage lies,
> And my soul only sees thy soul its own?
>
> O love, my love! if I no more should see
> Thyself, nor on the earth the shadow of thee,
>   Nor image of thine eyes in any spring,—
> How then should sound upon Life's darkening slope
> The ground-whirl of the perished leaves of Hope,
>   The wind of Death's imperishable wing?
>
> (Works, 75)

The language of love and worship is all appropriately in place, but it soon becomes apparent that it is not the woman who is worshipped, but rather the Love itself—the woman is a sort of medium for a love known *through* her. The woman is conspicuous for passivity and still-ness, for though she is "eloquent" it is only with "still replies." As in "Jenny," the "woman almost fades from view" (*Works*, 41) as her "twi-light-hidden glimmering visage lies, / And my soul only sees thy soul its own?" In one sense—perhaps the intended sense—the lines may be taken to suggest a full merging of souls, a complete and fully recip-rocated sense of union in love. But this taking possession of the wom-an's soul has none of the sense of subordination of the self that we see in, for example, Browning's "Two in the Campagna," where the speaker seeks not for the woman to become his soul, but rather for himself to experience her way of seeing and being:

> I would I could adopt your will,
>   See with your eyes, and set my heart
> Beating by yours, and drink my fill

At your soul's springs—your part my part
In life, for good and ill.

By contrast, the way of seeing described in "Lovesight" seems yearn-
ingly possessive—the speaker's desire is for the two to become one, but
more specifically, for the two to become *him*. The narcissism implied
in the octave is further expressed in the sestet, in the very strange line
grieving at the possibility that the speaker may not only lose the beloved, but may no longer see the "image of thine eyes in any spring."
The eyes one sees when looking into a spring are likely to be the reflections of one's own. The evident invocation of the myth of Narcissus
admiring his own reflected image hints at the narcissism inherent in
"Lovesight" generally.

Perhaps not too much could be made of the implications of this one
sonnet if it were not consistent with the much more pronounced imagery of narcissism in both "The Stream's Secret" and in the central
group of sonnets in *The House of Life,* "Willowwood" (49–52). This
group of four sonnets, which has sometimes been seen as establishing
the tone of the whole of *The House of Life,*[9] describes the speaker as he
sits with a personified Love "upon a woodside well" (*Works,* 91), sees
his beloved in the waters of the well as "lovesight" transforms the reflection of Love to the image of the beloved, strives to kiss her, but
loses her as "her face fell back drowned" (*Works,* 92). Clearly, the kiss
is no longer a more-than-Orphean song to bring the dead back to the
surface of life. The obvious narcissistic imagery should not be cited to
blame Rossetti in any way—he was working within a romantic tradition most familiar from Shelley's visionary quests for the beloved seen
as the soul within the soul. The lover of "Willowwood" is first cousin
to the questing poet of "Alastor," and is almost as closely related to
Keats's Endymion and Byron's Manfred. Except for Endymion, however, these narcissistic questers seeking their vision beyond the confines
of mortal life are all ultimately seeking not fuller life, but death. Not
just Rossetti, but the romantic tradition generally, makes the visionary
male all-in-all, and reduces the female to the unattainable vision that
keeps him questing. It does not take a terribly careful reading of *The
House of Life* to see that over and over, even from the earliest sonnets,
the fulfillment of love is often seen as impossible in life, possible only
in death. The only possible marriage of true minds is evidently in
"Death's nuptial change" (2, "Bridal Birth," *Works,* 75), and the closing lines of the sonnet preceding "Willowwood" present a "veiled

woman" who states unambiguously that "I and this Love are one, and I am Death" ("Death-in-Love," *Works,* 90).

The emphasis in "Willowwood," as throughout *The House of Life,* is not on union in death, but on the fragmentation of life spent without love, parted from love. As the speaker kisses the image (his image?) in the well, he becomes aware of

> a dumb throng
> That stood aloof, one form by every tree,
> All mournful forms, for each was I or she,
> The shades of those our days that had no tongue.
>
> (*Works,* 91)

In Wordsworth, or in Proust, the moments of the past press forward into the present consciousness, and the self consists of an ever-developing, ever-coherent flow of consciousness, but in *The House of Life* past memories are past selves, mute witnesses to a past that has not cohered in a unified life. The point is made more emphatically, more painfully, in "Lost Days" (86):

> The lost days of my life until to-day,
>> What were they, could I see them on the street
>> Lie as they fell? Would they be ears of wheat
> Sown once for food but trodden into clay?
> Or golden coins squandered and still to pay?
>> Or drops of blood dabbling the guilty feet?
>> Or such spilt water as in dreams must cheat
> The undying throats of Hell, athirst alway?
>
> I do not see them here; but after death
>> God knows I know the faces I shall see,
> Each one a murdered self, with low last breath.
>> "I am thyself,—what hast thou done to me?"
> "And I—and I—thyself," (lo! each one saith,)
>> "And thou thyself to all eternity!"
>
> (*Works,* 103)

The sonnet scarcely needs explication—there is perhaps no stronger account of personality dismemberment in the language.

Long before the end of part 1, the failure of love to supply meaningfulness and coherence to life had been abundantly demonstrated.

Not surprisingly, then, in part 2, "Change and Fate," the sonnets become ever darker in tone and outlook. Many, like "Lost Days," are retrospective poems about a wasted and ineffectual life, a life of futile days and hours that finally add up to nothing at all—or at least nothing but the pageant of disconnected memories that "clangs and flashes for a drowning man." The speaker has not abandoned the possibility that in a "life spent well" memories may bring joy in heaven, but the emphasis is on the life of one who has failed in life, in love, in art, and for whom the embittering pictures of the past "may be stamped, a memory all in vain, / Upon the sight of lidless eyes in Hell" (63, "Inclusiveness," *Works*, 95). Even some of the more hopeful sonnets in this section describe lost opportunities. "The Landmark" (67), for example, implies that a path may be found—but for the moment at least it has been lost. "Hoarded Joy" (82) is not utterly without hope, but its emphasis is upon lost opportunity:

> I said: "Nay, pluck not,—let the first fruit be:
>   Even as thou sayest, it is sweet and red,
>   But let it ripen still. The tree's bent head
> Sees in the stream its own fecundity
> And bides the day of fulness. Shall not we
>   At the sun's hour that day possess the shade,
>   And claim our fruit before its ripeness fade,
> And eat it from the branch and praise the tree?"
>
> I say: "Alas! our fruit hath wooed the sun
>   Too long,— 'tis fallen and floats adown the stream.
> Lo, the last clusters! Pluck them every one,
>   And let us sup with summer; ere the gleam
> Of autumn set the year's pent sorrow free,
> And the woods wail like echoes from the sea."
>
>   (*Works*, 102)

The poem may be said faintly to echo Tennyson's "Ulysses" ("Though much is taken, much abides"), but the emphasis here is on how little abides, and how much has been pointlessly wasted.

Retrospection yields only more disheartening results in the next poem, "Barren Spring" (83), where the regenerating power of nature has no influence over a mind wholly preoccupied with its own dead past:

> So Spring comes merry towards me here, but earns
> No answering smile from me, whose life is twin'd
> With the dead boughs that winter still must bind,
> And whom to-day the Spring no more concerns.
>
> (*Works,* 102)

And far more grimly, in "Lost on Both Sides" (91), memory only points to divided and fruitless selves, "separate hopes" that "roam together now" in the speaker's soul, "and wind among / Its bye-streets, knocking at the dusty inns" (*Works,* 105). Not only are youthful aspirations divided and defeated, but the soul itself is a ghost town. The next several sonnets, in various ways, continue to insist that the hopes of youth end in shame, heartache, and ashes—in a line worthy of Hardy at his bleakest, the "World's grey Soul" is heard to cry that "Inveteracy of ill portends the doom" (93, "The Sun's Shame, I," *Works,* 105).

The general movement of despair culminates in two of the most powerful sonnets in the sequence, "A Superscription" (97) and "He and I" (98). Rossetti singled out "A Superscription" in his comment that among his poems "suited only to distinctly poetic readers," those that "I think perhaps the most of myself" are the sonnets "and none more than . . . *A Superscription.* This is decidedly (painful as it is) a favorite of my own. Nothing I ever wrote was more the result of strong feeling, as you may perhaps think retraceable in it" (*Letters,* 2:760). The comment gives some warrant for taking the sonnet as an expression of Rossetti's own sense of failure—not so much as a lover or as an artist, but as a coherent self:

> Look in my face; my name is Might-have-been;
> I am also called No-more, Too-late, Farewell;
> Unto thine ear I hold the dead-sea shell
> Cast up thy Life's foam-fretted feet between;
> Unto thine eyes the glass where that is seen
> Which had Life's form and Love's, but by my spell
> Is now a shaken shadow intolerable,
> Of ultimate things unuttered the frail screen.
>
> (*Works,* 107)

The sonnet is somewhat enigmatic—is the persona of the poem the speaker or person addressed? That is, is the speaker a personification of "Oblivion" from sonnet 1 in a more powerful and terrifying form, or is the speaker himself cast as a nonentity, a has-been, or a never-was? In the end it makes little difference, since the persona of the poem is ruled by this power, and is characterized by its attributes. The final lines of the octave affirm that neither Life nor Love have given meaning to the life that remains hatefully meaningless—a life with nothing to say for itself: it "Is now a shaken shadow intolerable, / Of ultimate things unuttered the frail screen." Alienation from the self, or at least from what the Victorians like to call the "best self," the self formed by love and life, could hardly be more powerfully expressed than in the image of a man who cannot find himself reflected in the mirror. For an artist and poet who depends upon his own inner being or vision as the source of his self-expression, such a characterization of the defeated self must be especially terrifying.

The next sonnet, "He and I" (98), is still more enigmatic, but just as emphatic in its representation of some sort of self-division and self-alienation:

> Whence came his feet into my field, and why?
>   How is it that he sees it all so drear?
>   How do I see his seeing, and how hear
> The name his bitter silence knows it by?
> This was the little fold of separate sky
>   Whose pasturing clouds in the soul's atmosphere
>   Drew living light from one continual year:
> How should he find it lifeless? He, or I?
>
> Lo! this new Self now wanders round my field,
>   With plaints for every flower, and for each tree
>   A moan, the sighing wind's auxiliary:
> And o'er sweet waters of my life, that yield
> Unto his lips no draught but tears unseal'd
>   Even in my place he weeps. Even I, not he.
>
> (Works, 107)

The speaker, cherishing the memory of a year of vital life, does not recognize the disillusioned and disheartened self he has become. Horribly, even that vital year is found "lifeless" by the new self, and more horribly still, the very existence of a "new Self" indicates that the persona does not develop an organically whole self, but rather sees old selves die, replaced by ever more bitter and disillusioned selves. The process is enacted in the sonnet, when the alienated "he" becomes, explicitly, the no-less-alienated "I." The following sonnets, a pair entitled "Newborn Death" (99–100), also review what might have been, and draw the conclusion that no salvation has been found in Love or Art, that indeed these have died to bring the speaker to his present living death: "And did these die that thou mightst bear me Death?" (*Works*, 108).

Most readings of *The House of Life* have stressed the positive myth of redemptive love, and many of the early sonnets in the series are, to be sure, among the most beautiful love poems in the language. But despite the incoherences, the fits and starts inevitable in work combining material written over a lifetime, the series moves remorselessly toward disillusion and even dissolution of the self. The final poem speaks of hope, but only in the most desolate way:

> When vain desire at last and vain regret
>   Go hand in hand to death, and all is vain,
>   What shall assuage the unforgotten pain
> And teach the unforgetful to forget?
> Shall Peace be still a sunk stream long unmet,—
>   Or may the soul at once in a green plain
>   Stoop through the spray of some sweet life-fountain
> And cull the dew-drenched flowering amulet?
>
> Ah! when the wan soul in that golden air
>   Between the scriptured petals softly blown
>   Peers breathless for the gift of grace unknown,—
> Ah! let none other alien spell soe'er
> But only the one Hope's one name be there,—
>   Not less nor more, but even that word alone.
>   (101, "The One Hope," *Works*, 108)

It is impossible to say what the "one Hope's one name" may be— perhaps Cecil Lang is correct in saying that the "awful conclusion" compels "us to recognize that [it] is neither Love nor the name of any person but a mocking pun, *wanhope*."[10] It is surely significant that the speaker—rather like the speaker of "A Last Confession"—imagines the afterlife from books, and in this case, even *as* a book, and that his hope or despair are balanced on the one unuttered and perhaps unutterable word that could give meaning to life. The situation is reminiscent of "A Superscription," in which the dissolution of the self seems to have come about through a failure to utter "ultimate things."

The sequence from the start holds out Art even more than Love as the transcendent power that might redeem otherwise meaningless lives—though in the end even the faith in Art seems a forlorn and probably self-defeating hope. It is Art that might utter "ultimate things," that might speak "that word alone" that would redeem all. Even in the early sonnets, those most optimistic about the power of love, the saving force is not Love, but Art. In "Love Enthroned" (1), for example, it is not Love, but Fame (presumably artistic fame) that fans the dead ashes of the past and gives life significant form in its "signal-fires." And in "Lovesight," the subject is not only love, but sight, a certain way of seeing that imposes meaning on experience. And as we have seen, both "The Kiss" (6) and "Nuptial Sleep" (6a) are at least as much about art as about love, with their references to Orpheus and to the creative power of the male imagination, and with their dramatic representation of withdrawal and aesthetic detachment.

In "Heart's Hope" (5), even more clearly, the ultimate subject is not love, but the power of art or song to draw meaning from love, to make love redemptive:

> By what word's power, the key of paths untrod,
>   Shall I the difficult deeps of Love explore,
>   Till parted waves of Song yield up the shore
> Even as that sea which Israel crossed dryshod?
>
> (*Works*, 76)

Not "Love," but the word, or the "Song," will part the waters and bring the speaker out of the wilderness and toward the promised land. As in many of the other sonnets, without that word, without some landmark or sign, the paths that might give continuity to life are difficult to find. In the second quatrain, the speaker makes it clear that it is only through verse—or a hoped-for verse that has not yet been uttered—that the self and other, soul and body, love and God can be achieved:

> For lo! in some poor rhythmic period,
>   Lady, I fain would tell how evermore
>   Thy soul I know not from thy body, nor
> Thee from myself, neither our love from God.

Only *if* he could write such a poem could he "Draw from one loving heart such evidence / As to all hearts all things shall signify"—conspicuously, *whose* heart is specified as the source of wisdom is left vague. Presumably the lover's self-expressive art will draw from his own heart. If so, the beloved is once again factored out, and the love poem becomes almost purely about poetry. As Richard Stein has pointed out, "The sonnet is chiefly about love poetry and only secondarily about love. In it Rossetti projects an ideal poem he wishes to write, so that the title refers to the desired future poem, his 'Heart's Hope' for a verbal achievement" (193). "Heart's Hope" represents in miniature the aspiration of *The House of Life* generally: the constant hope is that "Art's transfiguring essence" (60, "Transfigured Life," *Works*, 94) will miraculously transform the apparent inconsequence of circumstantial experience into something immortal. Repeatedly, the point is made in *The House of Life* that youth, beauty, and even love must die, but in "Love's Last Gift" (59) it is made clear that poetry, at least, may endure—the blooms of spring fade and die, but Love's last gift, when all else is gone, is laurel, the emblem of the poet, and "laurel dreads no winter days" (*Works*, 94). Although in "The Portrait" (10), the artist's medium is paint rather than words, the sonnet shows clearly how the transient beauty of the flesh may be transfigured into the eternal beauty of art. When the work is done

> Her face is made her shrine. Let all men note
> That in all years (O Love, thy gift is this!)
> They that would look on her must come to me.
>
> (*Works*, 78)

Two fundamentally important points must be made about these lines. First, the last line illustrates the way in which the male artist appropriates his female subject, taking possession of her (in the commercial world of art, such "shrines" are sold as commodities). And second, the face is not the shrine, but the *portrait* is—not female beauty itself, but the artist's representation of beauty. Finally, the artist's "vision," not love or female beauty, is being transcendentalized as an immortal object of worship, worthy of a shrine.

The House of Life as a whole attempts to create a shrine—or, perhaps, to use Wordsworth's image for his epic work, a vast cathedral consisting of many shrines. The untitled and unnumbered sonnet introducing the series is significant in this respect:

> A Sonnet is a moment's monument,—
> Memorial from the Soul's eternity
> To one dead deathless hour. Look that it be,
> Whether for lustral rite or dire portent,
> Of its own arduous fulness reverent:

Carve it in ivory or in ebony,
    As Day or Night may rule; and let Time see
Its flowering crest impearled and orient.

A Sonnet is a coin: its face reveals
    The soul,—its converse, to what Power 'tis due:—
Whether for tribute to the august appeals
    Of Life, or dower in Love's high retinue,
It serve; or, 'mid the dark wharf's cavernous breath,
In Charon's palm it pay the toll to Death.

                                        (*Works*, 74)

This sonnet in praise of sonnets was written late in Rossetti's life, in
1880, and appended retrospectively to *The House of Life,* presumably
to suggest the aspirations of that work, and presumably in a wholly
positive way. The clear suggestion is that the sonnet is immortal, and
immortalizes the hours it commemorates: transfigured in sonnets, the
dead hours of the past are "deathless." But significantly, the oxymoron
does not get past the problem that the deathless hours are still, in fact,
dead. The implication of the sonnet, as of the entire sequence, is that
art immortalizes not life and love, but death, the dead past—after all,
a sonnet is a monument, a memorial, a shrine. The extreme artifice of
the work, its personifications, its archaisms, even its use of the rigid
Petrarchan sonnet, overwrought with its "arduous fulness," all seem to
aim at a kind of monumentality that cannot preserve the living past,
or even give coherence to the dead hours and lost selves, but at least
preserve and enshrine past incarnations of the self. James Richardson
points out that "the 'arduous fulness' of *The House of Life* is an intensity
on the edge of dissolution. . . . [Rossetti's] need to form a 'moment's
monument' begins and ends in his Tennysonian sense of the shadowi-
ness of life."[11]

Fredeman has compared *The House of Life* to Tennyson's *In Memoriam,*
another Victorian long poem written over a number of years as separate
lyrics and eventually assembled into a single poem.[12] The comparison
highlights the elegiac tone of Rossetti's poem, an elegy not for a friend,
but apparently for his own past. Yet the tone, sometimes celebratory,
more often despairing, implies that Rossetti was not always sure
whether he came to praise Rossetti or to bury him. In either case, *The
House of Life* comes to seem less a house, or a cathedral, than a mau-
soleum and, indeed, one critic has responded to the "arduous fulness"

as oppressive, and has referred to the poem as "that House which is a reliquary" (Welby, 33).

I come, however, to praise Rossetti, and not to bury him. In my opinion, *The House of Life* certainly does fail in any attempt to unify flesh and spirit, to escape the crushing sense of self-division and self-alienation, and even to reflect in its own unity the "consistent and closely knit personality" of a great artist. But it does succeed, along the way, in offering us single sonnets of extreme beauty or pathos. More significantly, it succeeds, because of Rossetti's difficult struggle with an impossible artistic ideology, in showing us the dangers inherent in nineteenth-century idealizations of love and art. Most obviously, the poem measures the heartbreak and despair of the speaker against the impossible ideal of love that he cannot ever achieve. In addition, it both represents and enacts the ways in which an idealism that separates art from life, that makes art an autonomous source of unquestioned values, can actually contribute to the fragmentation of the self that lends pathos to *The House of Life*. The romantic ideal of self-expression, an impossibility in itself since experience is not immediately translatable into words, is subtly shifted to an ideal of art as the interpretation of life, but to interpret it one must be distanced enough to study one's own emotions and thoughts and then translate them into the forms of art. Rossetti did not necessarily see this as a bad thing. He described his mood in writing one poem, for example, as "That sublimated mood of the soul in which a separate essence of itself seems to oversoar and survey it."[13]

But the condition neutrally if not positively described here, may also be regarded as the fundamental source of difficulty and misery for the self-conscious romantic artist. Coleridge, for example, describes his wretchedness, his loss of spontaneity and vitality, as the consequence of always, as a philosopher and artist, being detached from his own soul: "by abstruse research to steal / From my own nature all the natural man" ("Dejection: An Ode"). The later poems in *The House of Life*, particularly such poems as "A Superscription," painfully give the sense of a life that has somehow never been lived. Arguably the problem is that the life has never issued in a fully coherent art; but another way to look at it is that the self-division necessary to produce art that would "steal" from the natural man in order to produce transcendentally autonomous works made the integration of life and art impossible from the start. Finally, the point is not that Rossetti has failed to achieve certain ends in *The House of Life*, but that he has masterfully recorded a personal sense of the fragmentation of personality widespread at a time when people began to find themselves without a unifying idea of God, of a traditional stable society, or of anything else. For this reason Arnold said that his art was fragments because he was fragments, and that he similarly saw other poets, including Keats, Tennyson, Browning, and Clough, overcome by the chaos of experience. Partly for this reason, no doubt, no major Victorian long poem (with the exception of *Aurora Leigh*) was written except as a series of discrete shorter poems. *The House of Life* painfully demonstrates that the prevailing idealizations of love and art were not likely to supply the lost unity of the self.

Chapter Six
The Last Decade

After having all but given up "the writing of poetry as a pursuit of [his] own" during most of the 1850s and 1860s, Rossetti entered a period of prolific poetic production from 1868 to 1871. During this time he wrote such characteristic works as "Eden Bower," "Troy Town," "The Stream's Secret," and the great majority of the sonnets of *The House of Life,* and he so substantially revised much of his early poetry that the work of this brief period may be said to constitute the bulk of those works that represent his distinctive achievement as a poet. The publication of *Poems* in 1870, and the subsequent roar of critical acclaim (however well orchestrated) only increased his poetic self-assurance, so that throughout 1870 and 1871 he wrote more confidently and ambitiously than ever. Despite his shaky health, his difficult relationship with Jane Morris, his possible guilt over exhuming his wife's body, and even despite the first attack on the moral value of his poems by Buchanan, he seemed eager and able to live up to his press clippings as one of the great poets of the age. Buchanan's first attack, written in 1871 under the pseudonymous name of Thomas Maitland in the *Contemporary Review,* had stung, but Rossetti was seemingly able to laugh it off: "For once," he said, "abuse comes in a form that even a bard can manage to grin at without grimacing" (*Letters,* 3:1017). Finding the author's real identity to be that of a Scottish poetaster with a grudge against other members of his circle, Rossetti seemed able and willing to dispose of him with a brief and pointed response, "The Stealthy School of Criticism," in December 1871. Yet in June 1872, when Buchanan reissued the attack in the enlarged form of a pamphlet, Rossetti responded with a nervous breakdown, a suicide attempt, and a collapse in health from which he never fully recovered.

It seems astonishing that Rossetti should have been so affected by an article that, in its enlarged state, was even more absurdly puerile than in its earlier incarnation. Undoubtedly, Buchanan's attack only precipitated a crisis brought on by a decade of "hard work, difficult adjustment, mental strain, and physical decline" since the death of his wife, and by the insomnia and addiction to chloral that resulted.[1] Ironically, the poet of romantic self-expression now felt that somehow the deepest secrets of his soul had been discovered and were being broadcast in corrupt fashion to the world. William later described his brother's reaction to the pamphlet: "From his wild way of talking—about conspiracies and what not—I was astounded to perceive that he was, past question, not entirely sane. . . . I was dismayed to find my brother an actual monomaniac" (1895, 1:307, 309). William's description makes it clear that Rossetti, always averse to criticism, had now become deeply paranoid: "His fancies now ran away with him, and he thought that the pamphlet was a first symptom in a widespread conspiracy for crushing his fair fame as an artist and a man, and for hounding him out of honest society" (1895, 1:305).

Though he recovered from this acute mental crisis by the end of the summer, Rossetti never fully recovered his health, nor did he ever fully overcome his paranoia. The story of his breakdown and subsequent brooding seclusion has often been told, and with abundance of romantic frills, but for our present purposes it is important simply to note that Rossetti's romantic aesthetic of self-expression had collided violently with the social ethic of "manly reserve." The result for Rossetti's subsequent poetry was drastic. In the first place, Buchanan's pamphlet effectively silenced him for several years: from 1872 until 1878 he wrote only about a dozen sonnets and a handful of brief lyrics. And when he did turn again to poetry at the close of the decade, his work was marked by a newly impersonal aesthetic, an objectivity demonstrated mainly in ballads and occasional poems that revealed next to nothing of the poet's own thought or sensibility. Meanwhile, since he had never publicly exhibited his paintings, and had encountered no serious disapproval from his patrons, he felt free to continue with the sensuous paintings of beautiful women that had characterized his art since 1859. Seemingly, the earlier situation had been reversed: where he had previously felt free to express himself in the autonomous art of poetry, he now felt free only in the more evidently commercial art of painting. Yet, as we shall see, even as a painter he was not so much following his own dream as responding to the marketplace.

Many of the poems Rossetti wrote at the height of his confidence in 1871 were among his very best. In 1871 alone he wrote 26 of the best sonnets in *The House of Life,* primarily those concerned with the vicissitudes of love and loss. These poems include some of the darker sonnets of lost love, such as "Severed Selves" (40), "Without Her" (53), and "Love's Fatality" (54), but they also include many of the most serene tributes to the redemptive power of love, including "Silent Noon" (19), "Mid-Rapture" (26), and "Soul-Light" (28). At this time Rossetti was clearly committed to exploring the idea (subsequently labeled essentially Rossettian) that love may bring about a perfect merging not only of self and other, but of body and soul. "Mid-Rapture" may be taken as representative of these sonnets:

> Thou lovely and beloved, thou my love;
>> Whose kiss seems still the first; whose summoning eyes,
>> Even now, as for our love-world's new sunrise,
> Shed very dawn; whose voice, attuned above
> All modulation of the deep-bowered dove,
>> Is like a hand laid softly on the soul;
>> Whose hand is like a sweet voice to control
> Those worn tired brows it hath the keeping of:—
>
> What word can answer to thy word,—what gaze
>> To thine, which now absorbs within its sphere
>> My worshipping face, till I am mirrored there
> Light-circled in a heaven of deep-drawn rays?
> What clasp, what kiss mine inmost heart can prove,
> O lovely and beloved, O my love?
>
> (Works, 83)

The union of flesh and spirit is evident even in the modulation from "kiss" to "eyes" since, as Theodore Watts-Dunton rightly pointed out, for Rossetti, the mouth represented sensuality, while the eyes expressed the soul.[2] The point is made more emphatically, however, as the immaterial voice is likened to a corporeal hand to touch the ethereal soul, and the hand in turn is likened to the voice. The sestet beautifully suggests the sublime reciprocity of love in the traditional image of the worshipping face mirrored in the eyes of the beloved, raised into its "heaven of deep-drawn rays."

"Mid-Rapture" expresses Rossetti's ideal of love as fully as any poem in his works, and shows him working at the height of his confidence in 1871. At the same time, it also reflects the skepticism that characterized Rossetti's best poetry. The octave describes only what "seems," and depends for its effects on similes, not assertions, and the sestet consists entirely of questions. Even the image of the lover mirrored in the beloved's eyes, for that matter, can be read as an account not of mutuality and reciprocity, but of narcissism, and the exaltation of the beloved into a "heaven" may be regarded as dehumanizing. My point is not that the poem is a failure, but quite the reverse: it succeeds brilliantly in projecting both the ideal of love and the unavoidable doubts about the possibility of finding transcendent value in a mere mortal relationship.

Rossetti's confidence as a poet never went so far as to make him confident as a bard or prophet in the high romantic tradition. Despite his tendency to idealism, he was always too much of a realist and a skeptic to adopt a prophetic stance. The closest he came to such a position, however, was probably in two lyrics written in 1871, "The Cloud Confines" and "Soothsay." His letters reveal that he gave a great deal of thought to "The Cloud Confines" in particular, and was eager to say in it as much as he felt he *could* say about ultimate truths. As his brother put it, he "wrote this poem . . . in a highly serious mood of mind: he intended it to be a definite expression of his conceptions, indefinite as they were, upon problems which no amount of knowledge and experience can make other than mysterious and unfathomable" (*Works*, 669). The poem ponders the mysteries of mortality, of love, and of hate, but never goes beyond the condition of doubtful pondering itself:

> The day is dark and the night
>   To him that would search their heart;
>   No lips of cloud that will part
> Nor morning song in the light:
>   Only, gazing alone,
>   To him wild shadows are shown,
>   Deep under deep unknown
> And height above unknown height.
> Still we say as we go,—
>   "Strange to think by the way,
>   Whatever there is to know,
>   That shall we know one day."
>
> (Works, 219)

The refrain, repeated in each of the five stanzas (with only a slight variation in the last), implies a faith in some kind of afterlife, but the last stanza offers only ignorance and questions, not bardic insights:

> Our past is clean forgot,
> Our present is and is not,

> Our future's a sealed seedplot,
> And what betwixt them are we?—
>
> (*Works,* 220)

"Soothsay" promises prophecy in its title, but only to recommend against any attempts to see beyond our mortal bourne, beyond the sphere of nature: "Let no man ask thee of anything/Not yearborn between Spring and Spring" (*Works,* 221). The poem, for the most part, consists of good advice, sometimes differentiated from Polonius's advice to Laertes only by the lyricism of the verse, and in the end it refuses to say even whether the world is governed by God or chance: "To God at best, to chance at worst,/Give thanks for good things, last as first" (*Works,* 222). "The Cloud Confines" and "Soothsay" have been frequently praised, but their importance, I think, is to demonstrate Rossetti's agnosticism, his refusal to make ultimate claims for spiritual truths. In "Soothsay" he is emphatic and explicit about the most mere mortals should seek from life:

> Crave thou no dower of earthly things
> Unworthy Hope's imaginings.
> To have brought true birth of Song to be
> And to have won hearts to Poesy,
> Or anywhere in the sun or rain
> To have loved and been beloved again,
> Is loftiest reach of Hope's bright wings.
>
> (*Works,* 221)

Not surprisingly, art and love are held up as the highest human values, but at least in this considered statement they are not regarded as utterly transcendent, as spiritual in any ultimate sense. They *are,* however, carefully distinguished from mere "dower of earthly things." They *are* cordoned off from the more mundane matters of life, given a certain autonomy.

Rossetti's poetic ambitions in this period, however, generally took the form not of gnomic utterances, but of plans for narrative works about, usually, love's fatality. Though the only major narrative poem he actually wrote at this time was "Rose Mary," he wrote intriguing, and in some cases quite detailed, prose sketches for a number of others. Plans for "Michael Scott's Wooing" and "The Cup of Water," for example, provide full prose versions of tales of thwarted love, supernatural wraiths, and unnatural death. Even more fully elaborated plans were drawn up for "The Orchard Pit" and "The Doom of the Sirens" (actually planned as a three-act "lyrical tragedy"), and in both the course of true but mundane love is destroyed by the fatal attraction of supernaturally seductive temptresses who lure the hero to his death. The sketch for "The Orchard Pit" (which Rossetti began to turn into verse but abandoned after 25 lines) begins with the famous sentence that commentators have frequently regarded as an expression of Rossetti's own mind: "Men tell me that sleep has many dreams; but all my life I have dreamed one dream alone" (*Works*, 607).

The dream is the character's, yet it is a dream of love's fatality that Rossetti returned to over and over again in his works, a dream that unites forbidden love with the highest ecstasy, but also with death: "And now the Siren's song rose clearer as I went. At first she sang, 'Come to Love'; and of the sweetness of Love she said many things. And next she sang, 'Come to Life'; and Life was sweet in her song. But long before I reached her, she knew that all her will was mine: and then her voice rose softer than ever, and her words were, 'Come to Death'; and Death's name in her mouth was the very swoon of all sweetest things that be" (*Works*, 609). The concerns of the poem, though to be evolved in narrative rather than in the more apparently self-expressive form of sonnets, were obviously closely related to those of *The House of Life*. The Siren's song of Love, of Life, of Death is reminiscent of the title Rossetti gave to the 16 sonnets he published in the *Fortnightly Review* under the title "Of Life, Love, and Death." Both "The Orchard Pit" and "The Doom of the Sirens" were also clearly akin to such poems as "Sister Helen," "Eden Bower," and "Troy Town" in their intended embodiment of the "passion-woven complexities" described in "The Stealthy School of Criticism" as the kind of "arduous human tragedy" perfectly suited for "development in Art" (*Works*, 620).

It is impossible to say how many of these projects Rossetti might have carried out if his brief period of productivity had not been curtailed by the "Fleshly School" controversy and his mental and physical breakdown. The one long poem he finished in 1871, however, developed many of the themes and concerns of the other projected works. "Rose Mary" is a long—perhaps *too* long—narrative of thwarted love. The rather elaborately contrived story hinges on a magic beryl crystal that shows true images only to pure maidens, but deceives those who have sinned. Rose Mary must look into the crystal for information that will save her lover from his enemies, but because she has secretly "sinned" with him, the crystal deceives her, and her lover is killed.

Rose Mary, in her grief, smashes the crystal to destroy the evil spirits that misled her, and in consequence dies—but dies confident that she will be reunited with her lover in death: "One were our hearts in joy and pain, / And our souls e'en now grow one again" (*Works*, 135). What Rose Mary does not know, however, is that her lover had been unfaithful, and was in fact on his way to meet another woman, so while her soul is guided to heaven, his has been sent to hell. As the spirit guiding her to heaven says, however, she will remember nothing of her treasonous lover:

> "Already thy heart remembereth
> No more his name thou sought'st in death:
> For under all deeps, all heights above,—
> So wide the gulf in the midst thereof,—
> Are Hell of Treason and Heaven of Love.
>
> "Thee, true soul, shall thy truth prefer
> To blessed Mary's rose-bower:
> Warmed and lit is thy place afar
> With guerdon-fires of the sweet Love-star
> Where hearts of steadfast lovers are."
>
> (*Works*, 137)

Rose Mary ends up, in effect, as a Blessed Damozel, but in her case the gulf between her and her lover is absolute, even though she is not conscious of it. Her heaven of "steadfast lovers" is, consequently, rather a peculiarly lonely one.

It is difficult to say quite what the thematic point of "Rose Mary" may be. Rees is right, I think, in suggesting that the poem explores Rossetti's "sense of the shifting frontiers of vice and virtue," but that despite a "strong sense of powerful forces at work and of situations big with momentous significance," the "quasi-metaphysical framework" is a "ramshackle affair" (119–20). Clearly, infidelity in love is shown to be reprehensible, and even the illicit sexual union of the true-hearted Rose Mary with her lover is characterized as "sin" and leads to both her own and her lover's death. Despite her "sin," however, Rose Mary is elevated to a heaven of lovers after death. Presumably, we are meant to see that true love is eventually rewarded, and treason punished. Despite its supernatural machinery and its glimpse into heaven, in some ways the poem seems to reinforce the thematic points of "The

Cloud Confines" and "Soothsay" in its demonstration of the fatuity of attempting to see beyond the evident bounds of human knowledge. Rose Mary fails to see accurately both when looking into the beryl and when looking into her lover's heart: God's mysteries and human hearts are equally unreadable. Despite the more-or-less happy ending, the poem reinforces some of the pessimism of *The House of Life*. Rose Mary places her faith in love, but love fails her.

"Rose Mary" is not an entirely successful poem and suffers from faults characteristic of Rossetti's long narrative poems. Like "Dante at Verona" and "The Bride's Prelude," it consists of many splendid stanzas and local details, but is somewhat diffuse and unfocused. Still, it shows Rossetti working ambitiously with themes he cared deeply about: passionate but fated love, the limits of human knowledge. After his breakdown in the summer of 1872, Rossetti never again had the confidence to work with such themes on such a scale. With a few notable exceptions, such as "Ardour and Memory" (1879), and the first of the three "True Woman" sonnets (1881), his occasional sonnets written after 1871 are overwrought and rather too plainly reflect the truth of his late comment to his sister: "With me, Sonnets mean Insomnia" (*Letters,* 4:1838). Even when he returned to the writing of verse with some enthusiasm from 1878 to 1881, he chose subjects that could be treated more or less objectively, with little demonstration or revelation of personal emotion or involvement—such as sonnets about other poets, or even the famous sonnet about the sonnet itself.

The major works of this last period, "The White Ship" and "The King's Tragedy," are long verse narratives based on historical incidents and legends. Both works show Rossetti's masterful craftsmanship in transforming prosaic narrative to verse, and both have at times been highly praised, but neither does more than tell an old tale. "The White Ship," described by William as "second to nothing that my brother produced" (*Works,* 660), is the story of the fatal drowning of the son of Henry I as narrated by the lone survivor, and "The King's Tragedy" is the tale of the death of James I of Scotland as told by the woman who attempted to bar the door against his assassins. Walter Pater, who rather strangely stated that "The King's Tragedy" might be the best work to offer "readers desiring to make acquaintance with [Rossetti] for the first time," also noted that it was an uncharacteristically impersonal poem. ("Rossetti," 241–42).

The impersonality of these late narratives was evidently deliberate. According to Hall Caine, "Rossetti used to say in his later years that he would never again write poems as from his own person," and he tended to speak of his own work in terms of craftsmanship rather than of inspiration.[3] Perhaps sensing the emotional sterility of these late works, however, Rossetti was evidently rather ambivalent about his newfound creed of poetry as objective craftsmanship. It was, in fact, in 1880 that he wrote "The Song-Throe," with its insistence that poetry should be an anguished or ardent cry from the soul, not a mere display of the poet's "august control / Of [his] skilled hand" (*Works*, 95). And when his sister praised "The White Ship" and encouraged him to "write more [ballads] . . . as they leave no sting behind,"[4] he was less than pleased at the implications. At times he professed a deep emotional involvement in the work, as when he described the composition of "The King's Tragedy" to Caine: "It was as though my life ebbed out with it."[5] There is little evidence that any of it flowed into the poem.

Rossetti's recorded comments on these late poems indicate that he thought very highly of them, but it is difficult to overcome a sense that part of the inspiration for writing them—or at least for writing them at such length—was his belief that his poetic output had been exceedingly scanty. Comparing himself with the prolific William Morris, he tried to put the best face on the matter. Though he had "nothing of his abundance in production," he attempted to make his own limited output "faultless by repeated condensation and revision."[6] Along the same lines he praised Tennyson for having "husbanded his forces rightly" (*Letters*, 4:1857), and he boasted to Caine that "probably the man does not live who could write what I have written more briefly than I have done" (Caine 1928, 221). Similarly, he praised Keats, after a rather peculiar fashion, for his limited poetic production: "Keats hardly died so much too early—not at all if there had been any danger of his taking to the modern habit eventually—treating material as product, and shooting it all out as it comes" (Caine 1928, 169–70). Still, he was ambitious to produce a new volume of poetry, and his letters reveal a constant anxiety to produce enough material to fill it, even though he seems to have been aware that "inspiration" was assuredly not the word for his "method of production."[7] In fact, the only way in which he was able to publish a new volume toward the end of his life was by "treating his material as product." In this sense, at least, poetry became more clearly for Rossetti what painting had always necessarily been, the production of a commodity.

He seems to have felt greater freedom in his last years to pursue his personal "vision" in painting rather than in poetry. Although there is considerable disagreement about the quality of Rossetti's painting in the last decade, there is no dispute that his works of this period represent a continuation and a heightening (for better or worse) of his work over the previous decade. Certainly, the late works do not shy away from "fleshliness" or from Rossetti's fascination with what seemed to him the fatally seductive power of female beauty, and certainly, also, Rossetti himself and many of his contemporaries believed that the late pictures represented the culmination of the distinctively "Rossettian" vision of beauty. Not everyone has found this a gain, and it is has been argued that Rossetti's late work became exaggerated, grotesque, and subjective to the point of solipsism because his isolation encouraged his worst mannerisms.[8] Indeed, even his brother William saw some validity to objections current in Rossetti's lifetime "against the outre points of [his] style in painting—especially the peculiar & almost mulatto form of his mouths, & the tumid elongation of his throats, almost (so W[atts] holds) goitred in form."[9] To this day there remains considerable difference of opinion as to whether the late works created a new and exalted type of female beauty, or a gallery of "Goiter-Girl portraits."[10]

Despite the evidently increased pursuit of a personal ideal, it would seem that in painting, as in poetry, Rossetti was increasingly inclined to discount inspiration or subjectivity and to emphasize craftsmanship, speaking of painting as the simple production of a commodity: "Painting, after all, is the craft of a superior carpenter. The part of a picture that is not mechanical is often trivial enough" (Caine 1928, 80). Nevertheless, he continued to chafe under the need to produce paintings to meet the demands of the market. A complaint to Ford Madox Brown in 1873 is characteristic: "I have often said that to be an artist is just the same thing as to be a whore, as far as dependence on the whims and fancies of individuals is concerned" (Letters, 3:1175). As Fennell has argued, Rossetti's refusal to exhibit his pictures has almost invariably been regarded as a sign of his independence from the marketplace, his artistic autonomy, but in fact it left him a "prisoner, albeit a willing prisoner, of his own business arrangements" with his generally nouveau riche patrons (xxiv). He ceased to experiment in his art at least in part because these patrons had quite specific expectations that he would continue to produce works in the style that had first attracted them. Indeed, they demanded works that would complement those they already had, that would provide consistency in their schemes for decorating particular rooms in their houses. At times his dispirited comments on his works give the impression that he was not following his own vision so much as the vision of his patrons. After finishing *A Sea-Spell*, for example, he remarked to Brown that "I have somehow got through a new Leyland picture of the usual kind" (*Letters, 3*:1354), a remark that raises the question whether he was producing "Rossettis" or "Leylands."

His paintings both expressed his own interests and tastes and appealed to those of his buyers. The point is obvious enough, but it is important to recognize that Rossetti's works did not simply spring from the inspired, utterly idiosyncratic, and enigmatic depths of artistic genius, but from the shared sensibility and desires of the age. Part of the appeal of Rossetti's paintings was their high finish and brilliant coloring. They were admirably suited both to provide an air of high culture and to function as sumptuous wall decorations in the sitting rooms of wealthy men of business. But undoubtedly part of their appeal was also in the invariable subject matter: beautiful women portrayed in varying degrees of "fleshliness." It must be added, of course, that the "fleshliness" rarely extended far below the shoulders (one buyer once insisted that even a naked shoulder be painted over [Fennell, xxiv]), and that neither Rossetti nor his admirers would have admitted to any erotic appeal in the pictures. Nevertheless, this combination of "high art" and sensuality provides intriguing insights into Victorian attitudes about both art and sexuality. As Jan Marsh has said, it may be because "art provided an approved way of articulating questions of sex" that Rossetti's paintings, like those of many of his contemporaries, appear today "as lightly disguised eroticism or soft, submerged pornography dignified by 'high art' connections."[11]

The convergence of "high art" and sensuality in Rossetti's late art is consistent with his paintings of the 1860s but from the late 1860s on his paintings became more and more emphatically stylized, in part because he was attempting to overcome the polarization of women into "body's beauty" and "soul's beauty." His late images of women were to show both the beauty of the flesh and of the soul. As a result, the paintings themselves would share both the seductive beauty and the soulful mystery of women—art itself would be beautiful and mysterious. In practice, the paintings often reflect the conflicted attitudes inevitable in such multiple idealizations of flesh, spirit, and canvas.

A particularly clear example of conflicted attitudes is apparent in *La Bella Mano,* a painting of a characteristically Rossettian type of beautiful woman, with full, slightly parted lips, wide expanse of cheek, practically nonexistent forehead, vast shoulders, ample breasts, and a "neck like a tower." She is attended by two angels (young girls with wings), and is shown washing her hands in a scallop-shaped golden basin which, as the accompanying sonnet makes clear, is evidently intended to suggest the famous image of Venus rising from the sea. The symbolism of the painting is seemingly contradictory: the angels imply holiness, while the allusion to Venus implies eroticism. A comment by Rossetti, however, makes it clear that the winged girls who represent angels in other pictures (notably in *The Blessed Damozel*) are in fact "Cupids" (Fennell, 67), and F. G. Stephens, who functioned more or less as Rossetti's public relations agent in the *Athenaeum,* referred to them as "two white-robed and red-winged Loves."[12] Other elements in the picture, however, continue to suggest that the theme is holiness. A circular mirror behind the woman's head suggests a halo, and the washing of hands suggests purity, though it might be argued that the image of a woman at her toilet is thematically akin to *Lady Lilith,* and suggests vanity and self-absorption.

The sonnet Rossetti wrote to accompany the painting reflects the same tension between eroticism and purity:

> O lovely hand, that thy sweet self dost lave
> In that thy pure and proper element,
> Whence erst the Lady of Love's high advènt
> Was born, and endless fires sprang from the wave:—
> Even as her Loves to her their offerings gave,
> For thee the jewelled gifts they bear; while each
> Looks to those lips, of music-measured speech
> The fount, and of more bliss than man may crave.
>
> In royal wise ring-girt and bracelet-spann'd,
> A flower of Venus' own virginity,
> Go shine among thy sisterly sweet band;
> In maiden-minded converse delicately
> Evermore white and soft; until thou be,
> O hand! heart-handsel'd in a lover's hand.
>
> (*Works*, 253)

The sonnet insists on the purity and maidenliness of the woman, but at the same time it insists on the association with Venus, the goddess of love. The curious phrase "Venus' own virginity" hardly clarifies matters, unless it is meant to suggest that the very purity and maidenliness of the woman makes her more sexually desirable. Her desirability is explicit when her lips are made the source of "more bliss than man may crave." Finally, her virginity in the "sisterly sweet band" and her delicate "maiden-minded converse" are not sufficient in themselves, and the concluding lines of the sonnet make it clear that ultimately she will find fulfillment in the love of a man. The sonnet, like the picture, seems to epitomize a characteristically conflicted Victorian view of womanhood in its simultaneous desire for a more-than-human purity and a more-than-human sexual desirability—"more bliss than man may crave."

A contemporary review of the painting similarly reveals the simultaneous denial and revelation of its erotic appeal:

> The pictorial object of this work has been to show the brilliancy of flesh-tints and whites, relieved on a ground subdued to the eye, and yet everywhere replete with varied colour and material. In these respects the work is a marvel of art, the whole glowing with rich light, and being intensely deep in tone, wealthy in colour. The sentiment of the design lies in the face, and is discoverable in the light of a woman's hope which fills the eyes, has given a warmer rose tint to the full and slightly-parted lips, that are red in their vitality, and as the abundant, noble bosom is, voluptuous, not luscious. (Stephens 1875, 220)

The whole description attempts, not very successfully, to displace any and all erotic impulses into considerations of the "pictorial object" and "sentiment." The sentiment is apparently to be found in the "hope which fills the eyes," though the nature of this hope is not spelled out—it is implied, however, in the subsequent description of how hope suffuses also the warm lips and the "noble bosom." The "hope" would seem to be lover's hope, and is apparently closely akin to sexual desire, and the "sentiment" of the picture certainly seems related to the desirability of the yearning woman. The reviewer is not inclined to face such a possibility explicitly, or perhaps even consciously, but the odd care with which he distinguishes "luscious" from "voluptuous" is characteristic of a denial of eroticism so conspicuous as to call attention to precisely what it is trying to hide. The discussion of the "pictorial object," similarly, insists on the appeal of "varied colour and material" as though oblivious to what they represent. The "flesh-tints and whites" constitute a color harmony, not a representation of skin. The painting is above all a "marvel of art," and only incidentally a representation of a voluptuous, if not luscious, woman.

The reviewer was not being hypocritical or even disingenuous in his emphasis on formal elements in the painting. Rossetti's paintings are, after all, carefully crafted studies in color and form, and he himself was inclined to describe them as "studies" in color or even, perhaps following the lead of Whistler, as "harmonies." *Veronica Veronese* (1872), for example, was "a study of varied greens" (Fennell, 29) and *La Ghirlandata* (1873) was, more emphatically, "The greenest picture in the world."[13] But such formal considerations, however important, were always secondary to Rossetti, at least in the sense that they were intended to contribute to the development of an idea—not a painterly idea, but a poetic one. He was from first to last a literary painter, even to the extent that more often than not he sent off his major paintings with accompanying "readings" in prose or verse. *Veronica Veronese,* for example, may have been a study of varied greens, but it was also a painting of a characteristically large-necked, full-lipped Rossettian beauty, as Rossetti said, "in a sort of passionate reverie" as she listlessly draws her hand across a violin. Rossetti was careful to emphasize the poetic sentiment with an inscription on the frame: "Suddenly leaning forward, the Lady Veronica rapidly wrote the first notes on the virgin page. Then she took the bow of the violin to make her dream reality; but before commencing to play the instrument hanging from her hand, she remained quiet a few moments, listening to the inspiring bird, while her left hand strayed over the strings searching for the supreme melody, still illusive. It was the marriage of the voices of nature and the soul—the dawn of a mystic creation."[14]

It may be that Rossetti included the musical motif in this painting partly because his foremost patron, Frederick Leyland, collected musical instruments and liked to see them in his pictures: the beautiful women are given musical instruments in numerous pictures that Rossetti sold or offered to Leyland, including *La Ghirlandata, The Roman Widow,* and *The Bower Meadow.* But the combination of women and music had been characteristic of Rossetti's art from the early fifties and had provided a significant element in the enigmatic symbolism of the medievalist watercolors. The motif may have been, in part, intended to suggest the "harmony" of the paintings, as F. G. Stephens seems to imply in a review of *The Blue Bower:* "The music of the dulcimer passes out of the spectator's cognizance when the chromatic harmony takes its place in appealing to the eye."[15] But it was also, no doubt, intended to suggest the spiritualization of the flesh and, as the inscription for *Veronica Veronese* makes clear, to suggest the search for a transcendent inspiration, a "supreme melody, still illusive." It was in this sense that Walter Pater, in his essay on Giorgione, said that "All art constantly aspires towards the condition of music"—that is, art attempts to soar beyond its mere material restrictions to a realm of pure and autonomous beauty.[16]

But Pater seems to have owed his idea at least in part to Rossetti, perhaps via Stephens's review of *The Blue Bower:* "it is of the nature of a lyrical poem, which aims at effect quite as much by means of inherent beauty and melodious colouring as by the mere subject, which is superficial. Titian and Giorgione produced lyrics of this sort in abundance; many of their pictures are nothing if not lyrical" (Stephens 1865, 545). And Pater certainly had in mind Rossetti's sonnet "For A Venetian Pastoral by Giorgione," inspired by a painting in which the naked model's "hand trails upon the viol-string." The sonnet had celebrated both the moment and the painting with lines insistent upon their mystery: "Nor name this ever. Be it as it was,— / Life touching lips with Immortality" (*Works,* 188). Like Giorgione's painting, *Veronica Veronese* and the other pictures of women and music are meant to be about both flesh and spirit, female beauty and artistic inspiration: "It was the marriage of the voices of nature and the soul—the dawn of a mystic creation." Yet the painting remains primarily a picture of a beautiful woman. The extent to which the symbolic significance is imposed upon the painting—or at least insistently brought out by Rossetti's commentary—becomes evident when we recognize that the title was an afterthought, and that the inscription, supposedly from *The Letters of Girolamo Ridolfi,* was probably actually written as a kind of rhapsody on the painting by either Rossetti himself or by Swinburne (Surtees, 1:128).

It is not that Rossetti was deliberately disguising a prurient interest in his models by loading them down with mystic significance, but rather that he saw both the highest beauty of women and the highest beauty of art as the point at which both pass beyond the merely physical to spiritual beauty. In various forms this had been the theme of his poetry and painting from the start, so it is not surprising that late in life he maintained that he was "now more than ever at the mercy of my first sources of inspiration."[17] In 1877, partly perhaps because he was at the mercy of his first sources of inspiration, and partly because he was at the mercy of his patrons, one of whom requested it, he finally painted a version of one of his earliest and best-known poems, "The Blessed Damozel." The painting epitomizes Rossetti's attempts to combine the physical and the spiritual. The maiden is indubitably in heaven, and so a spirit, and the stars in her hair and lilies on her arm have the same vaguely spiritual resonance as in the poem. Three winged and haloed girls just below her in the composition, moreover, emphasize the heavenly locale—at least if we can assume that they are angels and not "Cupids." On the other hand, the Damozel, with the conventionally Rossettian features, is certainly fleshly enough to warm the bar she leans on, and she is surrounded not by heavenly maidens, but by embracing pairs of lovers. Her wistful, longing expression makes it clear that heaven is not enough—for her as for the Damozel of the poem and for Rose Mary, heaven is a lonely place.

Like the late version of the poem, the painting emphasizes not heavenly joy, but earthly loss, the separation of lovers, and so implies that human love is the highest value. Rossetti included a *predella* for the painting, representing the bereaved lover on earth, gazing longingly toward heaven. The barrier in the frame between the man in the lower picture and the Damozel in the higher one further illustrates the impassable gulf between the lovers, between earth and heaven. The picture as a whole represents an idealization of female beauty, soul peering out through the flesh, but it also represents the difficulty with that ideal. The woman so idealized is unreal, only imaginable in a remote and inaccessible heaven—her purity makes her at once desirable and unreachable. Further, the gulf between earth and heaven corresponds to a gulf between flesh and spirit that Rossetti obviously would have wanted to close. Both the Damozel and the painting itself represent a kind of beauty that transcends earthly bounds, and for precisely that reason lead only to a kind of frustrated longing, a condition of perpetually conflicted desire and idealization.

The Blessed Damozel, La Bella Mano, Veronica Veronese, La Ghirlandata, Roman Widow, and other pictures of the same kind were all painted from the same model, Alexa Wilding, but in all of them she is made to look as much as possible like Jane Morris, who seemed to Rossetti the absolute ideal of spiritualized female beauty. From the time of his deepened relation with her, in 1868, Rossetti drew and painted her over and over again. Or rather, he drew and painted the idealized version of her that became celebrated as the highest type of Victorian beauty. More often than not, at some thematic level the pictures of Jane Morris, like *The Blessed Damozel,* reflect the obvious biographical situation in their representations of a lonely, longing, but somehow inaccessible woman. He painted her, for example, as Shakespeare's (or more likely, Tennyson's) lonely Mariana in the moated grange, and as Dante's Pia de' Tolomei, the imprisoned and lonely wife of a cruel husband. The most celebrated paintings of Jane Morris, however, represent her as inaccessible because removed from the realm of humanity altogether. Unlike the Damozel, however, she is not elevated to heaven, but is associated with darker, infernal powers. In her fatal beauty she is the source of the troubles of the world. In *Pandora,* she is shown just opening the casket that lets out the spirits of evil (or as Rossetti called them, the "bogies") that would plague mankind. The sonnet written to accompany the picture suggests the malign nature of female power:

> Ah! wherefore did the Olympian consistory
> In its own likeness make thee half divine?
> Was it that Juno's brow might stand a sign
>   For ever? and the mien of Pallas be
>   A deadly thing? and that all men might see
> In Venus' eyes the gaze of Proserpine?
>
> *(Works,* 211)

The Olympian goddesses are all summed up in Pandora, a deadly beauty. The goddess of love looks out with the gaze of the goddess of death. Rossetti is once again intimating that "the perilous principle in the world" was "female from the first."

Not surprisingly, Rossetti also painted Jane Morris as both Proserpine and Venus—or at least, as the Syrian Venus, *Astarte Syriaca.* One of his most successful late paintings, both aesthetically and commercially (he was repeatedly commissioned to make replicas of the work), the *Proserpine,* in effect, relocates the Damozel from heaven to hell, or at least Hades, and consequently provides a somewhat more fitting locale for the expression of melancholy yearning. The painting depicts that moment when Proserpine has just eaten of the fruit of Hades and so become "enchained to her new empire and destiny. She is represented in a gloomy corridor of her palace, with the fatal fruit in her hand." Characteristically, it is both a representation of a beautiful woman and a study in color—Rossetti described it as "a graduation of greys—from the watery blue-grey of the dress to the dim hue of the marble, all aiding the 'Tartarean grey' which must be the sentiment of the subject" (Fennell, 44). In this case the woman is seen more as victim than as fatal temptress, though her associations with death and with Eve (through the fatal fruit) indicate the deadly nature of female beauty.

In *Astarte Syriaca* the threatening element in female beauty is unambiguously emphasized. The huge canvas and huger woman presented at three-quarter length uncompromisingly confront the viewer with an image as much of sexual intimidation as of temptation. The model was Jane Morris, but she was strangely distorted to accommodate Rossetti's notions of female beauty. She is colossal, with massive neck and shoulders, and she is given grotesquely inflated lips and virtually no forehead at all. More than any other figure, she calls to mind Lucien Pissarro's comment on the solipsistic tendency in Rossetti's late work: "if he recognizes no limits to the foreign sentiment and character he may impose [on the model], he will, little by little, fall to the creation of a type which is not far short of a monstrosity."[18] In *Astarte,* the powerfully built, broad-shouldered goddess is shown striding toward the viewer, and fixing him with her unflinching gaze—but she is also seductively clothed in a gown clinging enough to be suggestive, and loose enough to look about to fall off.

The expected viewer of the picture is clearly male, for it would seem that the sexual dynamics of the picture demand this, but it is important to realize that if this is the case, the underlying assumptions about art involve an exclusion of women except as the subject of male fears and fantasies. The complex Victorian male interpretations and representations of female sexuality are suggested not only in the peculiarly threatening aspect of the goddess of love, but also in the extraordinary strangeness of the symbolism, composition, and coloring of the picture. Flanking the goddess are two attendants, who are more than merely the erotically yearning women they at first seem if only because they have wings—and yet they are clearly no angels, and are rather too full-grown to pass as innocent "Cupids." Over the head of the goddess, the sun and moon are seen in strange conjunction—a fact that no doubt accounts for the extraordinarily odd coloring of the picture, the almost oppressive sea-green of the robes and the somewhat unnaturally purple flesh tones. All in all, the picture is so strange, so disconcerting, that critics continue to debate whether it is a masterpiece or a disaster or, somehow, miraculously both. One viewer, seeing the painting for the first time, responded to it as "a terrible work which, to my shocked and instantly averted gaze, announced itself as an unusually bad Rossetti. I saw—against my will—a lilac face with purple lips, huge lilac arms sprawling over lumpy fulvous folds, distorted drawing, tortured, 'gormy' paint." But the same viewer was nevertheless subsequently "haunted" by a strange sense of the power and beauty of the image.[19] A more recent critic has maintained that the picture "must be regarded as the summation of Rossetti's career as an artist; legend, religion, art and love are all combined in this awe-inspiring Hymn to Her."[20]

For good or ill, the painting is a kind of apotheosis of the Rossettian, and it is also, in its powerful evocation of both attraction and repulsion, a kind of apotheosis of Victorian attitudes toward sexuality. The accompanying sonnet emphasizes the sense of awe inspired by the mysterious and perilous power of women:

> Mystery: lo! betwixt the sun and moon
> Astarte of the Syrians: Venus Queen
> Ere Aphrodite was. In silver sheen
> Her twofold girdle clasps the infinite boon
> Of bliss whereof the heaven and earth commune:
> And from her neck's inclining flower-stem lean
> Love-freighted lips and absolute eyes that wean
> The pulse of hearts to the spheres' dominant tune.
>
> Torch-bearing, her sweet ministers compel
> All thrones of light beyond the sky and sea
> The witnesses of Beauty's face to be:
> That face, of Love's all-penetrative spell
> Amulet, talisman, and oracle,—
> Betwixt the sun and moon a mystery.
>
> (*Works*, 226)

The sonnet somewhat surprisingly ignores the threatening power of the image in its insistence on "sweetness," and indeed the reference to the massive neck as a "flower-stem" is reminiscent of Millais's disparaging comment that Sir Joshua Reynolds was capable of painting "the stem of a rose as big as the butt-end of a fishing-rod" (quoted in Hunt, 1:58–59). The poem does, however, represent Rossetti's central theme, the power of love to unite flesh and spirit, heaven and earth, and it does suggest the meeting place of the highest beauty and the highest art in the pictorial representation that itself becomes "Amulet, talisman, and oracle." The first and last word of the sonnet, "Mystery," effectively sums up Rossetti's preferred attitude toward both women— or "Woman"—and art. A modern critical viewpoint, however, would be likely to substitute the word "mystification," and note that the

idealization of both women and of art had less-than-fortunate consequences for Rossetti and for his age, that instead of closing the gap
between flesh and spirit, the world and art, the idealizations of love,
beauty, and art only reinforced harmful distinctions between men and
women, and between artist and public. Rossetti is not to be blamed
for this, but rather, in a sense, praised. His poetry and painting, like
all art, were necessarily the products of their age, but it was Rossetti's
achievement to bring into sharp focus the aspirations as well as the
fears and conflicts of his time, to represent in his work the highest
ideals of love, of beauty, and of art that his age had to offer.

Chapter Seven
Conclusion

It would be difficult to overestimate Rossetti's influence on the arts in the second half of the nineteenth century. As a founding member of the Pre-Raphaelite Brotherhood, he had a significant impact on Victorian painting almost before he knew how to paint. Not only did he contribute to the general shake-up of the art world in 1848, but according to Robert Schmutzler, his very first oil painting, *The Girlhood of Mary Virgin,* "started a movement in London which leads uninterruptedly and logically through half a century to Art Nouveau, thus marking a turning point in art history" (quoted in Lang, xxiv). And though he perhaps ended up receiving rather more than his fair share of the credit for the first wave of Pre-Raphaelitism, he was indisputably the leading spirit in the second, more influential wave. His influence on Morris and Burne-Jones, especially, contributed immensely to the Victorian arts and crafts movement and in the graphic arts the line of influence from Rossetti leads very clearly through Burne-Jones to Aubrey Beardsley in England and to Gustave Moreau and Alphonse Mucha in France. Finally, even his late, highly stylized paintings of women were cited by Oscar Wilde as proof that life imitates art, for Rossetti, along with Burne-Jones, had created a whole new type of female beauty: "We have all seen in our own day in England how a certain curious and fascinating type of beauty, invented and emphasised by two imaginative painters, has so influenced Life that whenever one goes to a private view or to an artistic salon one sees . . . the mystic eyes of Rossetti's dream, the long ivory throat, the strange square-cut jaw, the loosened shadowy hair that he so ardently loved."[1] As Pollock has forcefully observed, far from being confined to Wilde's "own day in England," Rossetti's type survives and even thrives today in the cosmetically altered and airbrushed models of high fashion. A recent television documentary made the same point, juxtaposing shots of Rossetti's painted women with shots of the cosmetically painted contestants in a Texas beauty pageant.[2]

Rossetti was at least as influential in poetry as in painting during the nineteenth century. Despite attacks by Buchanan and others, his reputation in the closing decades of the nineteenth century was extraordinarily high—especially among other poets. In fact, the critical current was running so strongly in Rossetti's favor that even Buchanan eventually recanted, proclaiming the once fleshly corrupter of public morals not only a great poet, but a pure and modest one.[3] The poets of the fin de siècle regarded him as an impeccable authority in all matters artistic. According to Arthur Symons, for example, "No modern poet ever had anything like the same grasp upon whatever is essential in poetry that Rossetti had; for all that he wrote or said about Art has in it an absolute rightness of judgment."[4] He provided what Symons called a "kind of leadership in art"[5] for a generation of writers who, according to William Butler Yeats, "All were pre-Raphaelite."[6] By Yeats's account, indeed, Rossetti provided perhaps the strongest single influence on his generation: "If Rossetti was a subconscious influence, and perhaps the most powerful of all, we looked consciously to Pater for our philosophy" (257). But Pater, for that matter, had been powerfully influenced by Rossetti, whom he regarded as the greatest, most significant, most influential man of the age. As he said to William Sharp, Rossetti "is the most significant man among us. More torches will be lit from his flame . . . than perhaps even enthusiasts like yourself imagine."[7] The evidence bears out Pater's prediction and Yeats's affirmation. As John Dixon Hunt has shown, the various literary journals of the late nineteenth century are rife with very obvious and direct, though somewhat enfeebled, imitations of Rossetti's diction and symbolism, Italianate mode, and introspection.[8]

But it has frequently been argued that the full extent of Rossetti's influence cannot be measured by simply looking at works specifically indebted to him. Jerome Buckley, for example, has suggested that the "Pre-Raphaelite movement as a whole"—of which Rossetti was certainly the dominant figure—"did much to establish the autonomy of art and the independence of the artist from didactic purpose and sectarian demand . . . by its stress on the quality rather than the variety of experience it ultimately did more than a little to quicken the aesthetic sensibility of a whole culture."[9] Even though I have been at pains to illustrate the problems inherent in this view of art, Rossetti's contribution to it has clearly had considerable cultural impact. But if Rossetti's work and example were as important and influential as I have been suggesting, it seems reasonable to ask why his reputation declined drastically in the twentieth century, and has only recently been somewhat restored—though certainly not to anything like its former heights.

One reason, no doubt, is that early appraisals of his reputation were indeed excessively enthusiastic, and that a reaction was bound to set in. A second is that the tendency of Rossetti's admirers had been, as we have seen, to praise Rossetti's "genius" at the expense of his works, to raise the man above his art, and even, as in Benson's comments, to make him a martyr to his own exquisite sensibility. Overwhelmed by his desire for beauty, "the upshot is that he stands alone, in a fever of sense and spirit, a figure clasping its hands in a poignancy of agitation, and rather overshadowed by the doom of art than crowned with its laurels" (Benson, 144). According to this notion, Rossetti's legend was at least as influential as his works. As Buckley puts it, "his dedicated life in art, no less than his poetry and painting, had become a legend and an ideal to the intense young men of the Aesthetic Movement" (5). His view is amply borne out by such testimony as that of Richard Le Gallienne, who referred to Rossetti's dwelling "in mysterious sacrosanct seclusion, like some high priest behind the veil, in his old romantic house in Chelsea" (quoted in Hunt 1968, 7). Insofar as it was the legend and not the achievement (except in the sense that Rossetti's generation of the legend may be described as an achievement in its own right) that inspired others, and generally inspired them only to the production of weak imitations, it is not surprising that such twentieth-century critics as Evelyn Waugh could dismiss Rossetti as a sort of fraud (223).

But his very influence may, paradoxically, have contributed to the eventual decline of his reputation. As Hunt has argued, "The imaginative energies of Pre-Raphaelitism seem exhausted by the century's end, dissipated often by the uncritical imitation of flatterers" (243). By 1911 Rossetti's undoubtedly enormous influence was said not only to have enfeebled English poetry, but to have all but killed it. According to Ford Madox Hueffer (now remembered as the novelist Ford Madox Ford), "the art of writing in English received the numbing blow of a sandbag when Rossetti wrote at the age of eighteen *The Blessed Damozel.* From that time forward and until to-day—and for how many years to come!—the idea has been inherent in the mind of the English writer that writing was a matter of digging for obsolete words with which to express ideas forever dead and gone."[10] Rossetti himself had denied that his poetry was, as Buchanan asserted, "aesthetic" (that is, that it valued "form" more than "content"). He was always at pains to disavow any connection with the coming generation of aesthetic young men, and after his death his brother William was equally eager to assert his unlikeness to the "intense young men": "whatever else Dante Rossetti may have been, he was a quick-blooded, downright-speaking man, with plenty of will and an abundant lack of humbug. People who take an interest in him may depend upon it that the more they learn about him . . . the more will the masculine traits of his character appear in evidence, and the less will room be left for the notion of a pallid and anaemic 'aesthete.'"[11] But he was, nevertheless, associated with what came to seem an unhealthy aestheticism, and his reputation suffered accordingly. As late as the 1950s as eminent a critic as F. R. Leavis could still dismiss Rossetti's poetry as "shamelessly cheap," "bogus," and "aggressively vulgar."[12]

From our rather more distant perspective, it should be possible to form a more balanced judgment of Rossetti's achievement, a judgment somewhere between the early excesses of adulation and the later contemptuous dismissals. Such an appraisal will not come by praising Rossetti for establishing the autonomy of art and the independence of the artist from the life of his times. Indeed, such assessments simply return us to the view of Rossetti as a champion of aesthetic withdrawal—and insofar as they emphasize his undisputed effort to uphold a romantic ideology of the transcendent, autonomous imagination, they may describe his achievement in his own terms, but fail to gain a detached perspective on the real sources and significance of his work. In fact, as Antony Harrison has recently shown, Rossetti's own poetry often fights to establish the ideology of "aestheticism," the idea of art's autonomy and independence, primarily through its own complex dependence on prior texts.[13]

As Jerome McGann has argued, and as I have suggested in the preceding chapters, Rossetti's efforts to uphold and promote an idealized view of autonomous artistic genius was the source of his deepest anxieties and difficulties as a painter and poet. His art is best understood as very much a product of its times, even as a commodity produced within a society increasingly obsessed with cultural consumption.[14] The widely current view that Rossetti and the Pre-Raphaelites in general should be seen as leading a countercultural insurgence against the dominant Philistine culture of Victorian England must be considerably modified. Barbara Munson Goff is right to say that "The Pre-Raphaelites created an art whose appeal cut across the traditional class lines,"[15] but only if it is understood that their art, as in the clear case of Rossetti's late paintings, was not in the uncomplicated service of Art with a capital A, but was very much a part of the emergent hegemony of middle-class culture. Rossetti's paintings, for example, may have run counter to the tastes of the established aristocracy, but they were quite consistent with the tastes of the bourgeois nouveau riche. It is not, after all, merely coincidence that advertisements of the late nineteenth century, most notably those using the drawings of Mucha, featured variations of the face peering out from Rossetti's canvases.

Far from being preternaturally independent of his age, Rossetti was profoundly in touch with some of its deepest currents of feeling, and his art was deeply satisfying to some of its most urgent needs. This, it seems to me, is a far more realistic and useful explanation of his immense influence than is the notion that he somehow, by sheer force of personality, imposed a fraudulent art on an unwitting culture. Matthew Arnold argued that the "real estimate" of a poet's works, "the only true one," must be absolute, and must be based on their "power of forming, sustaining, and delighting us, as nothing else can," and he warned against being misled by a "historic estimate": "The course of development of a nation's language, thought, and poetry, is profoundly interesting; and by regarding a poet's work as a stage in this course of development we may easily bring ourselves to make it of more importance as poetry than in itself it really is."[16] But in our postromantic age it no longer seems possible to offer an Arnoldian "real estimate," with its assumption that the greatest poetry presents transcendent and absolute truths. We are left with the "historic estimate," and by this measure Rossetti must be seen as an artist of very great importance indeed.

Notes

Chapter One

1. Walter Pater, "Dante Gabriel Rossetti," in *Appreciations* (London: Macmillan and Company, 1889), 242; hereafter cited in the text as "Rossetti."
2. *The Works of Dante Gabriel Rossetti,* ed. William M. Rossetti (London: Ellis, 1911), 607; hereafter cited in the text as *Works.*
3. Quoted in Arthur C. Benson, *Rossetti* (London: Macmillan, 1926); hereafter cited in the text.
4. R. L. Mégroz, *Dante Gabriel Rossetti: Painter Poet of Heaven on Earth* (London: Faber and Gwyer, 1928), 258; hereafter cited in the text.
5. Helen Rossetti Angeli, *Dante Gabriel Rossetti: His Friends and Enemies* (London: Hamish Hamilton, 1949), xii; hereafter cited in the text.
6. Susan Miller, "Introduction" to Marina Henderson, *D. G. Rossetti* (London: Academy Editions, 1973), 16; hereafter cited in the text.
7. The latter is the methodology of the still standard biography, Oswald Doughty's *A Victorian Romantic: Dante Gabriel Rossetti* (London: Oxford University Press, 1960); hereafter cited in the text.
8. Griselda Pollock, *Vision and Difference: Femininity, Feminism, and Histories of Art* (London: Routledge, 1988), 100; hereafter cited in the text.
9. William E. Fredeman, "Introduction, 'What is Wrong with Rossetti?': A Centenary Reassessment," *Victorian Poetry* 20, nos. 3–4 (1982): xvi; hereafter cited in the text.
10. George Meredith, *The Letters of George Meredith,* 3 vols., ed. C. L. Cline (Oxford: Clarendon Press, 1970), 1:418.
11. Christina Rossetti, "In an Artist's Studio," in *The Complete Poems of Christina Rossetti,* 3 vols, ed. R. W. Crump (Baton Rouge: Louisiana State University Press, 1979–), 3:264.
12. Florence S. Boos, "Dante Gabriel Rossetti," in *Dictionary of Literary Biography: Vol. 35. Victorian Poets after 1850,* ed. William E. Fredeman and Ira B. Nadel (Detroit: Gale Research Company, 1985), 229.
13. William Sharp, *Dante Gabriel Rossetti: A Record and a Study* (London: Macmillan, 1882), 297; hereafter cited in the text.
14. *Germ: Thoughts towards Nature in Poetry, Literature, and Art* (1850, reprint, Portland, Maine: Thomas B. Mosher, 1898), 25; hereafter cited in the text as *Germ.* The version in the *Germ* is somewhat different from the revised version printed in the *Works.*
15. Jerome J. McGann, "Dante Gabriel Rossetti and the Betrayal of Truth," *Victorian Poetry* 26 (1988): 342; hereafter cited in the text.
16. *Letters of Dante Gabriel Rossetti,* 4 vols., ed. Oswald Doughty and

John Robert Wahl (Oxford: Clarendon Press, 1965–67), 2: 849–50; subsequent references to this edition will be cited in the text as *Letters*.

17. Jeremy Maas, *Gambart: Prince of the Victorian Art World* (London: Barrie and Jenkins, 1975), 17; hereafter cited in the text.

18. For an excellent account of the new patronage, see Dianne Sachko Macleod, "Art Collecting and Victorian Middle-Class Taste," *Art History* 10 (1987): 328–50.

19. William Holman-Hunt, *Pre-Raphaelitism and the Pre-Raphaelite Brotherhood*, 2nd ed., 2 vols. (New York: E. P. Dutton and Company, 1914), 1:107; hereafter cited in the text.

20. Rowland Elzea, "Pre-Raphaelite Patronage," *Journal of Pre-Raphaelite Studies* 5 (1985):25.

Chapter Two

1. David G. Riede, *Dante Gabriel Rossetti and the Limits of Victorian Vision* (Ithaca: Cornell University Press, 1983), 77–104.

2. Joan Rees, *The Poetry of Dante Gabriel Rossetti: Modes of Self-Expression* (Cambridge: Cambridge University Press, 1981), 19; hereafter cited in the text.

3. D.M.R. Bentley, "Rossetti's 'Ave' and Related Pictures," *Victorian Poetry* 15 (1977): 33; hereafter cited in the text.

4. Algernon Charles Swinburne, "The Poems of Dante Gabriel Rossetti," in *The Complete Works of Algernon Charles Swinburne*, 20 vols., ed. Sir Edmund Gosse and Thomas James Wise (London: Heinemann, 1925–27), 15: 21; hereafter cited in the text.

5. David Masson, "Pre-Raphealitism in Art and Literature," in *Pre-Raphaelitism: A Collection of Critical Essays*, ed. James Sambrook (Chicago: University of Chicago Press, 1974), 82; hereafter cited in the text.

6. Christina Rossetti, quoted in *The Blessed Damozel*, ed. Paull Franklin Baum (Chapel Hill: University of North Carolina Press, 1937), xiii.

7. Jerome J. McGann, "Rossetti's Significant Details," *Victorian Poetry* 7 (1969): 50; hereafter cited in the text.

8. A. I. Grieve, *The Art of Dante Gabriel Rossetti: The Pre-Raphaelite Period 1848–50* (Hingham, Norfolk, England: Real World Publications, 1973), 9; hereafter cited in the text.

9. David Todd Heffner, "Additional Typological Symbolism in Rossetti's *The Girlhood of Mary Virgin*," *Journal of Pre-Raphaelite Studies* 5 (1985): 73–74.

10. Grieve quotes Scott in his catalogue note for Alan Bowness, ed. *The Pre-Raphaelites* (London: Tate Gallery, 1984), 64.

11. Perhaps it does not *altogether* forego perspective—Holman Hunt, Rossetti's teacher at this point as well as his "brother," later remarked that "To induce him to put the perspective right was . . . a business needing

constant argument, and had it been left according to his choice it would indeed have distressed the spirit of Paolo Ucello!" (1:83).

12. Quoted from Virginia Surtees, *The Paintings and Drawings of Dante Gabriel Rossetti (1828–1882): A Catalogue Raisonné,* 2 vols. (Oxford: Clarendon Press, 1971); 1:10; hereafter cited in the text. The version printed in the *Works* is considerably altered.

13. I quote the early version from a manuscript in the Fitzwilliam Museum, Cambridge University. A somewhat revised version was published as part of *The House of Life.*

14. A. I. Grieve, "Style and Content in Pre-Raphaelite Drawings, 1848–50," in *Pre-Raphaelite Papers,* ed. Leslie Parris (London: Tate Gallery, 1984), 43.

15. Herbert Sussman, "The Pre-Raphaelite Brotherhood and Their Circle: The Formation of the Victorian Avant-Garde," *Victorian Newsletter* 57 (1980): 8; hereafter cited in the text.

16. For a fuller discussion of these points, see Richard Stein, *The Ritual of Interpretation: The Fine Arts as Literature in Ruskin, Rossetti, and Pater* (Cambridge: Harvard University Press, 1975), 205–10.

Chapter Three

1. "Madox Brown's Diary," excerpted in William Michael Rossetti, ed.; *Ruskin: Rossetti: Preraphaelitism: Papers 1854 to 1862* (London: George Allen, 1899), 40, 19; hereafter cited in the text.

2. See Maas, *Gambart,* 175.

3. Quoted in Graham Hough, *The Last Romantics* (1947; reprint, London: Methuen, 1961), 42; hereafter cited in the text.

4. John Ruskin, *The Art of England* (1884; reprint, New York: Garland, 1979), 6–7; hereafter cited in the text.

5. T. Earle Welby, *The Victorian Romantics, 1850–1870: The Early Work of Dante Gabriel Rossetti, William Morris, Burne-Jones, Swinburne, Simeon Solomon and Their Associates* (London: Gerald Howe, 1929), 72–73; hereafter cited in the text.

6. Walter Pater, "Aesthetic Poetry," in *Appreciations* (London: Macmillan and Co., 1889), 215–16.

7. *Oxford and Cambridge Magazine for 1856* (London: Bell and Dalby, 1856), 512; all quotations from the poem are from this edition.

8. William Michael Rossetti, ed., *Dante Gabriel Rossetti: His Family-Letters, with a Memoir by William Michael Rossetti,* 2 vols. (London: Ellis and Elvey, 1895), 1:203; hereafter cited in the text.

9. Swinburne's use of the phrase "fleshly form" is decidedly friendly, but for the notoriously hostile use of the word, see Robert Buchanan, *The Fleshly School of Poetry and Other Phenomena of the Day* (London: Strahan and Co., 1872).

10. Virginia M. Allen, "'One Strangling Golden Hair': Dante Gabriel Rossetti's *Lady Lilith,*" *Art Bulletin* 66 (1984):294; hereafter cited in the text.

11. Evelyn Waugh, *Rossetti: His Life and Works* (London: Duckworth, 1928), 130; hereafter cited in the text.

12. F.W.H. Myers, "Rossetti and the Religion of Beauty," in *Essays: Modern* (London: Macmillan, 1885), 325.

13. See Francis F. Fennell, Jr., ed., *The Rossetti-Leyland Letters: The Correspondence of an Artist and His Patron* (Athens: Ohio University Press, 1978), xxvii–xxviii; hereafter cited in the text.

Chapter Four

1. Robert Buchanan, *The Fleshly School of Poetry, and Other Phenomena of the Day* (London: Strahan and Co., 1872):32; hereafter cited in the text.

2. Algernon Charles Swinburne, *The Swinburne Letters,* 6 vols., ed. Cecil Y. Lang (New Haven: Yale University Press, 1959–62), 2: 47–48; hereafter cited in the text.

3. Quoted from the manuscript in the Fitzwilliam Museum, Cambridge University.

4. Stephen J. Spector, "Love, Unity, and Desire in the Poetry of Dante Gabriel Rossetti," *ELH* 38 (1971): 435; hereafter cited in the text.

5. Florence Saunders Boos, *The Poetry of Dante G. Rossetti: A Critical Reading and Source Study* (The Hague: Mouton, 1976), 103.

6. Daniel A. Harris, "D. G. Rossetti's 'Jenny': Sex, Money, and the Interior Monologue," *Victorian Poetry* 22 (1984): 205–6; hereafter cited in the text.

7. Robin Sheets, "Pornography and Art: The Case of 'Jenny,'" *Critical Inquiry* 14 (1988): 321.

8. John P. McGowan, "'The Bitterness of Things Occult': D. G. Rossetti's Search for the Real," *Victorian Poetry* 20, nos. 3–4 (1982): 53; hereafter cited in the text.

Chapter Five

1. William Rossetti, *Dante Gabriel Rossetti as Designer and Writer* (London: Cassell, 1889), 181–82.

2. C. M. Bowra, *The Romantic Imagination* (Cambridge: Harvard University Press, 1949), 203; hereafter cited in the text.

3. Paull Franklin Baum, ed., *The House of Life: A Sonnet-Sequence* (Cambridge: Harvard University Press, 1928), 46; hereafter cited in the text.

4. William E. Fredeman, "Rossetti's 'In Memoriam': An Elegiac Reading of *The House of Life,*" *Bulletin of the John Rylands Library* 47 (1964–65): 312. The most conspicuous example is Oswald Doughty, whose biography

rather tendentiously and single-mindedly reads backward from the sonnets to draw conclusions about the life.

5. Joan Rees, *The Poetry of Dante Gabriel Rossetti: Modes of Self-Expression* (Cambridge: Cambridge University Press, 1981), 162; hereafter cited in the text.

6. For a discussion of Rossetti as a feminized Victorian hysteric, see Barbara Charlesworth Gelpi, "The Feminization of D. G. Rossetti," in *The Victorian Experience: The Poets*, ed. Richard A. Levine (Athens: Ohio University Press, 1982), 94–114.

7. Richard L. Stein, *The Ritual of Interpretation: The Fine Arts as Literature in Ruskin, Rossetti, and Pater* (Cambridge: Harvard University Press, 1975), 198; hereafter cited in the text.

8. John Keats, *The Letters of John Keats, 1814–1821*, ed. Hyder Edward Rollins, 2 vols. (Cambridge: Harvard University Press, 1958), 1:185.

9. See Douglas L. Robillard, "Rossetti's 'Willowwood' Sonnets and the Structure of *The House of Life*," *Victorian Newsletter* 22 (1962): 5–9.

10. Cecil Y. Lang, ed., *The Pre-Raphaelites and Their Circle*, 2nd ed., rev. (Chicago: University of Chicago Press, 1975), 504; hereafter cited in the text.

11. James Richardson, *Vanishing Lives: Style and Self in Tennyson, D. G. Rossetti, Swinburne, and Yeats* (Charlottesville: University Press of Virginia, 1988), 99.

12. See "Rossetti's *In Memoriam*: An Elegiac Reading of *The House of Life*," *Bulletin of John Rylands Library* 47 (1965), 298–341.

13. Quoted in Ronnalie Roper Howard, *The Dark Glass: Vision and Technique in the Poetry of Dante Gabriel Rossetti* (Athens: Ohio University Press, 1972), 167.

Chapter Six

1. William E. Fredeman, "Prelude to the Last Decade: Dante Gabriel Rossetti in the Summer of 1872," *Bulletin of the John Rylands Library* 53 (1970–71): 93.

2. Theodore Watts-Dunton, "The Truth about Rossetti," *Nineteenth Century* 13 (1883): 412.

3. Hall Caine, *Recollections of Dante Gabriel Rossetti* (London: Elliot Stock, 1882), 171.

4. William Michael Rossetti, ed., *The Family Letters of Christina Georgina Rossetti* (New York: Haskell House, 1968), 89.

5. Hall Caine, *Recollections of Rossetti* (London: Cassell and Company, 1928), 133; hereafter cited in the text.

6. John Bryson, ed., with Janet Camp Troxell, *Dante Gabriel Rossetti and Jane Morris: Their Correspondence* (Oxford: Clarendon Press, 1976), 27.

7. "I am the reverse of Swinburne. For his method of production inspiration is indeed the word. With me the case is different" (Caine 1928, 82).

8. See, for example, Quentin Bell's comment that Rossetti's painting "seems to express the decline of his later years, the recurrent illnesses, the too frequent potations of whisky and chloral, the persecution mania" (*A New and Noble School: The Pre-Raphaelites* [London: Macdonald and Company, 1982], 147).

9. Quoted in William E. Fredeman, ed., "A Shadow of Dante: Rossetti in the Final Years (Extracts from W. M. Rossetti's Unpublished Diaries, 1876–1882)," *Victorian Poetry* 20, nos. 3–4 (1982): 230.

10. The phrase is Fredeman's, in "Introduction: 'What is Wrong with Rossetti?'" xixn.

11. Jan Marsh, *Pre-Raphaelite Women: Images of Femininity in Pre-Raphaelite Art* (London: Weidenfeld and Nicolson, 1987), 78.

12. F. G. Stephens, "Pictures by Mr. Rossetti," *Athenaeum,* no. 2494 (14 August 1875):220; hereafter cited in the text.

13. Rosalie Glynn Grylls, *Portrait of Rossetti* (London: Macdonald and Co., 1964), 157.

14. The translation of the original French inscription is by Virginia Surtees, *The Paintings and Drawings of Dante Gabriel Rossetti,* 1:128.

15. F. G. Stephens, "Mr. Rossetti's Pictures," *Athenaeum,* no. 1982 (21 October 1865):546; hereafter cited in the text.

16. Walter Pater, "The School of Giorgione," *The Renaissance: Studies in Art and Poetry,* ed. Donald L. Hill (Berkeley and Los Angeles: University of California Press, 1980), 106.

17. The comment, quoted by Rossetti's friend John Skelton, is recorded in *Letters,* 4:1815n.

18. Lucien Pissarro, *Rossetti* (London: T. C. and E. C. Jack, 1908), 53.

19. W. Graham Robertson, *Time Was* (London: Hamish Hamilton, 1931), 86–87.

20. Timothy Hilton, *The Pre-Raphaelites* (New York: Oxford University Press, 1970), 187.

Chapter Seven

1. Oscar Wilde, "The Decay of Lying," in *The Artist as Critic: Critical Writings of Oscar Wilde,* ed. Richard Ellmann (New York: Random House, 1969), 307.

2. "American Chronicles: The Eye of the Beholder," produced and directed by Mark Frost. The program aired on the Fox Television Network, 15 September 1990.

3. Robert Buchanan, "A Note on Dante Rossetti," in *A Look Round Literature* (1887; reprint, New York: Garland, 1986), 152–61.

4. Arthur Symons, *Dramatis Personae* (Indianapolis: Bobbs-Merrill Company, 1923), 120.

5. Arthur Symons, *Figures of Several Centuries* (London: Constable and Company, 1916), 201.

6. William Butler Yeats, *The Autobiography of William Butler Yeats* (New York: Macmillan, 1938), 147; hereafter cited in the text.

7. See R. M. Seiler, ed., *Walter Pater: A Life Remembered* (Calgary, Alberta, Canada: University of Calgary Press, 1987), 83.

8. John Dixon Hunt, *The Pre-Raphaelite Imagination 1848–1900* (Lincoln: University of Nebraska Press, 1968); hereafter cited in the text.

9. Jerome H. Buckley, ed., *The Pre-Raphaelites* (New York: Modern Library, 1968), xxiv.

10. Ford Madox Hueffer, *Memories and Impressions: A Study in Atmospheres* (New York: Harper and Brothers, 1911), 58.

11. William Michael Rossetti, ed., *Preraphaelite Diaries and Letters* (London: Hurst and Blackett, 1900), 4.

12. F. R. Leavis, *The Common Pursuit* (London: Chatto and Windus, 1952), 47–48.

13. Antony H. Harrison, *Victorian Poets and Romantic Poems: Intertextuality and Ideology* (Charlottesville: University Press of Virginia, 1990), 90–107.

14. For an intriguing recent study of Rossetti's age in these terms, see Thomas Richards, *The Commodity Culture of Victorian England: Advertising and Spectacle, 1851–1914* (Stanford: Stanford University Press, 1990).

15. Barbara Munson Goff, "The Politics of Pre-Raphaelitism," *Journal of Pre-Raphaelite Studies* 2 (1982): 60.

16. Matthew Arnold, "The Study of Poetry," in *The Complete Prose Works of Matthew Arnold*, 11 vols., ed. R. H. Super (Ann Arbor: University of Michigan Press, 1960–77), 9:163.

Selected Bibliography

PRIMARY WORKS

Poetry

Poems. London: Ellis, 1870.
Ballads and Sonnets. London: Ellis and White, 1881.

Translation

The Early Italian Poets. London: Smith, Elder, 1861. Republished as *Dante and His Circle*. London: Ellis and White, 1874.

Collection

The Works of Dante Gabriel Rossetti. London: Ellis, 1911.

Painting

Surtees, Virginia. *The Paintings and Drawings of Dante Gabriel Rossetti: A Catalogue Raisonné*. 2 vols. London: Oxford University Press, 1971.

Correspondence

William Michael Rossetti, ed. *Dante Gabriel Rossetti: His Family Letters with a Memoir*. 2 vols. London: Ellis, 1895.
Oswald Doughty and John Robert Wahl, eds. *The Letters of Dante Gabriel Rossetti*. 4 vols. Oxford: Clarendon Press, 1965–67.
John Bryson, ed. *Dante Gabriel Rossetti and Jane Morris: Their Correspondence*. Oxford: Clarendon Press, 1976.

SECONDARY WORKS

Books and Parts of Books

Ainsworth, Maryan Wynn, ed. *Dante Gabriel Rossetti and the Double Work of*

Art. New Haven: Yale University Art Gallery, 1976. Contains a number of excellent essays addressing questions concerning the relations between poetry and painting at different stages of Rossetti's career.

Angeli, Helen R. *Dante Gabriel Rossetti: His Friends and Enemies.* London: Hamilton, 1949. A moderate and judicious biographical study, though written by a "friend" (and relation) to refute charges made by "enemies."

Bell, Quentin. *A New and Noble School: The Pre-Raphaelites.* London: Macdonald, 1982. An excellent introduction to the history and works of the Pre-Raphaelites.

Boos, Florence S. *The Poetry of Dante Gabriel Rossetti: A Critical and Source Study.* The Hague: Mouton, 1976. A perceptive and thorough study that provides readings of nearly all of Rossetti's poetry.

Bowra, C. M. *The Romantic Imagination.* Cambridge: Harvard University Press, 1947. Contains a reading of *The House of Life,* and discusses Rossetti as a late romantic.

Doughty, Oswald. *A Victorian Romantic: Dante Gabriel Rossetti.* London: Oxford University Press, 1949. Still the standard biography, though Doughty tends to treat the poetry almost solely as biographical data.

Ford, George H. *Keats and the Victorians.* New Haven: Yale University Press, 1944. Includes an excellent account of Keats's influence on Rossetti, and of the Keatsian qualities in Rossetti's verse.

Fredeman, William E. *Prelude to the Last Decade: Dante Gabriel Rossetti in the Summer of 1872.* Manchester, England: John Rylands Library, 1971. A careful biographical study that corrects misapprehensions about Rossetti's nervous crisis and about the last decade of his life.

———, ed. *Victorian Poetry: An Issue Devoted to the Works of Dante Gabriel Rossetti. Victorian Poetry* 20, nos. 3–4 (1982). Numerous essays about Rossetti both as a painter and as a poet.

Gelpi, Barbara Charlesworth. "The Feminization of D. G. Rossetti." In *The Victorian Experience: The Poets,* edited by Richard A. Levine. Athens: Ohio University Press, 1982. Argues that Rossetti is best understood within a context of middle-class, feminine Victorian values.

Harrison, Antony. *The Victorian Poets and Romantic Poems: Intertextuality and Ideology.* Charlottesville: University Press of Virginia, 1990. A chapter on Rossetti shows that his poetry is programmatically intertextual, both building on and subverting prior poems to promote a specifically aesthetic ideology.

Hearn, Lafcadio. *Appreciations of Poetry.* London: William Heinemann, 1919. A long, enthusiastic appraisal of Rossetti's poetry, based on lectures delivered in 1899.

Hilton, Timothy. *The Pre-Raphaelites.* New York: Oxford University Press, 1970. An excellent introduction to the history and works of the Pre-Raphaelite brothers and their followers.

Hough, Graham. *The Last Romantics.* London: Duckworth, 1949. Sees Rossetti's painting and poetry as a salutary break with Victorian philistinism, but also, finally, as somewhat precious.

Howard, Ronnalie. *The Dark Glass: Vision and Technique in the Poetry of Dante Gabriel Rossetti.* Athens: Ohio University Press, 1972. A chronological study of Rossetti's poetic career, with perceptive readings of most of the major poems.

Hunt, John Dixon. *The Pre-Raphaelite Imagination, 1848–1900.* Lincoln: University of Nebraska Press, 1968. Shows both the extent and the limitations of Rossetti's influence in the second half of the nineteenth century.

Johnston, Robert D. *Dante Gabriel Rossetti.* New York: Twayne, 1969. A substantial, reliable account of Rossetti's career.

Landow, George P. *William Holman Hunt and Typological Symbolism.* New York: Yale University Press, 1979. Includes an excellent discussion of Rossetti's use of typological symbolism.

Lucas, F. L. *Eight Victorian Poets.* Cambridge: Cambridge University Press, 1930. A chapter on Rossetti sees him as a tormented genius with an almost magical sense of beauty.

Myers, F.W.H. *Essays: Modern.* London: Macmillan, 1885. Contains an important early discussion of "Rossetti and the Religion of Beauty."

Parris, Leslie, ed. *Pre-Raphaelite Papers.* London: Tate Gallery, 1984. Contains essays connected with a major exhibition of Pre-Raphaelite paintings at the Tate Gallery.

Pater, Walter. *Appreciations.* London: Macmillan, 1889. Pater's essay on Rossetti set the tone for much subsequent discussion of Rossetti as a mystic for whom soul and body were indistinguishable.

Pollock, Griselda. *Vision and Difference: Femininity, Feminism, and Histories of Art.* New York: Routledge, 1988. Superb feminist discussion of Rossetti's relations with and representations of his female models.

Rees, Joan. *The Poetry of Dante Gabriel Rossetti: Modes of Self-Expression.* Cambridge: Cambridge University Press, 1981. Particularly good on Rossetti's use of Dantean material.

Richardson, James. *Vanishing Lives: Style and Self in Tennyson, D. G. Rossetti, Swinburne, and Yeats.* Charlottesville: University Press of Virginia, 1988. Subtle investigation of the stylistic peculiarities and implications of Rossetti's verse.

Riede, David G. *Dante Gabriel Rossetti and the Limits of Victorian Vision.* Ithaca: Cornell University Press, 1983. Examination of the ways in which Rossetti shaped his career as poet and painter.

Rossetti, William Michael. *Dante Gabriel Rossetti as Designer and Writer.* London: Cassell, 1889. Blandly descriptive and deliberately noncontroversial, but with invaluable information.

Sambrook, James, ed. *Pre-Raphaelitism: A Collection of Critical Essays.* Chicago: University of Chicago Press, 1974. Excellent essays on Pre-Raphaelitism generally and on Rossetti specifically.

/ Stein, Richard L. *The Ritual of Interpretation: Literature and Art in Ruskin, Rossetti, and Pater.* Cambridge: Harvard University Press, 1975. Particularly good on Rossetti's poems about paintings and on the ways Rossetti anticipated certain elements of modernist poetics.

Stevenson, Lionel. *The Pre-Raphaelite Poets.* Chapel Hill: University of North Carolina Press, 1972. A good general introduction to the poetry of Rossetti and his circle.

Sussman, Herbert L. *Fact into Figure: Typology in Carlyle, Ruskin, and the Pre-Raphaelite Brotherhood.* Columbus: Ohio State University Press, 1979. Contains excellent comments on Rossetti's uses of typological symbolism in his poetry and paintings.

Waugh, Evelyn. *Rossetti: His Life and Works.* London: Duckworth, 1928. A frequently caustic, witty, and insightful critical biography.

Vogel, Joseph. *Dante Gabriel Rossetti's Versecraft.* Gainesville: University of Florida Press, 1971. Examines the technical elements of Rossetti's prosody.

Articles

Anderson, Amanda S. "D. G. Rossetti's 'Jenny': Agency, Intersubjectivity, and the Prostitute." *Genders* 4 (1989): 103–21. A strong feminist reading of the poem, with an interesting discussion of Victorian notions about prostitution.

Bentley, D.M.R. "Rossetti's 'Ave' and Related Pictures." *Victorian Poetry* 15 (1977): 21–35. Discusses the connections between the poem and the Marian pictures, and sees Rossetti as more genuinely religious than has generally been accepted.

Buckley, Jerome Hamilton. "Pre-Raphaelite Past and Present: The Poetry of the Rossettis." In *Victorian Poetry,* edited by Malcolm Bradbury and David Palmer. London: Arnold, 1972. Emphasizes the medieval themes in Rossetti's poetry.

Fredeman, William E. "Rossetti's *In Memoriam:* An Elegiac Reading of *The House of Life.*" *Bulletin of John Rylands Library* 47 (1965): 298–341. Argues that the poem is best understood as deeply personal, but not literally autobiographical.

Harris, Daniel A. "D. G. Rossetti's 'Jenny': Sex, Money, and the Interior Monologue." *Victorian Poetry* 22 (1984): 197–215. An influential reading that sees Rossetti as exposing the moral complacency of his speaker and his times.

Harris, Wendell V. "A Reading of Rossetti's Lyrics." *Victorian Poetry* 7 (1971): 299–308. Argues that Rossetti's poetry is best when examining transient psychological states through vivid natural imagery and the dramatic portrayal of individual feeling.

Johnson, Wendell Stacy. "D. G. Rossetti as Painter and Poet." *Victorian Poetry* 3 (1965): 9–18. Discusses parallel effects in the literary paintings and the painterly poems.

Macleod, Diane Sachko. "Art-Collecting and Victorian Middle-Class Taste." *Art History* 10 (1987): 328–50. An excellent discussion of Rossetti's relations with some of his most important patrons.

McGann, Jerome J. "Dante Gabriel Rossetti and the Betrayal of Truth." *Victorian Poetry* (1988): 339–61. A reading of Rossetti as trapped between the romantic ideology of transcendent artistic genius and the actualities of commodity production in the Victorian marketplace.

———. "Rossetti's Significant Details." *Victorian Poetry* 7 (1969): 41–54. An influential rebuttal of the view that Rossetti's form overwhelms his content.

McGowan, John P. "'The Bitterness of Things Occult': D. G. Rossetti's Search for the Real." *Victorian Poetry* 20 (1982): 45–62. Argues that Rossetti believed that the artist's function was to express the hidden meanings of things, but that he self-consciously failed to do so.

Nochlin, Linda. "Lost and *Found*: Once More the Fallen Woman." *Art Bulletin* 60 (1978): 139–53. An important discussion of Rossetti's most ambitious effort to paint "the modern subject."

Roberts, Helene E. "The Dream World of Dante Gabriel Rossetti." *Victorian Studies* 17 (1974): 371–93. Sees Rossetti's early paintings as the representations of daydreams in which he plays the chief character, the later paintings as representations of a more passive dream, one buried deep in the unconscious.

Robillard, Douglas J. "Rossetti's 'Willowwood Sonnets' and the Structure of *The House of Life.*" *Victorian Newsletter* 22 (1962): 5–9. Argues that *The House of Life* is structured around the four Willowwood sonnets.

Ryals, Clyde de L. "The Narrative Unity of *The House of Life.*" *Journal of English and Germanic Philology* 69 (1970): 241–57. Sees the sonnet sequence as a carefully planned and unified poem, the order and meaning of which are discernible without recourse to the poet's biography.

Sheets, Robin. "Pornography and Art: The Case of 'Jenny.'" *Critical Inquiry* 14 (1988): 315–34. A provocative discussion of the looseness of the borders between "high art" and pornography.

Spector, Stephen J. "Love, Unity, and Desire in the Poetry of Dante Gabriel Rossetti." *ELH* 38 (1971): 432–58. An important disscussion of the fundamental late romantic themes in Rossetti's poetry.

Swinburne, Algernon. "The Poetry of Dante Gabriel Rossetti." *Fortnightly Review*, n.s. 7 (1870): 551–79. A hymn of praise to Rossetti's absolute mastery as a poet and painter.

Weatherby, Harold L. "Problems of Form and Content in the Poetry of Dante Gabriel Rossetti." *Victorian Poetry* 2 (1964): 11–19. Perhaps the best statement of the recurrent argument that Rossetti's poetry is overwrought and underthought.

Bibliographies

Francis L. Fennell. *Dante Gabriel Rossetti: An Annotated Bibliography.* New York: Garland, 1982.

William E. Fredeman. "Dante Gabriel Rossetti," In *Pre-Raphaelitism: A Bibliocritical Study,* 90–105. Cambridge: Harvard University Press, 1965.

————. "The Pre-Raphaelites." In *The Victorian Poets: A Guide to Research,* edited by Frederick Faverty, 251–316. Cambridge: Harvard University Press, 1968.

Index

The Author

David G. Riede received his Ph.D. from the University of Virginia in 1976, and is professor of English at the Ohio State University. He is the author of books on Swinburne, D. G. Rossetti, Matthew Arnold, and romantic authority.

The Pattern Artist

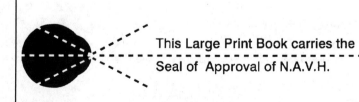

This Large Print Book carries the
Seal of Approval of N.A.V.H.

THE PATTERN ARTIST

NANCY MOSER

THORNDIKE PRESS
A part of Gale, Cengage Learning

GALE
CENGAGE Learning·

Farmington Hills, Mich • San Francisco • New York • Waterville, Maine
Meriden, Conn • Mason, Ohio • Chicago

GALE
CENGAGE Learning®

Copyright © 2016 by Nancy Moser.
All scripture quotations are taken from the King James Version of the Bible.
Thorndike Press, a part of Gale, Cengage Learning.

Thorndike Press® Large Print Christian Historical Fiction.
The text of this Large Print edition is unabridged.
Other aspects of the book may vary from the original edition.
Set in 16 pt. Plantin.

LIBRARY OF CONGRESS CATALOGING-IN-PUBLICATION DATA

Names: Moser, Nancy, author.
Title: The pattern artist / by Nancy Moser.
Description: Large print edition. | Waterville, Maine : Thorndike Press, 2017. |
  Series: Thorndike Press large print Christian historical fiction
Identifiers: LCCN 2016045090| ISBN 9781410496379 (hardcover) | ISBN 1410496376
  (hardcover)
Subjects: LCSH: Large type books. | GSAFD: Christian fiction.
Classification: LCC PS3563.O88417 P38 2017 | DDC 813/.54—dc23
LC record available at https://lccn.loc.gov/2016045090

Published in 2017 by arrangement with Barbour Publishing, Inc.

Printed in Mexico
1 2 3 4 5 6 7 21 20 19 18 17

To my mother, Marge Young
Thank you for teaching me how to sew
and be creative.

CHAPTER ONE

1911
New York City

"Annie Wood! I demand you wipe that ridiculous smile off your face. Immediately."

Annie yanked her gaze away from the view out of the carriage and pressed a hand across her mouth to erase the offending smile.

But as soon as the attempt was made, she knew it was impossible. The grin returned, as did her gumption. She addressed her accuser sitting across from her. "But Miss Miller, how can any of you *not* smile? We are in New York City! We are in America!"

The lady's maid sighed with her entire body, the shoulders of her black coat rising and falling with the dramatic disdain she seemed to save for Annie. She granted the street a patronizing glance. "It's a big city. Nothing more, nothing less."

"Looks like London," said the younger

7

lady's maid, Miss Dougard.

Miss Miller allowed herself two glances. "A city's a city."

If Annie could have done so without consequence, she would have made them suffer her own disdain by rolling her eyes. Instead she said, "If you'll pardon my directness, how can you be so indifferent? We've just crossed an ocean. We're in a foreign land, another country."

"Hmm," Miss Dougard said. "I much prefer France."

"Italy is the country of true enlightenment," Miss Miller added.

Show-offs. For they *had* traveled with the Kidds to many far-off places.

But Annie could play this game. "I happen to prefer China."

She earned their attention. "When have you — ?"

"I haven't, in body. But I *have* visited China in my mind. Multiple times. Multitudious times."

"Multitudious is not a word."

Annie rearranged her drawstring purse on her lap. "I am excited to be here because I've never traveled five miles beyond the village. Even when the Kidds travel to London for the social season I'm left behind at Crompton Hall."

Miss Miller smoothed a gloved hand against her skirt. "You wouldn't be along on this trip, excepting I knew her ladyship would get seasick."

What?

Miss Miller's left eyebrow rose. "Don't look surprised, girl. Even though you're traveling with the two of us, you are still just a housemaid, here to do our bidding as much as the family's."

Annie was tempted to let loose with an indignant *"I am not 'just' anything."* What about all the special sewing and handwork she did for the viscountess and her daughter? She had assumed *they* wanted her along because of her talent.

"Pouting does not become you," Miss Miller said.

Annie pulled her lower lip back where it belonged, hating that they'd witnessed her pain. Searching for a comeback, she bought time by yawning as if their assessment of her position meant little. Then she had it: "Considering her ladyship kept the contents of her stomach contained on the voyage, is it fair to assume my duties are now over? Am I free to enjoy myself at the Friesens'?"

"Don't be daft," Miss Dougard said.

"Or impertinent," Miss Miller added. She flashed a look at Annie over her spectacles.

"There will be chamber pots aplenty wherever you go, Annie Wood."

Annie felt her cheeks grow hot. *Under* housemaids had the burden of emptying chamber pots. As an upper housemaid Annie claimed cleaner duties that involved changing the linens and dusting the fine bric-a-brac that couldn't be entrusted to lower maids.

Except on the ship, when she *had* endured the wretched pot duty.

She drew in a deep breath, willing her anger to dissipate. As it waned, her determination grew deeper roots. Someday she'd rise high enough in the household that the Misses wouldn't dare make such a comment. Someday she'd be their equal.

Until that day . . . Annie revived her smile and returned her attention to the city passing by. She was in America, and she was not going to let anyone dampen her pleasure. No one in her family had ever even hoped to travel so far. When she'd told her parents about her opportunity, they'd scoffed. *"Who would want to go there?"* She should have anticipated their reaction but refused to let their naysaying ruin the adventure. *She* wanted to go to America. She wanted to experience *everything.* If they were content to live in the cottage where

Ma was born, taking in laundry or doing odd jobs to get by, let them. Annie had dreams.

The progress of the carriage was slow amid the teeming streets. On the ship, Annie had been astounded at the number of people gathered in one place. That number was a mere handful compared to the throngs capturing the streets of New York City. Everyone was going somewhere, in the midst of amazing missions. "They're so alive," Annie said, mostly to herself.

Miss Miller allowed herself a quick glance. "They look like ants rushing about, dizzy over a bread crumb. They don't realize life is ready to squash them. Like this . . ." She pressed her thumb against her knee and gave it a maniacal twist.

"Excuse me, ma'am, but if not for those busy ants, who would have built these enormous buildings? Who would grow the food that will be in abundance at dinner tonight? Who would do *all* the work a day requires? And if the truth be told, are *we* not ants, doing our work for the Kidds?"

The wrinkles in Miss Miller's face deepened. "I am not an ant!"

"Nor am I." Miss Dougard flipped a hand at the window. "If you can't see the difference between those of us who serve with

11

dignity and those . . . those . . ."

"People who also work very hard?" Annie offered.

Miss Miller hovered a finger in the air between them. "Never group the two of us with laborers who toil."

Two of us. Not three.

"*We* do not toil," Miss Miller said.

"Never toil," Miss Dougard said.

Although Annie knew she should nod and let it go, she heard herself say, "I agree."

The women blinked, and Annie changed the subject before they could dissect her full meaning. "Do you think the Friesen home is much farther?"

As those who did *not* toil discussed the correct answer, Annie let herself enjoy the sight of others like herself who did.

The two carriages — the one carrying the servants and the lead one transporting Lady Newley and her daughter, Miss Henrietta — parted ways when they reached the Friesen mansion as if a line of demarcation was drawn on the cobblestones dividing "them" and "us." The mistress waiting at the front entry for "them" was a distant cousin of Lady Newley's husband who'd married an American. Annie wasn't sure how Mr. Friesen had obtained his money but had overheard gossip back home that he *and* his wealth were uncouth and *nouveau riche.* Apparently new money was vulgar. Annie didn't see it. Didn't new money spend the same as old? From what she'd seen back home, old money had a hard time sustaining itself century after century. New was good. New was exhilarating. New was very American.

Annie set thoughts of the family aside when the servants' carriage stopped at the destination for "us." They were greeted by the mansion's staff, who offered a quick hello before everyone focused on the unloading and dispersing of the multitudious — she still enjoyed the word — Kidd family luggage. The two Misses did the pointing, and soon there were two stacks of large trunks and satchels, and one lesser one comprising the luggage of the three servants. The Friesen staff were swiftly organized and so began the hauling from the basement to the floor that held the family's bedrooms.

Annie waited for her traveling companions to assist with their personal luggage, but they made a quick escape into the house, chatting with the housekeeper, the butler, and various others who were their equals.

"They abandoned you," said a lad of twelve or thirteen who had helped with the unloading.

"They do that. I believe *I* am but baggage to them."

He laughed. "A steamer trunk or a carpetbag?"

"Definitely a carpetbag in hopes of becoming a grand trunk with brass fittings."

The boy swept a hand through a thick shock of wheat-colored hair. "I'm Danny. I'm the hall boy and do-whatever-they-don't-want-to-do boy."

She admired his pluck. "I'm Annie, an upper housemaid and do-whatever-they-don't-want-to-do girl."

"No one can call us lazy."

"But they might call us crazy."

He made his eyes grow too large and wiggled his hands by his face. "I won't tell if you won't."

She raised her right hand. "It will be our secret."

He nodded toward the luggage. "It's time to do whatever they didn't want to do. Tell me whose bag is whose."

Annie did so and was about to take charge of her own small satchel when Miss Miller appeared at the door leading inside. "Annie! Get in here. There's unpacking to be done."

"Coming." She gave the boy her thanks

14

and rushed inside.

"See you at dinner, Whatever-girl," Danny called after her.

How unexpected that her first friend in America was a plucky boy.

Annie unwrapped the tissue paper that encased Miss Henrietta's wardrobe and carefully lifted each dress out of the trunk and placed it on a hanger. Even if her ladyship took little notice, Annie recognized each costume as a vivid illustration of fashion — fashion Annie was lucky enough to touch and appreciate, alter and mend.

But never wear.

This limitation didn't bother her. Everyone was born into a certain position. Even in the animal kingdom a cardinal was born to be with other cardinals and a sparrow with fellow sparrows. Both shared the same overarching category, and both were content with their situation — or if not content, accepting of it.

As the daughter of a laundress and a ne'er-do-well who was usually half-rats with drink, Annie held no aspirations to be a countess or a queen. Being a lady's maid to such a woman was ambition enough. *Order above all* was a notable and noted English tradition. Although she was intrigued by the

15

idea of American freedom, it seemed a bit chaotic in its implementation. There was strength in knowing what was what and who was who. Or was it whom?

Annie worked very hard to speak and think as if she were educated, even though she was mostly self-taught. Her cause was aided by being a good mimic. She paid close attention when those of higher status spoke. Listening well was her school. To graduate would allow her to move up in the world. She would be ready when the door of opportunity opened.

Her thoughts were interrupted by Miss Henrietta as she rose from her dressing table, her hair freshened to go down for tea. She was assisted by Miss Dougard, whose black dress was a jarring swath against the sage-green silk that adorned every surface of the bedroom from wall to ottoman.

"I do hope this dress isn't too tight," Miss Henrietta said, using the pinched voice that signaled she was readying to hold her breath.

Miss Dougard glanced at Annie, and they shared the knowledge that Annie had recently — and not for the first time — let out the seams of the robin-blue afternoon dress. It was well known that the Kidds' only daughter had a tendency to overly delight in her scones and clotted cream. Annie had even overheard the Misses talking about their last trip to the fashion houses in Paris, where they'd given instructions that the seam allowances be extra generous to allow for future alterations.

Speaking of, Annie noted that the color of the let-out area along the newest altered seam differed ever so slightly from the rest of the dress, but she doubted anyone else would notice if they weren't spotting for it.

With an intake of breath on Miss Henrietta's part, the dress was put on and the hooks and eyes secured. Only then did she let out the breath, hesitate a moment, and smile. "I must be losing weight."

Miss Dougard did not respond but secured the clasp of a moonstone choker around the young lady's neck. The ensemble complete, Miss Henrietta headed to the door. "I wish to wear my rose chiffon for dinner. I forgot to mention before we left home, but the beading under the arms is quite abrasive."

"I'll see to it, miss," Miss Dougard said with a nod.

Annie nodded, her eyes downcast. As soon as their mistress was gone, Miss Dougard scanned the room — which was littered with clothes. "That girl is as fickle as a bee buzzing from flower to flower." She retrieved a mauve dress of faille silk, put it on a hanger, and handed it to Annie. "When the hooks on the wall are filled, use the few in the armoire."

There weren't enough hangers. There weren't enough hooks. It was clear six weeks' worth of clothing that would provide Miss Henrietta at least three changes a day would fill the lush bedroom to overflowing. "I wish we had a dressing room like we have back home," Miss Dougard said.

"At least it isn't winter," Annie said.

"Why would you wish that — other than the obvious fact that no one likes the cold?"

"Winter clothes would be bulkier and heavier than these — and there would be more layers to let out."

Miss Dougard's laugh renewed Annie's feeling that someday, when Annie was also a lady's maid, they might be friends.

Their work was interrupted when Miss Miller entered. She inspected the room with a single glance then said, "Miss Dougard, come. It's time for tea in the servants' hall."

"But Miss Henrietta asked that some beads be adjusted in her evening dress and —"

Miss Miller waved away her concern and said to Annie, "See to it, girl."

18

Annie expected as much. "I'll get to it right after tea."

"You'll get to it now. And you still have unpacking to do in this room *and* Lady Newley's."

But she was famished. Annie hadn't had a thing to eat since this morning on the ship.

"Don't give me that plaintive look. Work comes before pleasure. I'll have one of the under maids bring you something. The unpacking and mending must take precedence."

"Yes, Miss Miller."

Miss Dougard gave Annie a sympathetic look but showed her true allegiance by leaving for tea without fighting on her behalf.

The benefit of their departure was a chance to sit down. Annie fell into a brocade chair near the fireplace and closed her eyes. With all the family occupied on the ground floor and all the servants in the basement, the lone sound was the *ticktock* of the mantel clock.

Annie hadn't enjoyed silence since they'd left England. On the ship they'd endured the constant undulating pulse of the engine. Now she could only hear the occasional horse or automobile going by outside. The wide avenue in front of the Friesen mansion was a world away from the chaotic streets they'd passed through earlier.

Her mind raced, wanting to take advantage of the quiet, wanting to land on a peaceful thought that would offer rest. But in its racing it created an inner racket of to-dos and should-dos until Annie had no choice but to sit upright and address it. *Yes, yes. To work.*

She decided the unpacking should be attended to first, as there would be large heapings of trouble if she was found altering the dress when the bedrooms were in disarray. Once Miss Henrietta's belongings were in place, Annie moved to the bedroom of the viscountess. It was larger than the daughter's and had a small alcove assigned as a closet. There were only two gowns hung up, so Annie set to work. She was just about to move her ladyship's underthings from trunk to bureau when there was a knock. "Come in."

Danny appeared in the doorway holding a tray. "Tea is served, milady."

She laughed and curtsied then pointed to a table next to a chair. "Over there, if you please."

He set it down, and she saw it was indeed a pot of tea and three biscuits. The sight of them ignited her hunger and she fell into a chair. "You are a godsend." She poured a cup then wolfed down two of the biscuits in short fashion. Annie noticed the boy was still standing and had the most enjoyable twinkle in his eye. "Thank you for bringing me the tea, Danny — and the biscuits." When he didn't make a motion to move, she said, "Dare you sit with me a minute?"

"I'm always up for a dare." He claimed a seat. "And over here, they're called cookies."

Annie acknowledged the bit of information with a nod. "Did you miss your tea to bring me mine?"

"I volunteered." He stretched out on the chair enough for his hand to reach deep into his pocket. He pulled out his own three cookies. "But don't worry a smudge about me. I never miss a chance to eat."

"You sound like my little brother," Annie said. Her thoughts clouded. "You remind me a lot of Alfred. He was just your age. . . ."

"Was?"

"He died."

"Sorry," the boy said through a mouthful of biscuit. Cookie. "What'd he die of?"

"His appendix burst."

"Sounds awful. Were you close?"

"We were. But let's talk about happier things."

"I'll do my best." Danny stuffed a cookie

21

in his mouth, tried to talk, but ended up coughing. Crumbs spurted all over the carpet. Annie offered him some tea, and as soon as he was in control, he knelt on the floor to pick up the crumbs. "How long have you worked for the Kidds?"

"Five years. When I was fourteen I got a job at Crompton Hall. Ma and Pa didn't approve, but I did it anyway."

"Why wouldn't they approve? Being in service is a good thing — if there's no other thing, that is."

"There wasn't any other thing," Annie said. "My parents were always complaining about what they didn't have and how life wasn't fair. It was always someone else's fault. If the hen laid two extra eggs they complained it wasn't three." She took a breath. "I grew weary of it. I wanted to prove to them that there was more to be had if a person went after it."

"I'm betting they were proud of you."

She smoothed her skirt, as if making the fabric nice would make her memories the same. "They said I was nutters to try."

"But working for a highborn family like the Kidds . . . that's something."

"They didn't think of it that way." Annie remembered an incident to illustrate her mother's disdain for all those who *had* what she didn't. "One time the Kidds drove by in a fine carriage and everyone in the village stopped what they were doing and bowed and tipped their hats and such. Ma got peeved about it and said it didn't seem fair, them having everything and us having next to nothing." Annie adopted her mother's voice. " 'I'd like to see them wash clothes or mend a fence.' But I saw it differently. I said it was good the Kidds didn't do those tasks, because it meant they had to pay us to do them. We had jobs because of them."

"What'd she say to that?"

"She said, 'Whose side are you on?' " Annie sighed. "I suppose my parents are one of the reasons I want to be a lady's maid. Maybe then they'll be proud of me."

"But you're not a lady's maid."

"Not yet."

"Have the Kidds said you can rise up someday?"

"They implied it."

"But you're just a housemaid."

He was squashing her dream, and she didn't like it. "I came in as an under housemaid just to get my foot in. And now I'm an upper. I worked hard to earn that title."

"But you're still just a housemaid."

"This from a hall boy?"

Danny fell back in his chair and popped a

handful of crumbs into his mouth. "I'm not going to be a hall boy forever."

I would hope not. "What are you to be, then?"

"An adventurer."

She couldn't help but smile. "Do you have any specific adventure in mind?"

"I'm open to whatever comes my way. I refuse to jiggy up my life by making hard 'n' fast plans."

"You're a chancer." When he gave her an odd look, she explained, "You take risks."

"That's me. Wild and free. Free in spirit now, and free in body eventually."

"So you *do* have a plan."

He hopped to his feet, raising his right fist to the sky. "I plan to be deliriously happy!"

"You make *me* happy. You make me laugh."

He turned his declaration into a bow. "Then the main task of my day is successfully completed."

Task completed . . . Annie remembered all the tasks yet to complete. She drank the rest of her tea, put a cookie in her apron pocket, and handed Danny the tray. "I have to get back to work." As he headed to the door, she asked, "By the way, where did you take my satchel? Where is my room?"

"In the attic, milady. Where all captive

princesses reside."

She returned to her work, feeling rejuvenated by the food and the friendship.

The unpacking was complete, the alterations to Miss Henrietta's dress finished, and the dress worn to dinner. While the Kidds and Friesens enjoyed an after-dinner brandy in the drawing room, the servants had a short window of time for their own supper.

Upon seeing the bowls of beef, potatoes, beans, and bread that were spread upon the dinner table in the servants' hall, Annie's stomach growled loudly.

A footman standing close by grinned. "That's pleasant."

"I apologize for my stomach's anticipation."

He leaned close — too close — and whispered. "If you need anything, you call me. Grasston's the name. Got it, pretty filly?"

She got it. And rejected it. There was something about Grasston that made her want to be wherever he was not.

Annie waited to be told where to sit. At home there was a distinct seating chart, with the butler at the head, the housekeeper to his right, and the earl's valet, the lady's maids, and the first footmen next, followed through the ranks, ending with the kitchen maids and hall boy. Yet surely in democratic America, things would be different.

"You sit here, Miss Wood," instructed the housekeeper as she walked past Annie's seat to the head of the table, where she sat . . . to the right of the butler.

So much for democracy.

Annie settled in among the other house-maids and watched as the Misses took their places of honor at the other end. The situation made her feel oddly deflated. Hadn't America fought against the British to gain their freedom? Why copy what *was* when you had the chance to create something new and better?

When all were settled, the butler stood. "We'd like to welcome our visitors, Miss Miller, Miss Dougard, and . . ." His eyes scanned the table for Annie. "And their helper, Miss . . ."

"Miss Wood, sir," piped Danny.

"Yes, Mr. Dalking. I knew that." The butler nodded at Annie. "Miss Wood. You are also welcome."

She nodded, pleased at the extra attention — though with it came a crease between Miss Miller's eyes.

"Very well, then," the butler said. "Let us give thanks."

As he led them in prayer, Annie caught

Danny's eye, mouthed *Thank you,* and received a wink in return.

If Annie could have climbed the stairs to the attic with her eyes closed, she would have done so. Every inch of her body ached and begged for sleep. If the steps weren't so narrow and steep, she might have considered curling up right there.

But she didn't dare close her eyes, for the stairs were shadowed and the upper landing scowled in darkness. She had searched for a light switch at the bottom of the stairs but had found none. Which was surprising. She accepted sporadic electrical upgrades back at the Kidds' Crompton Hall that had been built in the 1700s, but she'd expected everything to be modern here.

When a figure appeared on the landing above, Annie nearly fell backward.

"So sorry," the girl said. "I didn't mean to scare you." She held an oil lamp high. The odd shadows made her face appear years older than the young tenor of her voice. "I heard you coming. Sorry there's no electricity up here. Guess they didn't think those of us in the attic were worthy of the expense."

"Us?"

"Just me anymore. They've taken to using

the rest of the rooms for storage. Come on, I'll show you to our room."

Our room? Annie didn't even have her own room?

"I'm Iris. I saw you at dinner. I'm Danny's older sister. You're Miss Wood, yes?"

"Annie." She remembered seeing the towheaded girl, but they hadn't spoken. As expected, supper conversation had been dominated by the butler, the Misses, and their American counterparts.

Annie leaned against the wall. "If you don't mind. I'm knackered." She nodded toward the attic.

" 'Course. Silly me."

Annie followed Iris to the first room on the right. It was like entering a cave. When Iris set the lamp on a dresser, it did little to improve Annie's first impression.

"We do have us a window," Iris said, displaying the curtained panes as though the darkness outside would benefit the darkness within. " 'Course it ices in winter something awful, so I cover it with a quilt, but in summertime I'd suffocate without it."

Sounds lovely.

Iris pointed to Annie's satchel sitting against the wall. "I didn't look inside. I promise."

28

"Nothing to see," Annie said as she moved the satchel to the only chair. She pulled out her nightgown.

"I emptied two hooks for you."

Annie hung up her one day dress and her formal uniform. She looked around for a washstand.

"Sorry. There's no water up here, neither. We have to share the bath with the female servants one floor down. But there is a pot." From beneath the bed Iris pulled out a chamber pot with a nicked rim.

All the comforts of home.

Needing sleep more than modesty, Annie began to undress. She shook out the uniform she'd been wearing since . . . had they only arrived today? It seemed weeks had passed since they'd left the ship.

Iris also began to undress and hung her uniform on a hook behind the door. "At least it's quiet up here."

That it was. Too quiet and very different from the quiet she'd enjoyed earlier in the day. Here in the dark attic the silence surrounded her like an ominous fog. "It's like we could be forgotten."

"They shan't forget us long. Not when they wake up and there's pots to empty and grates to sweep."

Annie decided to forgo washing her face,

and she removed her corset, taking a full breath for the first time all day. She let the folds of her nightgown fall over her like a familiar shroud. "I'm glad I don't have housecleaning duties while I'm here. I'm assisting Miss Miller and Miss Dougard."

"How do you assist them?"

"I sew and mend for both the viscountess and Miss Henrietta."

"Ain't that a task for the lady's maids?"

"They're not very good at it. And I don't mind because it's making me indispensable and shows my mistresses that I can be a lady's maid, too."

"They'll let you do that? Rise up from housemaid to lady's?"

Annie slipped between the sheets and was grateful she didn't have to share a pillow. "Miss Miller is over sixty. I've heard her talk about giving it up, and then Miss Dougard will rise from serving the daughter to the mother, leaving a space for me. At least I'm hoping that's how it will work."

"Hmm." Iris sounded skeptical.

"Miss Miller is always complaining about the stairs and talks about going to live with a sister in Brighton. I'm not going to be a housemaid forever."

Iris stood at her side of the narrow bed and braided her hair across her right shoulder. "I'm not, either."

"Do you want to be a lady's maid, too?"

"Not me. This world is too small, and I'm seventeen already. I want to work where I can meet people. I want to work in a shop." She exploded the *p* with special emphasis.

Annie thought of the tiny shops in the village of Summerfield back home. None held any appeal. "What kind of shop?"

"It don't matter to me, as long as I don't have to clean it." Iris pointed to the lamp. "Ready?"

Darkness swallowed the room.

Iris climbed into bed. When their hips touched they both moved an inch toward the edge. " 'Night," Iris said.

Yes, it was.

Chapter Two

The preacher's sermon echoed through the grand cathedral like the voice of God coming down from the heavens. Annie let her gaze move upward to the grandiose altar area with its brilliant stained-glass windows and intricately carved pulpit. The vaulted beams overhead captured the sounds of the service and returned them tenfold. Surely God lived in such a place. Their small country church back in England could fit inside this cathedral four times over. But as in England, the Kidds sat up front with the Friesens and other wealthy New Yorkers, while their servants sat in the back rows. Was the preacher talking to them first and the servants second? Or did his words rise toward God and the rafters, wrapping around them all equally?

Suddenly the preacher's voice echoed loudly through the sanctuary. " 'Praise, O ye servants of the Lord, praise the name of the Lord! From the rising of the sun unto the going down of the same the Lord's name is to be praised!' "

Danny leaned close. "Maybe after we get our work done."

He received a shush from the housekeeper farther down in the pew. Yet his words rang true. The servants of the Friesens and the Kidds were up with the rising of the sun and worked until it set — if not long into the darkness. It was a daily burden. The preacher was saying that the Lord's name was to be praised during all that? Annie had to admit she didn't think much about God during the day. She said her prayers at night and had done her share of praising Him on the trip to New York, but as the to-dos of the day demanded her attention, thoughts of God seemed very far away.

The preacher finished, and the massive organ played the introduction to the final hymn. The congregation stood and they began to sing together: " 'Take my life and let it be consecrated, Lord, to Thee. Take my moments and my days, Let them flow in endless praise. . . .' "

Praise. There it was again.

After finishing the midday meal, Annie stood on the basement stairs, staring out the small window on the landing. Rain pelted the glass.

"What's wrong?" Danny asked, as he and Iris came close.

"We have a free afternoon, but it's pouring. I hoped to see some of the city. I haven't been outside this house other than church this morning."

Brother and sister exchanged a glance and a grin. Then Iris took Annie's hand. "Follow us."

Annie expected them to detour on the main level, perhaps to some back covered stoop where they could bemoan the rain. Instead Iris led Annie up two more flights, to the attic. Annie hung back. "I'm sorry, but I don't want to spend the day up in our room. There's barely enough space to move around and —"

At the landing Danny edged past her and headed down the narrow attic hall. He swung open a door and stood aside, sweeping an arm to invite them in. "Enter, ladies!"

Iris went in first, running to a row of three dormer windows. "Welcome."

Annie walked through an aisle created from discarded furniture and trunks. Near the window she discovered a space hollowed out among the Friesens' discards, with two chairs framing a table, an oil lamp, a scattering of books, and an island of cushions, pillows, and coverlets on the floor. "What is all this?"

Danny flopped onto the cushions and immediately adjusted one under his head. "It's our hideaway."

Iris pointed to a chair and sat in the other one. "It was Danny's doing. One Sunday afternoon he got me exploring the storerooms up here, and we had the idea of making a place for us to spend our free time."

Annie scanned the room, which was larger by two than the bedroom she shared with Iris. "Why don't they let us have this room as ours and put their leftovers in our room?"

"Their things would never fit," Iris said. She retrieved three books. "And look at these: *Robinson Crusoe, Pride and Prejudice,* and *The Three Musketeers.*"

"The last one's my favorite," Danny said. "Just like us. We're the Three Musketeers. All for one and one for all!"

Annie leafed through the pages and looked at the spines. They were fine editions. "Where did you get these?"

"I borrowed them from the master's library. He'll never miss 'em."

"And if he does?"

Danny shook his head. "Nobody ever comes up here. This is the castoff room,

35

right, bug?"

Iris nodded.

His term of endearment made Annie ask, "Why 'bug'?"

Iris answered. "Cuz I hate 'em. Can't stand the crawly things and how they crunch when you step on 'em."

Annie laughed. "Brothers do like to pester, don't they?"

Danny winked at his sister. "I wouldn't pester you if I didn't love you." He looked to Annie. "Did your brother pester you?"

She thought a minute. "He used to hide my hairbrush."

"Any reason?"

"Because *he* always got in trouble for not combing his hair, he was such a yob, wanting me to get in trouble with him."

"I'll have to remember the brush thing," Danny said.

"No, you don't!"

Annie spotted a row of gilt-edged chairs, stacked two each. "You say this is the castoff room, but those chairs are posh."

"They were posh enough until Mrs. Friesen decided to redo the dining room last year."

It seemed like such a waste, yet who was she to complain? The Friesens' fickleness made for a fabulous nest among the rafters.

36

She eyed Danny's makeshift bed. "Maybe I could sleep in here so we wouldn't have to share a bed."

"We don't dare," Iris said. "If someone came for you in our room and you weren't there . . . We don't want anyone to ever find out about this room. It's our secret."

"A secret you shared with me."

Danny sat upright. "I do believe you've proved yourself trustworthy."

"And how have I done that?"

Danny moved to the window and pressed his hand against the glass as if challenging the raindrops to touch him. "You want something *more.* Just like us."

She remembered. "A shopgirl, an adventurer, and a lady's maid."

Danny wrinkled his nose. "Your dream is too small. At least Iris and I want to be something besides a servant."

Servants . . . "Did you hear the preacher talk about being servants of the Lord?"

"Sure. Getting up early and working late." Danny huffed against the pane then wrote his name in the fog.

"It's got to mean more than that. He was talking about it for everyone, not just us."

"The Friesens being servants? I don't think so." Danny rubbed the condensation off the window with his sleeve.

"God is their master just like they are ours."

He shook his head. "Too many masters."

Iris took her turn on the pile of cushions, not seeming to mind that her calves showed beneath her jumble of skirt and petticoat. "Being God's servants sounds high and good, but surely there's more for us than emptying chamber pots, or keeping the brass shining, or scrubbing a tub. None of those things sound like they're God's orders for us. At least I hope not."

Danny lifted his arm toward the sky and proclaimed, "I will strike you down for that, Iris Dalking! How dare you question Me!"

"Sorry, Lord," Iris said. "I know I shouldn't complain about what we do, and how hard it is. After all, God worked hard creating the world and all that."

Annie smiled. "And all that."

"But our work does get old, boring, and pointless. We do the chores then have to do them again the next day. A circle of chores that never ends."

"Don't you think there are repetitive tasks working in a shop?"

"Of course. But stocking shelves and getting to be around pretty things . . . and every day new customers will come in. That won't be boring at all."

Annie moved to the window next to Danny's, and Iris joined them at the third window. They could see the mansion across the street but were up too high to view the street below, or much of anything else beyond the roof and a few chimneys. "I would so like to see New York while I'm here."

"Next Sunday," Danny said. "I promise." He huffed on the pane again and wrote his name a second time. "See? I give you my signature, now you give me yours."

Annie did the same on her pane, and Iris followed suit.

"As I said, we're the Three Musketeers," Danny said.

They laughed together as their names faded away.

Miss Henrietta stood before the full-length mirror in her room as Miss Dougard attempted to fasten the hooks at the back of the lavender day dress. There was a good half-inch gap between hook and eye. After grunting and groaning, Miss Dougard gave up. "Perhaps the blue lawn?"

"I want this dress. I want to wear my straw hat with the lilac sprigs, so it has to be this dress." Miss Henrietta nodded to Annie. "You're a strong girl, you try."

Miss Dougard stepped away with a "you have a go" look. Annie took a fortifying breath then realized how insulting that might have seemed to her mistress. Luckily, Miss Henrietta didn't seem to notice.

Minding the impossible gap, and knowing there wasn't time to remove the bodice and tighten the already tight corset, Annie got an idea. "Would you please try to make your shoulder blades touch, miss?"

"What?"

"Put your shoulders back as far as they will go."

Her mistress thrust her ample chest forward and did as she was told. "There now," Annie said. "Hold that." She hurriedly fastened the hooks. The one at the waistline was the most difficult, but even it was secured. "Done! You can relax. Carefully, please."

Miss Henrietta slowly drew her shoulders forward. The hooks and eyes strained but held. She turned to face Annie. "Well done! Thank you. Now for the hat."

Annie assisted Miss Dougard by holding the hat pins. It was a lovely hat, so she could understand why her mistress wished to wear it to the tea at Mrs. Belmont's. Annie chastised herself for not checking the fit of the lavender dress before they sailed for

New York.

For there was still a problem. While seated, Miss Henrietta's bosom became the focus of her presence, as it was pressed to overflowing atop the squared neckline. The lace inset leading to the high collar strained against it. Annie vowed to alter the dress after this day's wearing was done so it would be ready the next time.

"I'll need my reticule and my shawl," Miss Henrietta said.

Annie had gathered the purse when the bedroom door burst open and Lady Newley strode in. "Come, Henrietta. You are making everyone late."

With a fit and fluster, Miss Henrietta grabbed the purse from Annie and followed her mother downstairs.

"She does not look seemly," Miss Dougard said as she tidied up. "She looks like a sausage overflowing its casing."

It wasn't that awful — though nearly. "I'll take out the dress when she returns."

"I don't think there's a smidgen left in the seams. I was against her bringing that dress at all."

"Perhaps I could add a gusset in the side seams?"

Miss Dougard eyed her over her glasses. "What do you know of gussets?"

Annie wasn't sure where she'd heard the term. "It would work, would it not?"

"You have no fabric to match."

"Perhaps we could go out and get some."

"Where?"

"I don't know where, but if there's a fashion problem, it needs to be addressed. She'll want to wear the dress again."

"The fashion problem has nothing to do with the dress and much to do with the lack of self-control of the woman wearing it."

It was a cruel statement, though Annie couldn't contest it.

Suddenly she spotted the shawl draped over a chair. "She forgot her shawl!"

"Run on then. Catch them if you can."

Annie sprinted down the stairs to the front entrance where Mrs. Friesen and Lady Newley were just entering a carriage, with Miss Henrietta last in line. Annie stepped forward. "Your shawl, miss."

Henrietta smiled. "Thank you, Annie."

Annie retreated toward the door, but as she passed Grasston, the footman said, "I hope that shawl's big enough to cover the big fat hen."

Annie was so shocked she stopped to face him. "How dare you. Show some respect."

He shrugged. Annie glanced to the carriage and saw by the look on Miss Henrietta's face that she'd overheard the rude words.

If Annie could have gotten away with slapping him, she would have left a mark on his cheek.

Annie was just finishing a cup of tea in the servants' hall when she heard the call bell for Miss Henrietta's room. "That's me," she said. "They must be back."

Once upstairs she rapped lightly on her mistress's door before entering, and was surprised to see that Miss Dougard was not present. "Yes, miss?"

Her mistress was still wearing her hat and had not begun to change clothes for the afternoon. She extended the shawl toward Annie. "Thank you for bringing my shawl."

"You're welcome." Annie folded it smooth. "Would you like me to help you change?"

She gave a quick shake of the head then a nod. "Yes, but first . . . I want to thank you for defending me this morning."

Annie wasn't sure what she was talking about.

"That footman?"

Ah. "Please don't take to heart anything he says. He's a bounder. From what I've seen he has the manners of a dustman —

though perhaps that's offending the latter."

Miss Henrietta smiled. "Be that as it may, I know what people think of me. I'm too young to be so . . . corpulent. Mother says I'll never find a husband if I don't trim myself up."

Annie could imagine Lady Newley saying such a thing — and not kindly. Especially since *she* was still a very handsome woman.

"Many men prefer a voluptuous woman," Annie said.

Henrietta looked down at her chest. "Voluptuous is fine, but fat is not."

Annie wasn't sure what her mistress wanted from her. Unfortunately, the vast menus that would fill the family's dining fare in New York would test Miss Henrietta's willpower past its limit.

"The dress can be altered to fit."

Miss Henrietta shook her head. "I don't want any more adjustments. I want to fit into this dress — which is one of my favorites. Perhaps overhearing the footman's comments was what I needed, for it has spurred me to take action and become a better, more desirable woman."

Annie admired her attitude but was distressed regarding its core. "You do whatever you wish to feel good about yourself, miss. But know that as you are, you have much to offer any man."

Miss Henrietta looked to the floor. "You are sweet, and I appreciate your words." She moved to the dressing table and allowed Annie to remove her hat.

After the evening meal, Annie headed toward the back stairs. Suddenly Grasston grabbed her arm and dragged her into the laundry. Two women ironing sheets looked up. He put his back to them and faced Annie. She yanked her arm away. "What are you doing? Leave me alone."

"Sorry," he said under his breath so the workers wouldn't hear. "But you've made that impossible."

"What did I do to you?"

"You made Mr. Brandon give me a reprimand."

"I did no such thing."

"Someone did. I've been demoted to second footman for a week."

So the news of Grasston's nasty comments had made their way to the butler's ears. "It serves you right for being so rude. Miss Henrietta is a wonderful woman and a guest in this house."

He took a step toward her, his grin smug. "A big, fat, ugly guest."

"You are the ugly one. Ugly inside and out."

Grasston grabbed her chin and squeezed it hard. "You'd better watch out, Annie Wood. You can't hide from me." He let go of her chin then swatted her behind before exiting the room.

Annie didn't know what to do. The two washerwomen stared at her, their eyes revealing their shock and compassion. But to acknowledge what they'd seen would make it worse, so Annie left the room and fled to the safety of the hideaway.

"Here you are," Danny said as he entered their attic gathering place. "Your mistress has been ringing for you, and Miss Miller sent me to find you."

Annie sat upright on the pile of cushions. "I needed some time alone."

"Not allowed. Not before the family goes to bed. You know that."

She nodded and held out her hand. He helped her to her feet, and she smoothed her skirt and apron. "Thank you for coming to get me."

He put a gentle hand on her arm. "What happened to upset you?"

Annie shook her head and left to find Miss Miller. Telling Danny about Grasston would

46

not better the situation.
   Nothing would.

CHAPTER THREE

After breakfast, Annie noticed the butler and housekeeper talking one-on-one with Danny. The butler handed him a note and with a hand upon his shoulder and the point of his finger gave him some instruction. Danny nodded, turned to walk away, and then turned back and asked a question. Both adults looked in Annie's direction, though past her. She turned around and saw Iris at the doorway. She heard a few more mumbled words then saw Danny leave the conversation with an enormous grin on his face.

"Come on," he whispered as he passed Annie. Danny corralled his sister, and the three of them found some privacy in the basement corridor.

"Why are you grinning so?" Annie asked.

"Mr. Brandon asked me to take a message to the Franklins, and Mrs. Grimble wants me to pick up a recipe for raspberry meringue pudding from their cook."

"You get to leave?" Annie said. "Lucky bloke."

"I asked if Iris could come along and they said yes — as long as she got her chores done."

Iris kissed him on the cheek. "I'll work at double speed."

Annie was happy for them but sad she was being left behind. But then Danny said, "Can you do *your* chores at double speed, Annie?"

Hope sped through her like a breath of fresh air. "Me? You want me to go, too?"

Danny glanced down the corridor where other servants bustled about the day's chores. "Just don't say anything to the rest of them."

Annie made a locking motion at her lips. "What time should we go?"

They each took a moment to weigh their tasks. Annie was the first to speak. "The Kidds are going to a charity luncheon at one. Perhaps after they leave?"

"One fifteen, then," Danny said. "Meet at the kitchen entrance."

"Outside the kitchen entrance," Annie said. "It will increase my chances of not being noticed."

Suddenly the butler's voice echoed down

the corridor. "Mr. Dalking? Miss Dalking? Have you nothing to do, because if you don't, I'm sure Mrs. Grimble can find something —"

"No, sir. Yes, sir. We're going."

Yes, they were.

Annie was torn.

Should she ask Lady Newley for permission to leave with Danny and Iris? Or should she ask Miss Miller for permission? Or . . . ?

Miss Miller's headache determined the answer to both questions. With Miss Miller indisposed — with instructions not to be disturbed — it was up to Annie and Miss Dougard to help their two mistresses get dressed for their outing. Lady Newley was the easier of the two, as the time helping Miss Henrietta was once again consumed with getting her dresses to fit. The chance for Annie to do any asking for anything at any time never presented itself.

As soon as the ladies were on their way, Miss Dougard informed Annie she was going to take a nap and she, too, wished not to be disturbed, thus closing the final door on permission.

Permission or not, she was going.

Annie rushed up the back stairs to her

room to find Iris already getting changed into her street clothes.

"Isn't this exciting?" Iris asked.

Annie wasn't sure *exciting* was the correct term for a simple errand, but she was very happy to be able to get out of the house. In a dash both girls were dressed and ready. At the last moment, Annie removed her hat. "I don't want to draw attention to myself. I'll put it on when I get outside."

"Should I go first?" Iris asked.

Perhaps. Annie let Iris leave the room and waited a short time before venturing out behind her. Her stomach was in double knots. She wasn't doing anything wrong by leaving for a short time, yet she knew she wasn't doing anything right, either. In spite of it all, she found bending the rules exhilarating.

What was it about America that made her think beyond what was into what could be?

As she approached the basement, Annie walked on her toes, slowing to check for witnesses. She heard the sound of workers in the laundry and saw a scullery maid moving from the storage closet to the kitchen. But otherwise the coast was clear. Tucking her hat beneath her arm, she slipped outside. She spotted Danny and Iris, but as she moved toward them, Grasston stepped out of the shadows.

"Well now. Who have we here?" He dropped the stub of his cigarette and ground it with his toe.

Annie ignored him, strode past, and linked arms with Iris.

"I'll see you later, Annie Wood."

She walked faster. As soon as they reached the street, Iris asked, "What did he do to you? You're practically trembling."

Danny stepped in front of the girls, stopping them. "If he hurt you in any way . . ."

The fact Danny assumed such a thing spoke volumes. "Has he hurt other girls?"

Danny's glance at Iris revealed the truth of it.

"Did he hurt you, Iris?" Annie asked.

"Not hurt me, but bothered me in a way I didn't like. At all."

Annie's ire rose. "Men like him should be stopped."

"How?" Iris asked, motioning for Danny to move so they could start walking again. "He's got the high position in the house. We don't."

"When I confronted him about Iris, he laughed at me," Danny said.

Annie wasn't surprised.

"He dared me to tell Mr. Brandon."

"Did you?"

Danny shook his head. "But when I get bigger, I'll take care of him no matter what he says. Our pa was six-foot-three, so I'll be tall like him someday."

Again Danny reminded Annie of her brother, Alfred, full of honor and high hopes.

"Enough of him," Iris said. "We have some time away, so let's enjoy it."

"Where is this house we have to go to?" Annie asked.

"A few blocks up Fifth. If we hurry and get that done, then I know a special place I want to show you."

Iris perked up. "Really, Danny? Do you think we have time to go to Macy's?"

"What's Macy's?"

Danny grinned. "Mrs. Friesen calls it 'a palace of product, pleasure, and profit.' And she's right. You have to see it."

Annie still wasn't sure what it was.

"It's a department store. Eight floors heaped with things to buy."

"But I don't have any money."

"Neither do we, but it's fun to look. Come on! We need to hurry."

The three young people finished the task at the Franklins' in quick fashion and soon found their way over to Herald Square.

"There it is," Iris said, as if viewing a holy relic. "Macy's."

The store loomed over the street corner, taking up more than an entire block. Windows ran the length of the building, with glorious displays of goods from iceboxes to boots to baby prams.

They stood in front of the window display of women's dresses. "Will you look at that blue dress," Annie said. "Don't you love how the lace on the bodice hangs free, making the waist look tiny? I'd add a bit of beading at the edges of the lace, though. It looks a bit raw."

"You care about the fashion of it," Iris said. "I don't care what the fashion is. I just want the chance to sell it, to be around it all day, to be around people."

"You're around people at the Friesens'," Danny said.

"I'm around other servants. I'm not around the family. They don't want to even see me, they just want to see my work."

It was a true statement. The majority of the servants were supposed to be invisible to the family they served, hence the back stairway and the careful timing of the chores so rooms were cleaned and beds were made while the family was elsewhere.

Once inside the store, all thoughts of the

Friesens evaporated as the threesome entered a land of plenty. Every kind of bits and bobs were on display. They walked through wide aisles that showcased glass cases of hats, shoes, gloves, lace, fabrics, and . . .

Annie stopped to gawk at a sewing machine. "May I help you, miss?" a clerk asked.

"I'm just looking. Admiring."

"Do you sew?"

"I do, but always by hand. To have a machine . . ."

"Would you like to see how it works?"

"Yes, I would, but . . ." Annie noticed Danny and Iris motioning her to move along. "Perhaps I can come back?"

"Of course. I am always here." She handed Annie a card with her name on it. "My name is Mrs. Holmquist. Feel free to ask for me."

Annie slipped the card in her pocket. If ever she could come back, she would.

There was no denying it was hard returning to the Friesens'. After experiencing a bit of New York and Macy's, Annie felt like a bird who'd jumped from the nest and learned to use its wings. She wanted to soar and explore, not return and yearn to be free again. Yet what choice did she have?

The three of them came in the back way, and Danny and Iris immediately detoured to report to Mr. Brandon regarding the message he'd had them deliver, and give Mrs. Grimble her recipe. Annie headed upstairs to her room to change back into her uniform. But as she reached the landing on the floor of the family bedrooms, she was surprised by Grasston, who popped out from a dark corner and pulled her into it. He pushed her back against a wall, angling her arm behind her. He loomed close. He smelled of cigarettes.

"You think you can come and go as you please?"

Annie glanced down the hall leading to the bedrooms and kept her voice low. "I am not beholden to you."

"They noticed you were missing. I made sure of it."

What? How dare he!

Fueled by anger, Annie pushed against him, but Grasston pinned her tightly against the wall, forcing her to turn her head to the side to avoid his warm breath on her face. He whispered in her ear. "I always wanted to taste an English tart."

He bit her earlobe. Then he stepped back, gave her a wink, and retreated downstairs

— into the bowels of Hades where he belonged.

Her strength drained out of her, and Annie found the wall a necessity. Her thoughts ricocheted with the bad news that her mistresses and the Misses knew she had left without permission, the lingering memory of Grasston's hands, and the fear it would happen again. Or worse.

She heard female voices in the hallway. Lady Newley's words rushed down the hall to her ears. "Annie is where?"

Miss Miller answered. "I have no idea, my lady. But I assure you I will find out."

Her wings clipped, Annie hurried upstairs to change into the clothes of a servant again.

She had just tied her apron when Iris came in their room, also ready to change back into her maid uniform.

"Mr. Brandon didn't say a thing about us being gone too long, so everything worked —"

"They know I left."

Iris put her coat on the hook. "How do you know they know?"

She decided not to mention Grasston — yet. "I overheard Lady Newley and Miss Miller in the hall."

Iris removed her hat and sat on the bed. "What are you going to tell them?"

"The truth. I have no feasible lie."

"What will they do to you?"

"I have no idea."

"They can't send you home. It's too far away. Can they?"

Surely such a punishment would be an overreaction. What had she done wrong except fail to ask permission?

Annie chose to check in with Miss Henrietta first. She knocked on her door and waited for permission to enter. Henrietta sat at the dressing table, removing her earrings.

"Good afternoon, miss. Did you have a pleasant time at your outing?"

Annie received a pointed stare. "Did *you*?"

Annie's insides flipped.

"The footman let us know of your absence."

Once again Annie was stunned by Grasston's gall. Yet it was best to face the issue head-on. She moved to help Henrietta with the removal of her other jewelry. "Actually, I had a very pleasant time. I haven't been out of the house except for church since we arrived."

"Really? Didn't you have Sunday afternoon free?"

"It was raining."

Miss Henrietta's nod eased Annie's

nerves. Then she locked her gaze with Annie's in the mirror. "You should have asked permission."

"Agreed, miss. But both the Misses were indisposed and didn't want to be disturbed."

"Perhaps you should have left a note."

Why hadn't she thought of that? "You are right. I should have. But I thought I would be back before you returned."

"Ours *was* a shorter outing than I'd hoped it would be. But Mother seemed peeved at the way the charity work was being handled, so she wanted to come home." She stood. "It was far too dramatic. I need a nap. I don't wish to wait for Miss Dougard. Help me undress."

That task accomplished, Annie fluffed the pillows and readied an afghan as Miss Henrietta lay down. "Did you come upon anything exciting on your outing?" she asked Annie.

Annie wasn't certain she should mention where they went, as it was out of the way from their initial errand, but decided to share because surely Miss Henrietta would be interested in Macy's. "The outside windows hinted at what they had to offer. Then once inside there were thousands of items to buy, floors and floors of pretty things."

Miss Henrietta snuggled into the pillows. "You haven't been to London with us, have you? You've never seen Harrods department store."

"It has display windows and many floors?"

"It does indeed." She yawned. "The window displays entice you inside to buy. It's quite impossible not to be lured in."

"They know what they're doing with that."

"Indeed they do. Now go. But tell Miss Dougard to wake me for tea."

Annie slipped out, feeling lucky to have no consequences.

"Annie Wood!"

She spun around and found the Misses exiting Lady Newley's room. Miss Dougard had a rose-colored dress on her arm.

Annie readied herself for another scolding but put a finger to her lips. "Miss Henrietta is resting."

The three women moved away from the bedroom doors. Then Miss Miller said, "Perhaps Miss Wood is exhausted from her own excursion? It seems you like to break the rules when others take a kip."

Annie stifled a sigh but repeated her explanation and her apology. "I should have left a note. I am sorry."

"You should be. Lady Newley is quite upset by your insubordination."

"It shan't happen again." As she said the words she felt a wave of sadness. She wanted to go out again. And again. And again. On any day of the week, not their free Sunday afternoon when nothing was open. Mrs. Holmquist and the sewing machine were waiting for her.

"Here," Miss Miller said, grabbing the dress from Miss Dougard's arms. "As punishment we have some extra work for you. Add some beading to the bodice of this dress. Lady Newley has realized the fashion of Mrs. Friesen overshadows her own."

If this was punishment, Annie would gladly accept it. Sewing for the Misses was nothing new. "Where do I get the beads?"

"Come to my room. I brought a store of them from home."

Annie held the dress at arm's length. "Any special instructions?"

Miss Miller pointed to the scooped neck bodice. "Something along there, but not like the beading you did on her sage dress. Something different."

"Use your imagination," Miss Dougard said.

That was hardly punishment.

Up in the hideaway, Annie enjoyed having time alone to do the beading. While she did

61

the work, she pondered two disparate issues: her newly born pleasure of exploring the city and her newly born fear of Grasston. As they were due to stay at the Friesens' for six weeks, she hoped for more weekday outings. To the other issue, she was wary of Grasston's unwanted attention. In the short time she'd been in residence, he'd shown a disturbing aggression that would probably get worse rather than better.

To fight back the fear, she reminded herself that he wasn't the first male who'd assumed too much and been too grabby. She might be only a maid, but she was a *maid* in the truest form of the word and planned to keep it that way. She'd known other girls who'd succumbed to temptation. Nothing good came of it. The only result was a ruination of their lives — never love. Annie wanted to fall in love someday, but not with someone who was merely handsome and charming. She wanted a man who challenged her, made her want to be more than she was alone, a true partner.

She finished the beadwork, tied off the thread, and cut it. She held the dress to inspect her work. "Lovely. As usual."

If she didn't say so herself. Yet if she didn't say it, who would?

CHAPTER FOUR

Upon hearing Mr. Brandon's chastising voice, Annie paused on the last step of the stairs leading to the basement. She didn't want to embarrass another servant by witnessing a scolding.

"Really, Mr. Grasston, this is the second time you've arrived for service without the proper gloves. I fail to understand what is so difficult about maintaining your proper uniform."

"I'm sorry, sir. I don't know what happens. I remove them to do other work and —"

"And they disappear?"

There was a pause. "They do, sir."

"Are you saying we have spirits in the house, Mr. Grasston?"

"No, sir."

"Are you accusing others of stealing your gloves?"

"Well . . ."

"Passing the blame is not acceptable. Unless you have proof that others are pilfering your gloves — which I have difficulty imagining — you must take responsibility. But know this, Mr. Grasston: I am giving you a warning. If you come on duty again without the proper gloves, I will dock your pay for a dozen pair. I believe that should rectify the matter if you cannot."

"Yes, sir."

"Very well then. You have work to do in the dining room."

In a split second, Annie realized Grasston would be using the stairs. She considered retreating upward but knew her footsteps would be heard. Best to continue down. She quickly backtracked three steps then came downstairs, passing Grasston as he started upstairs. Neither greeted each other, but after a few steps she heard him pause and felt chill bumps up her spine as she headed down the corridor. Was he wondering if she overheard?

She smiled at the thought. Let him squirm.

Then, ignoring common sense, she turned to look at him. "Lose something, Mr. Grasston?"

Only the sound of footsteps on the stairs saved her from his retort.

Or worse.

The Kidds and the Friesens were set to attend a formal dinner, which required extra care in the ladies' toilette. Annie moved between the rooms of Miss Henrietta and Lady Newley, assisting the Misses. She was thrilled to see that Lady Newley was going to wear the dress Annie had beaded. It was some of her finest work.

When Miss Miller left her ladyship's bedroom to retrieve her jewels from the Friesens' safe, Annie was left alone with her.

Ask her how she likes the beading. Now's your chance.

"Fetch my gloves, Annie," Lady Newley said.

Annie did as she was told, but as she was buttoning the twenty buttons that edged the inner seam, Annie took a chance. "I hope the new beading on your dress pleases you, my lady?"

Lady Newley put her free hand upon the beads. "It does. Miss Miller does such fine work. I couldn't ask for a more talented lady's maid."

Miss Miller's work?

Upon hearing the words of betrayal, Annie stopped buttoning the gloves.

"Annie? Come now. Finish up."

They didn't give me credit?

Two more questions came next, ricocheting against the first. *Have they ever given me credit? Do my mistresses truly attribute all the fine detail on their dresses, all the hours and hours of work, to the Misses?*

Somehow Annie finished buttoning the gloves. But then Miss Miller came in carrying two velvet boxes of jewels and shooed Annie away. "Go on, girl. There are towels to clean up in the bath."

"And I'd like a fresh pillowcase, if you please," her mistress said.

Annie walked into the hall in a daze. They truly thought of her as a housemaid. Nothing more.

That's because you are a housemaid. Nothing more.

All her hard work learning the details and intricacies of sewing and dressmaking so she could rise to the position of lady's maid . . . Had she ever had a chance? Or had she created her own dream and her own scenario that had never owned any basis in fact?

Annie went into the bathroom and cleaned up the towels, wiping down the floor. Maid's work. Anger stirred inside even as her body accomplished the work. She felt like a fool who'd been duped into striving for something that was impossible. She had more chance of building a skyscraper than she did of building a life as a lady's maid.

"They shan't get away with this" became her mantra as she scrubbed the tub. By the time her work was finished and the towels were taken downstairs to the laundry, she knew what she had to do.

Annie stood outside Miss Miller's room, her heart pounding in her ears. Inner warnings that she should let the betrayal pass collided with the need for justice and the unrelenting desire for her emotions to be released.

Please, God. Help me.

Help her what? Confront Miss Miller?

For better or worse.

With a fresh breath Annie knocked on the door, her first knock more forceful than the next two.

"Yes?" Miss Miller said.

Annie stepped inside and closed the door behind her. Miss Miller sat in an easy chair, reading a book.

"If you're wanting another outing, the answer is no."

"I need to talk to you."

With a dramatic sigh, Miss Miller shut her book and removed her spectacles. "But

I don't need — or wish — to talk to you. I need you to leave. I've had a hard day."

"Doing what?"

"What did you say?"

"What have you done today — or any day — that constitutes hard work?"

Miss Miller rose from her chair, the book thudding to the floor. "Leave!" she said, pointing to the door. "I insist you leave this minute."

Suddenly the door opened behind Annie, and Miss Dougard slipped in, closing the door behind her. "What's going on in here?" she whispered. "I could hear you in the hall."

"Annie was just leaving."

"I will leave as soon as I've said my piece."

"Your piece?" Miss Miller said. "You're the one in trouble."

"Not anymore." She cringed at her own word choice. It was too late to stop now. Annie drew in a breath and began. "I object to both of you taking credit for my beading work — for all the sewing work I've done for Lady Newley and Miss Henrietta. I thought they knew *I* was doing the work."

"And why would they know that?" Miss Miller asked as she retrieved her book.

It took Annie a moment to recover from shock. "Because you'd tell them. Because you wouldn't take credit for work you didn't do."

"You liked doing the work," Miss Dougard said. "You have a talent for it."

"I do like it, and I do have a talent for it," Annie said. "But that doesn't mean you should pass it off as your work." She pointed to a painting of a mountain scene on the wall. "The person who hangs the painting doesn't take credit for painting it."

"I don't like your tone."

"My tone?" She looked from one to the other, incredulous. "I did the work and deserve the credit. I did the work as training for when I become a lady's maid someday."

Miss Dougard looked at Miss Miller, and then the latter began to laugh. "You? A lady's maid?"

Miss Dougard shook her head. "Lady's maids are women of breeding and education."

"Not a girl who grew up cleaning pigpens and chicken coops."

A pit grew in Annie's stomach. "When I applied for a job at the manor house, I told them I was good at sewing."

Miss Miller was not fazed. "But you were hired as a maid. An under housemaid."

"That's the only position they had open.

But they saw my potential, I know they did. There are many who apply to work with the Kidds and not all are taken."

"They are if the vicar insists on it," Miss Miller said.

"What?"

"You'd just lost your brother and your father was a known drunkard. The vicar heard you were applying for a job and strongly suggested the Kidds take you on."

The foundation of Annie's position in the household cracked. "They were impressed by my sewing ability. I brought them examples of dresses I'd made for Ma and some neighbor ladies. I told them I wanted to be a lady's maid someday."

Miss Miller chuckled. "You had nerve, that I'll give you."

"Did they tell you being a lady's maid was a possibility?" Miss Dougard asked.

Annie's mind rushed back to her interview with the housekeeper at Crompton Hall. She remembered a vague *"We'll see, child"* but nothing else. Had those few words been an attempt to humor her, nothing more? Had Annie planted her hopes on the polite patience of a housekeeper who'd been instructed to hire her out of pity? As a charity case?

Miss Dougard touched Annie's arm.

"Don't feel bad about it. They hired you. People were looking after you."

Miss Miller pointed the book at her. "You should be thankful, girl. You have a job. You have a future with the Kidds."

"As what?"

Miss Miller looked taken aback, as if she didn't understand the question. "As a housemaid. It's an honorable position in an honorable house. I know dozens of girls who would fight for that honor."

The pit in Annie's stomach dug deeper. Why had she ever thought she could rise above her station? The Misses had never encouraged her. No one had.

"Go on now," Miss Miller said, opening the door. "Get up to the attic until we need your help when the ladies return home."

Miss Miller nudged Annie out the door and closed it on her heels. From the hall she heard their laughter.

She also heard the soft click of more than one other door in the servants' hallway.

Her humiliation was complete.

Annie went through the rest of the day and evening as if walking underwater, her movements slow, her gaze blurry. More than one person asked if something was wrong. She had no answer for them. For there were a thousand things wrong, yet nothing at all.

Nothing that could be shared. Nothing that would matter to anyone but herself.

When it was time to retire she returned to her attic room, longing for the oblivion of sleep. She dreaded seeing Iris, for Iris would sense something was amiss, and Annie didn't want to share the details of what a fool she'd been. She remembered the words of Iris and Danny when she'd first shared her dream. *"They'll let you do that? Rise up from housemaid to lady's maid?"*

Even young Danny had known what an impossibility it was. Why hadn't Annie realized as much? She'd been dumb as a plank for not seeing the truth.

Annie got ready for bed and slid under the covers, praying for sleep to come quickly. But her mind wouldn't let her body go, reliving every horrible moment again and again.

She heard steps outside the door and quickly closed her eyes, feigning the sleep that eluded her.

Iris came in with a lamp. "Oh," she said, immediately turning down the wick.

Annie was just about to congratulate herself on her ruse when she heard Iris crying — and not just a little.

She turned over to see her. "What's wrong?"

Iris shook her head back and forth. "Nothing. Really. Go back to sleep."

Annie pushed back the covers and went to her.

Iris fell into her arms. "He's such a brute. I hate him!"

"Grasston?"

Iris nodded. "He grabbed me and . . . and rubbed up against me, and . . . I don't know why he's bothering me."

Annie led her to sit on the bed. "I'm afraid I am to blame. I've rebuffed him more than once and got him in trouble about his rude comments to Miss Henrietta. If he can't get to me, he'll go after you because he knows we're close. I'm so sorry."

Iris nodded then put a hand on her upper arm as though it was sore.

"Did he hurt you?"

"He pinched me hard."

"Let's look at it." Annie helped remove her arm from the dress sleeve, revealing two distinct red finger marks on the outside and a thumbprint on the inner arm. "It's going to leave a bruise. We should show Mrs. Grimble or Mr. Brandon."

"No!" Iris said. "Nothing will come of it. And then he'll come after me more."

"We have to do something."

"I just want to go to bed."

73

Annie helped her then got in on her side. Sleep would come, but the problem remained.

Chapter Five

You must leave.

Annie sat up in bed, jarred awake by the words. Her bedroom was still dark but for the moonlight that cut a swath across the bed. Iris lay sleeping beside her, though she stirred at the alteration of the covers.

Annie took a fresh breath and blinked herself awake. Had she heard the words? They echoed in her mind as if they had been shouted.

You. Must. Leave.

Leave the Kidds?

Leave the Friesen household?

To go where?

Annie pressed a hand to her chest and made herself calm down. *God? Is this You talking? Am I really supposed to leave?*

Iris turned over and opened her eyes. "What are you doing awake?"

"I'm not sure."

"Then go back to sleep. It will be morning too soon."

She felt another prodding. "I can't sleep. And neither can you."

With a sigh Iris sat up. "What are you talking about?"

If only I knew for sure.

Needing to see if light dispelled the dream, the voice, the directive, or whatever it was, Annie lit the lamp then returned to the warmth of the covers.

"Your eyes are so bright, as if you've been lit from inside," Iris said.

"An idea has been lit. A big idea that includes you — and Danny."

Iris adjusted her pillow. "What is it?"

"It's hard to explain without sounding daft. But I was awakened by three words: *'You must leave.'*"

Iris glanced around the room. "In your dream or outside it?"

"I don't know. But they were clear enough for me to wake up."

" *'You must leave.'* Leave here?"

Annie's heart beat faster, and she said another quick prayer. *Yes, Lord?*

Receiving no nudge to tell Iris to go back to sleep, Annie continued, "Leave everything. Leave here, leave my job, leave the Kidds. Everything."

"And go where?"

"I have no idea."

"It would have been nice if the voice shared the details."

Agreed.

Now that Annie was fully awake the one idea expanded into many, like branches of a tree growing from its trunk. "The first day we met you told me you planned to leave, that you and Danny were saving up for it. You want to be a shopgirl."

"Someday."

"Then why not now? What's stopping you?"

Iris made a face, clearly thinking hard. Finally she said, "I know *here*. I don't know *there*. It's scary."

Annie felt the same fear but didn't tell Iris that. Instead she tossed the covers aside and faced her friend. "I'm going. That's why you and Danny should go, too. We'd be three instead of one. Being three would make us strong."

Iris's nod was weak.

"There's nothing for any of us here."

"What happened to becoming a lady's maid?"

Annie told her about the Misses taking credit for her work. And their derisive laughter when she confronted them. "I've been a fool, thinking I could rise up."

77

"So you think you could rise up out *there*?"

"Isn't America the land of opportunity?"

"To some, maybe. But for the three of us?"

Annie felt doubt threaten. She forced it away. "Why not us?"

Iris hugged her pillow. "What makes you think Mr. Brandon and Mrs. Grimble will let Danny and me go?"

"You're not going to ask."

"We're going to sneak away?"

"You can leave a note." Annie made a decision. "That's what I'm going to do."

"They'll never give us references if we leave like that."

"You want references so you can be a maid again?"

Iris bit the corner of the pillow.

"And remember Grasston. I doubt things will get better with him — for either of us."

Iris's shudder was the seal on it. They had to leave, or suffer under Grasston. Annie could probably handle him, but Iris . . .

"When do you want to go?" Iris said.

Annie let out the breath she'd been saving. "So you'll go with me?"

"If I don't go now I'll never go."

"What about Danny?"

"He'll be first out the door."

They laughed softly, knowing it was true.

Then they looked at each other and sighed at the same time, which elicited another laugh. "When do we leave?" Iris asked again.

Annie made a quick decision. "Tomorrow afternoon. My ladies have a function to go to, so the Misses will take their naps."

"Will you help me write a note?"

Annie glanced at the bureau. The Friesens provided their servants paper and pencil to write to their families. She gathered a piece of paper and the Bible to support it, and together they began their farewell notes.

With their departure day upon them, the notion of revenge grew. Each hour the details were refined, culminating in this moment when Annie stood in the hall of the servants' floor, looking at the door that divided the women's bedrooms from the men's.

"Boo!"

Her heart dropped to her toes as she turned to confront Danny. "Don't do that!"

"A bit jumpy, are ya? Just three more hours and we'll be free."

"I know. But first . . ." Maybe Danny could help. "I need you to do me a favor."

"Is it dangerous?"

"It could be. If you're caught."

He grinned. "What do you want me to

do?"

The Kidd and Friesen ladies left for the afternoon. On cue, Annie saw the Misses go off to take their naps. The coast was clear.

She slipped into Miss Henrietta's room and paused a moment to reread the note she was leaving:

Dear Miss Henrietta,
  Please share this with your mother.
  I am leaving your family's employ and am venturing out into New York City to find my new path. I am sorry to do this in such an abrupt fashion, but I have realized that as a housemaid there is no place to go, no ladder to climb. I have a stirring within me that forces me to take this drastic step. I know it is a risk, but it is a risk I must take.
  Please forgive the trouble this causes, and know that I truly appreciate your family's past kindness. Also know that I have greatly enjoyed serving you. Especially you. I wish you all the happiness in the world, Miss Henrietta, for you deserve it.

Sincerely,
Annie Wood

Annie had considered tattling on the Misses but hadn't wanted this final note to be tainted by a complaining tone. Besides, Miss Henrietta and her mother would find out soon enough that their lady's maids had no sewing talent. Being appreciative was the honorable way to leave.

She leaned the note against the dressing table mirror and closed the door behind her.

Annie was nearly through packing her few belongings when Iris came in their room, out of breath.

"Are you ready?" Iris asked.

Annie closed the clasp on the carpetbag. "I am now."

Annie helped Iris remove her uniform and put on her one shirtwaist, jacket, and a straw hat. Iris held up the apron. "I won't miss this. I vow to never wear an apron again."

Annie smiled but suffered a glimmer of dread. It might be a hard vow to keep.

"Do I leave my uniforms?" Iris asked.

"Did you pay for them?"

"No."

"Then you leave them. I had to provide mine, so I'm taking them with me. Perhaps I can alter them."

Iris carefully laid the clothes on the bed,

stroking a sleeve to make it lie flat. She retrieved her note for the butler and house-keeper and placed it on top.

"Well then," she said.

Their bags packed, they looked around the room they had shared. "Our last chance to change our minds," Annie said.

Iris let out a breath. "Onward. Quickly. Before I chicken out."

The plan was to meet Danny outside the kitchen door, behind the coal bin, hopefully out of sight.

Please don't let anyone see us. Please, God.

Iris and Annie waited in an alcove in the basement until the only noise came from the kitchen — which was unfortunately near the exit.

"I'll go first," Annie said. "Wait until I give you the signal."

Iris nodded, but her eyes were frantic with worry. Annie put a hand on her arm. "It will be all right."

Hopefully.

With one last look and listen, Annie walked quickly down the corridor. Cook was busy giving directions about how to slice carrots and had her back to the door-way. A kitchen maid looked up, but Annie didn't wait to be accosted.

At the door she motioned for Iris to follow. Iris ran on tiptoes, clutching her bag to her chest. Together they exited the home and ran behind the coal bin.

"You made it," Danny said.

"So far," Iris said. "Let's go before someone sees us. I feel like ants are crawling up my spine."

Annie led the way toward the street. She turned around and whispered, "Walk quickly. Don't run."

Somehow they managed to do so and turned left to walk away from the Friesens'. A delivery wagon passed them, and the driver gave them a second look.

As soon as they reached the end of the block Danny yelled, "Run!"

So run they did.

"Thanks for the ride, mister!" Danny said as the three young people hopped off the back of his wagon.

The man tipped his hat and went into a haberdashery to make his delivery.

They took a moment to look around the narrow, busy street, which even in the late afternoon was in shadow. "Where are we?" Iris asked.

"I don't care," Annie said, "as long as it's

away from *there.*"

"I'll tell you where we are," Danny said. "We're at the starting point of our adventure."

Iris tucked her hand around his arm, looking very vulnerable even if she was four years older than him. "There are so many people."

"Ah, don't be a baby. We've been to department stores before. We've been around loads of people."

"But we've never been around people when we don't have anywhere to go home to."

Annie had not expected to hear her doubt so soon. "Do you want to go back?"

"I just want to *be* somewhere, not here, out in the middle of nowhere alone, with all these strangers around."

What had the girl expected?

Danny patted her hand. "You have us, Iris. None of us are alone."

His strength fed Annie's.

"I'm hungry," Iris said.

"Never fear!" Danny said. He opened his satchel and took out a large roast beef sandwich and an orange.

"How did you manage this?" Annie asked.

"It pays to have friends in low places who appreciate that I'm a growing boy." He shrugged. "Cook likes me."

They sat on the stoop of a building full of apartment flats. Street vendors closed up their carts for the night. Annie heard a baby cry from inside the building and watched as a horse fouled the street. The city was shutting down.

Lovely.

Danny took out a pocketknife and divided the sandwich into thirds while Annie peeled the orange and did the same. There were ten sections, so she gave Iris the extra one.

"Our first meal on our own," Annie said, adjusting the bread around her meat. She shooed a stray dog away.

"But where will our next meal come from?" Iris asked.

"We all have a little money, yes?" Annie asked. "You said you've been saving for this."

"We have a little," Iris said. "Very little."

"We'll use our money to get a room for the night and tomorrow we'll find jobs."

"Where?" Iris asked.

Annie was weary of her helpless attitude. "You and I will get a job in a shop."

Danny took an enormous bite of his sandwich. "As for me? Give me a job and I can do it."

Annie appreciated his attitude. "I believe you."

Danny licked his fingers noisily. "Let's count how much money we have between us."

They each retrieved their coins, and Annie suddenly realized that she didn't have dollars and cents but pounds and pence. "What good will this do me?" she asked aloud.

"There's got to be a place to change it," Danny said. "Most everybody here came from somewhere else."

Another task for tomorrow. But for today . . . "Just counting yours we have $11.52."

"Is that enough for a room?" Iris asked.

"I don't know what boarding rooms cost."

"We probably shoulda checked into that," Iris said.

"Too late now, bug," Danny said. "We'll just have to —"

Suddenly a boy ran toward them and grabbed all the coins out of Annie's hands. "Hey!" she cried.

Danny ran after him as Iris picked up the few coins the boy had dropped. Annie rushed toward the people on the street. "Please! He stole our money!"

She received a few sympathetic looks from

passersby and scanned the street for a bobby.

No police anywhere. All she and Iris could do was look in the direction the boy and Danny had run and hope for the best.

A minute later, Iris said, "There's Danny!" She rushed to meet him. "Did you catch him? Did you get our money back?"

Danny opened his palm to reveal two coins. "He dropped these, but I couldn't catch him. It's gone. Our money is gone."

Iris began to cry, and Danny put his arm around her. "Don't cry, bug. We'll get jobs tomorrow and everything will be fine."

Annie knew he was overstating it but didn't want to make Iris more upset. Especially when evening was upon them. They had to find a place to sleep. Soon. They'd regroup in the morning.

She looked around for a church. It would be a safe place to stay.

But she couldn't spot a steeple in any direction. Shops and housing closed in around them, blocking out the last of the sun.

Men walked by and entered a pub with Beer on the signage. She didn't want to be anywhere nearby when they came out drunk.

"Let's find a quiet alley out of the way

where no one will bother us," she said.

They walked up and down the street, checking for a suitable choice, but many stunk from rubbish or rows of privies serving the flats. A woman heaved a bowl of table scraps out an upper window, and stray dogs rushed forward to clean the mess. Annie longed for the tidy streets of Summerfield village, where everyone knew everyone and lights illumined the cozy cottages as day moved into night.

"We should have stayed home," Iris said. "This is disgusting."

And though Annie agreed with her, she said, "Every day will get better. You'll see."

"How will it get better?" Iris asked.

"Because it can't get worse," Danny said with a laugh. He linked his arm through hers. "Did you really think our adventure would include soft beds and hot running water?"

"Yes."

He looked to Annie, apparently waiting for *her* to answer. "I didn't think about it much — at least not what would happen the first night or two."

"And we never could have predicted that our money would be stolen," Danny added.

"But it was. And so we'll make do. After we get jobs, everything will be fine."

Iris looked unconvinced. So be it. Annie had little patience for whiners.

"Come on, now," Danny said. "Let's keep looking for an alley. Maybe one paved with gold, eh?"

They finally found one that seemed the best of the worst. Danny rearranged some crates, moving them away from the brick wall, creating a hiding place for them to spend the night. They huddled together, Danny at the open end.

"Don't be afraid, girls," Danny said. "I hereby vow to protect you forever!"

Annie wasn't sure what a thirteen-year-old boy could do against the dangers of the world, but she appreciated his confidence.

She looked upward and saw the darkening sky between the four-story buildings on either side. Windows looked down on them. Laundry dried on clotheslines strung between the buildings, hanging limp and still in the autumn air. *At least it's not winter.*

Iris drew her knees to her chest, tucking her shoes under her skirt. She put her hands beneath her arms for warmth.

That gave Annie an idea. "I have a present for each of us." She dug into her carpetbag and retrieved three pairs of white gloves. "Here. At least our hands can be warm."

Iris turned a pair over in her hands. "These look like footman gloves."

"Because they are footman gloves. A particular footman's gloves." Annie smiled conspiratorially at Danny. "Danny did the deed."

"But it was Annie's brilliant idea."

Iris's eyes glowed with understanding. "These belong to Grasston?"

"Belonged," Danny said.

"He'll get in dire trouble with Mr. Brandon."

Annie nodded. "His trouble will be a small bit of justice against the trouble he caused us."

Iris put on the gloves — which were far too large. She spread her hands, grinning at the sight of them. "I'll take great pleasure imagining how it played out at dinner service — him with no gloves."

The pleasure was all Annie's.

CHAPTER SIX

Ooh, the cook made bread.

A groaning sound made Annie open her eyes. She wasn't at home at Crompton Hall. She was lying against a building, in an alley in New York City, with Iris's elbow in her stomach.

Danny lay on the outside of the three, the protector. He must have sensed her movement because he opened his eyes, blinked a few times, and then said, "I smell bread."

"Me, too," Annie whispered.

The two of them inched their way to sitting, causing Iris to lose her support. The girl opened her eyes. "It's morning? I smell bread."

Danny stood then helped the girls up. "We need to follow our noses and find the source."

"But we don't have money to buy any," Annie said, brushing off her jacket and skirt.

"Maybe the smell alone can ease the ache

91

in our stomachs," he said.

Iris stretched. "I want to eat it. Lots of it."

They gathered their things and left the alley in search of bread. All they had to do was follow the scent and the trail of people walking toward their morning sustenance.

The Tuttle Bakery was a block south, a narrow storefront with a window displaying rolls, biscuits, and bread. There was a line out the door. People with money.

The trio stood outside, gazing at the wares they couldn't buy.

Iris finally turned her back to the window, leaned against it, and pressed her hands against her stomach. "I'm starving!"

"You are not starving," Annie said, pulling her away from the bakery. She wanted to remind Iris that as a girl of seventeen she should act more mature than her younger brother, but Annie didn't think it would do any good. Maturity often had little to do with age.

The line lessened as people left the bakery with their goods and went on their way to work or home.

"I'm going in," Danny whispered.

"To do what?" Iris asked.

"To get us some breakfast."

The girls didn't have time to ask him more as he entered the bakery. They peeked through the window and saw him talking with a woman behind the counter, gesticulating with his arms, and finally pointing right at them.

The woman saw them, and Danny motioned them inside.

Annie and Iris went in, and Danny came to greet them. "This is my sister, Iris, and our friend Annie. Girls, this is Mrs. Tuttle."

That Danny had learned the name of the woman in such a short time was amazing. "Hello, Mrs. Tuttle," Annie said.

The woman wiped her pudgy hands on her flour-sprinkled apron and nodded at them. "Hello, girls. Danny says you've had your money stolen and are in need of some food to fill your stomachs."

Annie laughed. "It appears he's shared much in quick order." She wondered how much else he'd said. Surely he hadn't shared the full truth of where they came from.

Danny shrugged. "No need to dally around when we're hungry. Or starving." He gave Iris a pointed look.

"No need to be either when there's fresh bread. What will be your pleasure?"

She was giving them a choice?

"A bap would be wonderful," Annie said. "Thank you."

"I'd like the one there, with apricot jam," Iris said. When Annie nudged her she added, "Please. And thank you."

The woman handed over the rolls then looked at Danny. "And you, lad?"

"If you please, I think a loaf of bread would be wise. We could save part of it for lunch and dinner."

Mrs. Tuttle nodded and wrapped up a loaf, but her forehead was furrowed. "Where are you staying? I've not seen you in the neighborhood."

Annie tried to think of what to say, but Danny did the choosing for them. "We got laid off from our work — working for a family, we were. We slept in the alley last night."

Mrs. Tuttle blinked. "I don't like hearing that. Not at all. Where is your home?"

They glanced at each other, and this time Annie answered. "We are on our own, and our task today is to find jobs so we'll never have to ask for charity again."

"A work ethic, have you?" she asked.

"We *are* hard workers," Danny said. "All three of us."

There was a decided thump overhead then the sound of a scuffle and children crying. "My boisterous brood. They know better'n to misbehave during the morning rush." Then, with a blink, she looked at the girls.

"I could use some help with 'em."

"I love children," Iris said.

Annie was less enthused. "How many?"

"Seven."

"Seven?"

"The two oldest are my husband's children from his first wife before she passed. After he and I got hitched, we had five in quick succession. They're the ones who need tending. You interested?" She looked directly at Iris.

"How much does it pay?"

"Room and board. And maybe a little more if you handle it well."

Iris checked in with Danny, who nodded. "Yes. Please."

"Glad for the help," Mrs. Tuttle said. "Would you like to help around here, too?" The woman looked at Annie.

Although Annie had hoped for a job in a shop that sold clothing or hats, she certainly wasn't going to turn the offer down. "I would."

"Count me in," Danny said. He flexed a muscle. "I can do the heavy work."

Mrs. Tuttle laughed. But then Annie wondered if they'd asked for too much. "Are you sure you could use all three of us? We don't want to be a burden."

Mrs. Tuttle wiped some crumbs off the

counter onto her palm. "After child number three came along, I came to the conclusion that it wasn't that hard to add another one to the pile. Family is precious, and helping three young people in need is the Christian thing to do."

Annie had never met someone so generous. "We'll work hard. We'll not let you down."

"I know you won't." A customer came in the store. While he was looking at the baked goods, Mrs. Tuttle pointed toward the back. "There's a storeroom off the kitchen. See how you can arrange it for a space to sleep."

Danny led the way back through a kitchen where two men — one elderly and one less so — worked with a boy and girl aged about twenty and a little less. They looked up from their work, but briefly. Apparently three strangers walking through didn't faze them.

They spotted the storeroom. There were shelves of pans, bowls, and utensils. Sacks of flour and sugar were stacked on the floor. "There's not much space here at all," Iris said.

"We can sleep on the floor between the shelves," Danny said. "Maybe Mrs. Tuttle has a few extra blankets. We can use our carpetbags as our pillows."

He was being optimistic, yet Annie was

pleased to have a roof over their heads.

Mrs. Tuttle popped her head in. "It ain't much, but I'll get you some blankets and maybe you can arrange some of those pallets as beds."

"We appreciate it, Mrs. Tuttle," Annie said. "You're very kind."

"Don't thank me yet. Not until after you meet the hellions upstairs."

The five Tuttle children stopped jumping on the bed and throwing toy blocks at each other and eyed the three strangers warily.

Their mother stepped forward and removed a brush from a girl's hand — a brush that was en route to whack a sibling. "Children, I'd like you to meet three new friends who have come to help us. There's Danny and Annie who will help us in the shop, and Iris who will help take care of you."

Annie was relieved her name wasn't mentioned in the latter task.

The children were named and their ages given: Nelly, Nora, Nick, Newt, and Joe were aged eight, seven, six, five, and two.

Iris scooped Joe into her arms then sat on the floor near the largest pile of blocks. "Let's see how tall a tower we can build."

Shockingly, the children gathered round.

"Well then," Mrs. Tuttle said. "Would you

97

look at that." She put a finger to her lips and motioned Danny and Annie out of the flat and down the stairs to the store.

Once again the two young people looked up from their work, though there was one less, as the older man could be seen up front manning the counter. "Family, I'd like you to meet Danny and Annie who are going to be staying with us and helping in the store. Iris is upstairs saving the children from themselves." She nodded at the duo then at the man. "This is my husband, and the two others are our eldest."

Mr. Tuttle looked over his glasses. "They're staying in the storeroom?"

"I thought you could arrange some pallets for them. Maybe fill some old flour sacks with straw."

The expression on his face showed his exasperation at the arrangement and extra work but quickly changed to resignation. "Yes, m'love." To the guests he said, "Welcome."

The young man stepped away from his kneading, his eyes locked on Annie in a way she'd seen before. "Hello. I'm Thomas."

She gave him a nod, felt herself blush, and then looked past him and said to the girl, "And what's your name?"

The girl seemed to prefer the view of the

floor over making eye contact. She let her floured hands fall upon her apron and mumbled something.

"That's Jane," Mrs. Tuttle said. And to the girl she said, "I've repeatedly told you to speak up."

"Yes'm," she said softly.

Annie felt sorry for her. In a family of seven children, the quiet ones would have a harder time of it. Annie gave her a smile — which was returned.

"Gramps works with us, too," Mrs. Tuttle said, nodding toward the front. "But his knees get to hurting something awful so he needs to be spelled more often than most."

"I can do that," Danny said.

Mrs. Tuttle laughed. "I'm sure you can, but I think the best use of your young muscles is delivering."

"In a wagon?" Danny asked, his eyes wide.

Mr. Tuttle answered, "Unless ye want to haul the fifty-pound bags of flour and sugar on yer shoulders."

"I get to be out of doors?"

"In good weather and bad."

Danny looked as though he was about to burst. "When can I start?"

He earned their laughter, and even Jane smiled.

"Ye know how to tether a horse and drive

a wagon?" Mr. Tuttle asked.

"No, but you'll teach me, yes?"

Mr. Tuttle offered him a wink. "I'll teach ye, yes."

Thomas nodded toward Annie but looked to his stepmother. "What's Annie going to do?"

Mrs. Tuttle put a finger to her chin. "I'm not sure yet, but we have plenty of work to be done, that's for certain."

Annie was a bit disappointed that the other two had been specifically chosen for a task, but she used it as an opportunity to interject, "I was thinking of working in a store that sells dresses or shoes or hats."

Mrs. Tuttle gave Annie's outfit a once-over, clearly judging it for its lack of fashion. "More power to ya. But until then, how about cleaning that stack of pots and pans over there?"

Over there was a sink with a hand pump and an enormous stack of dirty kitchen utensils.

The bell on the front door dinged twice in quick succession, causing Mrs. Tuttle to say, "I needs to get up front and help Gramps. Back to work, everyone."

Mrs. Tuttle left them, and the other three went back to their baking.

Leaving Annie to tackle the pots.

Joy.

Dinner was served in the kitchen of the bakery, on the table where the bread was made.

Before the meal, Annie hadn't noticed the two benches pushed under the worktable, but as the bakery closed up shop and Mrs. Tuttle put on a huge pot of stew, the benches were pulled out and the table set.

The children descended from upstairs like a herd of cows coming in from a pasture. They were accompanied by Iris, and with little to-do everyone took a place. Mr. Tuttle sat at the head using an upturned crate as his throne.

"Grace," he said. That one word caused all talking to stop and all heads to bow. In unison the family prayed, "We thank the Lord for happy hearts, for rain and sunny weather. We thank the Lord for this our food and that we are together. Amen."

Annie was moved by the simple table grace. It seemed to suit the Tuttles. She imagined their lives to be more full of sunny weather than not and felt an aura of gratitude even amid their hard work. Annie was thankful for the chance to work at all, and mostly that they were all together. She much preferred this prayer over the longish ones the butler at the Hall used to say, the prayers that offered gratitude as a duty rather than a joy.

Mrs. Tuttle served up bowls of stew, and bread was passed. Annie was ravenous.

"Did ye work up an appetite?" Mr. Tuttle asked.

She forced herself to slow down. "I did."

"Nothing wrong with that." Thomas gave her a sympathetic smile. "We worked you hard today."

Annie rubbed her red and chapped hands. "At least it's done."

"Until tomorrow," Jane said softly.

"Aye," said her mother. "Unfortunately, that's the way of it. Every day it starts over again." She pointed to Annie's hands. "I have some salve. Jane can attest to its value on chapped skin."

So Jane's task had been the washing? Somehow knowing she was easing the girl's load made the work a little easier to endure.

"I worked hard, too," Iris said, with a look to Thomas.

He glanced at her and nodded. "Didn't say you didn't."

Iris's brow dipped.

"I'm going to drive the wagon tomorrow," Danny said.

"With my help," Gramps said. "Though

ye do seem a natural at it. The horses liked ye well enough this afternoon and that's important."

"Everyone likes me well enough," Danny said.

"That's because you're so humble," Annie said, taking a bite of bread.

Thomas passed the jam across the table. "Try this apple butter. It's as sweet as you."

Annie felt her face grow hot and looked around the table. The flattery had been noted by all the adults.

Everyone but Iris was smiling.

From beading gowns to stitching straw mattresses.

Annie tied off the thread, finishing the last of the six fifty-pound flour sacks they'd filled with straw, and took it into the storage room.

Danny and Thomas set empty pallets on two sides of the room, while Iris placed the makeshift mattresses on the pallets, two to each.

Jane arrived from upstairs with three quilts and one pillow. "Sorry there's only the one."

Thomas took it from his sister and handed it to Annie. "You can have it. I want you to be comfortable."

Iris put her hands on her hips. "And what

about me?"

Danny lightened the moment by mimicking her. "And what about me?"

Annie didn't appreciate Thomas's obvious favoritism — though she did like having the use of the pillow. "We'll take turns." She put the pillow on one of the beds. "Actually I'm so tired I think I could sleep directly on the floor."

"Sorry the work was so hard," Thomas said.

Although she'd enjoyed his extra attention, it began to grate. "I'll be well enough."

"Me, too," Iris said.

"Me three," Danny added, unlacing his shoes.

The oldest of the younger children appeared in the doorway. "Iris, Mama wants help getting Joe to bed. She says he's taken a liking to you and he never goes quietly for her."

Iris sighed dramatically. " 'Man may work from sun to sun, but woman's work is never done.' " She brushed her shoulder against that of Thomas when she left the room.

"My, my, that girl has a chip on her shoulder," Thomas said.

Danny was already stretched out on his mattress, punching and pushing the straw to find some comfort. "Chip or not, she's working as hard as any of us."

Thomas looked as though he wanted to say more but, with a nod to Annie, left them.

Annie released a breath she'd unwittingly saved.

"He's sweet on you," Danny said.

She sat on her mattress and removed her shoes. "You saw it, too?"

"Everyone saw it." He turned on his side to face her. "Trouble is, Iris likes him."

"She can have him."

"You're not interested?"

"Face the wall so I can get undressed."

Danny did as he was told. "You didn't answer me."

Annie unbuttoned her blouse. "I could be interested. He's a nice enough boy, and maybe a few days ago I would have been. But now I'm just not."

"He's not good enough for you?"

She stepped out of her skirt and hung it from a nail. "It's not that." She unhooked her corset, relished the freedom of full movement, and put it out of sight in her bag. She put her nightgown over her head. Then she lay down and arranged the blanket to cover herself. "You can turn around now."

Danny faced her. "Finish what you were saying about Thomas."

Putting it into words was like trying to

catch the mist. "I have a feeling there's something out there for me to do, to be. Something that's beyond anything I can imagine."

"I believe it. You certainly have a fire in your belly that goes beyond washing pots and pans."

His belief in her gave her courage. "I have no idea what *it* is."

"Maybe you don't need to. Maybe it will find you instead of you finding it."

She lay on her back and noticed water stains on the ceiling. "I do like the sound of that. It takes the pressure away, as if it's fate, not just folly." She looked at Danny. "Tomorrow I'll do my work here, but I'm also going to find a job in a store."

"Macy's?"

She hadn't thought of it, but yes, why not Macy's?

CHAPTER SEVEN

There was a detail Annie hadn't thought about before going to sleep in the storeroom the night before: bakers have to get up early to make their breads. To make their breads, they need supplies in the storeroom.

The door swung open, flooding the room with lamplight.

Thomas did the honors. "Sorry to wake you, but we need flour."

"No sorry to it," Mr. Tuttle said from behind his son. "People won't wait for their bread. We could use yer help."

Iris squinted at them. "What time is it?"

"Half past four." Thomas set the lamp on a shelf.

"That's earlier than we got up at the Friesens'."

Thomas looked at his father. "The Friesens? The banking Friesens?"

"I sees their name in the paper off and on," Mr. Tuttle said. "Surely ye didn't leave a position in a family as wealthy as them."

They couldn't renege on the name, so Annie went back to their original lie. "They didn't need us anymore, so they let us go."

"That's not very kind of them," Jane said from the kitchen. "Times are hard. What with all their money you'd think they could keep you on."

Annie wished they would leave so she could dress. They were having this discussion while she and Iris had their blankets pulled up to their chins. "Come in and get what you need and then we'll dress and get to work."

Sacks of flour, sugar, and dried milk were obtained, and the door was closed. "You get up first, Danny," Iris said.

Iris and Annie averted their eyes, and Danny dressed and was gone. The girls dressed and went outside to the communal privy in the dark alley. The stench was horrific, and Annie longed for a flush toilet, a bath, and warm water.

On their way back inside, she asked, "When you were upstairs with the children, did you see a bath or running water?"

"Only water is downstairs in the kitchen. Mrs. Tuttle said Saturdays are bath day."

Annie hated to ask. "Where is this done?"

"In the kitchen. A tub's brought in. Water

is heated."

The thought of it harkened back to her childhood, when her family shared a weekly tub at the fireside in the kitchen. Once she started work at the Kidds', she was happy to find they'd had indoor plumbing added to the centuries-old mansion, which included designated bathrooms for both family and servants. The Friesen household in New York was even more modern with tile walls instead of wallpaper, fancy painted water closets, and sinks with brass faucets. To go from those comforts to the primitive facilities at the Tuttles' was definitely a step back.

Wait until you get a job. Then you can let a proper room, with a proper bath.

The thought made her remember that today she needed to find another job. She'd work extra hard this morning to earn the chance to leave this afternoon. Surely they wouldn't object.

Upon reentering the bakery, Iris went upstairs to help with the children, and Danny left to see to the horses.

Annie approached Mr. Tuttle, who was measuring ingredients into an enormous crockery bowl. "Sir? Mr. Tuttle?"

He gave her a glance. "We'll have dishes to wash soon enough."

"It's not that, I —"

"Ye want breakfast ye'll have to wait till the bread's done. Unless ye want some day-old in the cupboard."

"I can wait." He was making this difficult.

Finally he stopped his work. "What is it then, girl?"

"I need to be gone this afternoon to apply for a job in a shop."

His eyebrows rose. "This shop ain't good enough for ye?"

"I'm not implying that. But since my talents lie in sewing and fashion, I thought it would behoove me to get a job more suited to my abilities."

"Well now. Aren't ye the fancy one?"

"Fashion?" Jane asked. "You know about fashion?"

Her father pointed a finger at her. "None of that wasted dreaming of fancy dresses, lass. Ye have no need for fashion other than some simple clothes on yer back."

Jane nodded once and slunk away. Annie wanted to defend Jane's natural female desire for pretty things but knew now was not the time. Her new job had to come first or there'd be no fashion for anyone.

"Where are you going to apply?" Thomas asked.

"Macy's."

"That's a grand store."

"Yes, it is. A grand store that has many employees. I hope they have an opening."

"If they don't you'll still work for us, won't you?" he asked.

The need to get another job increased. "I'm not one to give up easily," she said.

"Neither am I."

Oh dear.

With her chores at the Tuttles' accomplished, Annie walked to Macy's on Thirty-Fourth and Broadway. It was hard to believe that she and her friends had been in this very store a few days earlier. They'd been three servants out on a lark, seeing how the other half lived.

She wasn't a servant any longer.

She was a scullery maid.

She *had* to get a job here.

Annie entered the store at one of the three entrances on Sixth Avenue and saw it with new eyes. It wasn't just a palace of products she couldn't afford, it was a place where she could prosper as a person. She was guessing a clerk didn't make a lot of money, but the money was secondary. The goal she was pursuing had a larger name: purpose. The pit of her belly stirred, begging to discover what she'd truly been born to do. To be.

Annie considered seeking out Mrs. Holmquist in the sewing machine department but balked because she knew nothing about the product. Yet there were other products she *could* sell. . . .

She walked among aisles of merchandise that screamed, "Buy me!" There was the untrimmed hat department, which led to the vast display of flowers and ribbons to adorn them. Hosiery, jewelry, lace and embroideries, handkerchiefs, ladies' collars and cuffs — with similar products in a men's section seen across the store. Gloves, linens, curtains, and a vast shoe department that could have easily — and stylishly — shod the entire village back home.

Annie passed a display case of buttons and dress trimmings. *I can sell these.* She was drawn to the dress goods in every color and quality from silks, satins, and velvets, to cottons and worsteds. Signs announced the prices and the special sales: NOVELTY DRESS SILKS! 49 CENTS A YARD/VALUE $1.00 A YARD. Even she was drawn to the bargain though she had absolutely no use for silk — and no money to buy it.

And then she saw it. A sign on a counter: SALES HELP WANTED.

Her stomach pulled, then danced, causing her heart to pound. This was it. This was her opportunity. Her destiny.

She stepped toward the counter and waited for a clerk to notice her.

A middle-aged woman approached. "May I help you, miss?"

Annie nodded toward the sign. "I would like to apply for a position. The sales position."

The woman's gaze fell upon Annie's clothes then met her eyes. "It's a position that requires a knowledge of sewing, dressmaking, and . . . fashion."

The last word was said with a hint of disdain.

Annie stood taller. "I have extensive experience with alterations of fine gowns and the use of proper accessories."

"Where did you gain this experience?"

It was a challenge more than a question. "I worked for a viscountess and her daughter." *As a maid.*

The woman eyed her warily, and Annie could tell she took her words as a lie. "If you held such a position why would you leave it?"

Please give me the words. With her next breath she was fueled by a sudden surge of confidence. "I left England and came to America to follow a dream."

"And that dream is . . . ?"

113

"I want to become all I can be. I have a talent for sewing and designing and altering fashion to make it suit its wearer." She spread her hands and took a step back to showcase her own meager ensemble. "As a working girl I have no funds to apply what I know to my own clothing, but that will change once I find a job. I want to help women dress in ways that will make them feel on top of the world." She stepped closer, lowering her voice. "Please give me a chance. I shan't let you down."

The woman glanced at Annie's hands, which were clasped against her breast. "You don't have the hands of a seamstress."

Annie looked at her hands — which were chapped and red. She put them at her sides, out of sight. "I've been helping a neighbor with some cleaning."

A customer approached, and the clerk gave Annie one last look. "You need to speak to Mr. Jones, the superintendent. He'll get you set up."

"So I have the job?"

"It's not for me to say." She suddenly craned her head then said, "He's over there. By the thread."

Annie saw an older gentleman with a large gray mustache. Annie looked to the woman, who nodded.

"Good luck," the woman said with a smile. "And tell him that Mrs. MacDonald approves."

Annie bounced twice on her toes. "Thank you so much, Mrs. MacDonald." But as Annie approached the man, she found herself focusing on something other than the need for good luck. *God? Please help me get this job. Please open this door for me.*

Mr. Jones was jotting something in a small notebook. Annie stood nearby and waited until he was finished and looked up. "May I help you find something, miss?"

"No. I mean . . ." A fresh breath brought courage. "My name is Annie Wood, and Mrs. MacDonald over there . . ." She paused to nod toward the notions counter, where Mrs. MacDonald offered a discreet wave. Annie turned her attention back to Mr. Jones. "I spoke with Mrs. MacDonald about the clerk position. I gave her my qualifications, and she said I need to finalize my employment with you."

That wasn't exactly what was said, but Annie hoped the implied confidence would work to her favor.

Mr. Jones eyed her clothes a bit more discreetly than had Mrs. MacDonald. "There is a certain standard required of a Macy's clerk. A certain code of dress."

"I realize that, Mr. Jones. And if I could be advanced a small sum, I would be happy to buy an appropriate ensemble."

When he smiled his mouth disappeared beneath the swag of his mustache. "You're already spending your wages?"

"For the benefit of the position, sir."

His left eyebrow rose. "I admire your spunk, Miss Wood."

"Does that mean I have the job?"

"As I am busy today, and the need is great . . . it does. Follow me to my office and I will take down your information. Then report to the floorwalker, Mrs. Gold, and she will explain how things work."

Annie nearly curtsied but remembered she was in America. Instead she held out her hand and Mr. Jones shook it firmly. "Work hard, Miss Wood. That is all we ask." With a sweep of his arm he led them to the elevator and to his office.

She was officially a shopgirl!

Mrs. Gold read the note from Mr. Jones and then wadded it up in her palm. "Well then. I will have to assume you have been thoroughly vetted, but honestly, I have my doubts."

"I assure you, Mrs. Gold, I will not be a disappointment."

"Hmm." She strode toward the women's wear section and waved toward some black shirtwaists and skirts. "Choose two of each. And two white lace collars from that department."

"That is generous."

"It is not generous. A bit will come out of your wages until it is paid off. But take note that the proper costume is imperative. As a sales clerk you are the primary point of contact between the store and the public. Macy's reputation depends upon the manner and method in which you perform your work."

Mr. Jones had repeated the same lines — almost word for word. "I understand."

"Did Mr. Jones explain to you about wages?"

"Six dollars a week to start, with the chance of bonuses if I sell my quota."

"Which is two hundred dollars a week. Sell above that and you will get an additional one percent."

"I will achieve that quota — and then some."

Mrs. Gold shook her head. "Don't get cocky on me, girl. Collect your uniform then report to Mrs. MacDonald tomorrow by —"

"Twenty past eight."

"By eight o'clock since it's your first day."

"Yes, ma'am."

Mrs. Gold peered downward. "Let me see your shoes."

Annie lifted her skirt enough to reveal her well-worn but still functional boots.

"They will do. Go on, then. Gather the essentials and get a good night's rest. You will need it."

Annie was bursting with joy and longed to let out a whoop of rejoicing. Instead, she turned her gratitude inward. *Thank You, God! I shan't let You down!*

She hurried to the women's department to shop for ready-made clothes. It was a first. Her maid uniforms at the Kidds' were stitched on-site, though the shoes and undergarments were ordered from London. Annie had never shopped for herself other than to spend a few pennies on a stick of candy or a handkerchief at the Summerfield mercantile.

"May I help you, miss?" a clerk asked.

With full pride Annie was able to say, "I have just been hired as a clerk in the sewing department and I need to dress the part."

"And who is going to wash the pots and pans now?" Mr. Tuttle asked.

Annie set the parcel containing her clerk

uniforms aside and glanced at Jane. Jane's hands were covered with flour, but the task of washing would once again fall on her.

She looked at Thomas to see his reaction, but he was focused on forming the dough into rolls.

"I'm sorry for the inconvenience, Mr. Tuttle, but aren't you happy for me? I'm proud to work at such a prestigious store as Macy's."

"So we ain't good enough for ye?"

"You know that's not true. I appreciate you taking us in like you did, but I made it clear I was seeking another job." She noticed the sink overflowing with pots and pans. "I'll still do the washing today."

"We wouldn't want to put ye out." His voice dripped with sarcasm.

She ignored his tone, tied on an apron, and set to work. If she clanged and clattered a bit more than necessary, let them complain.

Jane came up behind her and whispered, "I'm happy for you."

"I'm sorry about the dish washing."

Jane shook her head vehemently. "Don't be. You getting a job at Macy's is ever so exciting."

"Girls?" Mr. Tuttle barked. "Work."

Jane had one last thing to say. "Be a grand

success, Annie. For both of us."

The awkwardness continued when the rest of the Tuttles came to the kitchen for dinner. Mrs. Tuttle was at the stove, and Iris was busy getting the children set at the table. Annie wanted to tell Iris when they were alone, but with the Tuttle clan teeming around them, it wasn't possible.

Just as the adults were sitting down, Danny and Gramps returned from deliveries.

"Smells great, Mrs. Tuttle. I'm starved to near wasted away."

"You are always starved, boy. Eating us out of house and home, you are."

He gave her a peck on the cheek before washing his hands at the sink.

Gramps sat at his place with a noisy *oomph*. "Don't get af'er the boy. He earns his keep."

Mr. Tuttle glared at Annie — implying she was *not* earning her keep. She might as well share her news now rather than later. "I was hired at Macy's. I start tomorrow."

Her news was received in silence. Danny was the first to respond. "Congratulations, Annie. It happened just like you hoped it would."

She looked at Iris, who was just sitting

down with the baby on her lap. "Are you happy for me?"

"Of course. Good for you."

That was all?

Mrs. Tuttle finished spooning out the soup. Only then did she look at Annie. "You're putting us in a bind."

How? Until two days ago Jane washed the pots.

"We let you have a room here if you worked for us, but now . . ."

"Once I get a paycheck, I will pay you rent."

Mrs. Tuttle exchanged a look with her husband. He was the one to answer. "One dollar a week for the room, and one dollar for the meals."

That would be a third of her paycheck. "I'll be eating the noon meal at Macy's," she said. "Apparently, they have an employees' cafeteria with reasonable prices."

"Seventy-five cents, then," he said.

How could she haggle? "Consider it done."

Done for now. One day she'd have a proper working-girl flat.

Annie draped her new uniforms over some bags of sugar in the storeroom. She carefully set her lace collars on top — one white

121

and one ecru.

Iris came in. "Fancy shopgirl clothes."

"They're not fancy," Annie said. "But they are the uniforms worn by all the girls. I bought two skirts, two blouses, and two collars."

Iris ran her fingers along the batiste fabric as if it were the finest silk. "You got the job I always dreamed of."

Annie hadn't thought of that. "You can get a job there, too. Mr. Jones says they have over five thousand people on staff."

Iris pulled her hand away from the temptation of the outfits. "I haven't seen five thousand people in my life."

"You know what a big store it is. Eight floors of pretty things to buy."

"Things you can't buy if you don't have any money."

Annie didn't want her to be miffed. Or discouraged. "The Tuttles said they would pay you something in addition to the room and board."

Iris shrugged. "Actually, *I* wanted to work in a small sort of shop with just a few clerks."

Her stipulation removed some of Annie's guilt. "Then Macy's isn't your cup of tea."

Their conversation was interrupted by two distinct pounds coming from the floor above. "Mrs. Tuttle needs me."

"That's how she calls you? She stomps on the floor?"

"I have to go."

As she left the room, Danny came in. "Well I'll be. Look at your fine duds."

"It's a uniform. All the clerks wear black with a collar."

"Fancy." He slumped onto his blanket. "I am happy for you, Annie."

"I am happy for me, too. But I don't want Iris to be green about it."

"Ah, don't mind bug. Though she won't admit it, I think she likes taking care of the children."

Annie sat on the straw bags that were her bed. "I couldn't do what she does. There are so many of them."

"Don't you want to be a mother some-day?"

The dreams of her future had never strayed in that direction. "I know I *should* want that."

"No *should* about it. And you don't have to decide now. What are you? Eighteen?"

"Nineteen, and no, I don't have to decide that yet. Besides, a husband needs to come first."

He grinned. "I know someone who's interested."

"I am *not* interested in Thomas."

He lay on his back, linking his hands behind his head. "New York is enormous. I didn't know how big it was till I got the chance to drive the streets."

"Do you like your work?"

"I do. I like being outside and driving the wagon. I like Gramps, too. He reminds me of my own granddad: feisty and full of good stories."

"Do you see him? See your own granddad?"

"Nah. He died. Grandma and our parents, too."

Annie felt a wave of compassion. "I'm so sorry."

"It happens."

"But all of them? What did they die of?"

"Some fever. Iris and me were spared because we were working at the Friesens'."

The implication was sobering. "Those jobs saved you."

He shrugged. "Those jobs, and now the jobs we have here."

"And at Macy's."

"It seems the lot of us are right where we ought to be."

"So it appears."

"God did a pretty good job arranging it,

didn't He?"

Annie had no complaints.

CHAPTER EIGHT

Annie tried the entrance door at Macy's, but it was locked. She moved to another one and found it, too, was locked. She felt panic rise within her. How could she be on time if she couldn't even get in?

But then a man inside noticed her, came to the door, and talked through the glass. "Store opens at eight thirty, miss."

"I'm a new clerk. Today is my first day."

The bald and bearded man studied her a moment then unlocked the door, letting her in.

"A little eager, are we?" He pulled a pocket watch from his vest. "It's only quarter of eight."

"A little eager, yes. And nervous."

"No need to be. Macy's wants you to succeed."

She liked the sound of that. "I never thought of it that way."

He leaned close, as if sharing a confidence.

"If you succeed, Macy's succeeds."

She laughed. "I will do my very best."

"Which department?"

"Dress goods and sewing supplies."

"Are you a talented seamstress?"

She considered this a moment. "I am a seamstress with aspirations of talent."

"Work hard and you will attain your aspirations."

For the first time Annie noticed that not all the lights were on. Was it this man's job to light the store? "I'm sorry," she said. "Did I take you away from your work?"

"Nothing takes me away from my work."

The door opened behind them, and Mrs. MacDonald entered. "Mr. Straus. Miss Wood."

"Good morning, Mrs. MacDonald. It appears you have an eager new clerk."

"I do, sir."

"Carry on, then. Good day, ladies." He left them.

"You are one lucky girl," Mrs. McDonald said.

"Lucky?" Annie asked.

"To meet Mr. Straus on your first day."

"Who is Mr. Straus?"

Mrs. MacDonald gawked. "You're joshing."

"I'm not. I don't know who he is."

"He's our boss. He's the owner of Macy's."

Annie looked back. "But he was so nice."

Mrs. MacDonald took her arm and got them walking. "He is nice. And he cares about his employees and their families. Among other things, he's the one who stopped the practice of keeping the store open until ten or eleven o'clock on the ten evenings before Christmas so we could spend more time with our families and stay in better health. Before then, I remember not getting home until midnight and then having to be back to work at eight. The new policy is much better for everyone."

"That was nice of him."

Mrs. MacDonald stepped onto some moving steps leading upward. Annie balked.

"Haven't you ever seen an escalator before?"

"I hadn't been in an elevator until yesterday."

Mrs. MacDonald was halfway to the next floor. "Come on. Don't be scared. Take the handhold and step on."

Annie watched the steps ever moving from flat to full. If she timed it just right . . .

She stepped on and grabbed the hold, only bobbling a little. Mrs. MacDonald stood at the top, laughing. "My, my, you have been in the sticks."

Annie wasn't sure what she meant by the comment but ignored her ribbing, as the stair was ending and she had to concentrate on stepping off without incident. As she did so, Mrs. MacDonald applauded. Annie responded with a bow. And a sigh of relief.

"By the time we get to the floor that houses the employee lockers, you'll be an expert."

They finally reached the area where they put their hats and jackets in lockers. Mrs. MacDonald nodded toward some other rooms. "Employee restrooms are in there. The public ladies' is on the second floor, right next to the boys' clothing department. But we are to use these facilities and leave the other to the customers."

"Understood." *Anything is better than the privies at the Tuttles'.*

Mrs. MacDonald checked her hair in a mirror. "There are also shower facilities for employees."

"Really?" Annie had never had a shower, and the last bath she'd had was at the Friesens'. "Have you used them?"

"I prefer baths. But it's there for you to use. Men's and women's, of course."

"Of course." Annie tucked a few stray hairs behind her ears. "It seems Mr. Straus has thought of everything."

"Most everything. I'll tell you more as we go along. Come, now. Let's get to work."

"Miss Wood, I would like you to meet Miss Krieger, the other clerk in our department. Mildred, meet Annie."

Annie extended her hand to a petite girl in her early twenties, whose sharp and pinched facial features made her look cross. Surely when she smiled, the look would fade.

Unfortunately, the smile did nothing to soften her expression. On the contrary, the smile seemed false, as though it was only for show and there was malice behind it.

Mildred ignored Annie's hand. "We don't need another clerk."

Mrs. MacDonald's eyebrows rose. "That's not for you to say."

"She'll just make it harder to sell over our quota, taking away any chance of a bonus."

With such a tetchy attitude, Annie wondered why any customer would buy from Mildred.

Mrs. MacDonald moved on. "Please watch the counter as I teach Annie the sales procedure."

Mildred had the audacity to shrug. How did she ever get hired with such an attitude?

Mrs. MacDonald brought out two sales books. "This one is for Monday, Wednesday, and Friday, and this one is for Tuesday, Thursday, and Saturday. When you have a sale, you list the items and their cost and then collect the payment and put it, along with your sales slip, in one of the pneumatic tubes over there." She pointed to a creeper vine of brass tubing on the wall. "It is sent to cashiers in the tube room, who send back change and your sales slip, stamped to show that payment was made. You call a parcel boy to wrap the package for the customer."

"What do I do with the paid sales slip?"

"You put it in your book for the proper day and turn them in at night to be checked against the money received. That's why you need a different book for alternate days."

It was all very logical. "It gives them time to do the checking and get the book back to us."

"Exactly. Well understood. Follow the rules and make shopping a pleasant experience for the customer and —"

"And a profitable experience for Macy's."

Mrs. MacDonald beamed. "I'm glad you were hired, Miss Wood."

Annie ran her hand along a bolt of gold shantung. The weave of the silk caught the light, making the cloth sumptuous.

A customer — her very first customer — strolled by, eying the bolts. "May I help you with your choice today, my . . . madam?" She'd caught herself before saying the familiar "my lady."

"I'm looking for cloth suitable for a walking suit. Something for autumn."

Annie chose the gold bolt and unrolled a yard or two of the fabric to best showcase its depth and texture. "This color mimics the rich hues of the season." She noted the woman's auburn hair. "It would also complement your coloring beautifully."

The woman blushed and put a hand to her cheek. "Do you think so?"

"I do, Mrs. . . . ?"

"Reinhold."

"Would you like to look at suit patterns and find a style that pleases you, Mrs. Reinhold?"

The woman ran a hand over the fabric as if they were getting to know each other. With a final pat she claimed it as her own. "I would. Thank you."

Annie led Mrs. Reinhold to the Butterick pattern catalogs and turned to the suit and coat section. Mrs. MacDonald was watching and gave her a nod of encouragement.

"Are you making this yourself or having it

made?" Annie asked.

"Myself," Mrs. Reinhold said. "I haven't sewn my own clothes much, but in the past year we've had a few setbacks and my husband wants to cut . . . wants me to be thrifty and wise."

"That is always a worthwhile goal." Annie sensed that a simpler pattern would be the best choice. "What about this one?" she said, pointing to a drawing of a streamlined three-quarter-length coat. "You could use a gold velvet for the stand-up collar and cuffs, and perhaps some wash braid sewn into a curved design down the front and along the bottom. See how clean the back silhouette is?" *Clean, meaning simple to sew.*

"I do see," the woman said, leaning close to the page to see it better. Annie hoped she had spectacles at home, or sewing anything would be difficult.

The woman stood upright and finalized the decision with a nod. "This one," she said. "I think I can conquer this one."

Annie smiled at her terminology. "I'm sure you can. Would you like a skirt to go with it? Let me show you another pattern that would complement the coat."

They quickly found a pattern for a simple A-line skirt to be sewn in brown lightweight wool, and the customer approved of Annie's

133

choice of a chocolate-brown soutache braid as an accent to be applied in a loop design.

While Annie measured and cut the fabric, Mrs. Reinhold studied the illustration on the pattern envelope. "I do like her hat. And with brown gloves . . ."

"I would be happy to accompany you to the hat department and see if they have anything to your liking. If not, Macy's has an extensive trim, ribbon, and silk flower department so you can make your own hat that will be every bit as grand as the one in the picture."

"Ooh. I'd like that."

It took an hour to complete Mrs. Reinhold's transaction. With the fabric, trim, pattern, thread, basic hat — and the silk flowers and ribbon bought to recreate the one in the picture, Mrs. Reinhold's total was $9.45. Plus fifty cents for brown gloves — $9.95.

Annie sent the receipt and the money up to the tube room where change would be made. A boy collected the goods to wrap as Annie and Mrs. Reinhold chatted.

"If you have any questions about the construction, come back and ask."

Mrs. MacDonald joined them. "I couldn't help but see the lovely ensemble you're going to make. The color is very becoming."

"Thank you," Mrs. Reinhold said. "I couldn't have done it without Miss Wood's help."

Mrs. MacDonald put a hand on Annie's shoulder. "She is a prize."

The change was made, the hat and its trims were safely in a hatbox, with the fabric wrapped in brown paper, tied on top to form a handle. "I think I'm ready," Mrs. Reinhold said. "I can hardly wait to get home and get started. Thank you, Miss Wood."

"You are utterly welcome."

As the customer walked through the store toward the exit, Annie felt as if she would burst with pride. "I did it. I knew I could do it, but I actually did it."

"That you did," said Mrs. MacDonald. "You seem to have an eye for fashion and design. And because of your suggestions, she also purchased hat supplies and a pair of gloves. Well done."

"Thank you."

The floorwalker, Mrs. Gold, walked toward them. "Things going well, Mrs. Mac-Donald?"

"Very well, thanks to Miss Wood." She gave Mrs. Gold the details.

"A notable first transaction, Miss Wood," the older woman said. They all spotted a woman approaching the display of batiste blouse fabric. "Don't stop now," she said to Annie.

"I wouldn't think of it."

Annie pinned on her hat and gathered her jacket and purse to leave. Her first day was finally finished. As was she. It would take the rest of her stamina to get home.

Just as she left the locker room, Mildred stepped in her path. Although they'd been introduced, Annie had been so busy throughout the day that they'd never had a chance to get to know each other.

"Hello, Mildred. Are you as knackered as I am, because —"

"Because you hogged all the customers?"

"I did no such thing." Annie had second thoughts, trying to remember if she'd stepped up when she should have let Mildred handle a sale. "Or if I did, I apologize. It being my first day I was probably overly zealous."

"You ruined everything." Mildred took a step closer, making Annie want to step back. But something about the girl's stance and the way she scowled made Annie understand that it was important to stand her ground. She'd dealt with bullies before and knew strength was the best deterrent.

Besides, Mildred was six inches shorter than Annie.

"I don't recall ruining anything," Annie said. "In fact, Mrs. MacDonald and Mrs. Gold commended my work."

"Bootlicker."

"Excuse me?"

"Don't think you can come into my department and take over, acting like a know-it-all."

Annie took a step back and then another, turning toward the mirror to adjust her hat. "I don't believe it is anyone's department — unless you are Mr. Straus." The hat properly adjusted, she faced Mildred. "When I saw him this morning he said if I worked hard I would attain all my aspirations. He's such a nice man."

Mildred's expressions revealed her battle between anger, frustration, and a tinge of envy and fear. "I've met him, too, you know."

"Jolly for you."

Mildred moved close and held a finger in Annie's face. "Watch it, Annie Wood. You don't want to cross me."

No, she didn't. With difficulty Annie masked her nerves with a smile and turned on her heel. "If you'll excuse me, I need to go home and rest up for another successful selling day tomorrow."

Annie left the room with a stride of bravado. Yet as she made her way toward the exit, she suffered a shiver. It was never good to make an enemy.

Annie didn't get home until nearly seven. Jane was washing the dinner dishes.

"You missed the meal."

"I apologize." She locked the bakery door behind her.

"I kept a plate warm for you." Jane removed a plate of roast beef and potatoes from the oven and set it on the table.

Annie removed her hat and jacket and sat at the table with a thud. "That's very kind of you."

Jane brought her a glass of water. "How was your first day?"

"Long."

"As a maid you're used to long days. Longer days than this, yes?"

Annie cut a piece of meat and chewed on it, along with her response. "Working at the store seems longer because my day is out in public. As a maid I worked hard, but I was alone much of the time." She rubbed her cheeks. "My face is sore from being cheery."

Jane laughed. "My hands are sore from washing."

"Again I'm sorry for giving you a respite then taking it away so quickly."

"From the moment I met you I knew you were destined for big things."

"How did you know that?"

Jane shrugged. "You have an air of success about you."

Annie liked the sound of that.

Annie was already in bed when Iris and Danny came down from the Tuttles' living quarters.

"I didn't know you were back," Iris said.

Danny sat on his bed. "You should have come upstairs. We had a rousing game of Whist."

"I don't have the energy to hold the cards." She wished they would turn out the light.

"Was being a clerk everything you thought it would be?" Iris asked.

Annie was unsure what Iris hoped to hear. She was too tired to come up with anything but the truth. "Actually, it's quite glorious. I enjoy helping customers put together a new ensemble from pattern to cloth to accessories. But it's also grinding work. My feet are throbbing."

Danny doused the lamp so he and Iris could get undressed. "I got to drive the wagon all the way to Chinatown today. It's like going all the way to China itself."

She heard the rustle of the straw mattress as he got under the covers.

"How about you, Iris? What did you do today?" Annie asked.

There was a long patch of silence. "I learned how to play jacks."

"What's that?"

"It's picking up little pieces of things before a ball bounces twice. I got to fivesies. And Nelly is an expert at doing the horse before carriage. But little Joe kept stealing the ball and . . ."

Annie had no idea what she was talking about, nor did she want to know. Sleep. Sleep.

CHAPTER NINE

Walking through Macy's on the way to her department, Annie paused at the display of sewing machines. She spotted Mrs. Holmquist, the clerk who had talked to her on her first visit to the store.

Mrs. Holmquist was setting up for the day and smiled at Annie. She began to give her the customer pitch: "May I interest you in the time-saving, high-quality aspects of our latest sewing machine? It is a must in any household that has an eye for custom fashion."

"That's a good line," Annie said.

"Thank you. I think the 'custom fashion' phrase is the clincher."

"Because every woman wants to think her fashion style is one of a kind?"

She touched the tip of her nose. Then she stared at Annie. "I've met you, haven't I?"

"I came in the store a few weeks ago, and you gave me your card."

Mrs. Holmquist looked at her more closely. "You're dressed differently, but it's more than that. You seem more . . . grown up."

Annie had to chuckle. "Life does that. And yes, I *am* more grown up now. And now I work here. Two weeks now. I'm Annie. Annie Wood."

"Edna Holmquist. And I've been here since bustles made our bottoms look enormous."

Annie liked her immensely. She glanced toward her department, not wanting to be late. "I am interested in learning how to use a machine. I know the basics of dress construction, but I've always sewn by hand."

"Are you hungry today?"

"Pardon?"

"Come by during your lunch break and I'll show you the basics."

"But you'll miss your lunch, too."

Mrs. Holmquist put a hand on her ample midsection. "I have stores enough to miss one meal."

They both saw Mrs. Gold coming down the aisle. "I'd better dash," Annie said. "But I'll be back."

Annie thought about the sewing lesson all morning. It seemed a bit sneaky to ask

142

another clerk for lessons behind Mrs. Mac-Donald's back — not to mention Mrs. Gold's eagle eye. So Annie decided on the up-front approach.

"Mrs. MacDonald, may I speak with you a moment?"

As they walked away to gain some privacy, Mildred eyed Annie suspiciously. Mildred was always eyeing Annie suspiciously. She seemed to have two expressions: suspicion and a false smile she pasted on when helping customers.

"Yes, Annie?" Mrs. MacDonald asked.

"I thought it might be advantageous if I knew how to run a sewing machine."

"You don't know how to use one?"

"I've only hand sewn."

"Dear, dear. I don't know how that point was missed during your interviews."

Did this mean her job was at stake? If only she hadn't brought it up. "I assure you I am a fast learner, and Mrs. Holmquist has agreed to teach me during my lunch break."

"Oh, she has, has she?"

"I think it would be advantageous to know as much as I can about sewing a garment from start to finish to best help the customers with specific questions, don't you?"

"I do. Of course I do." She looked toward Mrs. Holmquist's department then back.

"You *are* familiar with using patterns."

It was a statement. A challenge. Annie couldn't lie. "I've studied the envelopes. I've noted the different pieces that are involved in making a garment."

"But you've never actually pinned them to fabric, cut them out, and sewn them together."

Suddenly being sneaky about her lessons seemed the better option. "No. I haven't." When Mrs. MacDonald's eyes grew large, Annie added, "I'm going to learn that, too. Since I've received my first paycheck, I plan to buy some fabric and a pattern so I can start a garment from scratch, just like my customers have to do."

Two customers approached, thankfully ending their conversation.

For now.

"You slip the edge of the fabric just so," Mrs. Holmquist said, "then lower the presser foot to keep it in place. Left hand behind, right hand in front. But first use your right hand to move the wheel on the side forward, and then let your feet get the treadle going, making the needle create the stitch."

Before Annie started the seam, she took a deep breath. "So many things to remember."

"With just a little practice it will become second nature."

Annie began, at first making the needle go too fast with a surge then getting control so it made the stitches with a steady rhythm. "I did it!"

"You certainly did. You're a natural."

They stopped what they were doing when a customer approached and looked at another machine. Annie experimented with reverse and pivoting at corners, and she loved the sense of taming a machine. She'd never used a machine — any machine. It made her feel bold and strong and confident, as if the world was hers to conquer.

Mrs. Holmquist returned. "How are you faring?"

Annie lifted the presser foot and snipped the threads. "I'm enjoying this."

"You should. Creating something from scratch is very satisfy—"

"Ahem."

They turned around and saw the floorwalker close by, her hands clasped behind her back.

"Good afternoon, Mrs. Gold," Mrs. Holmquist said.

The elder woman ignored the greeting. "What's going on here?"

"I'm giving Miss Wood a lesson in using a

sewing machine."

"On company time?"

"During our lunch break," Annie said. "Mrs. Holmquist is a wonderful teacher."

"That may be, but I want no more lessons on the selling floor. Is that understood?"

"Yes, ma'am," Annie said.

"Yes, Mrs. Gold."

Annie stood. "I'm disappointed. I need to learn all of it. And Mrs. MacDonald informed me I need to learn how to use a pattern and sew a garment together from scratch."

Mrs. Holmquist spread her arms. "Then I'm your woman."

"But we can't —"

"We can't have the lessons here, but I have a machine at home. And a dining table that's perfect for cutting out patterns. Come to my place after work a few evenings a week and I'll make you an expert in no time."

Annie thrilled at the thought. "I'd be happy to pay you for your time."

"Nonsense," Mrs. Holmquist said with a flip of her hand. "I'm a widow and my son lives in Pittsburgh. You would be doing me a favor by providing me with companionship and conversation beyond the sound of my own voice — for it seems I've taken to

146

talking to myself."

Annie smiled. "Are you a good conversationalist?"

"Not really. I argue too much."

Annie noted the time. "I need to get back. Would tonight be too soon?"

"Just soon enough," the woman said.

Elated, Annie took a detour before returning to her duties in order to use the Macy's pay phone. She called the Tuttles and told them she would be late getting home.

All that accomplished, she returned to work, not needing food, not needing any fuel beyond anticipation.

During the rest of the afternoon, while helping customers choose patterns, fabrics, and notions, Annie had a chance to peruse the Butterick fashion catalogs with her own needs in mind. She decided on a shirtwaist blouse and a five-gored skirt — very practical, yet stylish — and during a free moment she retrieved the two patterns from stock.

Her fabric choice was made while helping a woman find the proper dress goods for an afternoon dress. A brown broadcloth would do well for Annie's skirt, and an ivory cotton with a faint print of leaves would make a lovely blouse. On a whim she decided to create a cummerbund from some burnished-orange velveteen. Elated by the purchase for herself, she bought a length of three different colors of ribbon for Iris, Mrs. Tuttle, and Jane.

When Annie saw Mildred was occupied, she approached Mrs. MacDonald. "Would you cut my fabric, please? And make me a ticket?"

"You were serious about sewing yourself a garment, then."

"Of course I was. Mrs. Holmquist has offered to take me through the process at her home, starting this evening."

"That woman is a gem. You should feel very lucky to have such a teacher."

The fabric was cut and buttons and thread added to the purchase. Annie got the package boy to wrap up the goods. "When you're done just slip the parcel under the counter, Robbie."

It felt wonderful to pay for the goods out of her own earnings. During all the time she'd worked for the Kidds and earned wages, there had never been much to spend it on in the village of Summerfield. She'd saved up twenty pounds over the years, but it could have been two hundred for all the access she had to it now that she'd run away and left it behind in England.

She truly was starting from nothing.

Wasn't that the American way? Pulling oneself up by one's bootstraps and making a success of it? Annie liked the sound of that challenge. And now, for the first time in her life, it all seemed very possible.

"There," she said, placing the coins in Mrs. MacDonald's palm. "All paid."

At the end of the workday Annie was hungry — after all, she'd skipped lunch for the sewing machine lesson — but she was not at all tired. Rather, she was eager to go to Mrs. Holmquist's for the sewing lesson.

She gathered her jacket and hat from her locker, and on her way out, she stopped to retrieve her parcel from under the counter.

Suddenly a man grabbed her arm. "We'll take that, miss."

Annie had seen the man in the store previously and had been told he was a plainclothes security man. His main job was to catch shoplifters —

"You think I'm stealing?" she asked.

He took the parcel from her and opened it on the counter. "We've been so informed." He seemed disappointed at the contents. "Sewing supplies?"

Annie was incensed. She saved the spool of thread from rolling off the counter. "Yes, sewing supplies. Supplies I paid for. You can check my receipt book from today."

Mrs. Holmquist approached, putting on her gloves. "What's the issue, Mr. Horace?"

"We were informed Miss Wood was stealing."

"I assure you she is not." She spotted Mrs. MacDonald and motioned her to join them. "Velma, tell Mr. Horace that Annie paid for the goods."

Mrs. MacDonald's face passed from confusion to anger. "She most certainly did." She pointed to the parcel. "Wrap it back up, Annie."

"But we were informed —"

"You were informed wrong," Mrs. MacDonald said. "And who, may we ask, was your informant?"

"I prefer not to say."

"I insist you do say," she said.

"As do I," Mrs. Holmquist said.

"As do I," Annie said.

He looked reluctant but leaned close and said, "Miss Krieger."

"Mildred?" Annie wasn't surprised.

"I'll deal with her tomorrow," Mrs. MacDonald said. "Now then, let us go home in peace."

Mr. Horace nodded and let them go.

The three women made for the exit. "That girl," Mrs. MacDonald said. "I don't know what to do with her. If it's not lollygagging in the department, it's scowling when she should be smiling, or . . ."

"Has she done anything like this before?" Mrs. Holmquist asked.

"No."

"She took a dislike to me the moment I started work," Annie said. "I have no notion why. I've tried to be friendly."

"She has a chip on her shoulder, that one does," Mrs. MacDonald said.

Mrs. Holmquist opened the exit door and held it for the others. "Maybe it's time to knock it off."

"I know it's necessary," Mrs. MacDonald said. "But I'm not looking forward to the repercussions."

"Repercussions?" Annie asked.

They turned south on Broadway. "She is a relative to one of the buyers."

"Relative or not, Macy's holds its clerks to a certain standard." Mrs. Holmquist said. "Falsely accusing another clerk of theft is unacceptable."

Mrs. MacDonald nodded. "I'll speak with Mrs. Gold about it tomorrow."

"That's settled then," Mrs. Holmquist said.

Annie had a bad feeling about it. Nothing about Mildred seemed "settled."

■ ■ ■ ■

"Forgive the walk-up," Mrs. Holmquist said as they reached the landing for her third-floor apartment.

"I'm used to stairs," Annie said. "As a housemaid I used to —"

Mrs. Holmquist stopped in front of her door, key in hand. "You were a housemaid?"

"All my life."

"Until when?"

They heard another tenant on the stairs above. "I'll tell you the entire story inside."

Mrs. Holmquist used the key. She flipped a switch and turned on the lights. "It's not much to look at," she said. "But it was enough for my Ernie and our son."

Mrs. Holmquist hooked their coats and hats on a coatrack by the door.

"This is far more than I've ever had," Annie said. She strode through the parlor, past a table with four chairs and a small kitchen beyond. There was a hallway leading to the right.

"Two bedrooms, indoor plumbing, and electricity. And plenty of windows for natural light — though with working the hours I do, I don't get to see much of the sun."

"It has all the comforts of a loving home."

"All the comforts that Ernie and I needed to bring up our boy."

"You said your son was in Pittsburgh?"

"Steven is an English teacher there. I'm very proud of him."

"As you should be."

Mrs. Holmquist stepped into the kitchen. "I have some leftover stew and bread. Care for a quick supper?"

"That would be grand. I'm famished." Remembering the reason she was so hungry, she added, "You must be, too, for you gave up your lunch break to help me."

"It adds to a person's character to be hungry once in a while." She pointed to one of two chairs next to a tiny table. "Have a seat."

"I'd be glad to help."

"Keep me company while I work."

Annie took a seat and watched as Mrs. Holmquist took a bowl of stew out of a small icebox. "You have an icebox?"

"Wouldn't do without one. Ernie liked to buy me the latest equipment." She moved to an odd-looking stove. "But this is my pride and joy. It's an oil cookstove." She pointed to the three receptacles beneath the burners. "See here? I put the oil in, light it at the top, and voila! I can cook." She lit

153

the wick, and a blue flame appeared.

"That's marvelous. Back at the manor the cook still uses an enormous cast-iron stove."

"I had one of those while Steven was growing up. But it took up too much room, and since I don't have reason to bake any-more . . ."

She sounded wistful about it, and Annie could sense her loneliness.

The smell of stew began to fill the room.

"Would you like some coffee, too, Annie?"

"That would be lovely. At least let me help with that." Mrs. Holmquist gave her the coffee grinder then put a pot of water on to heat.

She let Annie help with more than the coffee, showing her where the dishes were. Soon the meal was ready and they sat to eat in the dining room. "It smells delicious," Annie said, taking up her spoon. "Thank you for all you're doing for me, Mrs. Holmquist."

"You're welcome. And the name is Edna." She held out a hand and clearly expected Annie to take it. "And since you've thanked me, let us thank God." She bowed her head and Annie did the same. "Come, Lord Jesus, be our guest, and let Thy gifts to us be blest."

"Amen," Annie said.

But Edna wasn't through. "And thank You for the blessing of friendship. Amen."

"Amen again," Annie said. "The dinner grace makes me think of the Tuttles. They are probably sitting to eat this very moment."

"That's the family you live with?"

"Stay with."

"There's a difference?"

Annie wished she hadn't pressed the issue. "If I explain the difference I'll sound ungrateful, and I'm very grateful to them, for they took the three of us off the street when we had nothing and nowhere to go, and —"

"Three of you?"

"Danny and Iris are brother and sister. The three of us sleep in the storeroom of the Tuttles' bakery, amid the stores of flour and sugar. Before I was hired on at Macy's, I scrubbed their pots and pans. Their daughter was relieved of the duty, but then she had to go back to it when I got my job, and their son acts like he's interested in me, but I'm not interested in him — Iris is — and . . ." She sighed. "It's complicated."

"Thank God you've moved up in the world."

"I have, and I do thank Him for it."

Edna passed a jar of apple butter, and Annie spread it on her bread.

"How long have you known the two friends staying there with you? Iris and . . . ?"

"Danny. He's her little brother. We'd only known each other a short time when we all ran away from service together."

"You mentioned being a housemaid? This sounds like a story I need to hear."

And so, Annie told it. All of it. From her life in England as a housemaid, to her dreams of becoming a lady's maid for the Kidds, to the exciting trip to America, to the betrayal of the Misses, the tension with Grasston, escape, and being saved by the Tuttles.

By the time she was finished, they were done eating — and then some. They were on their second cup of coffee. "Iris, Danny, and I are the Three Musketeers. We're in this together."

"To begin with, perhaps. But you've moved on."

"But I am still their friend."

"Of course." Edna stood. "As we are friends. And as your friend, I think it's time I give you your first lesson on using a sewing pattern."

Their conversation had been so refreshing that Annie had nearly forgotten why she was

156

there. She helped clear the table and was told not to mind washing the dishes. Edna moved the dining chairs away from the table, giving them full access. "Now show me the pattern and fabric you bought."

It was after ten when Annie stepped off the streetcar. The door to the bakery was understandably locked, but she rapped softly on the glass. Danny came and let her in.

" 'Bout time," he said.

"I know. Sorry."

He locked the door behind them. "They were worried."

"I called. I told them I'd be late."

They walked back to the storeroom where Iris was just getting into bed. "You're late."

Annie held back her impatience and shooed Danny into the kitchen so she could get undressed. She kept the door open so they could still talk. "How was your day?" she asked.

"As if you care," Iris said.

"Bug . . . ," Danny said from the other room. "Be nice."

Iris got under the covers. "We never see you anymore. You've moved on and are making new friends and having adventures without us."

So that was the problem. Annie hurriedly

unhooked her corset and drew her night-gown over her head. Then she sat on the bed beside Iris. "I'm not sure *adventures* is the right word. I'm working — working very hard."

"But you have other friends."

"I have one friend, Mrs. Holmquist, and she's old enough to be my mother."

The crease in Iris's forehead eased. "Oh."

Annie took the ribbons out of her purse. "I bought something for the three women in the house, but you can have first choice."

Iris's face softened, and she chose the ribbon of emerald green. "Thank you."

Annie took the girl's hand. "You will always be my special friends. My first friends in America."

Danny knocked on the doorjamb. "You decent?"

"I am."

He came in and stood nearby. "Remember, we each have to make the most of today. Even if it's not doing the same thing in the same place as each other."

He was such a dear. "I agree," she said. "Make the most of today."

CHAPTER TEN

Upon entering the sewing department, Annie spotted Mildred speaking with the security man, Mr. Horace. Mildred was shaking her head as he pointed his finger at her.

"If Mildred disliked me before, she'll hate me now," Annie said under her breath.

Mrs. MacDonald overheard. "You have made an enemy."

"Unless they sack her."

"I doubt that will happen. After all, she can give the defense that she was watching out for the best interests of Macy's by trying to catch a thief."

"But I'm not a thief."

She shrugged. "I'll keep an eye on her."

Annie wasn't sure Mrs. MacDonald's care would be enough to save her from Mildred's wrath.

Luckily for Annie, the day was a busy one. With a constant stream of customers there wasn't any free time for her to interact with Mildred.

And then, Annie's day brightened. A handsome man with sandy hair and a winning smile entered the department. "May I help you, sir?"

His eyebrows rose, and he gave her a mischievous smile. "I am the one to help you, Miss . . . ?"

"Wood," she said.

He set a large sample box on the counter. On the outside was stenciled BUTTERICK PATTERN COMPANY.

"You're the Butterick salesman?"

"I am." He held out his hand, "Sean Culver, at your service." He leaned his forearms atop the case and grinned at her. "What next, Miss Wood?"

She felt herself blush. "I don't know what to say. I don't know the procedure."

"The procedure is that I win you over in such a grand fashion that you'll go the extra mile to sell Butterick patterns above all others." He leaned close and spoke behind his hand. "We show utter disdain for the McCall's product."

"But isn't competition the essence of American business?"

"By your accent I can tell you're not from around here. I bet you're from . . . Brooklyn perhaps?"

She had no idea where Brooklyn was but knew he was teasing. "I am from England. Kent, to be exact."

"You worked in a store there?"

She chose her words carefully. "I worked for the Kidds at Crompton Hall. Lord and Lady Newley and their daughter and son."

He eyed her a long moment, and she feared he would guess her past lowly position. To distract him, she said, "Do you need to check our pattern stock, Mr. Culver?"

"It seems you've caught on to the procedure quite well, though far too quickly, for I would have enjoyed chatting a bit longer."

In spite of his blatant flattery, she liked the twinkle in his eye. "We can chat while we check the stock, can't we?"

"I can think of nothing better."

He came behind the counter and pulled out drawer after drawer of numbered patterns that were kept in a large oak cabinet. "Care to hold the clipboard for me and mark the numbers?"

"Isn't that making me do *your* job?"

"Part of it."

She looked across the department and spotted Mildred staring at them. Scowling. Since there were no customers to occupy Annie's time, if she left Mr. Culver to

161

himself, a confrontation with Mildred would surely be imminent. "I would be happy to help you."

Annie entered the employee cafeteria and chose a glass of milk, a turkey sandwich, and a bowl of vegetable soup. She paid her dime and took her tray toward a table. She spotted Mildred, nearly finished with her meal, and thought of joining her. The stress of waiting for Mildred's wrath made her want to push for a confrontation so she could be done with it. Or — miracle of miracles — make peace.

But as she approached Mildred's table, the girl left.

So be it.

Mildred glared. Mildred stared.

And though Annie tried not to, Annie cared.

Her nerves got the best of her mid-afternoon, and she fumbled a box of buttons, scattering them over the floor. Mrs. MacDonald moved to help, but Annie waved her off. "I'm the fumble fingers. I'll get them."

She was nearly through when a man knelt beside her and said, "You missed one."

"Thank —"

"Hello, Annie."

Annie's heart flipped. She stood and stepped away from him. "Grasston."

"I'm glad you remember me."

"What are you doing here?"

He moved to the counter and fingered some lace. "I was just walking through, passing the time since I now *have* so much time. You see, I am no longer employed by the Friesens."

"What?"

"It seems that losing three pairs of gloves tipped the scales against me. I was sacked."

Because of the gloves I took?

"I'm sorry to hear that," she said, even though she wasn't. "Are you looking for other employment?"

"Actually, I'm looking for something more satisfying than employment."

She remembered his inappropriate behavior against herself and Iris. "Move along, Mr. Grasston. There will be none of that."

"You flatter yourself. I wasn't talking about *that,* I was talking about something even better."

She didn't want to ask.

"I'm talking about revenge."

Her breath caught in her throat, and she decided to feign ignorance. "Revenge for what?"

"For someone setting me up, for ruining my reputation."

He knew. For who else would have taken his gloves?

"I'm sorry my joke caused you —"

"Joke?" he said, taking a step closer.

His voice had risen, and people looked toward them.

"I meant no harm." *Not this much harm.* "Now please . . . go away."

She saw Mrs. MacDonald speaking with Mr. Horace. Help was on the way.

But Grasston saw it, too. With the parting words "We're not done, you and me," he quickly walked toward the exit.

"Are you all right, Miss Wood?" Mr. Horace asked. "Was that man harassing you?"

No. And yes.

"I can go after him, if you'd like."

The last thing she wanted was for Grasston to hold more against her. "I'm all right. No harm done."

"Who was he?"

"Just an acquaintance from my last employment."

"He seemed to take issue with you."

She smoothed the lace Grasston had touched then pulled her hand away, remembering that he'd touched it. "I believe Mr. Grasston takes issue with many more per-

164

sons than me. It's his nature."

"There are those sorts," Mr. Horace said. "I'll leave you to your work, but let me know if you see him again."

"I most certainly will, and thank you for your concern."

As soon as he left, Mrs. MacDonald came over, and Annie repeated her rendition of the event.

It was a mixed blessing that Mildred stayed away. But instead of bothering Annie, Mildred kept looking in the direction Grasston had gone.

The customer perused the Butterick catalog. "I don't like the sleeve in this dress but I do like the neckline and the skirt."

Annie made note of it then said, "Excuse me a moment, but if we go back two pages . . ." She found the pattern illustration she was looking for. "Is this the sleeve you like?"

"Yes, it is. But I don't like that pattern's bodice or skirt."

"Then combine the two patterns into one garment," Annie said.

The woman studied the pictures of both patterns, back and forth between the pages. "I can do that?"

"Of course you can. See how the set-in of

the sleeve is the same? This sleeve will fit into this other pattern and you will have exactly the fashion you want."

"Brilliant!" the woman said. "I'll take both."

"Now let's find you some fabric."

Annie perused her sales receipt book at the end of the day. She mentally added the numbers. It had been a good day. Her best ever. At this rate she'd get a bonus.

"Don't gloat."

Annie looked up to find Mildred standing in front of her. "Gloat?"

"You're stealing the best customers."

"I am doing no such thing. And how would either of us know who is a good customer versus a bad one until they start looking?"

Mildred huffed this off. "You got me in trouble and I don't appreciate it."

Annie had to back up her thinking. Was she talking about Mr. Horace? "You shouldn't accuse me of stealing when you know very well I paid for the items."

"I didn't know that. You hid the package like you were guilty."

"I put it under the counter, out of sight from the customers. If I wanted to steal, would I get Mrs. MacDonald to cut the fabric for me?" Annie was done, fully done with her. She crossed her arms in front of her chest. "Is there anything else you have against me? For if there is, let it out now. I want to know."

Mildred's expression was a mask of confusion. Had no one ever called her out on her behavior?

When she didn't say anything, Annie said, "Then I would appreciate it if —"

"Your flirting with Mr. Culver is disgusting."

This was unexpected. "If you must know, he flirted with me. And any banter between us is none of your business, and above all, is not disgusting or inappropriate or any other word you care to fling at me."

"Why does that button man hate you?"

Button man? Then Annie realized Mildred was talking about Grasston, who had helped her pick up the buttons. She'd had enough. "If you would spend more time focused on your own clerking skills and less on me, we'd both be happier and more successful."

Mildred shuffled her shoulders. "I'm a fine clerk."

"Good for you. Now if you'll excuse me, I want to get home."

The gall of some people.

■ ■ ■ ■

Annie first felt the *presence* as she waited for the streetcar, a distinct feeling that someone was watching her. She turned around, but the sidewalk was crowded and she saw no one out of the ordinary. The stop was populated by many Macy's employees, many who smiled or nodded at her gaze.

Then, she spotted a black-suited man slip around the corner of a building. Grasston had been wearing black.

The streetcar arrived and she was forced to let her suspicians go. She was being silly. A lot of men wore black suits. Most did. All of the male clerks at Macy's wore black.

She got on the streetcar and found a seat — which was a blessing, for the car was overloaded and many had to stand. She made small talk with her seatmate and let her nerves subside.

Until she was almost at the bakery door. Suddenly fear crawled up her spine. She spun around and scanned the street.

And saw no one.

But with all the alcoves and doorways, it would be easy for someone to slip out of sight.

Gathering her senses, she hurried to the

door, entered, and locked it.

Iris ran to greet her. "You're home for dinner! I'm so glad. I have much to tell you."

Annie let the tension outside be overshadowed by her friend's enthusiasm — which was a marked improvement over Iris being so irritable.

"I'd love to hear all about it," Annie said.

But then Mrs. Tuttle and Jane asked for help with dinner, so the conversation had to be postponed. Yet Annie noticed they were each wearing a new hair ribbon — Mrs. Tuttle's was royal blue, and Jane's was red. And Iris wore her green one. Annie was glad she'd thought to buy them the small gift. It would hopefully ease the friction of her working such long hours.

But then during dinner, Annie thought she saw someone looking in the window from the street. It was dark out, and hard to see, but she couldn't help but wonder if Grasston was out there. Waiting for her. Waiting for his revenge.

"Goodness, Annie," Mrs. Tuttle said. "Your face is pale as a baby's, the blush gone from your cheeks entirely. Has something frightened you?"

It showed? "I missed your fine cooking last night and am in dire need of it."

With that, the discussion moved to Edna

169

and her lessons. "How often are you going to have those lessons?" Danny asked.

"Every other evening," she said. "We have the skirt and blouse cut out, but next I have to learn how to sew it all together — on a machine, not by hand."

Mrs. Tuttle nodded. "Mrs. DiSalvo down the street has a machine. She's offered to sew some dresses for the little ones."

"In exchange for bread, I hope," Mr. Tuttle said.

"Yes, dear. I know the rule. Barter is better."

"I'd like to barter for a new horse," the elder Tuttle said. "Old Moss is limping."

As talk turned to other things, Annie tried not to glance at the window. Tried not to be afraid.

After the lights were out in the bakery, Annie ventured near the window, needing the darkness to cover her interest. She peered out and saw no one besides a couple walking together, and another man hurrying home late from work.

She started when Danny came up beside her. "You scared me!"

"I see that. The question is, why are you scared?"

He deserved to know, for he'd been a part

of it, too. "I saw Grasston."

"How is the clod?"

"Angry." She faced him. "He got sacked because of the gloves I pinched."

"Sacked for gloves? That can't be the only reason. Others besides us musta seen the kind of man he was."

"Whether they saw or not, he's blaming me. He wants revenge for costing him the job and ruining his reputation."

"He did that on his own."

"Tell him that."

"I will tell him, if I see him."

Annie felt a terrible foreboding. She put a hand on Danny's arm. "You will not tell him anything. If you see him you will give him a wide berth. Do not involve yourself."

"Too late. I am involved. Remember I promised to protect you forever."

She slipped her hand around his arm. "Are you sure you're only thirteen?"

Annie was dozing by the time Iris came down from upstairs. "Baby Joe would *not* go to bed. And his ma makes it worse by coddling him. Annie? You awake? Remember I have things to tell you?"

"I'm awake."

But only for a moment.

CHAPTER ELEVEN

Danny nudged her. "Get up! It's morning."

Annie heard him awaken his sister next then heard the door to the storeroom open and close.

The night had been too short, for she had been plagued with nightmares about Grasston popping out of hidden corners, being everywhere. A constant threat.

She tried to force the latest bad dream away. The details faded but the essence remained.

"Good morning, Iris," Annie said as they both got out of bed.

"She speaks."

"What?"

Iris smoothed the blanket on her makeshift bed. "Remember last evening how I wanted to tell you something important?"

Oh dear. "I'm sorry. I was preoccupied with —"

"With your very important life. I know.

Sorry to intrude."

Annie kicked herself. With all her Grass-ton worries, she'd completely forgotten her friend. "I'm the one who's sorry. Tell me your news."

Iris grabbed her clothes off a shelf. "If you'll excuse me. I'll dress elsewhere."

Again, the door opened. And closed.

Annie stood in the room alone. She sank onto her bed. She'd been so caught up in her new life she'd ignored the old one. Her old friends. Her best friend.

She looked upward when she heard the patter of children's feet overhead. The Tuttles were up. Iris was busy.

The thought of enduring breakfast with the lot of them made her lose her appetite. Iris wasn't good at hiding her feelings, and there would be more tension.

"I can't take more tension right now."

And so, Annie hurriedly got dressed and left early for work. It wasn't the courageous thing to do, but it was the best she could do.

It was too early to go to work, so Annie strolled around Herald Square. The elevated train that loomed above the street seemed ominous, especially considering her mood, so she walked to the Herald Newspaper building at the crown of the square. It was already humming with commotion. She could even look in the windows and watch the presses.

A young boy approached, a stack of newspapers under his arm. "Paper, lady?"

"No, thank you."

"Don't you care nothing for the World Series?"

"I'm afraid I don't know what that is."

He gawked at her. "Baseball, lady. The New York Giants are playing the Philadelphia Athletics. Third game is today up at the Polo Grounds at two twenty-five. We're tied one game to one."

Annie knew nothing about baseball, but the boy's passion made her believe it was a lack of knowledge that needed to be rectified. "You convinced me. I'll take a paper."

"Remember, two twenty-five. No need to even go because thousands stand right here outside the offices and get a play-by-play."

"I'll be working." She nodded toward Macy's.

"Just listen for the roar of the crowds. They'll let you know how we're doing." He tipped his cap and left to do his job.

Speaking of . . .

She checked the clocks on the Herald building and saw it was time to go to work.

"Good afternoon to you, Miss Wood."

Annie was glad to see Mr. Culver. "I'm surprised you're here," she said.

"Why?"

"Doesn't the baseball game start any minute?"

His eyebrows lifted. "You're a Giants fan?"

She retrieved the newspaper from under the counter. "Not yet. But I'm learning."

"Highly commendable. And you've caught me. I purposely timed my day to be around the Herald offices during the game. They have a Play-O-Graph posted outside that shows a miniature baseball diamond. They get the results telegraphed inside and then post the plays on the board."

"How ingenious." She didn't want to admit she had no idea what a baseball diamond was, or any details about how the game was played. But she was happy he was impressed with her interest.

"What can I help you with, Mr. Culver? I don't believe we've depleted our Butterick stock since your last visit."

He set his sales case on the floor at his feet. "Actually, I've come because of a complaint."

She put a hand to her chest. "About me?"

She saw him glance in Mildred's direction.

"Mildred is the complainant?"

"I assure you there isn't cause for worry, but my superiors insist that I —"

"Everything about that girl is cause for worry," Annie said, more to herself than to him. "How did she make this complaint?"

"She sent a note to the Butterick office, and they sent me to deal with it."

"Meaning?"

"I'm supposed to talk to you. See if there is any basis in the complaint."

Annie's heart pumped double time — not out of fear but anger. She hadn't done anything wrong, and the gall of Mildred to imply otherwise was unacceptable. "Since Mildred leveled the complaint, I insist she be present during your accusation. Mrs. MacDonald, too." Annie didn't wait for him to say yea or nay but called the two women over.

"What is it, Miss Wood?" the older woman asked as she joined them. "Afternoon, Mr. Culver."

Annie pointed at Mildred, who approached warily. "It appears Mildred has lodged a complaint against me to the Butterick Company."

Mrs. MacDonald's brow dipped. "Is this true, Miss Krieger?"

Her shrug turned into a nod. "When I witness wrongdoing I feel it is my duty to report it."

"Wrongdoing like the fabric I *didn't* steal?"

"I agree with your point, Miss Wood," Mrs. MacDonald said. "Miss Krieger, you do seem overly concerned with Miss Wood's behavior."

Annie's thoughts returned to Mildred's complaint. "There has been no wrongdoing. How can there possibly be wrongdoing selling sewing patterns?"

They all looked to Mildred. At least she had the decency to blush. "I . . ." She passed it off to Mr. Culver. "He has the complaint. Let him read it."

Coward.

Mr. Culver unfolded a piece of paper. " 'Miss Annie Wood has denigrated the Butterick product to customers by declaring their designs insufficient and inferior.' "

"What?"

Mr. Culver lifted a hand and continued, " 'Noting a customer's dissatisfaction with the fashion design of a pattern, Miss Wood did not try to sway her by mentioning the pattern's attributes, but openly discussed its flaws. This disloyalty should not go

177

unpunished.' "

Annie laughed. Then she laughed harder. "That's the all of it? That's your complaint?"

Mildred pointed to the note. "It's true. I witnessed you with that customer wearing the blue coat, talking with her about the flaws in the pattern designs."

This was absurd. "She didn't like a certain sleeve, but *did* like the bodice and skirt of a dress pattern. I suggested she combine two patterns to get the look she desired. In the end she bought two patterns instead of one. I doubled the sale."

Mildred blinked twice then took sudden interest in the cuffs of her blouse. "I . . . I stand by my complaint."

Mrs. MacDonald shook her head. "Miss Krieger. Really."

"But she —"

"I'll deal with you in a moment." She turned to the others. "Please forgive Miss Krieger her falsely placed . . . whatever it is. Miss Wood? I congratulate you on doubling the sale. Keep up the good work. Mr. Culver, I assume this is a nonissue with your employer?"

"It is now."

"Very good. Now if you'll excuse us." She took Mildred's arm and led her away. After they slipped behind a display of woolens,

178

Annie could see Mildred get a good ear bashing.

"She's hated me since my first day," Annie said.

"With good reason — no one likes her, and everyone likes you."

"How do you know that?"

"Oh, I know. You want to know how I know?"

"I suppose."

He moved to block the view of Mildred's scolding. "Because *I* like you, Miss Wood. Because you're irresistible."

She blinked. "Where did that come from?"

"I could say 'my heart,' but that would sound too sappy, don't you think?"

"It would."

He tapped a finger against his lower lip. "So . . . from where did my fondness stem?"

"Mr. Culver, I don't think you should talk like this."

"You're against the truth?"

"I'm against flattery. You shouldn't flirt with me."

His face turned serious, his mischief gone. "I don't want to flirt with you, Miss Wood. I flirt all day to gain sales. It's part of the job. But with you . . ." He waited until she looked at his eyes. "I knew very quickly you were special."

She smiled. "Flattery again, Mr. Culver?"

He shook his head. "I admit that the first Sean Culver you met was the salesman, but the Sean talking to you now is just the man. And that man wants to know the woman, Annie Wood, beyond sales and work and customers."

She didn't know what to say.

He took her hesitance as a rejection. "I'm sorry. I've gone too far and said too much too fast. I don't mean for my words to be off putting or alarming, only to be honest and —"

She touched his arm for the briefest of seconds. "Shh."

He sighed. "Again I've said too much — I'm sorry."

She sighed, too. "You haven't said too much, you've said just enough."

Relief washed over his face. "Just enough for . . . ?"

"For me to be interested. In Sean Culver, the man." She was surprised at her own words, yet they were sincere.

He beamed. "You've made my day, Annie Wood. My week." He leaned close, becoming the flirt again. "Perhaps my life."

She laughed. "Shut it down, sir. Don't get carried away."

He put on his hat and retrieved his sales

case. "I won't promise a thing. See you tomorrow, Miss Wood."

"What's tomorrow?"

"You and I are taking a late lunch so we can go outside and watch the game play out across the square."

Annie looked for Mrs. MacDonald, who was helping a customer. "I'm not sure I'll be able to get away."

"It's worth asking, isn't it?"

Yes, it was.

Thankfully, Mildred avoided even the proximity of Annie the rest of the day. Perhaps the humiliation and the scolding by Mrs. MacDonald had properly quashed her schemes. Annie began to relax, to breathe easier, to —

Annie did a double take when she noticed the customer Mildred was assisting. Odd enough that it was a man, but when he looked in her direction . . .

Grasston!

She gasped. How dare he come back here!

She looked around the store for Mr. Horace.

Grasston said something to Mildred then turned toward Annie, smiled, and waved.

Somehow his false friendship was more frightening than a direct threat.

Annie spotted Mrs. MacDonald, but she was busy with a customer. If Grasston approached, she would be on her own.

Only he didn't approach. He continued his conversation with Mildred and even got her laughing. He touched Mildred's hair, as if retrieving a thread from the tendrils near her face.

Don't you touch her!

Annie's heart beat in her throat. She didn't like Mildred, but the girl had no idea the sort of man she was flirting with. Annie stepped into the aisle when Grasston faced her and offered a proper bow and a tip of his hat. Then he walked toward an exit.

After watching him leave, Mildred looked at Annie and gave her a challenging smile full of contempt and satisfaction. *She doesn't know what she's doing.* Annie set aside her dislike and went over to talk to her. "What did that man want?"

"None of your business."

"Don't play coy with me. Now is not the time."

"Not the time because I happen to have a handsome man interested in me? You have Mr. Culver wrapped around your little finger. You want the button man, too?"

It was apparent that Grasston hadn't told Mildred his affiliation with Annie. "I know

182

him better than you, and he's smarmy, a conniving dolt, and —"

"I will know him plenty well myself after we go walking this Sunday."

"No!"

Mildred blinked at Annie's outburst then busied herself with a rack of trim. "I don't need your permission to have a gentleman caller."

"He's not a gentleman. He's a cad."

"He is no such thing. He's very nice and said he's been in Macy's before and has admired me from afar. It took all his courage to approach me today and talk with me."

She was utterly blind. "He's not here for you, he's here for me."

Mildred straightened to her full five-foot-nothing height and glared at Annie. "How dare you think you are the only woman who can attract male attention."

"I don't think any such thing. It's just that I know him. He's out for no good. He wants to hurt me. He's paying attention to you to get to me." Annie saw a flutter of pain cross Mildred's face. "I don't say it to be mean but to save you from grief, from heartache, and . . . and maybe worse."

"I don't need your warnings. I am quite capable of taking care of myself."

"But —"

Mildred glared at her and lowered her voice. "You wonder why I hate you? You come into Macy's and act as though you are the queen of the store. You can do no wrong and everyone loves you."

"Maybe if you didn't have such a sour look on your face all day and weren't such a dosser they'd —"

Mildred pointed toward the other end of the department. "Go on. Go back to your counter and stop trying to take away my chance at happiness."

Annie was stunned.

"Go!"

"Just be careful of him, all right?"

Mildred turned on her heel and walked away.

Annie returned to her post, saying a prayer of protection for Mildred. She might not like the girl, but she wouldn't wish Grasston on anyone.

It was closing time, and Edna stopped at Annie's department on her way out. "Are you coming over this evening for another lesson?"

Annie looked around at the mess in her department. "I will as soon as I clean up from my last customer. She bought dress goods for three ensembles, but it made quite a shambles of everything."

"Do you want me to wait for you?"

"Go on home. I'll be there as soon as I can."

"I'll stop at the butcher's to buy some pork chops and get supper going."

After the drama of the day, Annie was famished. "You are too good to me."

On the way to Edna's home, Annie found a seat on the streetcar and closed her eyes. Even a few minutes of rest would be helpful, for her day wasn't over. Tonight she was going to learn how to set in sleeves.

Instinctively, Annie sensed when her stop was close, opened her eyes to confirm it, and got out. But as she walked toward Edna's flat, she felt uneasy. The familiar sound of people walking behind her intensified and became significant.

She glanced over her shoulder and saw others making their way home after work, everyone intent on their own thoughts and their own destinations.

But then she saw him. A face intent on *her*. Staring after *her*.

Grasston.

She quickened her pace, needing to get to the safety of Edna's. She still had two blocks to go and the crowd behind her was thinning out. They were her buffer against him. Surely, he wouldn't do anything surrounded by witnesses.

But then she felt a swell of anger rise up. Unlike Mildred, she was not going to be a victim. She knew the truth about him, and with truth came power.

And so she stopped walking and turned to face him.

A few other walkers looked surprised at her action but handily sidestepped around her. But other than the lifting of his right eyebrow, Grasston wasn't fazed. He stopped in front of her and smirked as if nothing she did would rile him, and even worse, as if everything she did stirred him in a way Annie didn't want to think about.

"Mr. Grasston," she said. "Two times in one day? Really? Don't you have anything better to do with your time than —"

He grabbed her upper arm with a shocking strength and pulled her close to his side. Then he led her into an alley. She could feel his warm breath in her ear. With each step away from the community of the street, her fear intensified. *He's going to hurt me! Lord, please don't let him hurt me!*

She frantically looked around for an escape, but the alley was closed at the end and only grew darker at its terminus. She looked upward but only saw clothes hanging like flags on lines strung over the alleyway. The few windows were closed against the evening chill.

The possibilities of what could happen threatened to crush her. But then she thought of Iris and Danny and all they'd been through losing their family, and their courage combined with her own that had thrust them out of servanthood and into lives full of hope and opportunity. The thought of them gave her the power to shove aside her fear and ignited her choice to fight. She would not let this bully have his way.

With a surge of energy, she twisted her arm out of his grip and ran toward the street.

But he ran faster.

He caught the hem of her jacket and yanked, making her fall. He fell on top of her, turning her over, securing her flailing arms.

"Come on, Annie. Gimme what I want."

Please, God, help!

The weight of him . . . she found it hard to breathe. She knew his brute strength was no match for her own. And so she used all her energy and what oxygen was left in her lungs to do one thing. She screamed. "Help!

He's attacking me!"

He released an arm to cover her mouth, but she bit him and continued calling for help.

She heard a commotion at the entrance to the alley; then two men pulled Grasston off her. He ran toward the street and one man went after him. "Police! Police! Stop him!"

The other man, and then a woman, knelt beside her. "Are you all right?"

They helped her sit then stand. "I'm fine. Thank you, thank you so much."

No one asked what Grasston was doing to her. There was no need. His aberrant intention had been clear.

And she had been saved from it. God had heard her cries and saved her.

The couple helped her to the street, where a police officer rushed toward them. The man who'd run after Grasston returned and said he'd lost him. Annie thanked the couple and the man profusely, and they stepped away as the officer asked her for details of the assault. She did not hesitate to give him Grasston's name, though she hated that she didn't know where he'd been living since being sacked. "He's been harassing me at work and following me home. He blames me for losing his job."

"Where is your home?" the officer asked.

"Far from here, but I was going to my friend's flat a block away. Take me there, please."

She gave him the name of the Tuttles' bakery and her department at Macy's should he want to ask further questions. He accompanied her to Edna's, chaperoning her all the way to the door.

Edna opened the door saying, "I was wondering when you would get —" She looked taken aback by the officer's presence. "Sir? Annie? What happened?"

Annie turned to the bobby. "Thank you, Officer. I'll be all right now."

He tipped his cap and said, "The name is Officer Brady, miss. I suggest you stay here the night if you could. At least until we catch him."

Annie looked to Edna, whose eyes were wide with questions. "I can stay, can't I?"

"Of course, of course. Come in."

As soon as the door was closed behind her, Annie's legs faltered. She fell into the arms of her friend.

Dinner was eaten, the story was told, and the sewing lesson set aside. The horrors of what could have been consumed Annie and sapped her remaining energy, leaving her barely enough to button the nightgown

Edna lent her. The palms of her hands stung from the scraping they'd taken when she fell, and her muscles ached from the impact and the fight against Grasston. Even her face was sore from his hand trying to cover her mouth.

Edna finished smoothing the bedding in a small bedroom that used to belong to her son. "There now. Your bed is ready, and the Tuttles have been called and assured of your safety. There is nothing left for you to do but rest. Tomorrow is another day."

If only it were so easy. Annie lay down and let her friend tuck a sheet and blanket around her. "You've been so kind."

Edna ran a comforting hand over Annie's forehead. "Everything will be all right. They'll catch him."

"How? They don't know where he lives. He's but one man in an enormous city."

Edna nodded then gathered Annie's hands into her own. She bowed her head. "Father, thank You for saving Annie from that evil man. Help the police find Grasston and arrest him so he no longer causes harm to my dear friend, to Mildred, or to any other person. Give Annie the rejuvenating gift of sleep, and the courage and strength to deal with tomorrow, tomorrow. Amen."

"He *did* save me," Annie said. "God."

"Yes, He did. Now sleep."

She would try, but when she closed her eyes, Grasston's face loomed large and fierce.

CHAPTER TWELVE

"Are you sure you want to go to work today?" Edna asked Annie. "You have good reason not to."

She let Edna board the streetcar first and waited to answer until they were seated. "I have good reason to go in. I will not let Grasston stop me from earning a living."

"What if he comes back to Macy's? What if he follows you home tonight?"

She had no answer.

"Perhaps you should come and stay with me again," Edna said. "He doesn't know where I live."

"Can we be sure of that?" Annie asked. "I wouldn't put it past him to run away last night but circle back to see where I was heading. You may be in as much danger as I."

Suddenly Edna turned her head and looked at everyone in the streetcar. "I'm not sure I know what he looks like."

"He looks like evil," Annie said. She was tired of talking about him, thinking about him, dreaming about him.

"As soon as we get to work, you must inform Mr. Horace. He's seen him and talked to him. Have him be on the lookout."

It was a wise idea. As the streetcar jostled her to the left and right, forward and back, Annie closed her eyes and let the movement take her where it wished. Why fight it? She was clearly not in control.

Should I tell her?

Annie considered telling Mildred about how she'd been attacked. But every time she thought of it, Mildred would glare at her or blatantly turn her back.

"So be it," Annie finally said aloud. Luckily a customer came by and she was distracted. The busier the better.

She spotted Mr. Horace strolling by. He'd been true to his word that morning and made diligent rounds through Annie's department hourly. Every time he passed, he gave her a nod. His presence gave Annie a tentative peace.

A peace that could be shattered in a blink.

"Excuse me, miss," a customer said. "I asked for the blue ribbon, not green."

"Oh. Yes. I'm sorry." It was not her first error.

"What happened to your hands?" the woman asked, pointing to Annie's scraped palms.

"I fell." *I was tackled to the ground by a man who meant to force himself on me.*

"Put a potato poultice on them."

Annie had never heard of such a thing but thanked the woman and sent her on her way.

Mrs. MacDonald approached. "Go home, Annie. You've been through a very traumatic experience. No one expects you to act as though nothing happened."

Suddenly the stress of keeping a stiff upper lip combined with the stress of her attack, and she began to cry.

Mrs. MacDonald led her behind a pattern display and handed her a handkerchief. "That's it, then. You're going home right now." She looked around the store then called to Robbie, the package boy. "Robbie, I want you to accompany Miss Wood home. She's not feeling well. Can you do that for me?"

"Sure, Mrs. MacDonald." He looked at Annie. "You sick or somethun?"

Mrs. MacDonald reached into her pocket and gave him a few coins. "Here's money for the streetcar to her house and back. Now go up to the lockers and get her jacket, hat, and purse. Number . . . ?" She glanced at Annie.

"Number 387."

"Go on now. I'll make sure you stay on the clock."

He nodded and ran toward the stairs.

Annie dried her eyes. "I'm sorry to be such a bother, but I do think home is exactly where I need to be."

"My ma will love getting some fresh bread," Robbie said as he walked Annie from the streetcar to the Tuttles' bakery. "That's mighty nice of you to offer."

"It's nice of you to interrupt your day to bring me home," Annie said.

"Interrupting is good." Robbie walked with one foot in the street and one on the curb. "I likes getting out. Whenever they needs anyone to go on an errand, I'm their boy."

He was delightful. Actually, she thought of introducing him to Danny. Both boys had the same charming manner.

They approached the bakery, and Annie got her wish, as Danny was outside, painting the trim around the window.

"Annie! What are you doing home so early? Are you all right? We got the call last night from Mrs. Holmquist and were worried."

The thought of rehashing all that had happened made her stomach turn.

"She's not feeling good," Robbie said. "I brought her home. Got paid for it, too."

Annie hurried past his comments. "Danny, I'd like you to meet Robbie. He works at Macy's with me. Robbie, this is Danny, a very good friend who makes deliveries for the bakery."

Robbie's eyes grew wide. "You get to drive a wagon?"

"I do. And I get to paint, too, until the next delivery is ready."

She'd been right about their affinity for each other. She left them to talk and had her hand on the doorknob when she looked inside. Grasston was buying some bread from Mr. Tuttle.

She pulled her hand away and stepped back.

At that moment, he spotted her. He looked right at her and grinned. Then he tipped his hat as if nothing had happened.

Danny moved to her side. "What's wrong?"

Everything. She pointed at Grasston. It took Danny a moment to recognize him. "How did he get in there? I didn't see him go by me."

It didn't matter how, it just mattered why. "He's the one who attacked me last night." She held up her palms as evidence. "I called the police on him, but he ran away."

Robbie took a step toward the window to see him better. "Is he the man Mr. Horace told us about?"

She needed to make Robbie leave. She took him by the shoulders and turned him toward the streetcar stop in the next block. "Go on now. Get back to work before you get in trouble."

"But —"

"Go!"

Robbie reluctantly ran down the street.

Grasston chatted with Mr. Tuttle. Was there no end to his nerve?

Danny pulled the door open and, before Annie could stop him, stepped inside. "You!" he shouted, pointing a finger at Grasston. Annie followed him inside.

Grasston looked surprised — for a brief moment — then his smirk returned. "If it isn't Danny the hall boy. What'd you do? Run off with Annie? Isn't she a little old for you?"

Danny shoved him into the counter, making him drop his bread.

"Danny!" Mr. Tuttle said.

Thomas moved close, his hands covered with flour, his eyes alert.

Danny talked to the Tuttle men. "His name is Grasston and he used to work at the Friesens' with me and Iris, and —"

Grasston smoothed his coat and looked toward the back of the shop. "Is Iris here with you? I'd really like to see her. *Really* like to see her."

Although he was a good six inches shorter than Grasston, Danny swung to hit him in the jaw.

Grasston grabbed his wrist. "What do you think you're doing, you dumb kid?"

Danny yanked his hand away. "You attacked Annie last night. You hurt her."

Thomas moved closer, and Mr. Tuttle asked, "Is this true, Annie? This is the man?"

"Show 'em your hands," Danny said.

She did just that.

Mr. Tuttle called Jane from the back of the bakery. "Run down the street and get the police, Jane. Tell them to hurry."

She rushed past, giving Grasston a wide arc. Upon her exit Danny stood in front of the door, barring Grasston's escape. Thomas stepped around to Grasston's side of the counter.

He was cornered. The police would get

him, lock him up, and Annie would be safe again.

But then Grasston whipped out a knife, pointing it at each man. "Back away!"

Thomas raised his hands. "Annie, come here."

Gladly. She took cover behind him.

With a surge of motion, Grasston grabbed Danny's arm and yanked him away from the door so violently that he bounded off the wall and tumbled to the floor. He rushed outside and turned right, while Jane had turned left.

Annie ran to Danny's side. "Are you all right?"

Danny moaned as he got to his feet but immediately made for the door. Annie caught his arm, holding him back.

"Let me go! I'm not going to let him get away with this."

Annie held firm. "He has a weapon and he'll use it. Let the police handle it." *Hopefully they'll catch him this time.*

A customer came in, studied their faces a moment, and then asked, "You open?"

Mr. Tuttle ran a hand through his hair then said, "What can I get for you?"

Life goes on.

It was an odd fact to realize that Annie's

crises did not change the world.

Or stop it.

After Grasston ran from the bakery, there was still bread to get out of the oven, pans to wash, deliveries to make, and customers to serve.

After speaking with a constable, who assured Annie that Grasston would be caught, Mr. Tuttle suggested Annie go upstairs with the family. She could rest up there.

It was a nice thought, but impossible. With five children under the age of nine, there was seldom a quiet moment. They weren't naughty; they were just children.

Mrs. Tuttle was down in the bakery most of the time, leaving Annie alone with Iris and the brood. Iris got the older two girls interested in drawing pictures and the younger three boys playing with blocks: Nick and Newt built a tower, and two-year-old Joe knocked it down.

Iris brought Annie a cup of tea as they sat in the only two chairs that had cushions. "I'm sorry to hear Grasston is back."

Annie held the cup beneath her chin, enjoying the warmth and fragrance of its rising vapor. "He's not just back, he's vowed revenge. He's evil, Iris. Fully and completely evil." She noticed Iris wasn't drinking. "Aren't you having some?"

She shook her head. "Actually . . . can we move to the other room? I have laundry to take in."

They entered one of four small bedrooms and sat upon an oak chair in the corner. Iris opened the window and pulled in the laundry that had been drying on a line.

"I can help," Annie said, setting her tea aside.

"No, you sit. Relax. Talk to me while I fold it."

Annie felt guilty for sitting yet didn't feel up to doing much more.

"Do you really think he would have . . . forced you?" Iris asked.

"I do. He wants to hurt me. Shame me."

"As you shamed him?"

Annie was taken aback and was going to protest but realized Iris was right. "I did shame him, didn't I?"

"You took his gloves on a lark, but if it made him lose his job . . ."

She felt her defenses rise. "But he hurt you, too. He pushed himself on you, too."

"After you told on him about Miss Henrietta and he was scolded."

After I told. After I took his gloves. The wave of regret fell upon Annie's shoulders. "I never thought I'd say this, but he has a right to be angry with me."

"Angry is one thing, violent is another."

It was a relief to have it confirmed that despite his reasons, Grasston had gone too far.

Iris spread a shirt on top of the dresser and turned to Annie. "Sprinkle these shirts and aprons for me. Then roll them up to keep until I can iron them."

Annie took up the Coca-Cola bottle with a sprinkle attachment corked in the top and did as she was asked. Suddenly she remembered that she still hadn't heard Iris's news. "Tell me your news. I've been so consumed with my own troubles that I —"

"Yes, you have."

Annie accepted the rebuke. "I'm sorry I haven't been here for you."

Iris drew a clean nappy to her chest and faced her. "I was the one who wanted to be a shopgirl."

Annie suffered an inward sigh. "We've gone over this. The other day you said that Macy's was too large a store for you."

Iris nodded and looked to the floor then at Annie. "It was, and it is, and . . ." She smiled broadly. "The truth is, I've given up the notion of ever working in a shop. My future is set."

It sounded both ominous and hopeful. "How so?"

Iris looked past her to the main room. The children's voices could be heard, but none were close by. "Thomas proposed to me."

The sprinkle bottle slipped from Annie's hand, but she caught it before it hit the floor. "When did this happen?"

"A few days ago." She beamed. "He says he loves me."

If he did, Thomas had made quick work of it. Annie couldn't help but remember his initial interest in herself. "Do you love him?"

There was a moment's hesitation. "I think I do."

"*Think* you do?"

"I do. I do."

Annie hoped Iris wasn't getting married to be married. She was only seventeen and had only known Thomas a short time.

"Don't doubt me," Iris said. "Don't make me doubt myself. That's not fair. You've found yourself a new life, so don't begrudge me doing the same."

Annie pushed her doubts aside and embraced her. "Congratulations. I'm very happy for you. When is the —"

Annie's words were cut off by a horrific scream coming from the bakery below. It sounded like Mrs. Tuttle. Annie and Iris rushed down the stairs, with the children close behind. They nearly ran into Jane, coming up to get them.

"What happened?" Annie asked. "Is your mother all right?"

Jane's face was a mask of panic. "It's not her, it's . . ." She looked to Annie and then Iris. "It's Danny."

The girls ran into the bakery, looking this way and that for Danny. But he wasn't there. No one was. Everyone was outside.

Annie got there first. She fell upon Danny sprawled in the back of the delivery wagon. He was covered in blood.

Thomas held Iris back as she screamed, "No!"

So much blood, too much blood.

"Is he . . . ?" Annie asked.

"Yes," Gramps said. "He's dead. Beaten and stabbed."

Annie stared at Danny's bruised and bloodied face and torso. How could this broken being be her vibrant Danny? She took Danny's hand in hers. "Sweet boy, dear Danny. I'm so sorry."

"Why are *you* sorry?" Mrs. Tuttle asked.

Why couldn't they see the obvious? "It's Grasston. He did this. He was angry with me but took it out on Danny."

Iris broke away from the comfort of Thomas's arms and hurled herself toward Annie, pounding her with her fists. "You did this! This is all your fault!"

Thomas pulled Iris away so Annie was saved from her pummels.

But not from the truth.

Annie hugged herself and looked to the floor as she answered the constable's questions. If only she could disappear or wake up and find it was all an awful dream.

"What is this Mr. Grasston's first name?"

Shocked at the question, she looked up. "I don't know."

"Hmm. You say he had a grudge against you? What for?"

"He worked for the Friesen family as a footman. He bothered me and Danny's sister, Iris, and —"

"Bothered?"

It *was* too soft a word. "He made inappropriate advances on us."

"Oh."

"He did worse to me last night. He's been following me for days, showing up at my work, coming in the bakery just to intimidate me."

"So he was after you, not the young man."

There was the truth of it. "He blames me for him losing his job at the Friesens'."

"But hadn't he also 'annoyed' Mr. Dalking's sister?"

"I was the one who stood up to him." The rest of it would sound petty, but she had to say it. "I took his footman's gloves when the three of us left service, and he got in trouble for it. Told me that was the reason he was sacked."

The officer blinked. "Over gloves."

Annie realized how daft it sounded. How far fetched and false. She could honestly add, "I'm sure it wasn't just the gloves." She stood straighter and looked at the officer, emboldened by this truth. "He was a horrible man. He attacked me last night as I walked to a friend's house. He knocked me to the ground and would have . . ." She needed to just say it. "Would have had his way with me if my screams hadn't brought others to save me." She showed him her scraped palms. "See?"

His eyes grew wide. "I'm so sorry for your pain, Miss Wood."

"Thank you. I spoke with an Officer Brady. You might talk to him about it."

He nodded. "But the question remains, why would this Grasston kill Mr. Dalking if his beef was with you?"

She thought of Danny and his declaration to keep the two girls safe. "Danny was protective by nature. I'm sure he died defending me."

The officer nodded to the elder Mr. Tuttle. "That's what the old man said. Said a man approached them and started harassing the boy. Went away, but then must have caught him when he was alone."

To get to me. "You see what a despicable man he is? Instead of talking to me, why don't you go out and find him. Please. Before he hurts someone else."

"We're doing that, miss." He closed his notebook. "If I have any more questions, I'll come back. Until then, you have my condolences."

As the officer left, Annie did a double take when she saw Mr. Culver on the street nearby. He walked toward her.

Impulsively, she flew into his arms. "He killed him! He killed Danny!"

Mr. Culver held her close. "I'm so sorry."

Annie let his warmth and strong arms comfort her. She leaned her head against his shoulder and closed her eyes. *Don't let go. Don't ever let me go.* "Why are you here? How did you know where I live?"

"I went to Macy's for our baseball outing and —"

She pulled away. "I'm sorry. I should have sent word."

He shook his head, brushing away her apology. "Obviously that pales in relation to this horror. When I heard you'd gone home and pressed Mrs. MacDonald for why, she gave me your address so I could check on you. I hope you don't mind."

She longed to return to the safety of his arms. "I'm glad you're here."

He touched her arm. "I'm so sorry for this, and for what you endured last night. They'll catch him. I know they will."

Annie knew no such thing.

She spotted Iris coming toward them, her face sagging with grief and tears. Annie feared another pummeling and was surprised when Iris held out her arms.

Annie was glad for the embrace. "I'm so sorry, Iris," she whispered. "I never meant for any of this to happen."

Iris began her nod even before she left the embrace. "None of us did. He's an evil man. Our Danny died as he lived, protecting those he loved."

Annie drew in an enormous breath and let it out, relieving herself of the guilt that had restricted her breathing. "You forgive me, then?"

Iris nodded. "Of course I do." She returned to Annie's arms for a second embrace.

Chapter Thirteen

And God cried.

That's what it seemed like during the week of Danny's death. The morning after he died, the skies opened with the tears of every mother and sister and father and brother. God may have welcomed Danny into His everlasting arms, but those left without him couldn't grasp the whys of it.

There was no answer to that.

Annie had few memories of the wake and the funeral. The rain created a somber veil keeping the pain inside. She had vague memories of visits from Edna, Mrs. Mac-Donald, and Mr. Culver. Sean. For his care had shoved aside all formalities. He was Sean and she was Annie.

Annie awakened to commotion in the main bakery, and only by that sound realized it was time to get up. The first morning that Danny hadn't awakened her, she'd slept so long that Jane had been forced to come in the storeroom to get her up — for they were in need of more flour.

Not wanting to be embarrassed again, she'd started to sleep with the door ajar so she could hear them earlier. Hearing them now, she quickly rose, lit the lamp, and dressed. As she buttoned her work uniform, she worried about her day. She was going back to work for the first time since Danny's death. Macy's had been very understanding about her time off, but she could not take advantage of their largesse any longer. The Tuttle family and Iris had buried the dear boy, had found a proper pocket to keep their grief, and had gone back to work. Could she do any less?

Her eyes fell to the makeshift beds that used to belong to Danny and Iris. The covers and pillows were gone now. For even Iris had left her, moving upstairs to be with the family she now claimed as her own.

She paused in her buttoning. "I'm all alone here. I'm not family." And finally, as a natural conclusion to her statements, she said, "I can't stay here anymore."

The realization forced her to sit. Where could she go?

Edna's.

With the force of the answer Annie stood. She would ask her friend if she could be a lodger and felt totally assured Edna would take her in.

She finished dressing, and as a period to her decision, folded the linens of her bed and took them out to the bakery.

"Good morning, Annie," Jane said. Her eyes grazed over the linens. "Would you like me to wash them?"

Annie cleared her throat, needing all of them to hear. "I am moving out."

Mr. Tuttle, Gramps, and Thomas all stopped their work. "You're leaving us?"

She'd stated it too plain, without the proper preamble. "I am ever so grateful for the welcome you gave me and Iris . . . and Danny. The place to sleep, the meals, the care and sense of family."

"You are family," Jane said.

After a moment's hesitation, Annie shook her head. "Iris and Thomas are going to be married, and I am happy for them. It's a joyful event that will help ease our current pain. But . . ." She had no hard and fast reason. "I need to move on."

"But where will ye stay?" Mr. Tuttle asked.

"I've made a good friend at work. Mrs. Holmquist. I stayed with her the other night."

Mr. Tuttle nodded. Then Jane said, "We're going to miss you."

"And I will miss you. I am forever in your debt."

The sounds of the rest of the family coming downstairs for breakfast interrupted the conversation. Annie dreaded telling Iris, but the decision was made. The deed was done.

As the children swarmed around the table and took their places, Annie took Iris aside.

But instead of an argument, Iris said, "Are you sure?"

Annie felt the hint of disappointment rise then fall away. "I am."

Iris glanced at Thomas. "You will come to the wedding, though?"

"Of course. And I'll visit. Edna's isn't that far away."

With a nod, Iris hugged her. "Good-bye, then."

The finality of her words made Annie wonder if Iris still held Annie accountable for Danny's death.

So be it.

Since the good-byes had already been accomplished, Annie decided to forgo breakfast. She quickly packed her bag, took the hot roll offered by Mr. Tuttle — and a loaf to give to Robbie for seeing her home from Macy's a week ago — and left the bakery.

As the door shut behind her, she felt as if more than a door had been closed. A chapter of her life had ended.

And a new chapter had begun.

"Of course you can move in with me," Edna said.

Annie hadn't realized she'd been holding her breath. She breathed free. "Thank you so much. I shan't be any trouble, and I'll be a proper lodger and help with expenses."

"Not a worry. When can you move in?"

"Straightaway? Tonight?"

Edna chuckled. "You are a girl who makes quick decisions."

She hoped it wasn't a rash one.

It was odd being back at work, waiting on customers, smiling. Helping a woman choose a pattern and fabric seemed frivolous compared to the life-and-death situations she'd endured the past week.

Her only relief was that Mildred had kept to herself. Though others had offered condolences and wanted to know the lurid details and whether Grasston had been arrested — which he had not — Mildred offered accusatory glances. Accusing Annie of what, she wasn't sure.

It didn't matter. Mildred Krieger had no part in Annie's life. She was an annoying fly on the back side of a window.

As Annie was finishing up with a customer, she spotted Mildred talking to Mrs. Reinhold, the customer she'd helped during one of her first days on the job. She saw the woman pointing at Annie, and Annie waved. With a nod, Mrs. Reinhold said a few more words to Mildred and then came over to Annie's counter.

"Good morning, Mrs. Reinhold," she said. "I'll be with you in just a few minutes."

"I will wait," she said.

As Annie wrote up the other customer's purchase, Mrs. Reinhold addressed the woman. "You are smart to let Miss Wood help you with your sewing purchases," she said. "Look at what she helped me put together." She spread her arms and turned in a circle.

Only then did Annie realize she was wearing the gold coat and brown skirt they had designed together. "What a fine job you did," Annie said. "You are a very talented seamstress."

"And you are a very talented fashion designer. From skirt to coat, to hat and gloves."

The other customer pointed to the hat. "Did you make that, too?"

"I did — with Miss Wood's design expertise."

The new customer turned to Annie. "I'd

like to make a similar hat to go with the fabric I am purchasing. Can you help me?"

Annie feared the extra time required would offend Mrs. Reinhold. She need not have worried. "Don't concern yourself with the delay, Miss Wood. I have the time. And if you don't mind, I'd like to add my two cents to the process."

The other woman beamed. "I'd welcome your opinion."

Annie proceeded to help the ladies.

While Mildred stewed nearby.

Annie was cleaning off the cutting table when she looked up and saw the owner of Macy's standing before her.

"Mr. Straus."

"Good day, Miss Wood."

She put a hand to her hair, hoping the stray strands were neatly tucked away. "What can I do for you, sir?"

"Continue on as you have been doing," he said. "I've heard good things about your work."

"Thank you, sir."

His face grew serious. "I wanted to check to see how you were after the death of your friend. I offer my sincere condolences."

"Thank you, sir. I am coping. And I want to thank you for the time off. I enjoy working here, so to have my job still available after being gone a week is —"

"Paid time off," he said.

She gawked. "Paid?"

"It is the least we can do for our employees in their time of need."

"Oh, sir. Thank you so much."

"You're quite welcome." He looked embarrassed and quickly said, "Carry on."

She watched him walk away, his hands clasped behind his back. He greeted many of the clerks and customers, the store's attentive father.

Soon after Mr. Straus's visit, Sean stopped by. Annie was busy with customers, but he quickly wrote something on a slip of paper and handed it to her. When she was free she read it: *Skip lunch and let's have our baseball date today at 2:30. At least we can hear part of the game.*

They were still playing the World Series?

Annie asked Mrs. MacDonald about it. "Oh yes," she said. "They played the first three games, but then because of constant rain, game four in Philly and today's game here were postponed. Tomorrow is the last game — in Philadelphia. Unless we win both, and then they'll have to play a seventh game."

Annie was getting confused. "Are we winning the series?"

"We need a win today to stay alive. Philadelphia is ahead three games to one."

The only detail that mattered was that the Giants needed to win today, and Sean wanted her to be there. With him. She showed Mrs. MacDonald the note. "May I go? For a short while?"

The woman smiled. "Of course you can. You need some frivolity in your life."

The morning flew by, and soon she held Sean's arm tightly as they made their way through the crowd in front of the Herald Newspaper offices. A police officer shooed them up onto the curb and sidewalk, trying to keep Broadway clear. But both sides of the street were shoulder to shoulder.

"There," Sean said, pointing to the building. "That's the Play-O-Graph. See the diamond on it?"

"But what does it mean?"

He explained the game: bases, outs, strikes. He received help from men wedged on either side of them.

"I think I have it," she said, truthfully. "It's a bit like cricket where they hit a ball and run while it's being fielded."

One of the men laughed. "You could be right, miss. I don't know cricket, but your quick understanding of baseball means you've done better'n my wife. I've been trying to get her interested for ten years but she won't have nothing to do with it."

"You have a fan," Sean whispered in her ear.

"I hope I have more than one."

He winked at her.

She enjoyed the crowded conditions, for it enabled her to stand close to Sean without fear of seeming too fresh. She stood in front of him, enabling her ear to be near his lips. He put a protective arm around her, keeping her safe. And happy. It felt good to be happy.

But Grasston is still out there.

She shoved the thought away. He wouldn't dare bother her with thousands of witnesses.

A man stood beside the Play-O-Graph, getting news that was relayed from inside. "Miller on first!"

The crowd roared. And Annie's heart soared.

"Seeing you three times in one day is quite the treat," Sean said.

Annie retrieved her carpetbag from her locker and put on her coat. "You don't have to help me move to Edna's," she said. "All I have is this one bag — which I can easily carry."

Nearby, Edna secured her hat with a hat pin. "Quiet, Annie. If a man offers to help, you let him help." She winked at Sean. "Especially a handsome man."

"Are you flirting with me, Mrs. Holmquist?"

"Was I? Who knew I still had it in me. Come now, you two. I want to stop at the butcher's and get some beef. I'm going to make you Swedish meatballs."

"You don't have to feed me," Sean said. "I work for free."

"If a woman offers to feed you, you let her feed you."

Annie's few belongings were moved into Edna's extra room, and then dinner was enjoyed by all. Annie was impressed by how easily Sean kept the conversation lively. Between his stories about growing up in Brooklyn, Edna's stories about her early days at Macy's, and Annie's stories about working as a maid at Crompton Hall, time flew by.

Edna shoved her third cup of coffee away and stood, groaning as she arched her back. "Sitting so long makes these old muscles tighten like a clothesline in the winter."

Sean stood, too. "I should be getting home

219

myself. Tomorrow is a workday."

Annie hated to see him go. "I thoroughly enjoyed today," she said.

"Especially since the Giants won the game."

"It was fun to lark about and see a portion of it, and then hear the crowd cheering even after I was back at work."

"I'll make a fan of you yet," Sean said. He moved toward the door but detoured to the sewing machine where Annie's blouse was being sewn. "Is this the product of your lessons?"

"It is," she said. "And you'll be pleased to know I used a Butterick pattern. Sort of."

"What do you mean 'sort of'?"

She took up the blouse — which only had one sleeve set in. "Since I'm a bit taller than most women, Edna showed me how to alter the patterns to fit. Plus, I wanted to try a tight sleeve to the elbow and let it go into a wider flare and —"

"I'm not sure I understand."

Annie took up a pencil and paper and sketched it for him. "See? The upper sleeve is straight, but the bottom half billows out at the elbow and is secured again at the cuff." She studied it a moment. Something was missing. She took the edge of the pencil and smudged a bit of lead on the underside of the sleeve to better show it off. "There. That's better."

"I'm impressed."

"It was just an idea I had and —"

"I'm impressed by your sketching ability." He took the page and showed it to Edna. "Did you know she could draw like this?"

"I did not. Annie, why didn't you tell me you were an artist?"

"I'm no artist."

"You most certainly are," Sean said. "Look at how you captured the design with just a few lines. You even added shadow. You must have had some training."

She laughed at the thought. "I've been a housemaid since I was young. I've never had time or the inclination to draw anything, much less become an artist."

"I'm even more impressed," Sean said. "To have a talent you don't even know you have?" He shook his head. "Fascinating."

Edna handed the drawing back, and Annie looked at it with new eyes. It *was* good — though next time she would add the entire bodice to the drawing to give it context.

Sean put on his coat and hat. "You are full of surprises, aren't you, Annie-girl?"

Apparently.

■ ■ ■ ■

Before Annie turned out the light in her room at Edna's, she stepped across the hall and rapped on the other bedroom door. "You still awake?"

"I am. Come in."

Edna was sitting up in bed, reading the Bible. "Do you have everything you need?"

That one innocent question punched a hole in the wall Annie had built around herself, letting her emotions rush out in a torrent. She fell into Edna's arms.

"Oh my. Oh sweet girl."

"My best friend is dead!"

Edna stroked her back. "I know."

Annie thought of more. "I don't have a spot at the Tuttles' anymore."

"I know."

"Grasston's still out there. Who knows if he'll find me again and hurt me."

"I know."

Annie sat up to face her. "Iris is getting married."

"The gall."

The change in Edna's answer made Annie blink. "I'm not saying it's a bad thing. I'm happy for her."

"Are you?"

"Of course."

"You don't sound happy. You sound peeved."

Annie stood beside the bed. "I never expected her to find love — at least not so quickly."

"Before you."

The words could have stung, but oddly they did not. "I'm not seeking marriage."

"Was Iris?"

Annie didn't know. "She wanted to work in a shop, but then the Tuttles needed her help with the children, and . . ."

"And she was happy doing that?"

"I suppose."

Edna peered at her over her glasses.

"Yes. She was happy."

"Isn't that what you want for her?"

"I do." Annie didn't like how Edna flipped her grievances over upon themselves. "But Danny is dead!"

"A true tragedy. But are you upset because he died so young and lost the chance at a fuller life, or because he left you?"

"You're turning everything around."

Edna removed her glasses and set the Bible on the bedside table. "I'm merely pointing out that everything you mentioned had *you* as the focus. The truth is, it's not just about you."

"That's rude."

"Truth can be rude, but that doesn't stop it from being the truth." Edna patted the side of the bed, and Annie sat. "Yes, your best friend died, but he's the one who had his young life taken from him."

"I didn't mean to belittle his loss, but —"

Edna raised a hand, stopping her words. "It's true you don't have a room at the Tuttles' anymore — or perhaps, even a place in their family. But you are not on the street, not destitute. You do have a room — a real room with a bed to sleep upon, not a makeshift bed on some flour sacks."

Shame took a turn. "I'm sorry. I don't mean to downplay all you've offered me. I truly appreciate the room. Actually, I've never had a room of my own."

Edna cocked her head. "Never?"

Annie let her thoughts trail through her life. "When I was small I shared with my brother, and when I got a job with the Kidds I shared a room with another maid. Even here in New York I shared a room — and a bed — with Iris." She was shocked by her realization. "And at the Tuttles' I shared a room with Iris *and* Danny."

Edna spread her arms. "You have risen up in the world."

Why hadn't she thought of it like that?

"Thank you, Edna. For everything you've done for me. Befriending me, giving me sewing lessons, feeding me, giving me the room, encouraging me . . ."

"I did all those things — do all those things — because I care for you."

Annie took her hand. "I care for you, too. Immensely. You're like the mother I never had."

"You mother wasn't around?"

A snicker escaped. "She was around in body but had none of your loving and generous character."

"I *am* exceptional," Edna said with a laugh.

Annie clasped her hand harder. "Actually, you are. My parents begrudge the world its every smile or bit of happiness. They feel due, as if everyone and everything owes them. They can't see that they have nothing because they give nothing. They don't understand it isn't just about them."

Edna's left eyebrow rose, and Annie realized Edna had just said it wasn't all about *her.*

She tried to recover from the similarity. "But they are leeches, sucking the world dry. Nothing is ever good enough or enough enough. It's left them gorged with pessimism."

"I'm so sorry. What a horrible way to live."

Annie squeezed her eyes shut, ridding her mind of the memories. "Their attitude is why I went into service when I was fourteen. I had to get away *from* them or be pulled under *with* them."

"All the more reason to count your blessings. You are here, across the world, fully free to be all you can be."

"I am free, aren't I?"

"Completely. You have a job you enjoy, a warm bed, the most fabulous landlady —"

"Absolutely."

Edna held up a finger. "And you have a newly discovered talent to draw."

The idea was still hard to fathom. "I never knew I could do that."

"A talent uncovered is a talent recovered."

"Recovered?"

"It's always been with you, Annie. You just didn't know it was there. It's a known fact that God's gifts can't be returned."

God gave her that gift? It made her wonder what other talents lay hidden.

"You've forgotten one other blessing in your life."

"What's that?"

"*Who's* that?"

"Ah. Sean."

"Yes, ah Sean. He's a good man who likes

226

you very much."

"But —"

"Before you discount his interest, think about all he's done for you in the short time you've known him. He's defended you to his company against Mildred's complaint."

"A stupid complaint."

"Let me finish. After Grasston assaulted you, Sean sought you out to check on your well-being."

"He did."

"That took effort. He also was a comfort after Danny was killed, yes?"

She nodded. "He came to the Tuttles' every day. He accompanied me to the funeral."

"Which shows how much he cares."

It does.

"And," Edna said, "he took you out to listen to a baseball game during the World Series."

Annie laughed. "I never would have experienced that without him."

"I'm betting there are many things you can experience together." Edna's smile spoke beyond the words.

"I am not ready to be courted."

"You may not be ready to be courted, but you *are* being courted. By Sean and by someone else."

"Who?"

Edna lay a hand on her Bible. "The Almighty is working all around you if you just open your eyes. He's waiting for you to notice Him."

Annie wanted to respond but couldn't find the right words. "If you say so."

"I do." Edna squeezed Annie's hand. "Now go to sleep, girlie. And may all your dreams reveal wonderful surprises."

Annie snuggled amid the covers of her very own bed, in her very own room. Edna was right. Even through the hard times of the past few weeks, there had been good times, times of great blessing.

"The Almighty is working all around you if you just open your eyes. He's waiting for you to notice Him."

She was still a bit baffled by Edna's words. She believed in God. She even prayed occasionally.

When I need something.

Wasn't that all right? Didn't God want to hear her needs so He could provide for her?

More of Edna's words returned: *"It's not just about you."*

She sat up in bed. "Then who's it about?"

"Me."

The thought surprised her. What also

surprised her was the unexpected knowledge that "Me" was God. God was claiming that *He* wanted the attention? That it was all about *Him*? Wasn't that selfish?

"Come to Me first. You are Mine and I am yours."

The words that were unspoken yet felt frightened her. The concept of a God who gave Himself to her and drew her close was beyond any father-child relationship she'd ever experienced. Fathers weren't loving. They were judgmental, disparaging, and cruel.

"I love you, Annie."

God. God was telling her He loved her? This was too strange. Things like this didn't happen to her.

Annie lay down and pulled the covers close.

Chapter Fourteen

Annie looked up from a display case of scissors to see two police officers standing in front of her. One of them was Officer Brady, who'd spoken with her after her assault. Memories of that attack and Danny's death forced themselves to the front of her thoughts.

"Officer Brady, is everything all right?"

The two bobbies touched the brims of their hats, and Officer Brady said, "I believe it is, Miss Wood. For we have caught your assailant."

The fear that had rushed forward retreated like a tide going out to sea. "Grasston."

"Oscar Grasston, yes, miss," the other officer said.

"So he's going to jail forever?"

The officers exchanged a glance. "For assault, no."

"But he killed Danny."

"Allegedly," Officer Brady said. "We've

not found a witness."

"Yet," the other officer said.

"But he's guilty! He did it! Gramps saw them arguing then found Danny stabbed. All after Grasston threatened him with a knife at the bakery."

Officer Brady made a "calm down" motion with his hands, and Annie realized she'd raised her voice. She saw Mrs. Gold approach Mrs. MacDonald to talk, her eyes on Annie and the officers.

This was neither the time nor the place.

"We need you to come to the precinct and pick him out of a lineup."

"But I know he assaulted me. I don't need to identify him." She leaned over the counter and lowered her voice. "He knocked me down. He was on top of me."

Did bobbies blush? Both of them looked down, cleared their throats, and then looked back at Annie. "It's just a formality, Miss Wood, as we do have statements from others at the scene. You confirm he's the one and we'll take care of the rest."

Annie noticed too many eyes watching. She needed them gone. "May I come after work? Around six?"

"We can hold him that long."

That long? He needed to be jailed forever.

Brady handed her a card that showed the

precinct address, and they left.

Before they were even out of the store, they were accosted by Mr. Horace and another plainclothes security man. As that was happening, Mrs. Gold approached Annie. "Miss Wood, this sort of attention is not welcome in Macy's."

"It's not attention, ma'am, it's police work."

"I realize that, but uniformed officers disturb the customers."

"I don't understand why. They should feel more secure seeing officers here."

"I will not play tit for tat with you, Miss Wood. I merely mean to impress on you the need to maintain an enjoyable shopping experience."

Annie understood, but it rankled her. "If you're interested, they caught the man who assaulted me, the man who killed my friend. I will be visiting the precinct to identify him."

"On your own time, I assume."

"On my own time." This was wearying. "You're treating me as if I caused all this."

Mrs. Gold's hesitation was telling. "Carry on, then, Miss Wood. But please inform the officers that next time they need to speak with you, they can send you a note."

The silly thought of the two burly officers

writing a note made her smile.

"Do you find this amusing, Miss Wood? Because I assure you I take it very seriously."

"I take this seriously, too, Mrs. Gold. After all, my friend and I were the victims."

With the lift of an eyebrow the supervisor walked away, only to be quickly replaced by Mrs. MacDonald — and Mildred, who'd somehow made her way from fabrics over to the sewing notions section, where she busied herself sorting tape measures. Annie was beyond caring. Let her listen in.

"So?" Mrs. MacDonald asked.

"They caught him." She looked directly at Mildred. "They caught your friend, Grasston. He's been arrested for assault and murder." She forgave herself the embellishment.

Suddenly Mildred stopped her sorting and came close, her forehead furrowed. "He . . . he's arrested?"

"He is. I tried to warn you. I hope you didn't spend any time alone with him."

Mildred shook her head vehemently. But then she began to cry.

Tears? "What did he do to you?" Annie asked.

"Nothing."

"Then why are you crying?" Mrs. Mac-

233

Donald asked. "Did he hurt you?"

Mildred retrieved a handkerchief and dabbed at her eyes and nose. "Thankfully, no. He wanted to take me out, but we never went anywhere. He gave me attention here at the store and led me on then disappeared and never came back."

So it was an issue of pride. "He disappeared because he'd killed Danny."

Mildred turned away from them and blew her nose. When she turned back she said, "I'm crying because I finally get a man interested in me, and he turns out to be a criminal."

That *would* hurt.

Annie let Mildred cry on her shoulder.

Would wonders never cease?

"You're treating me as if I caused all this."

Although Annie's previous words to Mrs. Gold were said in her own defense, and though Mrs. Gold had not confirmed them, they hung over Annie the rest of the day as her own private condemnation.

For it was true. She was to blame for all the problems Grasston had caused, and who knew how many more people he had — or would — hurt because he was angry at *her*.

Oddly, during her lunch break in the cafeteria, she saw men talking among themselves — their glances revealing that she was the subject of their discussions. And the women . . . When she went to sit with some girls from the shoe department, they quickly left.

Now I know how Mildred feels eating alone. She had the notion to take her tray and eat in the locker room.

While she ate her soup and buttered her bread, her nerves tingled as if she were being electrified. When a group of young male clerks started giggling as they looked at her, she'd had enough. Annie pushed her chair back with a titter of its legs against the floor. She stood — though the moment she stood, she told herself to sit back down before she did something stupid.

She didn't listen to her own warning. Instead, she scanned the room and said, "Attention! I'd like your attention, please."

She got what she asked for. Talking stopped and all eyes were on her.

"I am ever so glad to provide you with your daily dose of gossip. But know this: the man the police have arrested, the man they want me to identify after work this very evening, is evil. Oscar Grasston attacked me, followed me for days, harassed me, threatened me, and stabbed a dear friend to death when he came to my defense. He killed Danny, a thirteen-year-old boy who will never have the chance to grow up and become the fabulous man he was destined to be. So if you wish to chunter on and giggle and talk behind your hands, at least get the story straight. Otherwise, keep your nonsense to yourselves."

She was glad the chair was there, because her last words did her in. She was about to pull the chair back toward the table to finish her meal when a man came close and helped her scoot it in. "Well said, Miss Wood."

As he stepped away, the rest of the cafeteria began to applaud. There were even a few shouts of "Go get 'em, Annie!"

The notion of eating in the locker room returned. But then someone joined her at the table.

"Mildred."

"I thought you could use a friend."

Well, then. Would wonders never cease?

"I think that lace would look lovely on your blouse, Mrs. Dresden. How many yards would you like?"

As Annie's customer did the calculations, Annie spotted Mr. Straus walking by. After her outburst in the cafeteria she hesitated to make eye contact. Surely he'd heard about the woman gone off her trolley, making a scene.

But as he strolled past, he caught her glance and in return offered her a wink and a thumbs-up.

She laughed aloud. Would wonders never cease?

Sean took her hand as they left Macy's at the end of the day. "This is not how I planned to spend our evening together. Although I will say visiting a police station is a unique outing."

"And not just visiting," Annie said, "but making sure an evil meater stays in jail."

"Meater?"

"Coward. For he is that, you know. Only a coward would hurt women and children."

Sean pulled her hand around his arm. "Don't be nervous. I won't let him hurt you."

"I *am* nervous because I'm afraid not you or anyone can stop him if he's set loose."

"Then we'll have to make sure he's not set loose."

"But they're only wanting me to identify him as the man who assaulted me, having nothing to do with Danny's death."

Sean stopped walking and looked at her. "I thought this was for —"

She shook her head. "They have no witnesses for it."

"But we all know he did it."

She shrugged. "Without witnesses . . ."

Justice would not be done.

Annie clung to Sean's arm as the men were
lined up in a viewing room at the police station. They each held a number in front of
them. Although they were in the light and
she was standing in the dark, she knew she
could be seen.

Grasston could see her.

And just as she zeroed in on him, he did
the same for her. His jaw clenched, and his
eyes bore into hers for just a moment before
he looked away.

"Number three," she said immediately.

"Wait a minute, miss," the officer said. "I
haven't even asked the question yet."

Sean intervened. "Then ask it, sir."

"Which man best resembles the man who
attacked you on October 17?"

Annie wasn't sure she had air enough in
her lungs to answer again, but she dug deep
and said, "Number three is the man. He's
the one who hurt me — and killed my
Danny."

She saw Grasston flinch. Let him.

"He's not here for that, miss. But thank

you. That will be all."

She couldn't get out of the room fast enough. The officer led her down the hall to the precinct offices. "So what now, Officer? When will he be tried?"

"Can't say at the moment, Miss Wood. We'll let you know. You'll have to come back and testify."

Annie let out a sigh. "Isn't identifying him enough?"

" 'Fraid not. But we thank you for coming down."

She needed more from them. "What about the murder of my friend, Danny Dalking? Have you found a witness yet?"

"Not that I'm aware of, miss. But be assured we're doing our best."

She left with Sean, feeling spent. "I fear their best will not be enough." The image of Grasston showing up at times and places of his own choosing haunted her. "Even if he's convicted of assault, that won't keep him in jail very long." She voiced a thought that had niggled at her for days. "Sometimes I wish he'd really hurt me. That way he'd be put away longer. Or maybe it would have delayed him enough so they would have caught him right then and there. Maybe he wouldn't have been free to kill Danny."

Sean put his arm around her shoulders.

"Don't say such a thing. We have to be thankful he didn't hurt you more than he did."

She was unconvinced. "I would gladly suffer if it would bring Danny back." Tears took over, and she let herself be comforted.

CHAPTER FIFTEEN

It was done. Her testimony against Grasston for the assault was over. Being in the same room with him, feeling the heat of his stare . . .

Now it was up to the judge.

Sean accompanied her out of the courtroom. "You're shaking."

An inner quaking started deep inside and overflowed to her extremities. She held her hand out, and seeing the result, pulled her fingers into a fist to stay them. "I don't know why I thought telling the truth would be easy."

They walked down the courthouse steps arm in arm. "I saw how he glared at you the entire time. But he had no defense. Explaining your fall by saying you tripped? Making him trip on top of you? Very lame."

As if minding Sean's words, Annie tripped on the steps. Without his help, she would have ended up at the bottom.

"I'm a jumble," she said. "The lid is off the teapot. My life is boiling over, making the fire go out."

Sean laughed. "I've never heard it described that way. How British of you."

"How would an American say it?"

He was quiet a moment then said, "Your life is a mess."

"That it is."

"I have a way to change all that," he said as they headed back to Macy's.

She felt a surge of panic. The only drastic *change* she could think of involved him proposing marriage. She was nowhere near ready for such a question. "I think I'm afraid to ask."

"You don't trust me?"

"I'm not certain how to answer that."

He pulled his hat off and thrust it against his chest. "I am utterly crushed. And just for that, I'm not going to tell you my idea."

"Now you have me curious."

"Too late," he said, returning his bowler to his head.

She was too drained to play games. "Please tell me. I do want to know."

"I think I'll tell you at dinner tonight, when I have the proper time to explain my idea."

"Explaining an idea" didn't sound like a

phrase associated with a proposal. Her mind eased.

After taking time off to testify against Grasston, Annie rushed directly to her department at Macy's. She folded her jacket around her purse and set her hat on top, all under the counter. She checked her reflection in a hand mirror, tucking the stray strands of hair where they belonged.

"So?" Annie turned around to find Mildred standing before her.

"I testified. Now it's up to the judge."

"He'll go to jail, won't he?"

The strained look on her face reinforced Annie's feeling that something *had* gone on between Grasston and Mildred beyond what she'd admitted. "I'm sure he will." *For how long is the issue.*

For Mildred's sake, Annie gathered a smile she did not feel. "Enough of Grasston. Let's not let the likes of him cloud our day." She looked around the department. "Have you been busy?"

Before Mildred could answer, Annie spotted Iris walking down the store aisles. She rushed to greet her friend, kissing her on the cheeks. "Iris! I'm so glad to see you."

"And I you," Iris said. She looked around the store. "Remember when you and I and . . . and Danny came to Macy's, exploring?"

"I do," Annie said. "That outing sparked the idea to work here." She wasn't sure whether she should mention Danny further, but it seemed wrong not to. "How are the Tuttles? How is everyone faring without him?"

Iris pulled an envelope from her pocket. "This is for you. Open it."

Annie broke the seal and removed a hand-lettered card. "It's an invitation to your wedding?"

Iris pointed to the card. "December 23. The church is a few blocks from the bakery."

It was only six weeks away. Annie embraced her. "I'm happy for both of you."

Iris's smile faded. "You don't think it's improper to get married so soon after Danny's death?"

"I think he'd want you to be together as soon as possible."

Iris nodded, making the daisy on her hat bob. "That's what we thought. Plus, we decided to marry soon because there's an apartment coming open in the building across the street, so we needed to make a quick decision and grab it up."

"Your own apartment . . ."

"I know. And me being married. Ain't it

strange?"

"It's wonderful. You deserve some happiness." Annie spotted Mrs. Gold giving her a disparaging look for chatting instead of selling. "May I interest you in a dress pattern, Miss Dalking?"

Iris looked confused then saw the supervisor. "I'd like that very much."

Annie led her to the catalog, and they leafed through it. Suddenly Annie got an idea. "What if I made you a wedding dress?" She turned the pages to the illustrations of fancier dresses.

"Ooh," Iris said. Then she shook her head. "I don't have the need for a fancy dress — nor a white one. But a new one I could wear to church Sundays? Yes, please."

"Perfect." Annie was a bit relieved. She's just finished her first skirt and blouse from scratch. To tackle a dress of satin and lace would have tested her abilities. Since the pricey fabrics were out of the mix, Annie had another idea. "In fact, I will pay for everything *and* do the work. As my wedding gift to you."

Iris flung her arms around Annie's neck. "You're so good to me. Thank you!"

Annie pulled out a chair so Iris could sit and properly peruse the pattern illustrations. Luckily, she wasn't choosy and quickly picked out a pattern for a dress. Annie studied it a minute to make sure she could sew it, and decided she could. The dress had a slim sleeve and silhouette that was popular. The neck was scooped with trim along the edge. The dress itself hung straight from a slightly higher waist, and an overskirt was cut short on the diagonal from knee to ankle, revealing the drapery of the main skirt beneath.

"I don't want a train," Iris said, pointing to the slight train of six to eight inches in the back. "I wouldn't want the risk of getting it mucked up on the street."

"That change is easy enough." Luckily, they had the right size in stock. "Now, for the fabric. What's your favorite color?"

"Blue," Iris said, without hesitation.

Annie made a beeline for the perfect piece, a dusty-blue moss cloth, a mixture of wool and silk that felt like a soft moss. Iris ran her hand over it, caressing it. "It's beautiful."

"You'll be beautiful in it — and it has enough body to hang nicely." *And sew easily.* "Perhaps the underskirt could be a crepe that would drape, and the wide decorative strip on the bottom of the overskirt could be a matching satin?"

"I put myself in your fashionable hands,"

Iris said.

They finished gathering the notions Annie would need — with her keeping track of the cost for her own sake — when Officer Brady approached.

A verdict already? Annie greeted him and introduced Iris — but he already knew her from the murder investigation. "Good news I hope?" Annie asked. "How long is his sentence?"

He swirled his mustache and did not meet her eyes. "I hate to tell you this, ladies, but Oscar Grasston escaped custody."

Annie and Iris exchanged an incredulous glance. "He's loose?" Annie managed.

"I'm afraid so."

"How could that happen?"

"As he was being led from the jail to the courtroom for sentencing, he pushed an officer down the stairs and ran out a side entrance — handcuffs and all. We ran after him, but he . . . Well, he slipped away."

He's free.

Mr. Horace approached and was filled in. "Do you think Miss Wood is in danger?"

"I do," Officer Brady answered. "He knows where she works and has come here before."

"He also knows where *I* live," Iris said. "He came in the bakery the day he killed

Danny." She clutched her drawstring purse, her eyes darting. "He doesn't like us, either. You interviewed all of us after Danny died." She looked at Annie with panicked eyes. "He's going to come after us!"

Brady sighed and spoke to Mr. Horace. "I think it would be best if we accompany both of these girls home to the bakery, for their own safety."

"I . . . I don't live there anymore," Annie said. "I have a room with another clerk."

"Does Grasston know where you live?"

She thought a moment. "I don't think so. He assaulted me nearby, but ran in the opposite direction after help came."

He twirled his mustache again, obviously thinking. "I think you can go back to your place, then. But I will provide an officer to accompany you."

Annie shook her head. "A male friend is coming to get me after work. He will see me home safely."

"But what about here at the store?" Mr. Horace asked Brady. "We certainly don't want that man coming in here and causing trouble."

"I'll put officers at the doors, and you make your security men aware." He turned to Annie and Iris. "We are heartily sorry, ladies. We are doing our best to catch him."

He spoke to Iris alone. "Are you ready to go home, miss? I will fetch an officer to accompany you."

"I can finish up here," Annie said. The girls embraced and wished each other well.

Mr. Horace left to alert his men. As soon as they were gone, Mrs. MacDonald and Mildred came close. "He's free?" Mildred asked under her breath.

"He is."

Her head shook back and forth, back and forth. "What if he comes after me?"

"Does he know where you live?"

She bit the nail of her thumb. "No. We met elsewhere."

"Then you should be all right."

Mrs. MacDonald had a solution. "I'll accompany you home tonight, Mildred."

Everyone was covered — as well as they could be.

Sean was a good sport about postponing their dinner so Annie could get safely home. Although Annie wanted to enjoy the time alone with him, she could not get Grasston out of her mind. Even as they got on the streetcar she searched the crowd for her tormentor. She held the parcel containing the supplies for Iris's wedding dress tightly against her chest, like a shield.

249

Sean must have noticed, because as soon as they were seated he said, "Surely he wouldn't be stupid enough to show his face."

"He's not stupid, he's obsessed. With me. With revenge."

"All because you took his gloves."

"And cost him his job."

Sean shook his head. "A footman could dye his gloves purple and it wouldn't be enough to get him sacked."

"You don't know the butler."

"Neither do you. How long were you visiting at the Friesens'?"

She had to think. "Five or six days."

"Less than a week."

"Yes."

"So in less than a week, as the maid of a guest, you single-handedly were responsible for making the head footman — which is a prestigious position — lose his job? You have that sort of power?"

It did seem far fetched. "But he blamed me. In person, the first time he came to Macy's."

Sean looked out of the streetcar window a few moments before turning back to her. "Perhaps he's simply one of those people who have to blame someone — anyone — for their own shortcomings and mistakes."

That made her feel better, until the truth pressed forward. "Be that as it may, Grasston's character flaws do not change the fact that he attacked me, did something to Mildred she won't talk about, and killed Danny. We could determine with one hundred percent certainty that the reason he's perpetrating these crimes is because he hates his mother or can't stand cloudy days. The whys behind his actions do little good other than help us wrap our minds around his actions. They do not *change* his actions."

Sean let out a sigh. "Where did you get your keen, logical mind, Miss Wood? It's quite impressive."

Accepting the compliment spurred her to answer with confidence. "I have done more than my share of dissecting character while trying to figure out my parents. I quickly learned that such an analysis — though interesting — made it clear that I had little choice but to accept them for who they are and make choices based on logic rather than emotion."

He leaned slightly against the outer wall of the streetcar to better study her. "Tell me about them."

"This is peculiar," she said. "I rarely think of them, yet just the other night Edna had

251

me talking about them, and now you."

"Why don't you think of them often?"

She placed the parcel in her lap and laid her hands upon it. "I shouldn't be here in America."

"They disapprove."

"They don't know."

"*That* is peculiar."

She nodded. "By saying I shouldn't be here, I mean that the opportunity to travel or to work in a fine store like Macy's are achievements I never dreamt of as a child, because I couldn't even conceive of such possibilities. I grew up poor."

"There's no shame in having meager beginnings. Many of us did."

Us? She'd ask him more about his roots later. She wanted him to understand hers. "Being poor in status is one thing. My family was poor in spirit. In their attitude." She looked at him, needing to see his eyes. "It *is* possible to be happy and poor." She put a fist against her chest. "Happiness comes from in here, doesn't it?"

Sean was quiet for a moment. "It should. But often the outer details of life complicate and cloud happiness. They stir people up and feed their discontent."

Annie nodded. "I know it's not as simple as I make it out to be, but I think there has to be a certain amount of will involved. People need to *will* themselves to be happy so the harsh particulars won't faze them."

Sean nodded. "God gave us free will to choose our own way."

"To choose happiness?"

"To choose Him and His way — which will give us that deep-down happiness and contentment, no matter what happens."

"Now, *you* make it sound too easy."

"It's not that difficult to say yes to Him. And the subsequent yeses get easier."

Annie remembered her last encounter with God at Edna's, when she felt His presence and love. *"Come to Me first. You are Mine and I am yours."* God wanted her to say yes to Him. Now Sean was telling her to say yes to Him. Surely it couldn't be as simple as that.

"Annie?"

She changed the subject. "Back to my parents —"

He smiled. "You're willing to talk about a flawed father rather than a perfect one?"

"I know the one better than the other."

"That's too bad."

She huffed at him. "Do you want to hear my story, or not?"

He gave her a by-your-leave with his hand. "Where was I?"

"Being happy in here." He put a fist by his own heart.

Her thoughts sped across the ocean to her family home. "I was determined to be happy, but my parents were just as determined to be unhappy, to be dissatisfied, to be victims of life, with no hope of changing it or making things better." Before he could respond, she finished her point. "Yet they did worse by begrudging everyone else of *their* happiness, wanting to pull the rest of us down into their hole to moan and complain."

"So you moved away from that hole."

"I ran from it. I ran to a life that offered hope and a chance to be something more, first with the Kidds, and now on my own."

He took her hand in his. "You've done well, Annie Wood."

His words filled her up. "I hate that your compliments mean so much to me."

"Why?"

"It's hard to explain."

"Do you want me to tell you why?"

She was amazed at his audacity. "Be my guest."

"To accept compliments means someone else has seen into your world and has judged it."

"I'm used to being judged."

"In the negative."

She felt the sting of tears and nodded.

"Having others point out the good in you means *you* need to acknowledge the good in you."

She swiped a stray tear away. "Where did you get your keen, logical mind, Mr. Culver? It's quite impressive."

Edna arrived home before Sean and Annie and was at the stove when they entered. The delicious smell of sausages and onions filled the flat.

"Dinner will be ready soon," she said. "Not as fine as in a restaurant, but I made bubble and squeak to honor Annie's British roots."

Sean hung his coat and hat on a hall tree. "I have no idea what that is."

Edna pointed at the stove. "Sausage served with mashed potatoes, cabbage, and onions."

"Thank you, Edna. It's one of my favorites." Annie began setting the table.

"Why the 'bubble" and why the 'squeak'?" Sean asked.

Edna smiled. "Listen." She leaned her ear toward the pan. The onions bubbled and the sausage squeaked.

Sean laughed. "Food that makes music. I

know it will taste as good as it sounds." He took on the job of slicing bread. Annie loved how he pitched in without asking.

"So, Sean," Edna said as she stirred the onions. "Annie said you were going to take her to dinner and share some great idea?"

Annie felt herself blush. She'd told Edna about it, never intending for Sean to know. What *if* his idea was of a more personal nature? He wouldn't want to share it here. "If you don't want to tell me tonight —"

"With me in the room," Edna said.

"You don't have to," Annie said. "I can wait."

"But I can't."

His enthusiasm fed her own and eased her mind about the subject matter. Within minutes they sat at the table, said grace, and set to work eating dinner.

"Hmm. The bubble and squawk is now a favorite."

"Squeak," Edna corrected.

Sean winked.

"Oh you," she said. "But enough about the food. Annie's dying to know your idea."

"Dying might be too strong a word. I'm interested."

"That's all?" Sean said, pretending to be annoyed.

She played along. "Very interested." *Just tell me.*

Sean ate another large bite to fuel himself, then stood. He stepped into the parlor and returned with Annie's drawing. "This sketch is going to change your life."

Really? "You have my attention."

"After seeing your talent, I approached my superiors at Butterick and told them about you, about your fashion sense, and your artistic ability."

"I hardly think helping a few customers choose the materials for a dress or skirt reveals any acute fashion sense."

"But you did more than just choose the materials; you looked beyond the patterns that were shown in the catalog and innovated a new piece of fashion altogether. You designed something that previously didn't exist."

"You did do that," Edna said.

Did I? "So what did your superiors say?"

"They want to hire you to work at Butterick in the pattern design department."

Annie felt her jaw drop. She pointed to the parlor. "I've only used two patterns. Ever. How am I going to help create new ones?"

"They are willing to hire you and help you learn."

It was all too much. "But why? They don't know me. They haven't even seen my sketch — my one sketch. Why would they risk so much on a girl who two months ago was a housemaid in England?"

He returned to his chair. "I can be very persuasive. And, there's an opening in that department."

Her thoughts collided, one into the other. "Let us say I am able to do a good job at Butterick. . . . What about Macy's? They've been nothing but kind to me, and have been so understanding about letting me take time off to deal with Danny's death and Grass-ton. I can't just leave them."

Her point was met with silence.

"Actually, you could," Edna said. "Clerks come and go all the time. It's the way of it."

"But you've been there many, many years."

"Because I found my niche selling sewing machines. Do you really think your destiny lies in selling fashion? Or designing it?"

The thought of abandoning Macy's over-whelmed: Mrs. MacDonald, Mildred, and even Mr. Straus . . .

"There is another reason you should take the new job," Sean offered.

Annie pressed a hand to her forehead. "More? I'm already at sixes and sevens."

"The other reason is that Grasston is loose. He knows where you work. But if you worked at Butterick, he couldn't find you and hurt you."

"Oh my," Edna said. "He's right."

It would be such a relief to not have to look for Grasston lurking around Macy's anymore.

Edna interjected. "If Annie is interested — which she most certainly *should* be — what is the next step?"

"I can't take any more time away from Macy's. I'm sure someone at Butterick would want me to come to their offices and interview and —"

"I thought of that. I got them to agree to an interview on the telephone." He retrieved a slip of paper from his pocket. "Here is the name and number of Mr. Burroughs. Call him tomorrow during your lunch break."

Annie stared at the number. "You've thought of everything."

"I've certainly tried." He took her hand. "I want you to become all you can be, Annie-girl. I also want you to be safe. Accepting this job will bring about both goals."

She thought of their discussion on the streetcar, the talk about free will, choosing God's way, and saying yes to Him. With a surge of certainty, Annie found herself saying, "Yes. I say yes."

Sean jumped out of his chair, pulled her to her feet, and encased her in a hug. Then it was Edna's turn.

"Once again, Annie makes a quick decision," Edna said.

"I hope it's the right one."

"I assume it is." Edna turned to Sean. "That's some idea you had."

He nodded but only had eyes for Annie. "You've made me very happy — in here." He put a fist to his chest.

She mimicked his motion, pressing a hand against her own happy heart.

CHAPTER SIXTEEN

Annie skipped lunch to call Butterick. As she stepped into the telephone booth in Herald Square she was glad she hadn't eaten. Her stomach clutched and rolled.

This one phone call will change my life.

Did her life need changing? She had already endured so many changes: coming to America, leaving her job as a maid, taking refuge with the Tuttles, getting a job at Macy's, moving to Edna's, losing Danny to Grasston.

Grasston was one of the biggest reasons she wanted to change her place of employment. Leaving Macy's would gain her much-needed distance from the threat of him.

She retrieved a coin from her purse and thought of yet another huge change in her life: Sean. If someone asked her to pinpoint when their relationship started, she would have a hard time giving them an answer. In so many ways Sean always *was.* He was indelibly linked to her time at Macy's. And now he would be a part of her time at Butterick.

If I get the job.

If she didn't make the call, there was 100 percent certainty she'd get a no. She had to risk asking the question.

But as she risked, she found herself turning to the One who knew all the answers. *God? Is this You at work? If so, let it happen. If not, I'll get back to work and be satisfied at Macy's.*

Annie hesitated a bit after realizing that her prayer was a bit confrontational, as if she was demanding God do the work to get *her* life where it needed to be.

Yet that's what she wanted Him to do. Sean had talked about saying yes to the Almighty. Doing so required surrender on her part but also demanded work on His part. Was He busy right now? Did God have more important things to do besides listen in on her phone call?

She shook the theological musings away. Whether God had time or not was out of her control. What *was* in her control was putting the coin in the slot, dialing the number, and saying "Hello" when someone answered.

With one last intake of breath, Annie did just that. "Butterick Pattern Company, may I help you?"

"I would like to speak to Mr. Burroughs. Please."

"I'll connect you."

Annie took advantage of the delay to breathe deeply. She saw a man standing outside the booth, waiting to use the phone. She covered the receiver and said, "Sorry, but I am going to be a while."

He shrugged and went on his way — which was for the best. She didn't need an audience.

"Burroughs here."

Annie's heart skipped a beat. "Yes, sir, Mr. Burroughs, my name is Annie Wood, and I was told by Sean Culver to —"

"Yes, indeed, Miss Wood. Mr. Culver has told me all about you."

What was she supposed to say to that? "Good things, I hope?"

"Very impressive things. Apparently you have a talent for fashion?"

She regretted that Sean may have over-stated it. "I have an interest in fashion." She thought of something to add. "And a desire to learn about the business."

"Very good. What is your background?"

She wanted to fudge about the maid part,

but not knowing what Sean had told him, she had to tell the whole truth. "I was a housemaid for the Viscount Newley and his family in England."

"Not much fashion involved there."

"At first, no, sir, there wasn't. But I quickly became involved in making alterations to the ensembles of her ladyship and her daughter."

"That doesn't sound like the usual duties of a housemaid."

"It wasn't. But I had an interest and helped the lady's maids do *their* jobs."

"So they taught you how to sew?"

Had they? "Not really. I learned by doing. By studying the dress construction of Lady Newley's couture gowns and dresses."

"Couture?"

She wasn't sure why he was asking the question. "She has all her clothes made in Paris after attending the fashion shows at the couture fashion houses."

"Your knowledge of such construction might come in handy."

Annie tried to contain her surprise. "I'm glad you think so. I am also currently working at Macy's and —"

"Mr. Culver has told us about your ability to sell multiple patterns to one customer."

She couldn't help but laugh. "I must

admit I didn't do it to gain sales as much as to fulfill the needs of the customer."

"That's a good answer."

Since he seemed impressed, she offered her own question. "What does the position at Butterick entail?"

"That depends on you."

"I . . . I'm not sure how to respond."

"Let's just say that with Mr. Culver's hearty recommendation and our conversation today, I am intrigued by the possibilities of having you work for our company. Are you interested, Miss Wood?"

And there it was. A *yes* or *no* stood between Annie and the path of her future. She found herself praying a very simple prayer: *Yes, Lord?*

With but a moment between the prayer and her answer, she heard herself saying, "Yes, Mr. Burroughs. I think I would be very interested."

"Very good. When can you start?"

Today would be ideal. But then she thought of Mrs. MacDonald and Mr. Straus. . . . "I will give my notice today and let you know. I don't want to cause Macy's more trouble than I have to." *Than I have already caused with the Grasston business.*

"Although I'd like you to start immediately, I find your loyalty and work ethic commendable. We shall be in touch."

"Thank you, Mr. Burroughs. I shan't let you down."

"I don't believe you will, Miss Wood."

Annie hung up and bowed her head in gratitude.

Annie needed to talk to Edna or she would burst with excitement. Luckily, Annie was helping a customer who was interested in sewing machines, so she had the chance to go to Edna's department.

As the woman tried a new Singer, Annie whispered to Edna, "I did it. I took the job."

Edna's eyebrows rose. "Congratulations. Have you informed Macy's yet?"

"I will as soon as there's a lull."

The customer looked up from the machine. "How do you make it go in reverse?"

Annie left her in Edna's care and returned to her own counter, eager for the chance to wrap things up. If only the customers would go home so she could talk to Mrs. MacDonald.

Finally, there was a lag in business, and she had her chance. "May I speak with you a minute, please?"

Mrs. MacDonald nodded, but the furrow in her brow revealed her concern. "Is everything all right?"

"It is. Yet . . ." She'd best just say it. "I need to give notice."

Mrs. MacDonald's head drew back. "I thought you liked it here."

"I do, and I appreciate everything that you and Macy's have done for me."

"Do you have another job?"

She nodded. "I'm going to work at the Butterick Pattern Company."

Mrs. MacDonald smiled, her face glowing with a revelation. "I'm betting this is Mr. Culver's doing."

Annie felt a bit of a pull in her stomach. "Yes, it's true he initiated it, but I had an interview and —"

Mrs. MacDonald waved her defensiveness away. "I'm sure you got the job based on merit. You *are* a very talented girl, there's no denying it."

Annie was embarrassed for overreacting. She touched her friend's arm. "I learned so much from you. I'm sorry to leave, but I can't ignore this opportunity."

Mrs. MacDonald patted her hand. "Nor should you. Have you spoken with the powers that be?"

"I have not."

"Best go do it. Mildred and I will cover for you until you get back."

Annie was going to miss this place.

Annie spoke to the person in charge of employees and resigned. It was as painless as such an act could be. They asked her to finish out the week. Only three more days . . .

But on her way downstairs, Annie spotted Mr. Straus standing outside an office. Of all people, he deserved to be told in person.

She walked toward him and waited until he was finished giving his secretary some instruction. He looked up, saw her, and smiled. "Miss Wood. How are you today?"

"I'm fine, sir, but may I speak with you a moment?"

He blinked once then nodded and led her into his office. "Have a seat."

She would have rather stood but didn't want to offend.

"What's on your mind?"

"I . . . I am leaving Macy's for another position."

His left eyebrow rose. "Is there a reason? Were you unhappy working here?"

She scooted forward in her chair. "Oh no, sir. Not at all. I am very thankful for the experience you've given me. I will be forever grateful for that, and for your kind sympathy and patience after Danny was murdered."

"Murdered," he repeated. "Have they found his killer?"

"They know who did it, but they don't have enough evidence to convict him." She considered telling him that Grasston was on the run but didn't want to go into it further.

"I'm sure he will be judged and jailed."

"I hope so, sir."

"So who is the lucky company who's stolen you away from us?"

"Butterick Pattern Company."

"A thriving company for certain. They just built a sixteen-story building. Very impressive."

Annie was unaware of these details but was glad to know them.

"What position will you have?"

She bit her lip. "I'm not sure. *They're* not sure where they're going to use me."

Mr. Straus laughed. "Which most likely means they see a myriad of talents in you and need to take time placing you to their best advantage."

It was a wonderful thought. "I hope so."

He stood and extended his hand. "I wish you the best of everything, Miss Wood. Don't be a stranger to us."

She was moved by his gracious farewell. She only hoped the people at Butterick would be so kind.

■ ■ ■ ■

As soon as she saw Mr. Horace walking toward her, Annie felt her entire body tense. The grim look on his face made her wary.

"Good afternoon, Miss Wood," he said.

"Good afternoon. Is something wrong?"

"Something isn't right." He handed her a note. "This is from Officer Brady. He didn't want to come inside because he knew his presence tends to disrupt business."

"How thoughtful of him."

"Read it," he said.

The note said: *Miss Wood, An update: Grasston is still at large. Continue your vigilance as we continue our efforts to capture him. Officer Brady.*

She sighed deeply, folded the note, and put it in her skirt pocket. "I was so hoping . . ."

"I know. We all were. You are being careful when you go home?"

"I am. I hope he still believes I live at the bakery." She thought of something. "Are the police watching the Tuttles? Watching for him there?"

"They are. But what about your new residence with Mrs. Holmquist?"

"I still don't think he knows about it."

"He could follow you after work."

Thanks for reminding me. "Did you hear I gave my notice today?"

His eyebrows rose. "Did he scare you off?"

"Partly. But I also received an exciting job opportunity I could not refuse."

"Good for you. Good for you in ways beyond the opportunity. Hopefully Grasston never finds out where you work."

"That was one consideration in taking the job."

He extended his hand for her to shake. "It has been nice knowing you, Miss Wood. I wish you a well and safe future."

Annie suffered a shudder. She wouldn't feel truly safe until Grasston was caught and convicted.

"I have a confession to make," Annie told Sean as they entered the restaurant.

"Is it something incredibly juicy and naughty?"

She batted him on the arm. "Sorry to disappoint. I was simply going to confess that this is the first time I have ever eaten in a restaurant."

"Ever?"

"Ever. When I was young we were too poor — and there were no restaurants in Summerfield anyway. In service for the

Kidds I ate with the servants. On the ship over to America I also ate with the servants, as I did at the Friesens'." She looked around the restaurant, which glowed with soft electric light and the sparkle of crystal and silver. "I have never ordered from a menu. Actually, I have never had much choice regarding what to eat at all, unless you count the cafeteria at Macy's."

"I don't count the cafeteria as proper restaurant dining." Sean pulled her hand around his arm and held it there. "I am honored to be the one who gives you a proper initiation."

A man dressed like a butler led them to a table and held out her chair, then Sean's. He placed a linen napkin in her lap with a flourish.

"Finally, our dinner out," Sean said with a wink.

"Are you saying Edna's dinners are lacking?"

They received menus. "I'm saying no such thing, and don't you ever imply that to her. I'm simply happy for the time alone with you."

She smiled at him then hid behind the menu lest he see her blush.

He guessed her ploy and pushed it down. "Is the feeling reciprocated?"

Annie pointed to the day's specials. "The codfish looks enticing."

Sean pressed the point. "Don't be coy with me, Annie. Or elusive. Or flirtatious."

"Then what should I be?"

"Open. Honest. And . . ."

"And?"

He looked at the menu. "I think I might try the mutton chops."

"You are so cheeky."

"I can be," he said. "And will no doubt continue to be." He set the menu aside and extended his hand on the table, waiting for her to take it.

Which she did.

"What I want from you, *for* us, is not a courting game that involves meaningless chitchat about nothing, but something very real that involves meaningful discussion about everything."

She was moved by his sincerity yet also a bit frightened by it. "I want that, too," she said.

"I hear a 'but' hanging nearby."

"But . . . everything in my life is happening so fast. Too fast. A very short time ago I was a housemaid. Then a clerk. And now a pattern artist."

"Your quick journey reveals your true inner talent."

"It's not just my career that has moved quickly, it's my private life, too. I went from knowing the Kidd family and the servants in the house to knowing Iris and Danny, to the Tuttles, to Edna and Mildred, and . . . and you."

"Saving the best for last."

She loved how he could make her smile. "I have no one left from my *before* life. Every friend is a new friend."

"That doesn't make us bad friends."

"Not at all. It's just . . ."

The waiter came and took their order. They stuck with their initial cod and mutton chops.

"It's just?" Sean prodded.

She adjusted the napkin in her lap, trying to return to the previous thought. "It's just that everything in my entire life is new. Even my so-called talent is new. I'm not sure who Annie Wood is anymore. I don't recognize her. I don't know her."

He found her hand again and squeezed. "But I do. Would you like me to introduce her to you?"

She laughed. "Are you going to make me blush again?"

"I certainly hope so." He let go of her hand and cleared his throat. "Annie . . . What's your middle name?"

"Louise."

He cleared his throat again. "Annie Louise Wood, aged . . . ?"

"Nineteen, but nearly twenty."

"So old." He continued, "Annie Louise Wood, aged nearly twenty, is an extraordinary modern woman. She knows her own mind, is not afraid to share it — even when she's wrong, and —"

"Blimey."

He held up a finger, stopping her objection. "*And* she has the ability to make everyone she's with feel special. She sees the world with wide-eyed eagerness, open to whatever life throws at her."

The thought of Grasston came. And went.

He had more. "She makes friends easily, has an incredible work ethic, and has excellent taste in male companions." He grinned. "I couldn't resist, but only because it's true."

"Are you finished?"

"You want *more* praise?"

"You have more?"

He sighed with feigned drama. "Annie Louise Wood has an amazing, fascinating, and surprising life in front of her. She will succeed in everything she does — with God by her side. There," he said. "Satisfied?"

"It sounded a bit like a eulogy. I'm not

dead, you know."

"In a way you are. The old Annie is dead and a new Annie has risen in her place."

His words took her aback, for they were full of truth.

Annie set her fork down and leaned back in her chair. "I cannot eat another morsel."

Sean did the same. "The apple tart crowned the meal — and then some."

She sipped her coffee. "The dinner was brilliant. I thank you for the meal, your delightful company, and for my new job."

"Your phone call with Mr. Burroughs cinched it. I merely put the idea in his head."

Remembering the interview . . . "Did you tell him I used to be a maid?"

"No. I didn't know if you wanted that mentioned. I focused on your work at Macy's, and your drawing ability. But —"

"Drat," she said. "Not knowing whether you mentioned it or not, *I* mentioned it. I hope he doesn't think less of me for my humble beginnings."

"You didn't let me finish. I spoke to Mr. Burroughs after your interview and he said that your experience as a maid under Lady Newley was the tipping point in giving you the job."

She was confused. "Why would that help my cause?"

"You told him you've altered couture gowns?"

"Well, yes. Lady Newley and Miss Henrietta went to Paris every spring to see the newest fashion. They had their clothes custom made. Of course I never went with them. But their lady's maids did."

"Ah. Paris. I'm betting that was the clincher for Mr. Burroughs."

"Why would the Kidds going to Paris matter?"

"Because Butterick sends handpicked employees to those same fashion shows."

"Why?"

"To make sketches that we turn into knockoffs for our home sewers. You play your cards right and you might get to go to Paris, too."

She had to laugh. "Me? Going to the fashion shows in Paris?"

"You, working as a pattern artist in the largest pattern company in the world?"

Annie put a hand to her heart and felt it pounding. "Why are good things happening to me?"

Sean studied her a minute. "What did you tell me yesterday? That you thought it possible to *will* yourself to be happy? That's what you're doing now."

"Am I?"

"You are. You're not letting the pain of Danny's death and Grasston rule your life. You've chosen joy and hope."

"Have I?"

He laughed. "You are either searching for more compliments — which I shall be happy to provide — or you're simply not allowing yourself to enjoy and accept the very marvelous woman you are."

Annie's heart swelled at his words — because they encouraged — but also because they revealed him to be an extraordinary man.

"There is one more thing I choose," she said.

"And what's that?"

"I choose you."

He leaned over the table and kissed her, sealing the moment.

CHAPTER SEVENTEEN

"Take a deep breath, Annie."

Annie did as Edna instructed, putting a hand upon her midsection. One breath then two for good measure. "I've got the collywobbles."

Edna smiled. "I've never heard that term before, but I understand completely. It's natural to be nervous about your first day on a new job."

Annie smoothed her new skirt. "Do I look all right?"

"You look lovely. They'll certainly be impressed you created your outfit with Butterick patterns."

She had second thoughts. "Is it too obvious? As though I'm a toady?"

"A what?"

Americans didn't use that term? "A flatterer. Buttering them up?"

"Ah," Edna said. "Don't point it out to them, but if they notice, you can certainly say something." She pointed to the toast on Annie's plate. "Eat. You need a good breakfast."

Annie wasn't sure her stomach was up to food, but she nibbled at the bread and drank her tea.

Sean had said it was approximately two miles from Edna's to the Butterick offices at Spring and MacDougal Streets. It should have taken her forty-five minutes at a brisk pace, but she'd taken a wrong turn and had to backtrack.

She was late. She hated being late.

The Butterick building loomed at the west end of Spring Street like a massive monster intimidating the three-story buildings around it. Its presence spoke volumes toward the company's importance and success.

Before she entered the building, she dabbed at her face and neck with a handkerchief. To "glow" prettily was one thing. To be sweaty was another. She looked at her reflection in a window and smoothed the stray strands of hair that announced her frenzied walk. Then she forced herself to take some deep breaths, hoping to calm her pulse. *Please, God. You brought me here. Help me do my best.*

She entered the lobby and approached a front desk. "Excuse me, but I'm a new employee. Today is my first day and I don't know where to go."

"Of course, miss," the receptionist said. "What is your name?"

Annie was instructed to go up the elevator to the fifth floor and report to Mrs. Downs.

As Annie walked away, the girl said, "Welcome to the Butterick Company, Miss Wood."

Her politeness reminded Annie to move out of her self-focus and reciprocate. "Thank you for the welcome and your help."

The girl's smile was genuine. "Don't be nervous. We don't bite."

Annie's laughter eased her nerves. "That's good to know."

The elevator operator greeted her warmly. "First day?"

"Is it so obvious?"

"Just a bit. Don't worry. You'll be fine."

The doors opened up to an enormous room filled with oak desks piled high with papers.

A man whose desk was in the front row asked, "Looking for someone?"

"Mrs. Downs? I'm Annie Wood. I'm new."

His gaze took in the whole of her, but she couldn't tell whether he was impressed or appalled. "We heard you were coming. Follow me."

By the way he said it, it seemed they'd been *warned* she was coming. She hoped her instincts were wrong.

"Mrs. Downs," the man said to an older woman with a pinched face. "This here's Miss Wood, come to work."

The woman eyed her, yet her gaze avoided Annie's face and took in her clothes. "I recognize the skirt — pattern number 8358, and the blouse is 3758, yet not completely."

Annie was impressed but immediately regretted altering the sleeve to her own design. "I changed the sleeve."

Mrs. Downs moved close and inspected it. "I do like the sleekness here, and the cuff . . . It is an interesting alteration."

"Thank you." Annie hastened to add, "It wasn't that I thought the initial blouse pattern faulty, I just had an idea and —"

"You are here to design, Miss Wood. To create. To take what does not exist and make it real."

Annie realized she'd been holding her breath. "I am eager to get to work."

"Hmm," Mrs. Downs said. "Come with me."

Annie was led into another room that contained an extremely long layout table in the center. Along the window wall were smaller tables, each four feet in length. A half-dozen women sat at those tables, while others fitted pattern pieces or fabric on headless dress forms that wore muslin ensembles in various stages of construction. A girl stood at the long table, using a curved ruler to mark on some paper.

Mrs. Downs clapped her hands to get everyone's attention — an act that was unnecessary as Annie had everyone's eyes from the moment she'd come in the room. As the man said, they knew she was coming.

"Ladies, I would like to introduce you to Miss Annie Wood, who has come to fill the position vacated by Agnes. As you've been informed, she has artistic ability illustrating designs, as well as an innovative eye. I trust you'll make her feel welcome." She pointed at the girl who was fitting some muslin on a dress form. "Maude? I place you in charge of Miss Wood."

"How grand. I've always wanted to be in charge of someone."

Mrs. Downs pointed a finger at her. "Be kind. Show her around the building and then lead her through the design process." She looked at Maude over her glasses. "Don't make me regret choosing you for the task, Miss Nascato."

Maude put a hand to her chest and feigned indignation. "I wouldn't dare."

Annie was shocked by her boldness. Yet Mrs. Downs must trust Maude or she wouldn't have chosen her.

As soon as the older woman left, the room erupted in giggles and comments such as "She lets you get away with murder, Maude" and "Be nice to Miss Wood, Maude" and "You'd better behave yourself, or . . ."

Maude turned to the last speaker. "Or what?"

The girl went back to her table. "One of these days . . ."

"I agree," Maude said. "One of these days I'm going to get what is coming to me: fame, wealth, and unimaginable happiness."

Her words quieted the girls and they returned to their work. But as Maude turned her attention to Annie, Annie wasn't sure what to think of her guide.

Maude stuck some stray pins into a cushion then headed for the door. "Come along, Annie Wood. Let me show you what you've got yourself into."

Annie was shown the press room where they printed up the envelopes for the patterns, as well as the pattern catalogs and copies of the *Delineator* magazine — which — Maude informed her, was the most successful women's magazine in America, with a circulation of 1.3 million readers. Annie had no concept of such numbers.

The sound in the press room was deafening, and the constant frenetic motion of the massive machines was almost frightening. Also frightening — in its own way — was the attention of the men manning the presses. They winked at her, whistled, and laughed among themselves.

Maude was not fazed. "Behave yourselves, boys," she called out above the noise. "She's not your type."

"How 'bout you, Maudey? Is you me type?"

"Nobody is your type, Calvin."

Another man yelled out, "You two are the jammiest bits of jam I's seen."

Annie was flattered and had to admit that she and Maude were a pretty pair. Maude was petite, dark, and curvy, and she, tall, slim, with creamy skin.

As soon as they were clear of the presses, Maude said, "Don't let their fresh ways intimidate you. They're good enough fellows. Actually, you won't have much contact with them."

"But you do?"

Maude grinned. "I have contact with everyone."

"Why?"

"Why not?"

"Then maybe I should know them."

Maude stopped walking and faced her. "Keep to the design department, Annie. There's only room enough for one know-it-all in this company, and that's me."

Annie studied her face a moment, trying to determine whether Maude was threatening her or teasing.

Maude flicked the tip of her nose. "Lighten up, chickie. Life's too short."

Annie wasn't sure what to make of the woman. She liked her, but she was also intimidated by her.

Maude led the way to another floor that was populated by dozens of desks, and dozens of workers. Each desk was piled high with letters. "This is the correspondence center. We get thirty thousand letters a week from women asking questions about our patterns, sharing ideas, or needing help with their sewing."

Again the numbers overwhelmed. "You answer them all?"

"Every one. A company doesn't have the money to build a huge building by ignoring the customers. And to let you know the massiveness of our jobs, Butterick puts out between seven hundred and nine hundred patterns per year. Patterns *we* have to design and create."

"That many new ideas? How do we do it?"

"You'll get the hang of it. And remember it's not just women's day fashion, but evening wear, sleepwear, undergarments, children's wear from layette to teen, and men's, too."

"I know nothing about the construction of men's clothing." *And little enough about women's.*

"We stick to the nontailored clothes for men. Shirts, vests, nightshirts."

"That's a relief. I can't imagine tailoring a suit."

Maude raised a finger and a point. "Neither can the average home seamstress."

It was a good point to remember.

"Don't worry about any of it. Nobody starts out knowing what they're doing — no matter what the job." She gave Annie a mischievous glance. "Unless you're . . . special."

It sounded like a challenge — one Annie was not willing to take. "I'm not special. Not at all."

"Noted, and filed for future reference."

They visited a floor where women were folding tissue patterns and stuffing them into printed envelopes. Maude shouted over the chatter of the workers. "Ladies! Meet Annie Wood, a new designer."

A chorus of "Hello, Annie" ricocheted off the tall ceilings.

"You *do* know everyone."

"Of course." She walked to a table and showed Annie a stack of pattern pieces. "I'm sure you're familiar with the patterns."

"I am. My skirt is number 8358, but the blouse is a variation of 3758."

Maude touched the sleeve. "You changed it."

My, these people were observant. "Do you like it?"

"It has possibilities." Maude turned back to the workers. "A cardboard template is made of each pattern piece, and then layers and layers of tissue paper are cut at once. And perforations are added to indicate the darts, the matching points, and to create identifying letters for each piece."

"Those perforations are very handy," Annie said.

"There's another department that takes what we've designed and what pattern pieces have been created and writes instruction sheets that go in the envelope."

"Another handy tool."

They took the elevator to the next floor where Maude announced, "This is the sales floor where —"

Sean rushed toward them, his face beaming. "Annie! My protégé!" He kissed both her cheeks.

Maude put her hands on her hips. "Ahem."

"Good morning, Maude." He winked at her. "You're looking especially lovely this morning, Miss Nascato."

She flipped his compliment away. "Too little too late, boyo."

"Don't say I didn't try."

"I'll let Sean show you around his department." To Sean she said, "Ticktock, Sean. Don't take too long."

"Yes, ma'am." Sean saluted her.

Sean showed Annie around, explaining how mail orders came in for fifteen cents and how there were agents like himself who called on stores to replenish their stock.

He was all business, so though she longed to take his arm, she dared not. Obviously he hadn't shared the more personal side of their relationship with people at work. She accepted that arrangement. In a way it was freeing. Annie wasn't certain she could handle dealing with a new job *and* a suitor on the job.

Sean led her back to her starting point, where they found Maude chatting with another salesman. Sean finished up by saying, "We have actual Butterick storefronts in Paris, London, Berlin, and Vienna. I am the lucky chap who gets to call on them in person."

"You get to go to Europe? For business?"

"I do. I'm going there in April. I'll attend the Paris fashion shows, too, getting ideas for the company." He grinned. "You want to come along?"

He'd already teased her with this possibility. "You know I would."

Maude approached, her hands beckoning Annie to follow. "Yes, yes, enough of the sales department. We need to be moving along. Ta-ta, Sean."

"Ta-ta, Maude." He gave Annie a special smile. "Miss Wood."

Maude led her to the stairs instead of the elevator. "The next bit takes some exertion. Are you up for it?"

"Of course," Annie said.

As they climbed floor after floor, Annie became winded. "Aren't we running out of building?"

"Almost."

They reached a landing with an exit door.

Maude opened it, and Annie found herself on the roof of the building. "You really are giving me the complete tour, aren't you?" She noticed enormous glass skylights cut through the middle of the roof.

"Natural light?"

"Two stories high. Saves on electricity." Maude pointed across the expanse. "No tour would be complete without seeing the famous Butterick sign in person." She swept a hand toward the east end of the building. They viewed the back of the sign amid extensive bracing. It was enormous.

"It's the largest illuminated sign in the world. The *B* is sixty-eight feet high — about the height of a five-story building. The smaller letters are fifty feet high. And it lights up at night." Maude led Annie to the side of the *B* where she could see hundreds of bulbs outlining the letter.

"How many bulbs are there?"

"Fourteen hundred — give or take. There's a man here who spends most of his time changing 'em out. Dwight takes his job very seriously, not wanting some letters to go black, lest the sign say 'butter' or 'ick" or worse yet, 'butt.' "

Maude was clearly gauging Annie's re-action to the slightly crude comment. Annie was not going to bite. "Protecting the

291

company's reputation is a noble job."

"And here I thought I'd get an indignant rise out of you."

"I'm not so easily scandalized."

"Good for you."

Maude led the way to a clear view of the city. "To the west there is the Hudson River, and Dwight says when he's up on the sign he can even see the Statue of Liberty, way down that way." She pointed to the south.

Suddenly Annie felt a little dizzy and took a step away from the edge.

"You all right?"

"I just realized I've never been so high."

Maude laughed and led the way back to the door. "Being in my presence will do that to a person."

Annie couldn't argue with her.

They made their way down the stairwell all the way to the floor that held the design department. But Maude paused at the door. "Are you sweet on Sean?"

Annie didn't know what to say, so she turned it around on her. "Are you?"

Maude flipped the notion aside with a hand. "Don't worry about me. I have no interest in Sean Culver."

Annie was taken aback by her tone. "You make it sound like the notion is revolting."

"Nothing against Sean, mind you. I simply

have no interest in the men who work here."

Annie caught the distinction. "So is there a man in your life? Who doesn't work here?"

Maude leveled her with a look. "You're getting mighty personal for the first day, don't you think?"

"You started it. You asked *me* about my personal life."

Maude tilted her head. "So I did." She opened the door and they were back at work.

Annie couldn't help but notice Maude hadn't answered her question.

"Enough of tour time," Maude said. "Now it's time to create some fashion." She stood with Annie in front of the huge layout table in the workroom.

It looked intimidating. There were rolls of paper, rulers, curves, pencils, scissors, and bolts and bolts of muslin. Annie had been assigned one of the tables that were set perpendicular to the wall of windows and had her own dress form.

"You do know how to use patterns, yes?" Maude asked.

Annie hesitated. "I have a basic knowledge." She remembered her lessons with Edna. "I have altered a pattern to fit my taller frame, and as you noticed, I changed a sleeve."

Maude stared at her, offering a slow blink. "That's the extent of it?"

Annie looked around the room, seeing that many of the girls were listening. She lowered her voice, hoping to reach Maude alone. "I want to learn. Teach me. Please."

Maude studied her a moment. "All right, then. Let's get to work." She moved to a muslin dress on a form. "Every dress has the same design elements to work with: the neckline, neck edge, armhole, sleeve shape, cuff, waistline, hem length, and skirt silhouette."

"All that."

"All that." She pulled a chart close. "These are the basic body measurements for our patterns. And over there are the basic patterns for our dresses, skirts, and blouses. We can start there and adapt the existing pieces to our ideas." She cut off a length of tissue paper and placed it over a bodice pattern piece on the table. "Let's say we want to have a scoop neck. We can draw it with the curve and trace over the basic piece." With a sweep of a pencil along the curved edge, Maude showed how it was done.

"You make it look easy."

"It can be — with practice."

Annie pointed to the finished dress. "How do we get from this to that?"

"Trial and error. After we make the new pattern we carefully cut it out in muslin, sew it together, and fit it on the dress form — seam-side out. That's where we make adjustments and alter the pattern until it's right. Only then is it made up in real fabric so the art department can make sketches for the catalogs and the *Delineator.* Then it goes into production."

Annie took a deep breath and let it out slowly.

Maude laughed. "It will be fine. You will be fine."

"I'll take your word for it."

The rest of the day went by in a blur. Annie worked with Maude on a blouse pattern with an interesting wide collar. They had trouble getting the collar to lie just right. It was a tedious process but one that provided much satisfaction. Creating something from nothing was a new experience, one Annie embraced.

The girls were nice enough: Suzanne, Wilma, Dora, Sofia — or was it Sophie? Annie tried to remember their names, but by the end of the day, with all the information thrown at her, she took the safe way out and said her good-byes without using their names.

"You survived," Mrs. Downs said when Annie clocked out.

"I did. But there's so much to learn."

" 'All I know is I know nothing.' "

"What?"

"Socrates."

Annie had no idea who that was but had the feeling she *should* know. "Thank you for the opportunity, Mrs. Downs."

"Don't thank me yet. You'll need to prove yourself, prove the buildup is true to your talent."

"Buildup?"

"Mr. Culver was beyond complimentary as to your potential."

"I hope he didn't overstate."

"So do we, Miss Wood. See you tomorrow."

Sean waited for her in the lobby. "Would you like some company on your walk home?"

"Of course."

They left the building amid the crowd, and only when they were a block away did he pull her hand around his arm. "So. Tell me everything."

She laughed. "I'm not sure I could detail

the color of the sky at the moment. My mind is a-jumble with new things I need to learn."

"You'll do it. I believe in you."

"Which brings up the point . . . I hope you didn't oversell my talent. I have very little experience. I fear they expect a Rembrandt while I am but a crude sketcher."

"I'm betting Rembrandt was a crude sketcher at one time. As Butterick is giving you a chance to excel, you need to give yourself a chance to excel and grow."

She leaned her head against his shoulder. "I don't know what to do with you, Sean Culver."

"I'll think of something."

Annie started up the steps of Edna's building then noticed Sean wasn't following her. "Won't you come to dinner?"

"Not tonight. I have some paperwork to do back at my place."

A new thought made her freeze in place. "I don't even know where you live compared to here."

"It's a ways away."

She descended the steps to face him on the sidewalk. "How selfish of me to never realize that you coming here, and walking me home, might be an inconvenience."

He touched her hand. "You're worth it."

Annie didn't feel worth it. She pressed the palm of her hand to her forehead. "I'm so angry at myself for not thinking of you, for only thinking of myself. I'm so sorry."

"You're forgiven." He kissed her cheek then turned to leave. "I'll come by tomorrow morning to walk you to work."

"But you said it's out of your way."

"And I said you're worth it."

She stood on the sidewalk and watched him walk away, his hands in his coat pockets, a spring in his step. "What did I do to deserve you?"

"Pardon?" said a man walking by.

" 'Evening." She went into the building and up the flights to Edna's — to *her* home.

At the sight of Edna in the kitchen, making dinner, Annie was faced with another failing. "I can make dinner sometimes," she said. *Though I have little idea of how to cook.*

"I know you can," Edna said, stirring a pot. "And once you're settled in your new job I'll take you up on it. Now, tell me about your day."

"What did I do to deserve *you*?" Annie said under her breath as she put her hat and jacket on the hall tree.

"What?"

"I'm noticing what good friends I have in

you and Sean."

"We are a golden pair, aren't we?"

Annie wouldn't let her flip the compliment away. She went to the stove and stopped Edna's stirring with a hand. "I mean it. If it weren't for you two, I might be heading back —" She stopped herself. *Oh no. Could it be?* "What is today's date?"

Edna hesitated a moment. "The thirteenth, I believe."

Annie took a step back, stunned by the fact.

"What's wrong?"

"Tomorrow is November 14."

"So?"

Annie's legs puddled beneath her, and with Edna's help she found a chair. "The Kidds sail back to England on the fourteenth."

Edna took the pot off the stove and sat at the table. "Your ride home."

"My ride home."

Edna wiped a few crumbs from the tablecloth onto her hand, where she held them captive. "You could still go."

"Could I?"

"I don't believe 'could' is the right word. *Would* you go? Do you want to go?"

Annie pressed a hand to her chest, trying

to calm her frantic heartbeat. "I don't know."

Edna's eyebrows rose. "Really?"

Her question — and her surprise — was justified.

"I wouldn't think you could leave Annie. Not with your new job, new friends — a special male friend."

Annie's nod had no strength in it.

"You're not agreeing with me," Edna said.

Annie rose from the chair, needing her body to move along with her thoughts. "I love my new life here, and appreciate everything about it."

"But . . . ?"

Annie stopped pacing and wrapped her arms tightly around herself. "Letting the Kidds go, and not being on that ship, is so final."

"A closed door."

"A locked door."

Edna shook her head. "Not locked. You can always return to England on your own."

"Perhaps."

"The larger question is what would you be returning *to*. Surely you don't want to be a maid again."

"Of course not. Never."

"Do you wish to go home and live with your family?"

"Of course not." *Never.*

"Do you have other job prospects there?"

"In Summerfield? None. It's a tiny village."

"How about in a city? London?"

She was embarrassed by her lack of experience. "I've never been." She returned to her chair. "I've never been anywhere but Summerfield and here."

"A village to New York City is an enormous jump."

"An enormous leap."

"Of faith?"

Annie was taken aback. "Is that what it is?"

"Seems so to me. You left the Kidds with the expectation you'd find something better."

"I had no idea what I'd find."

"Exactly. You took the leap — on faith — that there was something better out there. And there was."

"I did that."

"Is that a question or a statement?"

"Both."

Edna retrieved a Bible from her bedroom. She leafed through it then handed it to Annie, her finger pointing at a verse. "There. Hebrews 11:1. Read it aloud."

" 'Now faith is the substance of things

hoped for, the evidence of things not seen.' "
Annie put a hand on Edna's forearm. "I just
got the shivers."

"I always take such shivers to mean that
God approves of what I'm thinking. As if
saying, *'Yes, Edna. You've got it.'* "

"Surely not."

"You want to argue with me? Or Him?"

Annie's soft laugh broke through the
seriousness of the moment. "I do like the
notion that God is right here, letting me
know I'm on the right go of things."

"So you're all right with staying? With
turning your back on what was and fully
investing in what could be?"

Annie let a deep breath come and go.
"Sean said the old Annie is dead and a new
Annie has risen in her place."

"Has she?"

This time Annie's nod was filled with
certainty. "She has."

"Very good, then. Give God a 'thank You,'
and welcome to *now.*"

Now seemed a very good place to be.

Thank You, God.

CHAPTER EIGHTEEN

Annie was deep at work, trying to perfect the pattern for a draped overskirt on a dress, when suddenly all the girls in the department turned toward a sound in Mrs. Downs's office.

Through the glass window of the office Annie could see a visitor, a woman wearing a lavender wide-brimmed hat with a plume. She was talking very loudly to Mrs. Downs, gesticulating wildly with her hands.

"Who is that?" Annie asked Dora.

"That's just Mrs. Sampson, a rich lady with too much time on her hands."

"At it again, I see. Or rather, hear," Suzanne said.

The other girls giggled.

As the woman's voice grew more animated, Annie turned to Maude for a more detailed answer. "What's the story with her? She's a giddy kipper for sure."

There was a pause, and then the girls

laughed. "Giddy kipper?"

"She's overly excited."

"That she is," Maude said. "Always is."

"She comes here often?"

"Too," Suzanne said.

"What are they arguing about?"

"She's a fashion rebel," Maude explained. "If she had her way we'd all go around naked."

More giggles.

"If she's for nakedness, why is she visiting a company that designs clothes?"

"Don't take me too literally," Maude said. "She's one of the rational-dress reformers, those who are against corsets and clothing that binds."

"I'm against corsets, too," Annie said, adjusting the pinch of boning under her arm.

"But you wear one," Dora said. "We all do."

Suzanne shook her head. "It's improper to do otherwise."

"Scandalous," another girl said.

The subject got her thinking. "I know that's the way it's always been, but wouldn't it be nice not to be bound up? When I was a —" She caught herself before she admitted to being a maid.

"A what?"

She found a different tack. "When I was younger I was all excited to wear a corset, not knowing what a discomfort they could be."

"A torture."

"A cruelty to women."

As if on cue, all the girls made adjustments to their corsets.

Maude put a halt to the subject and pointed at the designs at hand. "Back to work, girls. After dealing with Mrs. Sampson, Mrs. Downs will be in a foul mood. We'd better be getting something done."

The four girls returned to their work. Maude looked over Annie's shoulder at the pattern pieces for the skirt and offered no suggestion. Then she placed a sketch in front of her.

"What's this?" Annie asked.

"Mrs. Downs wants us to add more hobble skirts to our catalog."

Annie looked at the drawing. The skirt of the dress was wide at the hips but at the knee narrowed drastically toward a tight tube above the ankles. "I've seen a few women around town in these, but they look ridiculous."

"It's fashion," Maude said. "From Paris."

"I don't care where it's from," Annie said. "Women can't walk in them. I saw a woman trying to get in a cab and she had to receive assistance, and then virtually had to lift the skirt quite high to get in." She pointed at the ankles of the woman in the illustration. "She's showing her ankles even before she tries to get in a cab."

"It's the fashion of women's rights," Maude said. "No more heavy petticoats. No more tripping on our skirts."

There was no "right" to it. It was illogical. "So we are free from the length, but create a new restriction in the width?"

"It's modern," Suzanne said from her table.

"It's silly."

"Yes it is. My point exactly."

None of them had noticed Mrs. Sampson leave Mrs. Downs's office until she stood beside Annie. "It's nice to hear the voice of reason in the design department." She gave Annie a look-see. "Are you new?"

"I am. Very." Annie caught Mrs. Downs's scowl. "Since I don't know much about fashion yet, I probably shouldn't voice my opinions."

"Of course you should voice them," Mrs. Sampson said. "We need a clear voice of reason in this company." She nodded at Mrs. Downs. "This is exactly why I continue to delight you with my visits. Think of me as the woman repeatedly coming before the judge in the Bible, wearing him down." She gazed directly at Mrs. Downs. "I *will* wear you down."

Mrs. Downs swept an arm toward the elevator. "Thank you for your visit, Mrs. Sampson, but the girls have work to do."

"Fool's work, if they're creating more patterns for that insipid fashion."

Mrs. Downs was insistent. "If you please."

With a dramatic sigh, Mrs. Sampson turned to leave. Then she paused and turned back to Annie. "What is your name, miss?"

"Annie. Annie Wood."

"I look forward to winning you over to my side. Carry on."

When she left she took a good portion of air with her.

"She exhausts me," Mrs. Downs said, pressing a hand to her brow.

"She seems interesting," Annie said.

"You will *not* be swayed by her rantings."

"Some of what she says makes sense." Annie pointed at the drawing. "This isn't a fashion for the everyday woman who needs to move about easily in order to get through her day. Home sewers don't want this."

Annie heard Dora gasp. And Suzanne took a step back. Maude crossed her arms and shook her head.

Now I've done it.

Mrs. Downs glared at her. "You are an instant expert as to the needs and desires of our customers? We've been in business since 1863, we have over a hundred branch offices and over a thousand agencies, and are second only to the United States government in the size of our publishing department, yet you know best?"

Annie wanted to hide under the table. "I'm sorry. I misspoke."

"Indeed you did. Focus on our company's goals, Miss Wood, not the absurd rantings of a rebellious malcontent." Mrs. Downs stormed into her office and shut the door hard enough to rattle the glass.

"Oh dear. I dropped a clanger on that one."

Maude laughed. "That you did."

Dora and Suzanne moved back to the main table. "I do see your point," Dora said. "The hobble skirts *are* a silly fashion."

Suzanne shook her head. "They may be silly, but if it's good enough for Paris and the Wright brothers, then —"

"The brothers who invented the aeroplane?" Annie asked.

"Rumor is they's the one who started it," Suzanne said. "They were taking some ladies up in their planes and tied a sash around their skirts below the knees so the fabric wouldn't flap around."

It made an odd sort of sense. "But very few women go on aeroplanes."

Dora shrugged. "Doesn't seem to matter. It became fashion."

"And as such, we need to work with it," Maude said.

As they turned their attention back to the drawing, Annie had one last question. "If Mrs. Downs doesn't like Mrs. Sampson, why does she let her in?"

"She and her husband have more money than spit," Dora said.

"That's hardly a nice way to put it," Suzanne said.

"It's all I could think of on short notice."

"She and her husband are friends with the Astors and Vanderbilts," Maude said. "Powerful families. Powerful businessmen."

"With power comes a voice that demands to be heard?" Annie asked.

"Exactly."

"You are right about one thing, Annie," Dora said.

"What's that?"

"Mrs. Sampson *is* a giddy kipper."

With work going well, there was still another

issue that needed to be addressed, and a phone call to make.

Since the people at Butterick knew nothing of Annie's personal life — beyond her friendship with Sean — she didn't want to risk anyone overhearing the call, so she left the building and found a phone booth. She held a business card for reference and dialed the number. When the call was answered, she asked, "May I speak to Officer Brady, please? Annie Wood calling."

While she waited for him to pick up, she recognized a few coworkers walking on the sidewalk, gave them a nod, and then discreetly turned away.

"Miss Wood," the officer said. "I *am* glad to hear from you."

Her hopes swelled. "You've caught him?"

"Uh, no. I was wanting to check to see if you'd seen him."

There was something pitiful about his question. "No."

"That's good."

"It is, but as I explained, I changed jobs. He doesn't know where I work."

"That's a plus."

"It is, but . . . the reason I called is this. I need to go to the Tuttles' to fit a wedding dress for Iris. But now that I hear he's not been caught, I'm hesitant to show myself there."

"You have reason to be hesitant. My men *have* seen him near the bakery."

"Then why haven't they caught him?"

"Seeing and catching are two different things."

His words were the antithesis of encouraging. "I'm not sure what to do. I really need to see Iris. Plus, I want to visit the rest of the family."

"This won't solve the latter issue, but perhaps Iris can come to you for the fitting?"

"Wouldn't Grasston follow her?"

"Not if he doesn't know where she's going. Since she left the Friesens' he's never been after Iris, has he?"

"Just me. And Danny." *And Danny's dead.*

"Then if she's aware and wise — and if someone accompanies her — I think it's a valid solution. I'd prefer that you stay away from the places he used to find you. No Macy's. No bakery. I'm sorry, but until we catch him . . ."

What choice did she have?

Annie thanked him — for what, she wasn't sure — then called the bakery. Saturday would be a good day for the fitting.

Thomas answered. Thomas, Iris's perfect

311

chaperone.

A boy ran into the workroom, an envelope to his chest.

"Yes, boy?" Maude asked.

"I got here a message for a" — he read the envelope — "a Miss Wood? And I's supposed to wait for a reply."

"That's me," Annie said, raising her hand.

There was a chorus of oohs and teasing comments. "A secret admirer, perhaps?"

"There's no secret. It's Sean Culver who admires her."

"Maybe this is a rival."

"Girls!" Maude said, shushing them. "Enough speculating." She turned to Annie. "Read the note."

"Thank you," Annie said.

But Maude wasn't through. "Then let us know what it says."

"Thatta way, Maude," Suzanne said.

Annie enjoyed their banter because it made her feel like one of them. She stepped toward the window and dramatically turned her back to read it. She assumed it was from Sean and planned to chastise him for being so bold.

But when she saw the elegant cursive of her name on the front of the envelope, she knew it wasn't from him. It was a female's

312

hand. Maybe a note from someone at Macy's?

Inside was a letter written on fine stationery, folded in two. There was a printed letterhead.

Eleanor Sampson.

What would Mrs. Sampson want with her? They'd only met this morning, with Mrs. Sampson being a blustery wind that had blown in and out of the room.

"Come on, Annie," Dora said. "What's it say?"

She hadn't gotten that far — yet the message was short: *You've impressed me, Miss Wood. I invite you to dine this Friday with myself and my husband. Eight in the evening. You may bring a companion. Relay your answer to the boy. I look forward to getting to know you better.* There was an address at the bottom.

"Come on, chickie," Maude said. "Spill."

Annie was hesitant. It had been made very clear that Mrs. Sampson and her rebellious ways were not looked upon kindly at Butterick. Plus, there was the question of why the woman would want to meet with *her*.

Before she could make the decision to share or not share, Maude plucked the letter from her hands.

"Wot! That's personal."

Maude read it quickly. "Why would she want to meet with you?"

There were many questions of "Who?"

The cat was out of the bag — and running about the room. "Mrs. Sampson."

Maude handed the note back and addressed the others. "Annie's been invited to dine." The last word was expressed with a haughty tone.

"Mrs. Sampson is giddy rich," Dora said.

"Very," Maude added. She gestured toward the letter. "They live at 451 Madison Avenue."

"Ooh," Suzanne said. "La-di-da."

Annie was intrigued by their response. "That's a posh address?"

"The poshest."

Annie was rather embarrassed with her first thought. "I don't have a thing to wear. I have work clothes, not dinner dresses."

"Miss?" It was the boy. "I needs an answer?"

Maude did the honors. "She says yes."

"And thank you," Annie added. The boy left Annie staring at the letter. "Why does she want to talk with me?"

"You and a companion," Dora said. "Who you taking with you?"

"I know," Suzanne said in a singsong.

Annie didn't like that they thought Sean

was a foregone conclusion. "Perhaps I'll bring my landlady. She's a dear friend."

"A landlady?" Dora said. "Don't be ridiculous. You must go with a man on your arm."

"And Sean's your man," Suzanne said.

They were right. If she asked Edna, Edna would be just as nervous as Annie. Sean's presence would hopefully keep her calm. "Fine," she said. "I'll ask Sean to go."

"Now *there's* a modern woman for you. She's doing the asking." Maude motioned toward the other girls. "We best get back to work or Mrs. Downs will have our heads."

"She still needs something to wear," Dora said, going back to the dress form she was draping.

"There's no time to make anything," Annie said.

Maude stared at the door, a hand to her chin, her thoughts clearly whirling. Annie left her alone. If anyone could find an answer, it would be Maude.

An hour later, Maude came to Annie's workstation and said — more loudly than necessary, "I'm afraid I was negligent about the tour of Butterick. Follow me, Miss Wood. There's one more area I'd like to show you."

"But where —"

"Shh."

When they were in the stairwell they could talk. "Where are you taking me?"

"To your very own personal closet."

"What are you talking about?"

Maude's face glowed with excitement and adventure. "We often fully make up the patterns with nice fabrics. Some are for fashion shows, and some for photographs, but all are stored together in a large closet."

Annie took the knowledge to its logical conclusion. "Do you think they'll let me borrow a dress?"

Maude started up the stairs and answered over her shoulder. "We aren't going to ask."

Annie tugged on the back of Maude's skirt. "But shouldn't we?"

Maude looked down at her from two steps up. "Do you want to risk a no?"

"Do I want to risk my job? And yours?"

Annie saw a moment's hesitation in Maude's eyes. "Opportunities such as yours don't come often into a working girl's life. You can't *not* go."

"I could still go, and just wear a blouse and skirt."

Maude shook her head. "Mrs. Sampson said you impressed her. So do that. Impress her by wearing something fashionable, something that shows you appreciate the invitation and are aware of what's proper and what's not."

"It's very tempting."

Maude put a hand on her shoulder. "They don't go through the closet often. The dresses that have already been utilized are just sitting there, gathering dust. We can choose one, borrow it, and you can bring it back on Monday."

The thought of dressing up — really dressing up — was enticing. Yet once again reality reared its head. "How do we get it out of the building?"

Maude glanced past Annie, revealing that this was an issue. Then her eyes brightened. "Occasionally I take home a garment to work on the design with my own machine."

"They let you do that?"

"I choose to do that, to get the thing done so I can move on to something else. I put the dress in a garment bag to take it home."

Annie nodded, understanding. "We could slip the dinner dress behind the other one?"

"It would work."

"But then you'd have to work. At home. On your days off."

Maude grinned. "So it is. My only payment will be hearing about everything — in detail — on the Monday morning after."

Consider it done.

CHAPTER NINETEEN

I am not meant to be a thief.

Annie hated that word. She preferred "borrower." Yet in all honesty, that term indicated an open arrangement, an ask-and-be-told-yes arrangement.

To just take the dress without asking . . .

She had to trust Maude. Maude had worked at Butterick for years. She knew the ropes. She knew the people. She knew the ins and outs of every department.

Maude knew how to steal a dress, but more importantly, Annie hoped she knew how to wangle not getting caught.

Maude's plan to slip the dinner dress behind a work-in-progress dress in a garment bag seemed possible. As long as something didn't muck it up.

When it was nearly quitting time. Annie's stomach flipped and grabbed. She put a hand to it and took a deep breath.

"Gracious goose, Annie," Maude said as

she came close. "It's not good form to look guilty before the crime."

Crime?

Maude held up a garment bag where she'd placed the dress she was going to finish at home. "I'm ready for the other one, and have even slipped a second bag in this one, so you won't be carrying a bare dress around when you go to your home, and I to mine."

Annie made sure no one else was looking. "Did your man, your contact . . . ?"

"Bertie, and he's just a boy. And yes, the item should be in a box in the storeroom on fifth, just where we arranged."

Annie needed this over and needed to be safely away. "I haven't been this nervous since I ran away from —" Once again, she'd nearly said too much.

"Ran away from what?"

She quickly put it to rest. "You don't need to know everything about me, Maude Nascato."

"Of course I do." Maude retrieved their jackets and hats. "But that will wait for another time."

Annie and Maude left with the other girls of the department, many chatting about their plans for their days off. No one mentioned the garment bag.

"Good night, Mrs. Downs," Maude said as they passed their boss.

"Good night, ladies." Mrs. Downs glanced at the garment bag but said nothing more.

As they entered the stairwell and made their way down two floors, Annie was impressed by Maude's confidence. She had a way about her that implied she knew exactly what she was doing and had full authority with what she was doing, which meant there was no reason to question her.

The girls detoured from the stairs into the fifth-floor offices, going against the tide of workers exiting toward the stairs.

" 'Night, Maude," a few of them said.

" 'Night, ladies." Maude strode toward the far side of the large room, and with a glance around, stepped inside a storage area, tugging Annie in with her.

And there it was. A box.

Maude lifted the lid to reveal the lovely peach gown Annie had chosen from the company's closet. But before she could admire it longer, Maude put the dress in a garment bag.

"I'm certainly glad it's not one of those old-fashioned dresses with huge leg-o'-mutton sleeves. I'd never get it to fit. Hand me the other dress."

Annie did as she was told, and within

seconds the garment bag within a garment bag was completed.

"By the way, you owe Bertie a bag o' sweets."

"Who?"

"The boy who brought this down here for you."

"Certainly." But then she had a question. "Why didn't we just get it directly from the closet upstairs?"

"Because it was upstairs." Maude nodded in the direction of the stairwell. "It would be a mite hard to explain the two of us going *up,* against the tide going *down.* I had to get it to a floor below ours."

Annie was impressed. "You think of everything."

"I try." She draped the bag over her arm. "The hard part is done. Are you ready to go?"

"More than ready."

When they exited the storeroom they found the entire floor empty. They rushed to the stairwell and joined the sea of workers going home.

Maude was smooth. Maude was unflappable.

When Annie met Sean outside the building — as per their routine — Maude walked with them for a while, giving no indication that anything was awry. As the corner approached where Maude would go north when they continued south, Annie felt a wave of panic.

For she had not told Sean anything about the dress. Although she felt she knew him well, to ask him to ignore their scheme was asking a lot.

"Down here," Maude said, stepping into an alley.

"What are you doing?" Sean asked.

"Close your eyes, Seanie," Maude said. "That way you won't be held as an accomplice."

"Accomplice to what?"

Maude already had the garment bag open and removed the second bag. She handed it to Annie. "There you go. Wear it in good health."

Sean's forehead was furrowed. "What just happened here?"

Maude offered a dramatic sigh. "You're accompanying Annie to the Sampsons' for dinner tonight, yes?"

"I am."

"What are you wearing?"

"I suppose I'll wear my Sunday suit. I haven't thought about it much."

"Of course you haven't," Maude said.

"But Annie has given great thought to her attire. She wants to wear something pretty and appropriate for such a grand dinner."

"I expect she would."

Annie couldn't take their vague banter any longer. "I had nothing to wear so I borrowed a dress from the Butterick closet and will bring it back on Monday."

Sean's gaze moved from Annie to the bag she was holding. "That belongs to the company?"

"It does."

"It does now, and always will," Maude said. "She's not keeping it, she's just borrowing it."

His eyebrows rose skeptically. "That's a fine line."

"Not fine at all," Maude said. "She wants to make a good impression. You can't fault her for that."

"Did you get permission?"

"Well . . . no."

He shook his head. "Breaking the rules, Annie. Really?"

Annie shoved the garment bag back into Maude's arms. "He's right. I can't do it. If the Sampsons don't like what I'm wearing, that's too bad. They know I'm a working girl and only have ordinary, functional clothes. They can't expect me to wear a

324

dress that's so . . . totally lovely." She gazed at the bag, remembering the fine detail of the dress inside.

"There," Maude said, presenting Annie's words as a cause to be championed. "Do you wish for our dear Annie to feel ordinary and functional, or totally lovely?"

Sean gave Maude the look she deserved. "There is no harmony between what's right and the answer you wish to hear."

"Of course there is. Choose the woman over the rule."

It was time for Annie to make her final petition. "I *would* love to wear it. Just this once. I promise I'll be exceedingly careful with it."

Sean looked from Annie to Maude then back again. "I am surrounded."

"And won over?" Maude asked.

"Stampeded is a better word."

Maude slapped him on the back. "Good for you, Seanie. Now take our Annie home, and have a marvelous time at dinner." She walked out of the alley to the street and then turned back to Annie. "Please don't spill anything on it."

Her departure showcased the silence. "Thank you," Annie said to Sean.

He took possession of the garment bag and offered her his arm — along with his reluctant consent to look the other way.

Annie stood before the mirror on the bureau. The dress made her feel lovely and sophisticated. She almost didn't recognize herself.

It was created from a peach-colored dupioni silk with a high waist and a daring scooped bodice that gained modesty with a dark brown chiffon covering the upper chest. The neckline was adorned with a wide flat collar of brown satin, with matching cuffs on the three-quarter sleeves. The shorter overskirt was edged in the brown satin that curved from the center front to the back, ending in a short train. Annie had never worn anything so beautiful. To go from wearing the uniform of a housemaid to this?

But then she remembered the source of the dress, and her elation waned. "Oh, Edna. I hope it's worth the risk."

"You're testing the bounds, that's for sure."

Annie wished Maude were here. Maude could convince Edna just like she'd convinced Sean. Even Annie could use an extra dose of convincing, because every time she thought about borrowing the dress, she felt a stitch in her stomach. Yet the anticipation of the evening always put a salve on the stitch, calming it.

For the moment.

Edna gave a little gasp. "Wait! I think I have the perfect accessory." She opened a bureau drawer and pulled out a worn velvet box. Inside was a necklace of golden-brown stones. "Wear this."

Annie let Edna hook the clasp at her neck. "It's beautiful. What are these stones?"

"Amber. It was my mother's."

"It's precious to you. I don't think I should."

"You should, because *you* are precious to me. I insist."

Annie pulled Edna into an embrace. "You are so good to me. You are the mother I always wished for."

Edna whispered in her ear, "And you are good to me. Good *for* me, the daughter I never had. I thank God for you."

Annie held back happy tears and whispered back, "As I thank Him for you."

There was a knock on the door.

Edna pulled back, flicking a tear away. "There's your escort."

Annie took a deep breath, wanting to hold on to the moment a little longer. For the first time in her life she felt fully complete and whole. She didn't need a fancy dinner or gorgeous dress to feel special, she only needed the presence and love of this dear, beloved friend. She had a fleeting but profound impression: of all the people who would move in and out of her life to come, the one she would treasure the most was Edna.

"Are you ready?" Edna asked.

Annie smoothed her skirt. "I am."

Edna answered the door, and Sean stepped in. As soon as he saw Annie his jaw dropped.

"Say something, man," Edna said.

"You're lovely. Breathtaking."

Annie felt her face flush. "Thank you. You look quite smart yourself."

Edna handed Annie a brown wool shawl. "There you go now. I don't want you to catch your death."

As they were leaving, Sean said, "Go to the window, Edna. I want you to see something."

Together Sean and Annie walked downstairs. "What do you want to show her?"

"You'll see."

Outside there was a motorcar with a driver. "What's this?" Annie asked.

"I hired him for the evening. I decided we needed to go to dinner in style."

Annie looked upward and saw Edna fling

open the window sash. "Well done, Sean!"

He tipped his hat then helped Annie into the car, and the driver closed the door behind them.

"I've never been in a motorcar."

"Me neither," he said. "I hope this is the first of many new experiences we share."

Annie could think of nothing better — or no one better to do it with.

"Oh my."

It was all Annie could say when their car motored in front of 451 Madison Avenue. It was not just one building, but three built in a horseshoe configuration with a court-yard between.

"This is one family's home?" Sean asked.

"I don't know. I assume so, but I know very little about Mrs. Sampson."

"You know her enough for her to invite you to dinner."

Suddenly the absurdity of the entire evening fell about her. "We shouldn't go. I met the woman once — in passing. We've only exchanged a dozen words. Why would she invite me here?"

Sean looked out the window at the im-mensity of the home. "Perhaps she's lonely. I think a person could get lonely in such a place."

The driver opened the door for them. "So?" Sean asked. "Are we going in?"

"We are." Annie would forever regret it if she didn't.

When they exited the car, Annie saw that they were directly across the street from an enormous cathedral. "What church is that?"

"St. Patrick's," Sean said. "How would you like such a monument for a neighbor?"

The next issue was finding the entrance. Sean asked the driver, "Where do we go in?"

"I believe you enter through that gate, sir. Then to the right."

Annie saw the ornate metal gate with a lantern hanging at the top of it.

"What time should I come to retrieve you, sir?"

He looked to Annie. "Ten . . . thirty?"

She nodded. If the dinner was done sooner, they'd go sit on the cathedral steps to wait.

The driver tipped his hat. "Enjoy your evening, sir. Miss."

As the driver drove away, Sean offered Annie his arm. "Shall we, *mademoiselle*?"

She gathered her courage. "We shall, *monsieur*."

They walked through the gate into a courtyard with manicured hedges. Electric lanterns lit the entrance on the right-hand building.

Annie was not encouraged when she heard Sean say under his breath, "Lord, help us." But his entreaty spurred her to add her own.

They didn't need to knock on the stained-glass door as it was opened as they approached. A butler nodded to them. "Good evening, Miss Wood, sir."

They entered a room where every surface was decorated, from the mosaic tile floors, to the marble walls, to intricately carved wood moldings, to columns that looked to be inlaid with mother-of-pearl. The furniture was secondary and consisted of a few chairs that were upholstered in a silky fabric with designs of orange and yellow.

"Blimey," Annie said, finding no other word adequate.

"This is just the foyer." Sean's eyes were wide, taking it all in.

"May I take your coats?"

As soon as Annie removed her shawl she was glad she'd borrowed the dinner dress, for her surroundings demanded posh attire.

"Right this way," the butler said and led them through a reception area into a drawing room. Annie couldn't help but compare it to the drawing room at Crompton Hall. The present room won the comparison with an intricate coffered ceiling, more columns clad with mother-of-pearl, and an inlaid wood floor.

"Miss Wood." Mrs. Sampson rose from a chair of golden velvet and came to greet them, her arms outstretched. She took Annie's arms and kissed her cheek.

This was completely different from how Lady Newley would greet an acquaintance. There was little touching among the titled in England. But in America — where no titles existed — such boundaries were obviously crossed.

"You look lovely, my dear."

"Thank you." Annie left it at that.

A mustachioed man joined them and shook Sean's hand. "And you are?"

"Sean Culver, sir."

"Glad you could join us."

Mrs. Sampson led Annie to a settee and shared the seat with her. "I am so glad you accepted our invitation. And that you brought a . . . friend?"

Annie hastened to explain. "Sean *is* a friend, but he also works at Butterick. He was instrumental in getting me the job."

"He obviously recognized your talent."

"I did," Sean said, standing by the fireplace with Mr. Sampson. "Annie has an innate design and artistic ability. She didn't even know she had the talent."

Mr. Sampson looked confused. "How could you not know?"

Annie glanced at Sean, not sure how much she should say. She knew so little about their hostess.

Mrs. Sampson touched her arm. "This is America, Annie. Humble beginnings are a badge of honor. It's not where you begin, but where you end up."

"Hear, hear," her husband said.

The butler returned with a footman, and hors d'oeuvres were offered. And wine. Annie took a glass to be polite, took a sip, and tried not to make a face when she disliked the taste.

"Now then," Mrs. Sampson said. "Back to humble beginnings?"

There was something about the woman that spurred Annie to share. "I was a housemaid in an English country estate. I started when I was fourteen."

"My, my," Mrs. Sampson said. "You have come a long way."

"Very commendable," Mr. Sampson said, "but I do believe I have you beat, Miss Wood. I started out shining shoes on the street. The horse dung I had to wipe away . . ."

"Yes, dear. That's enough of that."

Annie was impressed with his candor.

"I've had my share of such unpleasantries in the form of chamber pots."

"Oh, the things we have dung," he said with a chuckle.

"Stop it, Harold. Really."

Annie could tell that their banter was something they enjoyed about each other.

She had her own question. "If I may ask, what do you do now? How did you get from there to . . ." Her eyes scanned the room. "To here?"

"Shoes, Miss Wood. Shoes. As a boy I saw thousands of men's shoes and learned which ones were well made and which ones were going to fall apart. I decided to make quality shoes, and —"

"Sampson Fine Shoes!" Sean said. "I know of them."

With a glance to Sean's shoes, Mr. Sampson said, "I'll see you get a pair. Size ten?"

"How did you guess?"

He spread his arms. "It's my business."

"Now then," Mrs. Sampson said. "Back to Miss Wood's accomplishments."

Annie was more at ease talking about the shoe business. "It's a short list," she said. "I've only worked at Butterick a week, and before that, I worked at Macy's." She looked down at her dress. "This dress isn't even mine. It's borrowed. I don't own anything near this nice."

"Wearing your work clothes would have been fine," Mrs. Sampson said. "Just be who you are, Annie. Who you are is enough."

"But I want to know more, be more."

"You can add wisdom to your list of accomplishments."

Suddenly the flattery was too much. "I appreciate your kind words, but really, I know very little about a very little."

"More wisdom."

She sighed. "Why did you invite me here?"

Mrs. Sampson shared a laugh with her husband. "To the point. I like that."

"You warned me she was a feisty one."

"That she is," Sean said.

The three of them continued the discussion a few moments longer — as if Annie wasn't even there. It made her nerves rise to attention. The stress of the invitation coupled with the tension of borrowing the dress . . . "Stop. Please."

Silence.

"We don't mean to upset you, dear," Mrs. Sampson said.

"I'm not upset," Annie said. "Just confused. You talk about talent and being feisty and accomplishments when I haven't done anything to deserve your praise. Truly, I'm just starting out, trying to wend my way from being a maid to a working girl. I know bits about life, and am scared to pieces about all I *don't* know." She took a breath. "Why am I here? Tell me. Please."

Mrs. Sampson took her hand in hers and let both rest upon her knee. "You may be feisty, but I have been accused of being a whirlwind."

"Or a hurricane," her husband said.

She continued, "We speak of talent. My talent is identifying a spark in people. When I see it — as I saw it in you during our brief encounter the other day — I waste no time fanning that spark into a flame."

Annie was still confused. "What spark did you see?"

"The spark of practicality, creativity, and conscience."

Annie tried to remember the circumstances of their first meeting. "We were talking about hobble skirts."

"Exactly," she said. "You pointed out how ridiculous they are. Impractical. And I believe you called them —"

"Silly," Annie said, remembering. "They are silly. How is a woman supposed to live a normal life, hobbled in such ridiculous fashion?"

Mrs. Sampson looked at her husband.

"You see, Harold? I told you she was the one."

Annie blinked. "The one what?"

"The one to champion our cause."

"What cause is that?"

Mrs. Sampson opened her mouth to speak then closed it and raised a finger. "Have you ever heard of the Reform Dress Movement?"

"No."

"It started in the 1840s, rejecting the unhealthy confinement of the female form, and promoting practical clothing. Harold and I agree with its principles." She stood and set her plate and glass aside as if needing her hands free to make her point. "If women want the freedom to vote, then shouldn't they be allowed to wear fashion that offers them freedom of movement? Now is the time to let women break the bonds of corsetry and the confinement of petticoats!"

"Step off your soapbox, dearest," her husband said.

Mrs. Sampson nodded and took a fresh breath. "It's a steep step down. I apologize."

"Don't apologize," Annie said. "I like what I hear."

"Actually, I do, too," Sean said. "At least in theory."

"But there you have it," Mrs. Sampson said. "It has to be more than theory. Freedom of dress needs to become the new wave of fashion. And you, Annie Wood, are just the one to bring it into being."

At that moment, the butler entered the room. "Dinner is served, ma'am."

Sean accompanied Mrs. Sampson, and Mr. Sampson offered Annie his arm and a whispered "To be continued."

She wasn't certain whether to be eager or petrified.

Every surface of the Sampsons' dining room was embellished with carving, tile, mother-of-pearl, gold, brass, or silk. The item that was most unadorned was the top of the enormous dining table, which had its own decoration within the swirling grain of the polished oak.

Where the oak left off, the painted china took over, as each gold-edged plate — there were four different plates so far — presented a different exotic bird in its middle, with sweeping leaves and floral sprays surrounding it. The goblets were intricate cut glass, and the sterling silver flatware was far from flat as the handles were created through an interweaving of curlicues dotted with flowers.

Although awed by the decor and finery, Annie was heartily glad she knew which knife and fork to use. Although she'd never sat at such a fancy meal, she'd been exposed to a proper place setting at Crompton Hall. Sean seemed less informed and looked to her for guidance. She picked up the proper utensil, and he followed her lead. It was rather satisfying to know something that he did not.

The conversation about freedom of fashion did not resume until well after the fish course, as they were enjoying a fine cut of lamb.

"So, Annie," Mrs. Sampson said. "May I call you Annie?"

"Please."

"And you may call me Eleanor."

Annie was taken aback. "I'm not sure I can do that."

"Why not?"

She raised a hand a few feet off the table. "You are here, and I am . . ." She lowered her hand to just above her plate. "Here."

"Nonsense," Mrs. Sampson said. "Harold told you about our humble roots."

"It was very nice of you to share that. I like to hear such stories. They give me hope."

"A question, Annie. Do you wish to have

a house such as this?" Mr. Sampson asked.

She knew the answer straightaway but didn't want to offend, so she chose her words carefully. "I wish to be successful at something, but I don't much care if it brings me wealth."

"What would you like it to bring you?" Mrs. Sampson asked.

"Satisfaction." She let the word stand on its own.

Sean had his own requirement. "And a sense of purpose. I'd like to think I was doing what I was supposed to be doing."

"According to whom?" Mrs. Sampson asked.

Sean glanced at each of their faces before answering. "God."

Mr. Sampson slapped a hand on the table, making them jump. "Well said, sir. Well said."

Annie was surprised. She'd been taught never to talk about God or politics or the latest cricket match at the dinner table. The butler and housekeeper at Crompton Hall had been very strict about this during the servants' meals.

Mrs. Sampson leaned back in her chair so the footman could serve her more brussel sprouts. She nodded after receiving four.

"So you believe there is a divine plan, Sean?"

"I do." He looked at Annie and nodded once. "I believe we each have a unique purpose — a God-given purpose. The trick is to find out what it is."

"Now *that's* a good trick," Mrs. Sampson said.

"But not impossible," he said.

It was Annie's turn to ask a question. "So how does one know they are on the right path?"

Sean answered with confidence. "Practice and peace."

Mr. Sampson cocked his head. "You have my attention."

Sean's face reddened, and he refolded the napkin in his lap. "I am no expert, but from what I've ascertained from personal experience is that I need to pray for direction, be aware of the nudges the Almighty sends me, and act on those nudges to the best of my ability. If I'm on the right path, I feel a sense of peace."

"A very businesslike way of approaching the spiritual," Mrs. Sampson said.

"It's practical. And it works. I am proof of it."

Mr. Sampson made a motion to the footman to replenish the drinks all around. "I love a good story. Proceed."

Sean's blush deepened. "I didn't mean to take the attention away from Annie. She was the one you invited here. I am simply her dinner companion."

Mrs. Sampson smile was a wee bit wicked. "Oh, I think we have all determined you're more than just that."

Annie deflected her own heated cheeks by taking a drink of water.

Sean looked across the table at her. "If it's all right with Annie for me to tell my story?"

"Of course it is," she said with full sincerity. "I'd love to hear it."

Sean set his fork down and took a cleansing breath. "My life has been a series of stepping-stones, one step leading to another until I reached a door."

"A door you opened? Mr. Sampson asked.

"And walked though."

"In order to tell the story, I need to go back eight years. I was thirteen and working at my father's general store in Brooklyn. I was good at sales. He'd order in too many match safes and would ask me to push them until our stock was depleted. Or bowler hats. Or wire whisks — he overbought terribly the wire whisks."

"You were a salesman then as you are a salesman now," Annie pointed out.

"It seems that is my talent."

"Your purpose," Mrs. Sampson said.

"Not completely. Just a part of it."

Mr. Sampson motioned for the dinner plates to be removed. "Don't interrupt him, ladies. Let the man continue."

Mrs. Sampson made a locking motion to her lips, which made Annie smile.

Sean took up where he'd let off. "I befriended Ebenezer Butterick, who lived in Brooklyn, too." He must have seen Annie about to speak because he added, "Yes, the founder of our company. He was retired then, in his mid-seventies. A frail man, but very wise and sharp of mind. He lived quietly and simply, and gave much of his wealth to good causes. He had a soft heart for children — he created the first sized patterns to fill a need for home-sewn children's clothes."

"I didn't know that," Mr. Sampson said.

"Shh!" Mrs. Sampson said with a wink.

"Ah. Yes. Hush."

Sean smiled, too. "Mr. Butterick created his highly successful company from a single idea. In the early years they'd cut and package the patterns on their kitchen table in Sterling, Massachusetts."

"More humble beginnings," Mrs. Sampson said.

There were nods all around.

"The year we met, the company was constructing the building where Annie and I work. Mr. Butterick was very proud of how the business had grown, and attributed its success to God."

"A wise man."

"Very wise. That spring he grew ill. I made deliveries from the store to him, and he said I reminded him of his nephew, and we would talk. A lot. He seemed to need someone to talk to. His wife had died decades earlier, and his son in infancy. His only daughter, Mary Ellen, came to visit, but he seemed to like my company."

"I understand that." Annie's compliment was heartfelt.

"We talked about business, and sales, and using our success to help others."

"He sounds like a wonderful man."

Sean confirmed this with a nod. "We also talked a lot about God and how there's no such thing as a coincidence. He said that my making a delivery to his house was God's plan to bring us together. And when his health grew worse, he made me promise to go to his company and apply for a job. He even wrote a letter of recommendation."

"You went, and you got the job," Mrs. Sampson said.

"I did — against my father's wishes. He saw no reason for me to take a job in Manhattan when we lived in Brooklyn and I had a perfectly good job in the family store. But I really felt this was the path I was supposed to take, so I walked across the Brooklyn Bridge — and back — every day for five years until I got my current sales position, which allowed me to afford my own apartment closer to work. I was in the stockroom at first, but I worked my way up to sales. It all came about from me working in my father's store, from *me* making a delivery to Mr. Butterick instead of the other boy who worked for us. One thing led to the other. One stepping-stone led to the next and to the open door."

"And you felt it was right," Annie said.

"I knew it was right because of the peace I felt inside. I still feel that peace."

"What a marvelous story," Mrs. Sampson said.

Sean looked to his plate, which now contained a piece of multilayered chocolate cake. "I don't know if it's marvelous, but it's my story." He looked at Annie. "I think Annie is on her right path, too. The door to Butterick opened for her just as it did for me."

345

"Because you recommended me," Annie said.

"How could I not?" he said softly.

"I will not contradict you, Sean," Mrs. Sampson said. "But we asked you here tonight to open another door that leads to another room."

Mr. Sampson nodded. "I do believe it is time to get to the point. Go ahead, my sweet."

Mrs. Sampson took a large bite of her cake, pushed the plate aside, and then dabbed at her mouth. "Harold and I have been looking for a new beacon in the fashion industry, someone who can design for real women who live real lives. Someone who dares to be unconstricted by the designs of others who show more care for fad over function."

"Ooh, I like that, Eleanor," Mr. Sampson said. "Fad over function."

"Thank you, dear one," she said before continuing. She looked directly at Annie. "We believe you are that beacon."

Annie was confused. "You met me once — on my first day on the job. You know nothing of my talent or lack of it."

Mrs. Sampson shook Annie's logic away. "As I stated, my talent is having a sense about people. I am an extremely good judge of character. When good character and a zest for new ideas show themselves in a person, I will not remain silent. I must make every attempt to tap into it for the common good."

Annie looked to Sean for his reaction. His eyes were slightly wide, his eyebrows raised. He looked as confused as she felt.

"I know how odd this is," Mrs. Sampson said, "but before we move on, I need to finish it and put a cherry on its oddness. We want you to design a fashion line that combines style and utility." She looked to her husband, who nodded. "We will provide all the funding, and Harold has the business contacts for distribution."

"You will be paid well for your efforts," Mr. Sampson said.

"So what do you think of our grand scheme?" Mrs. Sampson said.

Annie had no idea how to respond. The idea was absurd.

Mr. Sampson looked across the table at his wife. "She needs time to think on it, my sweet — which again, shows her wisdom."

"Which further increases my desire to have her work with us." Mrs. Sampson stood, suddenly ending the evening. "We are so glad you took time out of your busy week to meet with us. And now you have the whole of the weekend to think about our proposal."

In minutes, Sean and Annie were out the door amid a flurry of thank-yous and good-byes.

"What just happened?" Annie asked.

"You were ambushed and they wanted us gone before you could object." Sean looked at his watch. "The car won't be here for a half hour. Shall we go across the street and sit on the steps of the church?"

Annie was glad for the suggestion because her legs felt weak. At the cathedral, Sean helped her sit upon a step before joining her. She tucked her skirt around her legs and wrapped the shawl close. The churning inner turmoil made the solidity of the stone steps a necessary foundation. Without it she would surely walk in an aimless circle, or faint away like some weakened woman of the past.

"They want me to quit my job — a job I just started. They want me to design clothes when I have no experience other than designing a different sleeve or collar."

"They want you to go against the entire fashion industry."

Annie remembered what Maude and Mrs. Downs had said about Mrs. Sampson. "They called her a fashion rebel, a nonconformist, and a zealous malcontent."

"Do you want to be associated with someone like that? Now, when you're just starting out?"

"No. I don't. I have too much to learn at Butterick to leave before I've started. Maybe at a later date, I'd —"

"So you'd consider it?"

She was surprised by the incredulity in his tone. "It sounds intriguing, and I like the idea of function over fad. You have to admit the hobble skirt is laughable and defies and denies all logical function."

"But that's what fashion is — a fad. Women like change. If fashion didn't change we'd still be designing hoopskirts or bustles."

"Two other fads."

Sean put his arm around her against the night chill. "Fads keep us employed."

"Even if what we're designing is wrong?"

The only answer he had for her was a shrug.

At this point it was as good an answer as any other.

Chapter Twenty

There was no time to talk about the Sampsons' offer with Edna.

Annie had arrived home late from the dinner party the night before, and in the morning — being Saturday — she immediately dove into working on Iris's wedding dress. Today Iris and Thomas were coming over so it could be fitted. *That* was the task for the day. Pondering some far-off, far-fetched future as the Sampsons' "it" girl would have to wait.

Edna fluttered around the apartment moving a candlestick to the right an inch, dusting some porcelain chickadees, fluffing a pillow that had NIAGARA FALLS embroidered on the front.

Annie looked up from some seam-work on Iris's dress. "Be still, Edna. The place looks grand."

"It does not look grand, it can never look grand." She put a hand to her mouth, her eyes scanning the space for offending bric-a-brac. "I don't get many guests."

"Iris and Thomas are hardly guests."

"They're your friends."

"They are. And this apartment is far more than what they're used to above the bakery. Remember Iris was a housemaid like me." Annie stopped her seaming and went to her friend, taking hold of her upper arms. "Be calm. Relax. They are coming so Iris can try on the dress, not to inspect your home."

"All right. *You're* right." Edna stepped to the couch and turned the pillow upside down. "How's that?"

Annie laughed. "I dare you to keep it like that."

Edna stared at the pillow as if it were a threat. There was a knock on the door, and Edna rushed to the pillow and turned Niagara right-side up again.

Annie opened up the door and made the introductions.

Thomas looked around the apartment then pointed to the pillow. "My father and stepmother went to the Falls after they were married. Jane and I went with them."

Edna took up the pillow, gave it an extra fluff, and then returned it to its place. "My husband and I visited there after our marriage, too." She looked at the couple. "And now you will be married. Congratulations."

"Thank you." Iris wove her hand around Thomas's arm and looked up at him adoringly. "We are very happy."

Their love gave Annie's insides a little twinge. She wanted such a love, even as the thought of it frightened her. Sean was a good man, and all evidence suggested their friendship could be much more. But was she ready for that?

As if summoned by her thought, there was another knock on the door. Sean joined the group easily, as he'd met Iris and Thomas after Danny's death.

"I'm so sorry you had to come all the way here," Annie said. "But Officer Brady thought it best."

"I'm glad to come," Iris said. "Glad to get away from the bakery for a while." She looked at Thomas with a panicked look. "I mean no offense. I love your family."

He patted her hand. "No offense taken. And I agree with you. Any time I get to spend with you away from their prying eyes is a bonus."

Again, the loving looks. Annie took the subject in a new direction. "Have you seen Grasston?"

"Once," Iris said. "Gramps saw him standing in the alley across the street, staring at

352

the bakery. He went outside, called a police-man over, and the coward ran away."

"Pa and I warned him never to go out there alone again," Thomas said. "I don't trust the wretch."

"Nor should you," Annie said.

"Ma didn't even want us coming today because she was afraid we would be fol-lowed," he said. "But I did a good scan of the neighborhood before I brought Iris outside, and we kept an eye out for him as we came here. We weren't followed."

That you know of. "I hope he doesn't know where I'm working now."

Edna smoothed the fringed scarf on the mantle. "We haven't seen him around Ma-cy's. No reason to think he knows you aren't there anymore."

"Except if he's been waiting for me before and after work and hasn't seen me," Annie said. "Maybe he's asking around. Maybe he's figuring things out."

Sean put a calming hand on her shoulder. "Don't borrow trouble. We're being careful. So are the Tuttles. And Officer Brady is on top of things. There's not much more we can do."

"Except keep praying for safety," Edna said.

"And justice," Annie said.

"We're doing that," Iris said. "I've got all the children adding it to their bedtime prayers."

Annie was moved at the thought of all those little heads bowed in prayer.

Iris shook the subject a way with the flip of her head. "I came here to talk about my wedding dress, not Oscar Grasston. Where is it?"

"It's in the bedroom," Annie said.

Edna shooed the men outside. "It's time for the males of this company to take a stroll through the neighborhood."

"But I'd like to see Iris in the dress," Thomas said.

"Not until the wedding," Edna said. "You know it's bad luck."

Annie had heard such superstitions but thought them preposterous, yet practical for today since there was work to be done.

She was nervous about Iris seeing the dress for the first time.

Her fears were unfounded when Iris put her hands to her mouth and gasped. "It's the most beautiful dress I've ever seen."

It was an overstatement yet also a relief. "Let's see how it looks on you."

The high-waisted dress of gray-blue moss cloth had straight three-quarter sleeves, a scooped neckline, and a straight overskirt with a diagonal hem, edged with a twelve-inch band of satin. The overskirt was short enough to reveal the soft drapery of the crepe underskirt. There was little trim, just some braid at the cuff of the sleeve and neckline.

Annie was glad she'd cut it a bit big. "Have you gained a bit, Iris?"

The girl sucked in — which removed an inch from her midsection. "I suppose it's possible. Working at a bakery makes it hard not to nibble the wares. Can you fit it?"

Annie tugged at the back seam and found there to be just enough. She took pins from a pincushion and pinned it shut. "It doesn't have the hem in yet, but you can get the feel of it. Go in Edna's room and take a look-see."

The three women moved into Edna's bedroom, and Iris had her first look. She touched the neckline, the cuffs, the curve of her hips underneath. "I look all growed up."

"That you do," Edna said.

That you should be if you're getting married.

Suddenly Edna bounced on her toes. "I have the perfect accessory!"

She stood on a chair and retrieved a hatbox from the top of her chifforobe. With a flurry of tissue, she removed a wide-brimmed straw hat with an ivory ostrich plume on it. There were pink silk roses in a spray on top of a wide blue ribbon. "Voila!" Edna said, presenting it to the ladies.

Annie took possession, giving it a good study. "It's very lovely. I think the pink flowers complement the blue of the dress perfectly."

She handed it off to Iris, who held it reverently. "I've never worn anything so . . . so *chick.*"

"It's pronounced 'sheek,' " Edna said. "And yes, that hat is indeed chic. I don't wear it often, but when I do, I feel quite glamorous."

"You wouldn't wear it during the wedding," Annie pointed out.

Edna agreed. "But for the occasional Sunday . . . you can borrow it sometimes, if you'd like."

Annie helped place it on Iris's head, tilting it back just a bit so her pretty face could be seen. "There."

Iris looked at her reflection and began to cry.

"What's wrong?"

"It's the most lovely I've ever looked. I am so blessed to be marrying Thomas and becoming a part of the Tuttle family." She turned toward Annie. "It was a good thing we ran away, wasn't it?"

Annie pulled Iris into her arms but couldn't help but think of Danny — Danny who would still be alive had they not run away.

Annie peered out the front window of Edna's apartment, looking for the men. Oddly, she saw them coming out of the brownstone across the street. Sean was carrying a piece of paper, and they were talking with a middle-aged man. Sean shook his hand.

What was going on?

Annie opened the window and called to them. "We're done, boys. Come back up."

Within seconds they heard feet on the stairs in the hall, and with a burst of energy, Thomas and Sean came inside.

"You'll never believe what just happened," Sean said, holding the piece of paper behind his back.

"You'll never believe what Sean just did," Thomas added.

"Do tell," Edna said. "But don't start until I get some coffee water on the stove."

The four of them sat in the parlor, with Iris and Thomas sharing the sofa. Edna quickly returned and stood at the mantel. "So, Sean. What is this amazing feat?"

"It's not a feat," he said. "But it is amazing. It's God's doing, plain and simple." Sean's smile couldn't get any wider. "While Thomas and I were sitting on the front stoop getting to know each other, I saw a man come out of the brownstone across the way. A Mr. Collins."

"Mr. Collins?" Edna asked. "The landlord?"

Sean nodded. "He was posting this on the door." He pulled the piece of paper front and center. It said Apartment for Rent. "All of a sudden I'm walking across the street and talking with him. And then I looked at the place and rented it. It's mine!"

"Were you looking for an apartment?" Edna asked.

"I wasn't. But I was swayed because it's so close to here, to Annie."

"That was quick work," Iris said.

Sean nodded at their reaction but looked to Annie. "Aren't you pleased? Now when I walk you to and from work I only have to cross the street to be home myself."

Annie knew what she should say, but for some reason the words wouldn't come. As each second passed without her reaction, Sean's smile diminished until it was extinguished completely.

"I thought you'd be happy for me. Happy for us."

A glance to Edna nudged Annie to respond — if not with total honesty, at least with the words Sean needed to hear. "I'm very happy for you."

"For us."

"That, too."

His brow dipped, but he was clearly too excited to let his mood be dampened too long. "Mr. Collins and I shook hands on it, and I'm moving after work on Monday. Luckily, I have very little to move so it won't be much of a bother."

"I'm going to help," Thomas said.

The sound of water steaming in the pot was heard from the kitchen. "Coffee's coming. And some scones." Edna nodded to Iris. "Would you like to help me, Iris?"

With a glance at Annie, Iris left the room.

"I'll help, too," Thomas said.

Leaving Annie alone with Sean.

Annie immediately regretted the delay of her response. If only she'd given Sean what he needed and not hesitated to dissect her own contradictory feelings.

Sean moved to the chair nearest her. "I thought you'd be truly happy."

"I am."

"But?"

She couldn't go down that road just yet because it had no clear direction. "It *will* be

359

much more efficient for you. I've felt guilty about you having the extra walking every day. You don't have to see me home. I am quite capable of —"

He popped out of his chair. "You're quite capable of making something I did because I want to be close to you into something completely pragmatic and convenient. Are you really so cold as to not be happy for the same reason I'm happy?"

She rose and touched his arm. "I'm sorry. I didn't mean to hurt you. You just caught me by surprise." She thought of something in her favor. "You caught yourself by surprise, too, correct?"

"I did. If Thomas and I hadn't been sitting on the stoop I may never have noticed the sign." His enthusiasm took over. "It's truly as if God put it together for me."

She said the words that would make him happy. "For us."

He beamed and kissed her lightly on the lips. "For us." He drew her into his arms where her doubts could be held at bay.

Iris and Thomas were gone. Sean, too. Annie had sent him away, claiming she had a bad headache.

She did. In a way. She suffered from a mental ache due to decisions left to make, and decisions already made by others.

"Would you like me to get you some aspirin?"

Annie took up Iris's dress and sat at the sewing machine. "I'll be all right."

Edna plucked the dress out of her lap and took Annie's hand, leading her away from the machine and to the sofa. "Sit."

"Did I do something wrong?"

"Lying is wrong. You lied about your headache to get Sean to leave — and don't deny it."

Annie drew the Niagara Falls pillow to her chest and leaned back with an expulsion of air.

"The question is why? You and he should be out celebrating his move to the neighborhood."

"I suppose you're right."

"Suppose?" Edna stood and stared down at her. "What is wrong with you, girlie? You have the interest of a wonderful man and you shoo him away like a mongrel puppy."

A wave of regret fell over her. "I did that, didn't I?"

Edna returned to the sofa. "You did. He was so pleased finding the apartment and you're acting as if having him close offends you."

"It doesn't offend me."

"Then what is it?"

Annie fingered the fringe on the pillow, giving herself time to find the right word. It came to her quicker than she expected. "It frightens me."

"Sean Culver is the least frightening man I've ever met. He's a true gentleman."

"I know."

"What other man would walk blocks and blocks out of his way — twice a day — to accompany you to and from work?"

"No one I know."

"Moving across the street will make life easier for him. Or don't you want things to be easier for him? Maybe you're a selfish flirt who wants to manipulate men to her bidding, keeping them on a leash she can yank at her every whim?"

Annie tossed the pillow aside. "I am not like that. I appreciate his extra care. I like having him around."

"But not too close."

Annie suffered a deep sigh. "I don't know what I feel about him. And then there's the Sampsons, offering me the world and —"

"What world? You haven't told me about the dinner party. What happened?"

Annie described the evening in detail, ending with the Sampsons' offer. "They want me to design a line of clothes for everyday women that combines function with style. They want me to leave Butterick."

"But you just started there."

"Exactly. And to add to the temptation they'll pay me well — better than what I earn now. By the looks of their mansion, I know they have the money to do everything they say."

"But it's an enormous risk. Going off on your own like that . . ."

". . . when I know so little about fashion and design. It's like leaping from scullery maid to housekeeper with no experience in between."

"So what are you going to do? You've been offered a new job and the love of a man. Two very large, very important decisions have been laid at your feet."

"Therein lies the problem. A few months ago I lived a life where every decision was made *for* me, where having a beau was frowned upon. Now I'm smack-dab in the middle of a life where *I* am in charge, where enormous life-changing decisions are mine to make. The responsibility overwhelms me."

Edna nodded and her face softened. "It was similar for me when Ernie died. Before his death he was in charge of most of the decisions of our life, and honestly, I was glad to leave him to it. But with him gone I was flung into a world where my happiness — and even my survival — depended solely on me."

"Spot on!" Annie said. "That's how I feel. How did you manage to get past it?"

"I didn't get past it, I trudged through it, one decision at a time."

"But how did you know which decision was the right one?"

Edna looked at Annie over her glasses. "You know the answer to that."

Ah. "I pray?"

Edna touched the tip of Annie's nose. " 'A threefold cord is not quickly broken.' "

"What's that mean?"

"Think of a rope. One strand is good, two strands wrapped around each other is better, and three strands woven together is not quickly broken." She pointed to herself. "One." Then to Annie. "Two." Then to heaven. "Three."

Annie nodded with understanding and acceptance. "You have an answer for everything."

"I don't, but God does." Edna offered Annie her hand. "Let's begin."

Annie took her hand and their fingers intertwined, becoming strong. They bowed their heads.

The prayers of the two women wove their way to the Almighty, merging with His immeasurable, unbreakable strength.

Chapter Twenty-One

The dress. Oh dear, the dress.

As it was borrowed, so it had to be returned. Yet there was a flaw in their plan. For going into work on Monday morning, Annie didn't have the help of Maude or Bertie. She was on her own.

Sean carried it for her as they walked to work. "How are you going to get it back where it belongs?" he asked as soon as they left their neighborhood.

It was the main problem of the day, yet she had to address something else first. "I want to apologize for my lukewarm reaction to the news that you are moving across the street."

"Tepid. Utterly tepid."

"I am sorry for it."

"Can you explain it to me?" He took her arm and helped her around some rubbish in the street.

"I can't explain it completely or well," she

said. "I must leave it at the fact that I am unused to being around gentlemen who are kind and thoughtful and think of my needs over their own."

"I think there is a compliment in all that."

"There is." She stopped walking and faced him, stepping out of the flow of pedestrians. "You are a wonderful man, Sean Culver, and I appreciate all that you are, and our friendship."

" 'Friendship' sounds too lukewarm for my taste."

Here was the difficult part. "I am a novice at being courted and wooed."

"I love that word, *wooed*. And *swooned*, too, if you ever choose to use it. Very descriptive words."

Annie smiled but would not be deterred from her point. "Recently I have been faced with many decisions, with more forthcoming. This freedom of choice is also new to me, and I don't take the blessing of it lightly. And so" — she took a fresh breath — "I wish to take the time to be wise. I am not saying no to everything you so generously offer me but am asking you to give me some time to choose wisely and right." She took his hand. "Is that acceptable?"

"Acceptable yes, but pleasing? No." He lifted her chin and looked into her eyes. "I am in love with you, Annie. If I had my way I would take you in my arms right here and give you a kiss that would create a public scandal."

She felt herself blush. "I didn't take you for a rogue."

"I am many things. Just give me time as I will give you time."

They resumed their walk, and Annie felt better for the discussion. At least that was taken care of. "Which leaves the dress . . . ," she said.

"You should never have taken it. It didn't impress Mrs. Sampson. She said as much. You risked much for little gain."

"Although I enjoyed the wearing of it, it was a bad decision. Unfortunately, I am sure it will not be the last."

"Perhaps you should just walk right up to the closet where you got it, put it away, and hope no one sees you."

"Last time I checked, I was not invisible."

"I see no other way."

She did. "Could you go ahead of me, and make sure the way is clear?"

He didn't answer, and she realized she was also putting his job on the line.

"Never mind. I'll get it done myself."

Somehow. Some way.

■ ■ ■ ■

Annie slipped into the stairwell with the garment bag over her arm. Dozens of employees walked past her up the stairs, going to their respective departments. No one asked about the bag. Maybe she *could* just put it back without incident.

But what if I get caught? Surely I will lose my job. I will be shamed.

I should be ashamed. I am ashamed. I took what wasn't mine.

Then another word fell upon the rest, sinking heavily to the bottom like a pebble in a pond. *Confess.*

With the thought of confession came a hint of hope that all would not be lost. Confession was good for the soul, but was it good for the job?

"It's the only way," she said under her breath.

A man walking by said, "Excuse me?"

She shook her head and joined the others heading up the stairs. With each step she prayed. *Help me. Help me. Help me.*

At her floor, Annie strode toward Mrs. Downs's office.

"Good morning, Annie," the woman said, looking up from a desk full of paperwork.

Annie shut the door, making Mrs. Downs set her pencil down. "Miss Wood?" Her eyes fell upon the garment bag then met Annie's gaze. "Is there a problem?"

Annie draped the bag over the back of a chair. "Last Friday I borrowed a dress from the company's storeroom."

Mrs. Downs blinked. "Why?"

"I was invited to Mrs. Sampson's for dinner and had nothing suitable to wear."

"Mrs. Sampson. Mrs. Eleanor Sampson."

Annie nodded. "And her husband."

"What would they want with you?"

The full truth would not do. "As you are curious, so was I — which is why I accepted." She thought of a point that might make the entire excursion more legitimate. "Mr. Culver in sales accompanied me."

By the furrow in Mrs. Downs's brow it was clear this point made things worse.

"So Mr. Culver was in on the borrowing of the dress?"

Why did I mention him! She hurried to explain. "No. Not at all. Mrs. Sampson simply said I could bring a friend, so I invited him."

"Perhaps you should have invited me. After all, Mrs. Sampson comes to Butterick to speak with me."

But you hate her.

"I apologize for my oversight. I was flattered by the invitation — and curious. I'd heard the Sampsons were wealthy, and I knew my work clothes would not be smart enough, so . . ." She sighed. "So I borrowed the dress. My vanity overrode my common sense."

"How did you even know we had a cache of dresses?"

Annie thought of Maude and didn't want to get her involved, too. "I saw them when I had a tour of the building."

"Maude showed you."

Annie thought fast. "She showed me the printing presses, too. And the order room and shipping bays." She was running out of words. "I'm sorry. I know it was wrong, and I shan't do it again."

Mrs. Downs just sat there, clearly not knowing what to do. The silence was almost worse than if she'd yelled.

Finally she said, "This is unacceptable."

"I know."

"I'm not sure how to deal with you."

Mercy? Empathy? Forgiveness?

With a shake of her head, she flipped a hand at Annie. "Take it back where you got it and get to work."

That was the lot of it? Annie didn't wait to hear more. She retrieved the dress and

371

scurried up the stairs to the company's closet.

As she was taking it out of the bag, a woman confronted her. "What are you doing?"

"Returning a dress," Annie said. "Mrs. Downs's orders."

The woman looked confused, but Annie folded the empty garment bag under her arm and left.

She hurried back to her floor, her steps light, her burden lifted. Confession had been the right choice. She'd never imagined getting off so easily.

When she entered her department Maude rushed toward her. "Mrs. Downs caught you?"

Annie kept her face neutral and her voice low for the sake of those who might listen. "I confessed."

Maude grabbed her arm none too gently and yanked her into the hall. "Did you tell them about my part in it?"

"I did not — other than to say I knew about the dresses because of the tour you gave."

"You didn't."

"I had to say that much. She asked how I knew the dress existed. But I did not tell her you came up with the idea, or your part in sneaking it out of the building for me."

Maude's chest heaved, and she stared at the air between them. Finally she looked at Annie again. "Why did you confess? Why not just put it back?"

"I feared I would be caught, so I chose to head it off by owning up to it."

"That was stupid."

Was it? "I feel better for having it in the open. I don't deal with fear well. All day I would have worried someone would find out and I'd get in trouble."

"So you chose to get yourself in trouble?" She shook her head. "Don't ask me to help you again." Maude walked away.

But you suggested it. I never would have even known about it if it weren't for you.

Annie noticed people looking at her as she stood oddly in the middle of the corridor.

What was done was done. She went back to work.

"Make sure the sleeve seam hits the cap of the shoulder just so," Maude said.

They stood before a dress form, where Maude taught Annie how to create the sleeve piece of a pattern. "How much seam allowance do you add?" Annie asked.

"Three-eighths of an inch."

It seemed an odd number. "Why not just

make it an even half inch?"

Maude glared at her. "And they call Mrs. Sampson the fashion rebel?"

"It was just a thought."

Maude shrugged. "You haven't told me about your dinner Friday — which *was* part of our bargain."

"It was very nice. Delicious. And their house is truly a mansion."

"All vague details, and assumed. I want to know the reason she invited you in the first place."

Annie wanted to tell Maude the gist of things, and she would have valued her opinion about the Sampsons' offer, but there was still a tension between them regarding Annie's confession. Now was not the time.

"I'm not quite sure of her reasons," Annie fibbed. "Apparently when she was here that Monday I caught her fancy."

"Again, assumed. But why? Why you? Why not me? I'm far more interesting than you."

Annie was relieved to see Maude smile. Perhaps the tension was easing.

"You certainly have far more confidence than I."

"If I don't believe in myself, who will?"

They stopped their conversation when Mrs. Downs came in the room and made a beeline toward them. The woman stood with her back to the others and said, "You are wanted in Mr. Burroughs's office."

A wave of panic swept over Annie. "But I thought —"

"You thought wrong."

She set aside the muslin sleeve.

"You, too, Miss Nascato."

"Me?"

Mrs. Downs lowered her voice. "Don't make a scene. Just go."

The two girls had everyone's attention when they left the workroom. As they waited for the elevator, Maude said, "Your confession may be good for the soul, but it may also put us on the dole."

"Surely not."

Maude leveled her with a look. "One does not get summoned to talk to the boss if there are not consequences to be meted out."

They were being sacked? Annie found it hard to breathe. She'd known that was a possibility, but after Mrs. Downs's mild rebuke, she'd thought she was safe. Why hadn't she simply returned the dress in secret?

The elevator came. The operator gave them a nod. Without privacy there was no chance to say all that Annie wanted to say, except a whispered "I'm so sorry."

There were two chairs in front of Mr. Burroughs's desk. Maude sat in one, her hands in her lap. Her expression revealed nothing.

Annie adopted the opposite posture. She sat very straight and on the edge of the seat. Her nerves were on the alert. *Please help me, God. Please. I'm so sorry.*

Mr. Burroughs sat behind the desk, his silver mustache and neatly trimmed hair giving him the look of an older man of wisdom.

And mercy. Please mercy.

His secretary stood beside him, showing him some numbers in a large binder. The two perused the opened page, pointed at various items, and spoke softly to each other. When they were finished, the secretary glanced at the girls with a disapproving look then made to leave.

Suddenly she dropped the ledger. The sound made Annie jump.

"A bit skittish, Miss Wood?" Mr. Burroughs said.

"Yes, sir. I am nervous, sir."

"As you should be." He glanced at Maude, but Annie was his main focus. "I hear you took it upon yourself to borrow a dress from our stores?"

"I did, sir. And I'm very sorry for it. It was an imprudent thing to do."

"That it was." He straightened some papers into a tidy pile. "You could have asked."

Annie was shocked. "You would have let me borrow it?"

"No," he said. "With over two thousand employees we cannot allow such borrowing. Even *if* it was for a special occasion initiated by a wealthy New York family."

"Of course, sir." Annie chided herself for not thinking of all this before the act. "I was so caught up in the excitement of my new job here, and somewhat overly flattered by Mrs. Sampson's invitation, that I overlooked common sense."

"And right and wrong."

Her stomach flipped. "That, too."

Mr. Burroughs looked at Maude. "You've been with us a long time, haven't you, Miss Nascato?"

"Five years, sir."

"I hear you showed Miss Wood the closet."

"I did, sir. Mrs. Downs asked me to give her a tour of the entire building."

Annie chimed in. "It's quite an impressive arrangement you have here, sir. Sixteen floors. Very large yet very efficient."

Mr. Burroughs closed his eyes then

opened them. "At times excessive flattery can be very unflattering, Miss Wood."

"I only meant to say that . . ." What did she mean to say? "I don't want Maude to get in trouble for something I did. I take the blame. I accept full responsibility for my actions." She risked a glance at Maude, but the girl was looking straight ahead.

Mr. Burroughs leaned back in his chair, his elbows on the armrests, his fingers tented. "What do you think I should do about you, Miss Wood? If you were me."

Annie didn't know whether to suggest leniency or a sterner punishment. "I would consider firing the offender, but I would decide against it because I would realize that the guilty party *did* confess and did apologize, and has great potential to be of benefit to the company if she were allowed to stay."

He smiled. "Great potential, you say?"

She felt herself redden. "Good potential?"

He leaned forward. "I prefer the 'great' designation. Prove me right, Miss Wood. Five dollars will be docked from your paycheck as a rental fee — a one-time rental fee."

"Yes, sir. I understand completely, sir."

"Be assured you do. Now carry on."

That was the full of it? They were free to go? With their jobs intact?

"Thank you, sir."

The two women stood, but Annie didn't dare risk a look to Maude. They opened the door to leave but saw Sean sitting by the secretary.

"You may go in now, Mr. Culver."

With only a glance, Sean walked by Annie into Mr. Burroughs's office. Had her mention of him to Mrs. Downs caused him to be in trouble, too?

She turned to the secretary. "Excuse me. Did Mr. Burroughs summon Mr. Culver, or did he arrange the meeting?"

There was a disapproving glint in the woman's eyes as she said, "He was summoned."

Annie's relief evaporated.

The girls took the stairs down to their floor, but not before Maude asked, "You got him called up, too?"

"I only mentioned him coming to dinner with me."

"Learn to keep your mouth shut, Annie Wood."

At lunch, Annie saw Sean sitting at a table with two friends. There was an empty place across from him so she sat down. As soon as she did, the two friends excused themselves. *What have they heard? What do they know?*

"Hello," she said to Sean as she took a sip of milk. She wanted to ask him about his visit with Mr. Burroughs but wasn't sure how to go about it.

She didn't have to. "You've already had a busy day," he said.

Annie set her glass down. "Meaning?"

"Ruining your career, Maude's, and mine. Quite the accomplishment."

With a glance around the cafeteria she saw she had the attention of many others. So they all knew? She pushed her tray away. "What did Mr. Burroughs say to you?"

"He asked if I knew what you'd done. I had to tell him I did."

"But you didn't condone it. You were against it."

"Yet I let you keep the dress for the weekend, and accompanied you to a dinner where you wore the dress." He looked at his plate then up at her again. "I should have made you take it back immediately. I knew it was wrong."

"*I* knew it was wrong," she said. "It's my fault, not yours. I'm being docked five dollars as a rental fee for the dress."

Sean harrumphed. "A pittance compared to the fact our reputations *were* priceless.

380

Now, they are tainted and tarnished. God's given us free will to make choices. We chose wrong."

"I'm sor—"

He shook his head. "All because you wanted to play dress-up and pretend to be someone you weren't."

Annie felt the breath go out of her. Was that what she'd done?

The truth of it made her next breath difficult. "You're right. But if that's true maybe working here is a farce, a part I'm playing. Maybe I should go back to being a maid."

He dabbed a napkin at his mouth and stood. "Maybe you should."

Annie was left alone at the table. Surely he didn't mean it. Surely *she* didn't mean it. Her days as a maid were over. She'd worked hard to get out of that life.

No, you didn't. You simply ran away.

But she'd worked hard to become a clerk at Macy's, and now a pattern artist.

Luck got you the first job, and Sean got you the second.

Now she'd ruined her biggest chance by putting on airs, *and* she'd hurt Maude and Sean.

It was Maude's idea.

She shook the thought away. As Sean said, she'd been given the choice. She could have said no when Maude first mentioned it. She could have said no when Maude showed her the dresses. She could have said no when Maude detailed the scheme or when she'd seen the dress where Bertie had placed it, or out on the street on the way home, or that evening when it was time to get dressed. She'd been given a dozen chances to say no.

Her shame increased with the gaze of her coworkers, their whispers and soft laughter.

Annie forced herself to stay and finish her lunch. The discomfort was just what she deserved.

Halfway through the afternoon, Maude came up behind Annie and said, "Move it along, chickie."

"Move what along?"

"Your mood." She pointed to Annie's wrinkled brow. "You want to look fifty before you're twenty?"

Annie pressed a hand on her forehead and could feel the worry lines there. She looked around the workroom, but luckily the other girls were busy. "You're angry at me, Sean's angry at me, Mrs. Downs is angry at me, Mr. Burroughs is angry at me, and I'm angry at me."

"As I said, move it along. It's over. Water

under the bridge, the cookie's been crumbled, the train has left the station."

Annie chuckled.

"That's better," Maude said.

"So you forgive me?"

"Of course I do. It won't be the last time I get my hands slapped. And as I get to know you . . . I'm betting it won't be your last time, either."

"Oh yes, it will," Annie said. "No more borrowing dresses."

"I believe you. But something else will come up where you will cross some line — with two feet I'd guess."

Annie thought of the Sampsons' offer. Quitting would certainly be crossing a line.

But that was a decision for another day.

"He'll be here," Maude said.

"I'm not so sure." Annie was doubtful Sean would meet her after work to walk her home. They hadn't parted on good terms at lunch. She'd caused him strife. She'd damaged his reputation and their relationship.

Beyond mending? Even though she didn't know exactly where she wanted their friendship to go, she valued the bond they shared.

Gazing through the mass of workers leaving the Butterick building, Annie didn't see him. He usually stood to the right of the main door, just outside.

He wasn't there. *Serves me right.*

But then Maude said, "There he is. As always."

There he was. Behind a group of men, talking.

He stepped out to greet them. " 'Evening."

"Yes it is," Maude said.

They began their walk home, but it wasn't "as always" at all. Sean did not draw her hand around his arm. Nor did he ask about her day, and she didn't dare ask him about his.

"This is a delightful conversation we're having," Maude said after a block walked in silence.

"I'm just tired," Sean said.

Annie nodded. She was tired, too. Drained. She glanced at Maude and made a short shake of her head, hoping Maude would let it go. Perhaps it was best to just let him be.

They approached the corner where Maude turned. "Have a nice evening, you two," she said. "If you can."

Why did you add that last bit?

"Maude, wait," Sean said. "I'm turning, too."

"You are?" Annie asked.

"If you remember, I'm moving today.

384

Thomas is meeting me at my apartment to help." He looked her straight in the eye. "I'm moving to be closer to you."

It was not said with tenderness, but as a reminder of his sacrifice. What should she say? What could she say but "Thank you."

He blinked, as if surprised by her answer. His face softened. "Will you be all right getting home?"

"Of course."

He hesitated a moment. "Good-bye, then."

Although he'd said good-bye dozens of times before, this time seemed different. Final. "You don't have to move if you don't want to," she said.

His countenance fell. "You don't want me to?"

"Of course I want you to, but considering . . . I don't want you to feel you have to."

He broke their gaze and looked to the ground. "I'd better go."

She watched him walk away as Maude's voice resounded in her head: *"Learn to keep your mouth shut, Annie Wood."*

Then she walked toward home, her gaze down, her arms wrapped tightly around her body. *I certainly mucked that up.*

She started as a church bell began to

strike the hour. . . . *Four, five, six.*

With the resonance of the bells still hanging in the air, Annie stopped walking and turned toward the church. She climbed the steps and took a seat at the top, pulling her skirt and coat over her legs against the cold.

She was immediately reminded of last Friday when she and Sean had sat on the steps of St. Patrick's. They'd discussed the job offer.

So much had happened since then.

She leaned her head upon her knees. *What should I do? I need direction.*

"Hey, missy."

She looked up and saw a disheveled man standing on the steps nearby. "Yes?"

"That's me place."

Even though it made no sense to do so, she stood and apologized. The man sat where she had sat then unwrapped a cloth and pulled out a heel of bread — half-eaten.

Annie dug a coin from her pocket and handed it to him. Then she headed in the direction of home.

Edna had to work late, so Annie had the flat to herself. She put a pot of soup on the stove so they could eat later and then went to the window of the front room where she could see the brownstone across the street.

And then she saw Sean and Thomas walking up the street carrying two suitcases and a carpetbag. She was relieved to feel glad to see him. Perhaps she did want him to move close.

Then why haven't you told him that?

When he looked up at her window, she slipped to the side, out of sight. *Coward.*

Then she saw Edna going over to the men, greeting them. She pointed to her apartment, and Annie feared she was inviting them to dinner.

It would be the right thing to do.

But Sean shook his head and they parted. A minute later Annie saw the light in Sean's new apartment turn on.

"I'm home," Edna said, taking off her coat and hat. "I smell soup."

"It should be ready soon," Annie said as she went to stir it.

"How was your day?"

Annie paused in the stirring, deciding whether she should share. "It was fine," she said.

Edna had endured enough of her dirty laundry.

Annie couldn't sleep. The knowledge that Sean was right across the street, and that he was angry at her . . .

She glanced at the clock. Two in the morning. There was nothing she could do about it now.

Or was there?

On a whim she tiptoed out to the parlor and retrieved a piece of stationery and a pencil from Edna's desk. She returned to her room and wrote a note:

Dear Sean,

Please forgive me for all the trouble I have caused you, and not just trouble but confusion and doubt.

I am very glad you have moved close, and I appreciate your constant care and concern for my well-being.

I suffer many regrets, but you are not one of them.

Sleep well.

She paused, unsure how to sign it: "Sincerely"? "Affectionately"? "With love"?

She decided on simply *Annie*.

She folded it in half then slipped on her shoes, a skirt over her nightgown, and then her jacket. Her hair fell upon her shoulders — totally unacceptable for a girl her age, but odds were, no one would see her.

Annie was glad Edna was a deep sleeper, but she left the apartment with as much stealth as possible and took the stairs in the same manner so as not to disturb the other tenants.

Being outside at this time of night reminded her of the first night she, Iris, and Danny had slept on the streets. This was a better locale than the alley they'd chosen, but there were still dangers about. Generally people who were out in the wee hours were up to no good.

Except her. Hopefully her note would do a lot of good toward mending the rift between herself and Sean.

She spotted two men talking at the far intersection, so she scurried across the street before they noticed her. The entryway was dark, with only one electric bulb on an upper landing. There were four stories to the building, and she'd seen that Sean was on the third. At the street side. She gathered her skirt and nightgown and made her way upward. There appeared to be four apartments per floor. She tiptoed to his flat and, with a kiss to the page, slipped it under his door.

It was done. There was nothing more she could do.

Her heart raced as she retraced her steps back home. But as she reached the street, she heard the sash of a window open. Sean's window. He leaned out. "Annie, wait," he whispered. He closed the window, and she stepped near the building, trying to be inconspicuous. Luckily, the men on the corner had moved on.

A few minutes later, Sean emerged, clutching his coat closed over his shirtless torso. He wore trousers and slippers. He looked wonderful. "I got your note," he said.

She could only nod. "You're moved in?"

"I am, but . . ." He shook the topic away. "Not everything can be fixed with an 'I'm sorry.' "

"But this *can* be? Please?"

He touched the hair around her face, letting his fingers glide its length. "This can be."

She fell into his arms, wrapping herself in his forgiveness, needing his strength. "Thank you."

He kissed the top of her head then gently stepped away. "Till tomorrow, then."

"Till tomorrow."

She noticed that he waited to go inside until she was at the door of her building. She waved. He kissed his fingers.

Thank You, Lord, for Your many mercies.

Finally, sleep could come.

CHAPTER TWENTY-TWO

"What if we did something like this?" Annie drew a sleeve with a slight bell shape at the forearms. "Nothing drastic, but something a little more graceful than the usual tight sleeve."

Mrs. Downs perused the drawing. "It's not done. Slim sleeves are the norm."

"But isn't that the point?" Annie said. "Taking what exists and innovating it into something a bit new?"

Dora gave the sketch a glance then went back to her dress form. "Those sleeves will catch on things."

Annie listened yet ignored her. In the weeks she'd been working at Butterick she'd learned that Dora was the naysayer in almost every design. Annie offered her defense. "It will provide more ease of movement. And air. We're designing for summer. We're trying to show something new."

"Suit yourself," Dora said.

"Curb your attitude, Dora," Mrs. Downs said. "Butterick is rooted in innovation." To Annie she said, "Carry on. Piece it out for me."

"Yes, ma'am." Once again Annie was given the go-ahead to create a pattern from one of her designs. Not every idea had been met with enthusiasm, and some had been discarded for this reason or that, but the rejections only heightened the sweetness of each victory.

Annie had just cut a new length of muslin when Mrs. Sampson walked into the department.

"Mrs. Downs. Ladies," she said with a nod.

This was the second time Annie had seen her since the dinner and the job offer, yet far from the tenth time that the woman had contacted her via notes and even letters. She was nothing if not persistent, each time asking if Annie had made a decision. And each time — if Annie responded at all — she asked for more time.

Annie had been praying for an answer, yes or no, but so far hadn't received any heavenly nudge that sent her toward a certain decision with confidence. And so she'd hedged, waiting for God to make things clear.

As Mrs. Downs and Mrs. Sampson chatted in the office, Annie tried to focus on her work. She even called another girl over to the table, hoping her presence would deter a personal conversation with Mrs. Sampson. No one but Sean and Edna knew of the job offer, and Annie hoped to keep it that way.

Then why not just tell her no and be done with it?

She knew that was the only way to rid herself of Mrs. Sampson, but she just couldn't shut the door on the opportunity quite yet.

Her attempt at evasion was to no avail. The two women came out of the office, and Mrs. Downs beckoned Annie to join them.

"Mrs. Sampson wishes to speak to you alone. I've given her use of my office for the sake of privacy."

Annie was immediately alarmed by this assertiveness and regretted the attention it brought. Yet she had no choice but to comply.

Once in the office, they both remained standing, which Annie hoped was an indication the meeting would be short. She put on a smile for those watching from the workroom — which she had to fake — and a curious look, which she did not. "Yes,

Mrs. Sampson?"

"You've evaded me long enough, my dear."

"I know. And I'm truly sorry. It's such a big decision. I simply need more time."

"I'm afraid you've run out of time. Tomorrow Harold and I are leaving on a ship bound for the warmth of Italy. We will be gone until the spring." She adjusted her gloves. "By the way, you know one of the other passengers."

"I can't imagine who."

"Mr. Straus and his wife. From Macy's. We know them quite well — and by the by, he speaks very highly of you."

Annie was glad for the compliment, yet Mrs. Sampson's ultimatum remained.

"I'd like to say it's now or never," the woman said, "but I'm afraid I'm too much of an optimist for that. Yet I do wish for your decision. It's the polite thing to do, don't you think?"

"I agree." Yet faced with the need for a decision, Annie still balked. But then, without her bidding, words began to spill out — words determining her future. "I can't leave Butterick. They've been so kind to me."

"Harold and I will be kind to you." Mrs. Sampson nodded toward the workroom.

"Do they believe in you like we do?"

"I am giving them reason to. I am working very hard to learn from them."

"Learning to do their bidding."

"You wish for me to do *your* bidding."

"Touché, my dear." She straightened a piece of paper on the edge of the desk with a single finger. "Yet our bidding leads to the freedom to design what you wish to design. Do you have that freedom here?"

The word *freedom* held such power. "Partially."

Mrs. Sampson raised an eyebrow.

"Perhaps not true freedom to fully design. No. Not as yet."

"And you won't. Ever."

"Neither of us know that. But I do know my limits. I'm not proficient enough in design and construction to have full freedom. If I ever go out on my own, I need to know much more than I do now. To build anything you have to have a firm foundation."

"You are a practical sort."

"It's not a negative trait."

"I suppose not." She adjusted her gloves a second time. "I do wish you the best, Annie."

"I wish you the same. I will always remember the faith you had in me. Perhaps someday I'll be ready to deserve it." As the woman turned to leave, Annie asked, "What should we tell the ladies in the workroom about our conversation?"

"Leave it to me."

They walked out of the office, and Annie returned to her workstation. Mrs. Sampson thanked Mrs. Downs for the use of her office. "Alas, Miss Wood doesn't feel proficient enough to make me some dresses."

Dora raised a hand. "I'll sew them for you, Mrs. Sampson."

With a blink, Mrs. Sampson said, "Perhaps in the spring, after we return from Europe."

As soon as she left, Mrs. Downs clapped her hands. "Back to work, ladies. And Annie? You made a wise choice not to dive into dressmaking. You have much to learn."

"That I do, Mrs. Downs."

There was a general murmuring among the other girls about what they would have done with such an opportunity, and Annie was glad to let them chatter on. On her own part, she felt exhilarated. Although she had not expected to make a choice today, God had nudged her to the point of decision. The result? She felt a burden lifted. She felt . . . peace.

She remembered the dinner conversation at the Sampsons' when they'd discussed knowing when you were making the right decision. Sean had suggested "practice and peace." Through today's decision Annie had gained both.

Smart man, that Sean.

On the last Thursday in November, Annie was awakened by the fragrance of nutmeg and cinnamon. But before she could wallow in the heady, cozy smell there was a knock on her bedroom door.

"Get up, girlie. I need your help in the kitchen."

Ah yes. Today was a holiday. Thanksgiving Day.

She'd been looking forward to this day ever since Edna had told her about it, for she had much to be thankful for. Plus, it would be a time when she could reveal her big decision to Edna and Sean. It had been hard to keep it quiet all week, but considering the weeks it had held her captive, she'd decided a more formal announcement on a day of celebration would be the proper time.

Annie got dressed quickly and joined Edna in the kitchen where she was putting a turkey in the oven. Fresh pumpkin pies sat on a sideboard.

"I do hope the turkey is large enough."

"There's enough there for many more

than six. What time did you get up?"

"Four. I needed to get the pies in to free up the oven for the turkey."

"You should have awakened me."

"There's no need for two of us to be tired. Besides, I wasn't sleeping well. I am so excited to have a real party for Thanksgiving. It's been far too long."

Annie tied on an apron. "I'm excited, too — for it's my first holiday. Set me to work."

"You can shuck the corn then peel potatoes. I'm going to get the cranberries on the stove for the cranberry-fig chutney. And I need to punch down the dough for the rolls."

The friends made a good team, each intent on their work. "This is also my first holiday off," Annie said.

"What do you mean?"

"At Crompton Hall we had a free day every week, but as far as days free due to a holiday? The servants only got a few hours off for Christmas and Easter. We still had to work. The food did not cook nor the house clean itself."

"English Pilgrims started the Thanksgiving tradition over here. In the 1600s they celebrated good harvest with native Indians." She nodded to the cranberries. "I believe it was the Indians who introduced them to berries."

"So it's been a holiday since then?"

"Oh no, for *we* have not been a country since then. It was celebrated here and there but it was only during our awful Civil War that our president, Abraham Lincoln, declared it a national celebration."

"It's a good tradition. We have so much to be thankful for."

"That we do."

Annie was glad Sean was the first to arrive. She needed a moment alone with him and Edna before the other guests came for dinner.

The aroma of freshly baked rolls accompanied her announcement. "Can you stop a moment, Edna? I want to share something important with the two of you."

Edna gave the corn an extra stir then gave Annie her full attention. "Important?"

"I made a decision regarding Mrs. Sampson's offer."

"It's about time," Edna said. "I'd bragged that you were a girl who made quick decisions, but this one has dragged on for weeks."

Sean's eyebrows rose. "When did you decide?"

"Monday last. Mrs. Sampson came into

work and gave me an ultimatum of sorts since they are traveling to Italy for the winter."

"And you said . . . ?" he asked.

"I declined their offer. I'm staying at Butterick."

Sean spun her around, nearly knocking over a chair. "I'm so glad!"

She hadn't expected his exuberance. "I didn't know it meant so much that I stay."

"I didn't either until I heard your decision. I like that we work together. I like walking with you to and from. If you worked elsewhere, when would I see you?"

His point was well taken.

"What was your reasoning?" Edna asked.

"A pragmatic one. I need more time to learn about fashion before I can be held responsible to fully design it."

"Good for you," Sean said.

"You could always take the job in the future," Edna said.

"That's what Mrs. Sampson implied."

Sean's smile faded, and Annie felt a wee bit peeved. Did he truly expect her to stay at Butterick forever?

The moment was saved by the sound of footsteps on the stairs, voices in the hallway, and a knock on the door.

"Oh, the heavenly smells, Edna," Mrs.

MacDonald said as she entered. "I'm eating before I'm eating."

Mildred nodded. "I haven't had a meal like this since I left home years ago. I thank you for inviting me, Mrs. Holmquist."

"You are quite welcome," Edna said.

"I thank you, too," Maude said, eyeing the pies.

"You're all welcome," Edna said. "Sean, take their coats, please."

The apartment was alive with happy chatter, with everyone pitching in. Finally it was time to eat.

Edna directed them to the dining table, which was decorated with gourds and small branches of brightly colored autumn leaves. "Let us give thanks, and then Sean, I was wondering if you would carve the turkey."

Sean eyed the bird on the platter as if it were a foe to be conquered. "It will be a new experience and may be more of a massacre than a carving. But if you're not choosy about the end result, I am your man."

"You're the only man," Maude pointed out.

They each took a seat around the table with Edna and Sean taking the ends. Then Edna held out her hands. Down the row the guests clasped hands then bowed their heads. "Dear God Almighty," Edna began, "thank You for the food upon the table, the roof above our heads, and the jobs to provide a living. But most of all, thank You for these friends, old and new. I want to say a special thanks for dear Annie, for she is the one who brought us together. Bless us and guide us to do Your bidding. In Jesus' name, amen."

Both Sean and Maude squeezed Annie's hands, and she felt herself blush at the extra mention. "Thank you," she said softly, looking at all of them. "Thank you for letting me be a part of your lives."

"Amen, again," Edna said. "Now to the turkey. Mr. Culver? If you please?"

Sean stood at his place and got to work, giving them their choice of white or dark meat. Annie had some of each. Then bowls of mashed potatoes, gravy, chutney, corn, and rolls were passed, and each guest filled their plates edge to edge.

More praise and thanks were offered as everyone enjoyed the bounty before them. When people began asking for seconds, Annie thought of something else to be thankful for.

"I am thankful that Grasston — though not caught — has not bothered us."

"Perhaps he's moved on to some other

target," Sean said.

Annie noticed Edna, Mrs. MacDonald, and Mildred exchange glances. "What's wrong?"

"He was at the store the other day," Mrs. MacDonald said.

"Edna? Why didn't you tell me?" Annie asked.

"Mr. Horace and his men shooed him away and the police were called."

"Was he caught?"

Mildred shook her head. "If only."

Annie felt an all-too-familiar tug in her stomach. "I truly thought he had moved on."

Edna picked up the bowl of potatoes. "Who wants thirds?"

Annie had lost her appetite.

CHAPTER TWENTY-THREE

"This is the life," Sean said as he walked to church with Annie on one arm and Edna on the other.

"Oh, you," Edna said. In her free hand she carried a hatbox with a ribbon tied around it. The box contained her straw hat that matched Iris's dress so well — her gift to the bride.

Annie was happy to share Sean with her best friend. Today was December twenty-third. Today Iris and Thomas would be married.

It was hard to believe that little Iris, the immature housemaid whom Annie had met on her first day in America, was going to be a married . . . woman. Married or not, she was still a girl of seventeen.

Annie remembered their first conversation up in the tiny attic room at the Friesens', when Iris had expressed her desire to leave service and be a shopgirl. She wasn't picky about what kind of shop, just so she was around a lot of people.

The Tuttle family certainly fit that bill. From the very first day, Iris had been assigned the duty of taking care of their five small children. She'd fit with them and them with her as though they'd all been waiting for each other.

Danny had fit in, too. Getting to help Gramps with deliveries fulfilled Danny's desire for adventure, to be outdoors, drive a wagon, and make friends along the way.

"Danny would have loved this day," Annie said.

"I wish I would have known him," Sean said.

"He sounds like a delightful boy," Edna said.

"That he was." She raised her free arm in the air. "Make the most of today!" She lowered it and explained, "That was his rallying cry to Iris and me."

"Carpe diem," Sean said.

"What did you say?"

"It's Latin. Carpe diem. Seize the day."

"What an inspiring saying," Edna said.

"How do you know Latin?" Annie asked Sean.

"Mr. Butterick. He would say the line often. I'm afraid it's the only Latin I know."

"It's enough," Edna said.

"Danny had no reason to know the Latin of it," Annie said. "But he was wise beyond his years." The sight of the church up ahead forced her to set the sadness aside. Today was a day for joy.

As soon as they entered the narthex, Annie left Edna in Sean's care. Since she was responsible for the wedding dress, she wanted to find Iris and help in any way she could. She asked an usher and was directed to a room off the sanctuary near the front of the church.

She heard Iris's voice inside and knocked. Mrs. Tuttle opened the door. "Annie! Come help with the ribbons woven through her hair. Jane and I can't get them quite right."

Annie stepped into the room to help, but at the sight of Iris, she stopped. "Oh. Iris, you're beautiful. Truly and fully beautiful."

Iris turned toward her, smoothing the blue dress. "It's because of the dress. I can't thank you enough."

"It's not the dress," Annie said. "It's you. You're radiant."

Iris beamed, which added to her happy glow.

With the words *I now pronounce you man and wife,* Sean squeezed Annie's hand.

The simple gesture surprised her. With that one squeeze was he truly saying he wanted to marry her? Pleasure and panic collided, and Annie found herself retracting her hand from his grip.

He gave her a questioning glance. She felt immediate regret, so she appeased him with a smile. He smiled in return, and she was struck by how much his mood was dependent on her own. There was power in that. But also responsibility.

The happy couple kissed and strode down the aisle with a confidence that two become one was a force to be reckoned with.

"I'm so happy for them," Sean whispered.

"As am I."

He held her gaze a moment, as though pondering his next words. Annie looked away, not wanting to encourage their release.

The ushers came to their row, indicating it was time to go to the church reception. Annie was glad for the distraction of getting from here to there. They were led into a large room scattered with tables. Several women set out various pastries around a two-tiered wedding cake — no doubt due to the expertise of the Tuttles. For an instant, Annie's thoughts flashed back to various party receptions at Crompton Hall when she'd helped out, dressed in her dress uniform of black with a crisp white apron. She'd come a long way — a world away. A lifetime away.

She thought of Lady Newley and Miss Henrietta. How were they getting on? And more to the point, how were the Misses handling the sewing work without her help?

"Let's greet the bride and groom," Edna said.

The three of them went through the reception line that consisted of the happy couple and Thomas's parents. It was rather sad that Iris had no family there to share her day. No parents. No Danny. The lack reinforced the special blessing of the Tuttles in her life.

The rest of the reception was a blur of Tuttle children running amok with other children of the neighborhood, the murmurings and laughter of friends celebrating one of life's milestones, the cutting of the cake, and numerous toasts with delicious spiced punch.

Annie sat at a table and closed her eyes, letting the noise of the party turn into a mesmerizing hum. If she let herself, she could easily doze.

Go outside. Now!

The inner nudge shocked her to full attention.

"What's wrong?" Sean asked from his seat nearby.

"Nothing."

"It was something. You jerked as if someone had shouted at you."

She put a hand to her forehead, trying to recapture the moment. "It was the opposite of a shout, but it *was* a voice — an insistent voice. From in here." She pointed to her heart.

"What did it say?"

" 'Go outside. Now.' "

After only a moment's hesitation Sean stood. "Come, then. I'll go with you."

"I'm sure it's nothing. I don't even know what it means."

"Did you hear the words, or not?"

"I heard them."

"Then we go. You'll never know what they mean unless we go outside."

They collected their coats. When they passed Edna on the way out, Annie whispered, "We'll be right back." There was no need to get her involved in this bizarre goose chase.

They stepped outside, where a light snow was falling. Annie raised her shoulders

409

against the chill. "It's too cold. Let's go back in."

"Just give it a minute," Sean said. "Look around."

Feeling ridiculous, Annie looked left, where she saw only pedestrians and carriages hurrying to their destination before the snow accumulated. And then right, where she saw more of the —

She gasped. "It's Grasston!"

"Where?" Sean said.

"He just ducked behind those barrels. He's over there!"

Sean ran after him.

"No, Sean! Don't!"

But it was too late. Grasston spotted Sean and escaped into a building. Sean ran after him.

Annie's thoughts dashed to horrible scenarios of Grasston lying in wait for Sean, hitting him over the head. Or did he have a knife? Or a gun?

She spotted a policeman talking to a street vendor who was closing up shop against the snow. "Officer!" she yelled. "Help!"

The officer came running, and Annie pointed at the building. "An escaped murderer, Oscar Grasston, just went into that building, and my beau ran after him. You have to catch him, stop him from hurting —"

"Is he armed?"

"I don't know."

The officer blew a whistle, summoning assistance. He instructed the other officer, "Go 'round back. Watch for a man . . ." He looked to Annie. "What's he look like?"

"Black hair, tall. Mustache. My beau is blond."

The officers nodded. One went down an alley toward the back, and the other went inside.

The whistle must have alerted the wedding guests, for a few of the men came outside and Annie filled them in. She was glad to see Mr. Tuttle and Thomas. "It's Grasston! He was here. He ran inside that building. Sean ran after him."

"Let's go," Mr. Tuttle said.

Annie took his arm, holding him back. "There are two constables involved. I think it's best we stay back."

But the two men would have none of it. "He's a slippery one. We can't risk him getting away yet again."

"That's my building," another man said. "There's a way out in the back. Come with me, men."

The women gathered close around Annie.

411

It was surreal to see Iris with a coat around her shoulders, wearing her wedding dress, her hair ribbons waving in the winter wind. "I'm sorry. I never meant to disrupt the wedding."

"Nothing could make my wedding happier than catching the man who killed Danny."

"Up there!" A man pointed to the flat roof of the building. "They're on the roof!"

They could see glimpses of men running around the roof, and they heard them shouting.

Edna took Annie's hand then Iris's. "Father God, keep our good men safe. Help them capture the man who's perpetrated such evil. Settle this now, Lord. Bring about Your justice, and relieve this horrible man's victims of his wicked —"

A scream sliced through her words, and they watched as a man fell from the roof onto the street not twenty feet away.

Most of the women screamed and looked away, shielding their eyes from the sight. But Annie and Iris did not. They looked upon the broken victim, needing to see, needing to know.

"It's him!" Iris yelled. "It's Grasston!"

Annie stared at the bloodied body with no aversion. The way his limbs were askew, and the blood . . .

The curious ventured close, but most gave him a wide berth. A stream of men filed out of the building, looked at Grasston, and then joined their families on the church steps.

Last out were the officers then Thomas, Mr. Tuttle, and Sean.

Annie ran into his arms. "You got him! I was so afraid for you."

"He got himself," Sean said. He put a hand to his arm. His coat was slashed.

"You've been stabbed!" Annie said.

"He sliced at me, but the coat saved me. I don't think I'm even cut." He shook his head, turning their attention. "As I said, Grasston got himself."

"That he did." Thomas wrapped his arm around his bride. "We had him cornered on the roof, and an officer was talking to him, trying to get him to turn himself in."

Mr. Tuttle took over the story. "But then he turned toward the edge and dove over it."

Sean nodded. "He was standing there, a knife in his hands, ready to fight us all. But then he stood upright and got the oddest look in his eyes."

"As if he was being talked to. As if he wasn't quite *there*," Thomas said.

413

Sean finished it. "And then he jumped."

Edna drew in a breath. "We'd been praying for your protection, and for God's justice."

They all looked at Grasston. A light blanket of snow began to cover him, a pure blanket for a very impure man. The officers stood nearby talking among themselves.

"Danny finally has justice," Annie said.

"Indeed he does," Mrs. Tuttle said.

There was a moment of silence among the wedding guests, as all looked upon the scene, letting its gravity and significance settle.

But then Mr. Tuttle said, "Inside now. We have a wedding to celebrate. A new beginning for our bride and groom."

"And for you," Sean whispered to Annie.

Annie turned her face toward the sky and let the snowflakes fall upon her.

Annie tied a bow around the vest she'd made Sean for Christmas. "What if it doesn't fit him?" she asked Edna.

"He'll love it anyway. Come help trim the tree before he gets here."

The fir tree was small and sat upon a table by the parlor fireplace, but it was more than Annie had ever had. "The Christmas tree at Crompton Hall was enormous and was

414

always placed in the front hall in the crook of the sweeping stair. Each servant could put on one ornament, and I always chose a little silver bird with its wings outstretched. I just loved the shape of it. The glisten of it."

Edna looked through the box of ornaments. "Look what we have here." She held up a silver bird. "You may do the honors."

Annie placed it on the tree, her old and new lives merging.

"Did you have a tree when you were a child?" Edna asked.

"No. Christmas was just another day, with Ma complaining and Pa yelling about who and what had done him wrong."

"I'm so sorry for that. Every child should experience the magic of Christmas, even in the simplest of ways."

Annie nodded, knowing that what every child *should* experience and *did* experience were often widely disparate.

She chose to think of happier times. "The tree at the Hall used to be ablaze with candles."

"Not here," Edna said with a sharp shake to her head. "Not anymore."

"Did something happen?"

Edna draped a string of beads on the branches. "Steven was ten and thought it would be fun to light them in the middle of the night so St. Nicholas could see better. He knocked a lit candle over, and if I hadn't been awakened by his not-so-quiet boyish noises, the entire apartment would have gone up in flames." She walked to the candles on the pine-draped mantel. "Since then, these do."

"They do just fine."

There was a knock on the door, and Sean came in, smelling of winter winds. "Merry Christmas!"

"Merry Christmas Eve to you," Edna said, kissing him on both cheeks. She brushed snow off the shoulders of his coat. "I didn't realize it was snowing."

"Quite hard, I'm afraid. I was glad my only trip was across the street."

"Not too much snow, I hope. Tomorrow we're going to see your family in Brooklyn," Annie said.

"We shall see. If not tomorrow, we can see them on New Year's Day. Mother won't mind. She wouldn't want us venturing out in a blizzard."

Annie was disappointed yet also relieved. Meeting his parents made her nervous.

"The tree is lovely," Sean said, straightening the star on top.

The clock on the mantel struck six. "We

have an hour until church begins. Would you like to open our presents?"

Annie saw that Sean hadn't brought anything. She didn't want him to feel bad. "That's not necessary," she said. "I am happy for the company."

He winked at her. "Fear not." He pulled a round tin from one coat pocket and a small box from the other. "I do bring gifts."

Annie was glad for it, for she was eager to distribute hers.

"Let me serve us a cup of wassail and we can commence."

Annie helped Sean remove his coat and, once again, noticed the slashed sleeve. "If we are snowed in tomorrow I will mend this for you — all the layers. How did your arm fare?"

"I was cut."

He hadn't said that yesterday. "Badly?"

"Hardly. Calm yourself. I am well."

Her thoughts strayed to yesterday's wedding and Grasston's death.

He pressed a finger on the space between her eyes. "There will be none of that. Tonight is a night of joy, celebrating Christ's birth and being together."

She loved how he could bring her back from darkness and into the light.

"Here we are," Edna said, carrying a tray

with three mugs of spiced cider. When they each had one, she raised hers in a toast. "To us."

"To happiness," Annie added.

"To the God who brought us together."

They clinked their mugs and drank. The warm liquid was a balm.

"My presents first," Edna said as they took seats in the parlor. She handed a present to Annie, her face glowing with expectation.

It was nearly flat, the size of her lap. Edna had wrapped it in a bit of calico and tied it with a ribbon. Annie pulled the bow free and gasped.

Edna was quick to explain. "It's a pad of drawing paper, new pencils, an eraser, a sharpener and . . . guess what's in the skinny box."

The box had the words Faber-Castell in large letters. Then two more words . . . "Colored pencils?" She opened the end and couldn't help but say, "Oooh. So pretty!"

"Now you can colorize your designs."

Annie was truly moved and set the presents aside so she could give Edna a hug. "You are far too generous."

"Not at all." Edna handed Sean a small box with a ribbon.

Sean opened it. "A tie tack."

"The stone is a tiger's eye."

He unfurled his tie and set it in place. "I'm quite the dandy."

"You're quite the gentleman," Edna corrected.

He gave her a kiss on the cheek.

"Me next," Annie said. She gave a present to Edna and knew it needed some explanation. "It's a tea cozy. I quilted it myself — on the machine. It should keep your teapot warm."

"Very nice, girlie. Thank you."

Annie's heart beat a bit faster as she handed her wrapped bundle to Sean. "I hope you like it."

"I'm sure I will."

The brown tweed vest was revealed. It had a satin lining and back.

"I made it myself. It has a pocket for your watch."

Sean made note of that detail and immediately removed his suit coat and vest to try it on.

Please let it fit!

When he began buttoning it — and it was not too tight — Annie breathed freely. "I'm so relieved."

"A mirror?" he asked Edna.

"In my room."

He went into the bedroom and admired it. "It's very sharp, Annie. You do fine work."

"It matches the tie tack," Edna added. "A coordinated effort."

He flashed a pose as if for an advertisement, his chin high, a hand on his hip.

The women clapped and laughed. "Fit for the *Delineator*," Annie said. "For it is a Butterick pattern."

"Of course it is," he said.

They returned to the parlor, where Sean gave Edna the tin. Inside were assorted chocolates.

"You'll make me plumper than I already am."

"More of you to love," he said. Then he handed Annie the small box he'd had in his pocket. "For you, my sweet Annie-girl."

Inside the paper box was a royal-blue velvet box, flattish, with a hinged edge. "I love the box."

"I hope you love what's inside."

She cracked the hinge open and saw a gold cross necklace with intricate etching and a reddish stone in the middle.

"The stone is a piece of coral," he said.

She removed the necklace from the box, fighting back tears. "I've never had any jewelry of my own."

"Ever?"

She shook her head. "Would you clasp it for me?"

Sean moved behind her and clasped the gold chain around her neck. "My turn for the mirror," she said as she moved to Edna's room. Seeing her reflection, she pressed the cross against her chest. The length of the chain was perfect, allowing it to be showcased within her neckline. "It's lovely."

He stood behind her. "You're lovely."

She turned toward him and encased him in her arms. "Thank you."

For so many things.

God is here.

There was no other explanation for the fullness in Annie's heart as she sat between her two dearest friends for Christmas Eve services. The sanctuary was filled to capacity, with each person holding a lit candle. There was no other light. Yet the combined illumination created an undulating, heavenly glow. Surely God Himself was here among them.

A choir up front sang carols for the Christ child. Annie pressed a hand to the golden cross at her neck and let the music wrap her in a warm embrace. Some songs were new to her, some familiar.

But then the choir began a song she knew from her time at Crompton Hall — one the entire household sang together on this very evening.

"Silent night, holy night . . ."

The congregation began singing with the choir, standing one by one, and then in groups, their voices joined together as if they *had* to sing along. Sean held out his hand, and Annie stood with the rest. Then she let her voice join in, the music an offering of thanks to God for His beloved Son.

Sleep in heavenly peace. Sleep in heavenly peace.

CHAPTER TWENTY-FOUR

"Don't be nervous."

"Nervous about walking across the Brooklyn Bridge, or nervous about meeting your family?"

"Both."

Annie held his arm tighter. "We're up so high over the river."

"The East River. And yes, we are."

"Until coming to New York I'd never been up high. Crompton Hall had three stories aboveground, and that was the extent of my experience."

"And now you work in a sixteen-story building, and even risked going on the roof."

She shook her head, in awe of her new experiences.

He pointed to the south. "Look there. The Statue of Liberty."

They stopped, and Annie was glad to grip the sturdy rail. "We saw her when we sailed into the harbor." The memory seemed distant and separate, as if it belonged to someone else. "It seems years ago when it was only a few months."

They began walking again. "A lot happened in 1911." He patted her gloved hand. "A lot will happen in this New Year. Your life has just begun, Annie-girl." He noticed her shiver and put an arm around her. "Are you cold?"

"A little. At least the sun is out and it's not snowing."

"The optimist."

"Hardly. The sun *is* out and it *isn't* snowing."

"You see what's there, don't you?"

She didn't understand. "Of course I see what's there."

"But you don't see what isn't there. You don't see what could be there, the larger scope of things."

"And you do?"

He stopped her, and they moved to the side to let other pedestrians pass. "Don't you ever dream of something that is beyond what you see in the moment?"

She was slightly offended. "Of course I do. I dreamt of being a lady's maid when I was a maid. When that didn't happen I dreamt of being a shopgirl."

"You got a job at Macy's because you

needed a job, not because of any dream. The same with Butterick. Your job there is not the fulfillment of any long-held dream."

"Why are you harassing me?"

"I'm sorry. That was not my intent."

She looked at the ships cruising under the bridge. All going somewhere. Everyone on the bridge going somewhere.

Where was she going? "What do you dream of, Sean?"

"Fulfillment."

She shook her head. "That is far too vague. Everyone dreams of fulfillment."

"You're right." He set his arms on the chest-high railing, leaning against them. He peered out at the water, the ships, and the horizon.

She thought of talking then decided this was a time for silence. She *was* interested in his answer.

Finally he looked at her. "You put me on the spot."

"Tit for tat."

"But I do have an answer for you. I dream of knowing I made a difference. I dream of knowing there is a definite reason I was born, a reason I exist now — not a hundred years from now or a hundred years ago. I dream of knowing that a portion of God's greater plan gets fulfilled through me."

Annie felt shivers that had nothing to do with the cold. She put a hand on his arm. "You shame me."

"That also was not my intent." He pulled her hand around his arm, and she felt his warmth through her jacket. "I merely want you to see with a larger scope. Think beyond our jobs — which may or may not have much to do with our true purposes." He turned them around and nodded to the other walkers. "What do our lives have to do with *them*?"

"I . . . I don't know them."

"But our lives can touch them. Somehow. Some way."

She watched a Jewish family walk by, the men with long curls and beards, the women with their heads covered. "What we do at Butterick touches people we don't know."

"It does. And perhaps that is part of it. I don't know all the right answers, or even the right questions. But I want to know. And I want you to want to know. For you, for me, for us."

"I'm not used to thinking this way. I relate to facts. One plus one equaling two, not some number I can't fathom."

He touched her cheek. "God made us different, you and I. I fantasize and you organize."

"Perhaps together we make a whole?"

His eyebrows rose. "Is that a proposal, Annie Wood?"

She looked away.

"I wish it were."

She risked a glance at him. "You know I'm not ready."

"But you will be. One day."

"You sound so certain."

"I can dream, can't I?"

Annie snuggled close to Sean in the cab he'd hired to drive them from the bridge to the Culver home. "One last chance to tell me what your parents are like."

"I'd prefer not."

"Why?"

"You'll know who they are immediately."

"Their personalities are so obvious?" It didn't sound very inviting.

"Although my parents are as different as night is to day, they are fully committed to who they are."

"Are they . . . likable?"

He cocked his head. "Each in their own way." He pointed up ahead. "There. Just up there."

The cab stopped in front of a lovely three-story residence. "You live here?" Annie gazed at the beautiful tan-brick home with

427

an iron gate, arched front door, and roofline edged with intricate molding.

"My parents live here."

"I thought you were poor."

"We started out poor, but the family's store is quite successful." He opened the wrought-iron gate for her then accompanied her up the stone steps to the front door.

Her heart began to pound. This was not a mansion near the size of the Sampsons', but it was a far step up from the rather ragged brownstones where she and Sean lived now.

"Ready?" he asked before he knocked.

The fact he even asked the question set her nerves on end. "I suppose."

His knock was answered by a butler, who smiled warmly. "Master Sean, how nice to see you."

"You, too, Baines."

They had barely entered when his mother swooped in. "Sean!" She embraced him warmly then smiled at Annie. "You must be Annie." She took Annie's gloved hands in her own. "Ooh, so cold."

"We walked across the bridge."

"Shame on you, Sean. You must promise to take a cab back."

"I enjoyed the walk," Annie said. "The view is incredible."

"That it is." She swept a hand toward the

parlor. "Take off your wraps and come in by the fire."

A man stood by the fireplace, lighting a cigar. "Son," he said, with no emotion, as if simply declaring his existence. "Smoke?"

"No thank you, Father." He led Annie closer. "Father, I would like you to meet Annie Wood. Annie, my father."

Mr. Culver tossed the match away and gave her half a nod. "Miss Wood."

She'd heard it said that you only get to make a first impression once. So it was with meeting Sean's parents. Within those few seconds her impressions were set. Mr. Culver was proper, controlling, and a bit cold, while Mrs. Culver was friendly, warm, and generous. As Sean had said, each personality was immediately evident.

What do they immediately know about me? What do I want them to know?

Choices rushed forward. Should she be sweet and flattering? Confident? Nervous and meek?

The thoughts sped through her mind in seconds, yet three attributes stepped toward the front. Annie wanted the Culvers to know she was honest, grateful, and a bit unpredictable. "I'm very happy to meet the parents who raised such a remarkable son."

Mr. Culver stopped puffing on his cigar.

"Really."

Mrs. Culver beamed and ran a hand across Sean's shoulders. "I happily take credit."

Sean blushed. "Mother . . ."

"Remarkable, you say?" Mr. Culver said amid a cloud of smoke.

"Absolutely," Annie said. "He discovered me."

Mrs. Culver raised her eyebrows. "Do have a seat and tell us all about this discovery."

Mr. Culver remained standing, but the other three sat upon maroon tufted chairs. "Now then," Mrs. Culver said. "How exactly did Sean discover you?"

Annie told them about working at Macy's and Sean seeing her sketch at Edna's. "I would not have the job at Butterick if not for him."

"What she isn't telling you," Sean said, "is that I had selfish motives." His smile was utterly sincere. "With both of us working there, I see her every day."

Mrs. Culver's eyes grew large. "So you are . . . ?"

"No," Annie said. "We aren't."

A shadow brushed over Sean's countenance then moved on. Sean slapped his hands on his thighs. "Today is the New Year, a new beginning."

"I do like New Year's," Mrs. Culver said, "when everything begins again, fresh." She looked to her husband.

"Hmm," was his only response.

There was a moment of silence then Mrs. Culver said, "So what do you do at Butterick, Annie?"

"I —"

"She's a pattern artist," Sean said.

"A designer?" his mother asked.

"To some extent," Annie said. "I work with others in taking an idea and turning it into a pattern for home sewers."

Mrs. Culver rose. "Well then, Annie, come with me. I have stacks and stacks of fashion magazines, and no female to share them with. You must give me your insight as to the new trends for 1912."

Annie was glad to leave the impenetrable wall that was Mr. Culver, but as she left the room, she saw a flash of panic on Sean's face.

"I'll return soon," she said.

"Do."

It was a cry to be rescued.

Annie followed Sean's mother into a room bright with sunshine. "I don't think we should be gone long," Annie said.

With a glance to the parlor Mrs. Culver

said, "We won't be, but it's good to let them stew a bit in each other's presence."

"Does anything good come of it?"

"Not really. But I can only play the peace-keeper so long."

"Sean told me his father was angry that he wasn't working at the store."

Mrs. Culver moved some fringed pillows off a padded window seat. "I think if Mr. Butterick hadn't died on his own, Richard would have killed him."

"He blames Mr. Butterick — ?"

"For stealing him away. Yes. Absolutely. And he blames himself for sending Sean for that first delivery instead of our usual runner."

"But it opened a new world for Sean. He's very good at what he does. He's a wonderful salesman."

"Which would have been of good use in the store."

"Of course."

"Enough of them," Mrs. Culver said, removing the long seat cushion. "Voila!" The window seat was hinged and, once opened, revealed stacks of magazines: *La Mode, Femina, Collier's, Young Ladies' Journal, The Designer, Vogue, The Delineator, McCall's* . . .

"I know," Mrs. Culver said. "There are a

lot of them. That's why I keep them hidden. Richard would pitch a fit."

Annie laughed then put a hand on her mouth to stop it.

"I'm sorry, but it just struck me as funny."

"It is funny in theory, but not so in reality." Her face was drawn.

"I'm sorry. I meant no offense."

Mrs. Culver negated the moment with a shake of her head. "None taken." She put her hands on her hips and nodded toward the stash. "You like?"

"Oh yes," Annie said.

"Then have a look. Enjoy."

Annie was surprised when Mrs. Culver sat on the floor and did the same. They pulled out magazine after magazine. When Annie chose a *La Mode* she said, "Lady Newley had this issue."

"Lady Newley?"

Annie renewed her choice of attributes: honesty, gratefulness, and being unpredictable. "I was a maid at an estate in England under the Viscount and Viscountess Newley. A housemaid."

"My, my."

"But I used to work on her ladyship's couture ensembles, making alterations."

Mrs. Culver clasped her hands beneath her chin. "You actually got to touch couture gowns?"

Annie was a taken aback by the sound of wonder in her voice. "I did. For both Lady Newley and her daughter. You see, Miss Henrietta's weight fluctuated, and it was my job to alter her dresses so they continued to fit."

"That doesn't sound like the job of a housemaid."

"It wasn't. But the two lady's maids at Crompton Hall weren't adept at alterations. They could repair an occasional seam or button, but ripping out and adjusting?" She shook her head. "They most certainly did not possess that talent."

"But you did. You do."

To hear it put so bluntly . . . "Yes, I do." Annie randomly turned the pages of a magazine in her lap. "I thought I would be asked to move up. I thought Lady Newley knew that I was the one doing the alterations."

"Ah. So the others took the credit?"

"That's why I left. Her ladyship and Miss Henrietta were here in New York visiting a relative when I finally realized what a dupe I had been." She shrugged. "I ran away, got a job at Macy's, met Sean, and am now at Butterick."

"You have ambition."

There was admiration in her voice. "Perhaps too much." Annie considered speaking of her relationship with Sean and how her ambition complicated things.

But Mrs. Culver did it for her. "Sean wants to marry you and you're not sure."

Annie suffered a laugh. "How did you figure all that out?"

"I saw the love in his eyes. He's never brought a girl home to meet us. But then you were quick to tell us you were *not* engaged."

"He hasn't actually proposed."

"He will. I guarantee it. And when he does, what will you say?"

Annie turned more pages, buying time. "I don't know. I think I love him, I do care for him tremendously, but marriage . . ."

Mrs. Culver shut Annie's magazine. "Don't do it."

"Excuse me?"

"Don't say yes — at least not yet. How old are you?"

"Nearly twenty."

"Still young. Very young."

"Don't you want us to marry? I know you just met me, but —"

Mrs. Culver put a hand on her arm. "I wanted to be a fashion designer when I was young."

It took Annie a moment to let her thoughts move from her engagement to Mrs. Culver's talent. "You did?"

She motioned toward the stash of magazines. "It's in my blood. Yet before I could do anything with my interest, Richard proposed marriage and I said yes, and then . . ." Her forehead tightened, and she cleared her throat before looking at Annie. "I love my husband and my children. I love my life. I have no real complaints."

"But . . . ?"

"But I never had the chance to even attempt making my dream a reality. That was twenty-five years ago, and women didn't have the choices they do now. Now, you have a career and a talent that needs to be nurtured so it can blossom. Sean will wait. Babies will wait — even though I am very eager to have grandchildren." She beamed. "Our daughter, Sybil, is expecting."

"Congratulations." Sean didn't mention having a sister. "Where does she live?"

"Chicago. We don't see her often enough. But when the baby comes, I'm going out to spend some time with them — with or without Richard."

It was clear this subject had been previously discussed.

Mrs. Culver continued, "I know it's im-

436

portant to support our husbands' careers and their dreams. For they are the breadwinners and the head of the household. I am very proud of our store and all Richard has accomplished. I simply advise you to think of the bigger picture of the future, rather than be confined to a future that involves the usual female choices, and *when* those choices are made."

"I merely want you to see with a larger scope." "Between the two of us, your son is the dreamer. He sees all the colors. I see things in black and white."

"Then you make the perfect pair." Mrs. Culver chose a new magazine for each of them. "Let him know your dreams and merge them with his own. Then you — being the practical one — can help them both come to pass."

Annie's throat was tight. "That sounds rather perfect."

"Only because it is." Mrs. Culver opened a magazine and pointed at a hobble skirt. "What do you think of this silly fashion?"

"So?" Sean said as they got in the cab to return home. "You and Mother seemed to get along well."

"She's wonderful," Annie said, adjusting the crate of fashion magazines on the seat beside her. "Did you know she wanted to be a fashion designer before she was married?"

"What?"

"She loved fashion and wanted to work in the field, but . . ."

Annie was relieved he filled in the blanks. "But then she got married and helped Father attain *his* dream."

"She loves her family very much, loves you very much."

"I know." He bumped her shoulder with his own. "Can you keep a secret?"

"Of course."

"She encouraged me to get a job at Butterick. If it weren't for her urging, I would still be working at the store."

Annie's respect for the woman grew. "I apologize for leaving you alone with your father so long, but your mother and I were having such a marvelous time."

Sean shrugged. "I suggested he show me the store and bring me up to date."

"How did it go?"

"He made constant digs about how all the improvements were done without me, and how I should have been there."

"So sorry that he holds a grudge."

"A wall of grudges, which he adds to every year I'm gone." He took her hand. "But

438

enough of him. I'm so glad you had the chance to meet them, and they you. I've never brought anyone home."

Annie hesitated. "Your mother said as much."

He turned to her. "What else did she say about *us*?"

There was little about that subject Annie wanted to share — at least at this point. "She is happy we work together and have the same interest in business and fashion."

"That's all she said?"

"She likes me. She approves of me."

Sean drew her hand to his lips and kissed it. "Of course she does."

"So?"

Back home, Annie laughed at Edna's simple question. "That's what Sean asked me after I'd spent time with his mother."

"And what did you say?"

Annie wasn't ready to share the conversation she'd had with Mrs. Culver, even though Edna would surely enjoy the details. Somehow that special time seemed almost sacred.

"She likes me and I like her." She moved to the box Sean had carried in from the cab. "Look at what she gave me."

Happily, the oohing and ahhing over the

fashion magazines prevented any further questions.

CHAPTER TWENTY-FIVE

The New Year ignited a new passion in Annie for her work. Although she didn't say as much to Sean, his mother's encouragement had been instrumental in her zeal to excel.

The first day back at work after New Year's, she brought a stack of Mrs. Culver's fashion magazines to the workroom. "I come bearing gifts," she said.

The girls rushed forward as if they were starving and the magazines were a feast. Perhaps they were: a feast for the eyes and the imagination.

Dora chose a copy of *Femina.* "French. How fancy."

Annie opened a specific copy of *Vogue.* "Look at this . . . what if we changed this detail a little? Here, I'll show you." She retrieved a piece of tissue paper and spread it over the page. With a sweep of lines, she drew a revised version of the dress. "I think the side draping is too complicated for a home sewer, but if we simply add a few tucks instead . . ."

"Interesting."

Annie hadn't seen Mrs. Downs approach, but since she had her attention, she handed her the drawing. "Do you think it would work?"

Mrs. Downs looked at Annie's sketch a moment then at the design in the magazine. "If we showed it in a variety of fabrics I think the design could be made for many occasions."

"I agree," Annie said. "That's why I brought these magazines in. There are so many couture designs that could be adapted and simplified."

"Couture," Mrs. Downs said, tapping her bottom lip. "I do remember when you were hired that Mr. Burroughs mentioned you know something of couture, but I've forgotten the details."

The voices of Mrs. Culver and Mrs. Sampson combined. *"You have a career and a talent that needs to be nurtured so it can blossom. . . . Be who you are."*

"I used to be a maid for a viscountess whose clothes were all couture designed in Paris fashion houses."

"You were a maid?" one of the girls asked.

"I was. But I often made alterations and

442

even improvements on her ladyship's dresses, and those of her daughter. I'm familiar with couture construction and design. And since leaving that position, I've become familiar with the simpler construction and design preferred by the home sewer."

"Well la-di-da," Dora said.

Instead of being offended, Annie embraced the comment. "That's a fair description of those gowns."

Mrs. Downs paged through a few of the magazines. She closed the covers. "Get back to work, ladies."

Annie was disappointed at her response. She'd seemed so interested.

"Don't mind her," Maude said as they went back to their tables. "If the First Lady, Mrs. Taft, walked in, old Downs wouldn't be impressed."

"But she was — for a moment."

"That's more interest than I've ever gotten from her. Come help me piece out this bodice."

Annie arched her back against the strain of bending over a worktable and cutting out muslin to shape the pattern pieces. She groaned at the excruciating, delectable stretch. "At times like this I wish I were shorter — or the tables higher."

"You're lucky to be tall," Suzanne said. "I often get mistaken for a twelve-year-old."

"That has nothing to do with your height," Maude teased.

Suzanne glanced down at her bodice and made herself useful elsewhere.

"You're nasty," Annie said.

"I tease. That's not the same thing."

Annie wasn't so sure and was about to get into a discussion about the difference when Mrs. Downs came in the workroom and walked over to her.

"Come with me, Miss Wood."

Her face was stern.

"Did I do something wrong?"

"Come."

Annie followed Mrs. Downs out to the corridor, sneaking glances at the girls she left behind. They looked curious, and Maude looked worried.

What could be wrong? This morning Mrs. Downs had seemed genuinely interested in her ideas. She couldn't imagine how she had offended her since then.

They took the elevator to the sales floor. Annie spotted Sean, but as he rose to greet her, she shook her head. *Not now.*

Mrs. Downs led Annie to a corner office. She knocked on the door and then entered.

A striking middle-aged woman sat behind the desk. Her hair was pulled up in the loose fashion of the Gibson girl, yet looked modern with two ribbons woven through it in a haphazard yet determined way it.

"Madame LeFleur," Mrs. Downs said. "I would like to introduce you to Annie Wood. Annie, this is our head of international sales and design, Madame LeFleur."

The woman made no attempt to rise or shake Annie's hand, so Annie nodded. "It's nice to meet you."

"So zis is the artiste."

Artist?

"Sit."

Annie let Mrs. Downs choose a chair first then sat beside her. With a glance she saw the walls were covered with beautiful fashion prints. On a table were stacks upon stacks of magazines, making Mrs. Culver's stash minuscule by comparison.

Madame LeFleur *was* fashion.

"So," the woman began. "You have ideas to adapt couture?"

"I . . . I do. I believe every woman deserves to wear beautiful fashion. If they can't afford couture, they still deserve to enjoy the essence of those designs — adapted to their specific financial and functional needs." Annie was rather surprised at her own eloquence.

Madame exchanged a look with Mrs. Downs. "As I explained," Mrs. Downs said.

Madame rose and beckoned Annie to the table where the magazines were stacked. She pulled one from the top and opened it at random. "There. Design." She handed her a piece of tissue and a pencil.

Put on the spot, Annie studied the dress on the page and quickly made adjustments. She placed the tissue on top and, with a few glances back to the original, made a sketch. "I think the key to most of these redesigns is removing the fussiness and simplifying the line. The spirit of the fashion remains, but the function and subsequent price is modified."

The two women held her drawing between them. Mrs. Downs traced a finger along the sleeve line. A silent decision was made, and the drawing was returned to the table. "How would you like to go to Paris with me in ze spring?"

Annie wasn't sure if there was anything Madame could have said that would be more shocking. "Me?"

Madame explained, "Each season a contingent from Butterick — led by myself — travels to ze Paris fashion shows to keep abreast of ze latest fashion. We return and adapt zat fashion to our patterns."

"Similar to what you just did," Mrs. Downs said.

"You are quick with ze ideas. Quickness is needed to study, remember, and adapt ze fashion we see."

Sean had mentioned such a process, but now to be asked? *Lord? What are You doing here? This is beyond anything I could have asked or imagined.*

Mrs. Downs straightened the magazines. "In the past I have gone on the trips, but I find that my time is better utilized here, keeping my department in line. And Maude has gone. She has an eye for the details others miss."

"Maude?"

Madame nodded. "And another woman, Mrs. Brown, has accompanied me, but she is off having ze baby."

Thank You, God, for Mrs. Brown's baby.

"So?" Madame said. "Would you like to go with us?"

There was no hesitation, no need for deliberation. "Yes. Very much so."

"Très bien. Bon," Madame said.

"When do we leave?"

Madame laughed. "You are eager, yes?"

"I am eager, yes."

"We do not leave until ze mid of March."

Annie remembered Sean mentioning sales trips to Europe. Could it be? Could he? "Does anyone else go?"

"A few others perhaps," Madame said.

Annie only needed one other.

Upon leaving Madame LeFleur's office, Annie desperately wanted to share the news with Sean. But his desk was empty. Telling Maude would be the next best thing.

But as she and Mrs. Downs reached their floor, Mrs. Downs said, "I would advise against sharing your news with the other ladies."

"Why?"

"Envy is a sin."

That is their problem.

"So is pride."

That is my problem.

"They will wonder where I've been, why you called me away."

Mrs. Downs plucked a scrap of muslin from the corridor. "I can only give the warning. Whether you heed it is your choice."

They entered the workroom, and the presence of Mrs. Downs was the only reason Annie's coworkers didn't swarm around her.

Maude sidled up close. "Well?"

Annie's excitement determined her choice

— though shared in a whisper. "I'm going to Paris, to the fashion shows. With you."

Maude blinked. "I worked here four years before they invited me to go."

Annie was surprised. "I thought you'd be happy for me."

Maude's countenance changed from surprise to glee. "Of course I am. The two of us in Paris! Can you imagine?"

"What's going on?" Dora asked.

Before Annie could suggest to Maude they keep it to themselves, she told the entire group. "Annie and I are going to Paris in the spring!"

There were groans all around, and a few comments that were far from kind, but it was nothing Annie couldn't handle.

She was going to Paris!

All day, Annie had but a single focus: she wanted to tell Sean about Paris, talk to Maude about Paris, and dream about Paris. But after the mixed reaction she received from the other girls in the workroom, she had to keep her excitement to herself — as best she could.

She was only partially successful.

"You need to stop smiling so much," Maude whispered as they sized out a waist-line.

"I can't help it. I've never been offered something so exciting."

"I agree. But you're acting like the child who gets a pony on Christmas when all her siblings get a new pencil box."

Point taken. And yet, "Blast them if they find my excitement offensive. Maybe if they'd shown some initiative and had some talent they'd be going, too."

Maude's eyebrows rose. "Too much truth, Annie. Rein it in."

"I'm sorry. But surely you've felt it, too. After all, they also chose you."

Maude angled her back to the others as she pinned a dart in the waist. "My mother used to tell me that of those who are given much, much is demanded. For whatever reason, you and I have been given some talent the others don't have." She shrugged. "Mother always said it's my responsibility to use what I have." She gave a slight nod toward the others. "Use your talent boldly when possible and discreetly when necessary."

Annie laughed. "That may be the best advice I've ever received."

A young man in a uniform stepped into the workroom. All eyes turned toward him. "Telegram for a Miss Annie Wood?"

Annie raised her hand. "That's me."

The women gathered close. "Telegrams are always bad news," Dora said.

Suzanne nodded. "We heard my uncle Jed died with a telegram."

Annie immediately thought of her parents. Were they all right? Yet it couldn't be from them. They didn't know where she was.

Dora offered a snide opinion. "Maybe it's some fancy Paris designer inviting you to dinner."

"Very funny," Maude said. "Come on, Annie. Open it."

Annie removed the note from the envelope. She read it through and smiled. "It's from a friend who's traveling in Europe. Just wishing me a happy New Year."

The group of ladies deflated with disappointment. "That's all?" Suzanne asked.

"You'd rather my uncle had died?"

They straggled back to work. Annie slipped the note in a pocket.

Maude sidled close. "What's it really say?"

"Just what I said." She flipped a hand, shooing her away. "You're as bad as the others." Then she had a thought. "How do I send a response?"

"There's a telegraph office down the street. You just stop in, write it up, and pay."

"How much?"

"Not much. But you're charged by the

word, so be brief. What do you want to say?"

Annie shook her head. "I'm just asking."

Annie desperately wanted to reread the telegram but made herself wait a half hour before she went to the ladies' and the privacy of a stall. Only then did she open the envelope a second time.

EUROPE LOVELY. OFFER STANDS. HAPPY NEW YEAR. MRS. S.

Lately Annie hadn't thought much about Mrs. Sampson's offer. Yet to know that it still stood added to her elation.

Mrs. Sampson is in Europe. I'm going to Europe. What if we could meet?

Annie fished a stub of a pencil from her pocket and wrote on the back of the envelope.

COMING TO PARIS MID-MARCH. FASHION SHOWS. TALK THEN?

She read it over, hoping to make it shorter, but there were no words to cut.

There were also no words to convey all she was feeling. Yet there *were* three she had to express: *Thank You, God!*

After work Annie couldn't wait outside for

Sean but instead met him at the stairwell, grabbing his arm.

"Well, hello."

"I have exciting news," she whispered as they headed outside.

They joined Maude. "She's been bursting at the seams all day."

Annie pulled him out of the stream of pedestrians, and Maude followed. Annie bounced on her toes. "I'm going to Paris in mid-March, to the fashion shows!"

His face brightened, and he lifted her off the ground and spun her around. "How did it happen? Who asked you to go?"

She told him the story of the magazines, Mrs. Downs, and Madame LeFleur. "They said there was another woman who usually goes, but she's having a child and —"

Sean looked at Maude. "Mrs. Brown?"

Maude nodded. "She's due around then. You're still going for your sales trip, aren't you, Sean?"

"I believe I'm going the first of March because I need to go to Berlin, London, and Vienna as well as Paris, but I'm sure I can arrange to meet up with you, and perhaps take the same ship home." He held Annie's chin and kissed her once. "We can see Paris together."

They began to walk again. "It's like a

dream."

"That it is," Sean said. "A dream come true."

Chapter Twenty-Six

"You're what?"

Iris blushed. "I'm expecting. A baby."

Annie drew her into an embrace. "I'm so happy for you." She pushed her at arm's length and took a discreet look at her abdomen. She did not look pregnant. "When are you due?"

"In the fall. October."

Edna put an arm around Iris. "Plenty of time for Annie and I to sew up a proper layette."

The blast of the ocean liner's horn deafened them. "I think that means it's time to board." Annie looked toward her travel party. Madame LeFleur was instructing some porters as to their luggage.

Annie hugged Edna and Iris. "Take care of yourselves — and the baby."

"Have a marvelous time," Edna said.

"You will see Sean?" Iris asked.

"He's already been in Europe two weeks

but will join us in Paris a few days after we arrive." She saw Maude motioning her over. "I have to go. Good-bye."

"Bon voyage," Edna said.

Annie rushed to join the others. With a shake of her head, Madame turned toward the gangway. "Come girls, *faites-vite*! *Plus vite!*"

As the girls scurried after Madame, Maude handed Annie two enormous hatboxes, keeping two for herself. "Madame doesn't trust porters with her beloved *chapeaux.*"

By the way Madame strode onto the ship, one would have thought she was a queen. The ship's attendants snapped to and gave her the attention she demanded.

"Do they know her?" Annie asked Maude.

"They know her type."

"But she's not wealthy."

"Madame acts as if she deserves deference, so she gets it."

A crewman walked alongside Madame, leading her to her stateroom. The men at the top of the gangway merely nodded to Annie and Maude. No one asked to take the hatboxes.

The two girls followed Madame and her guide up some stairs and then into a lush corridor. Annie was impressed that Butterick was letting them travel first-class.

The man opened a paneled walnut door. "For you, Madame LeFleur."

Madame perused the room with a glance to the *en suite* bath and water closet area.

"Does it meet your approval, madame?" he asked.

"I believe it suits." To Maude and Annie she said, "Go get settled. We shall meet later."

The hatboxes were relinquished and the girls left the room. "I just realized that I half expected her to ask me to do her unpacking," Annie whispered.

"You are not her maid."

"Last time I was on a ship, I *was* a maid." It seemed a lifetime ago, when she was a different Annie.

Maude looked at the papers that noted their cabin assignments then strode down the corridor and made a turn toward the center stairs. She descended the stairs.

"We're not on this level?"

Maude spoke over her shoulder. "You are not a maid, but neither are you first-class. We have second-class accommodations."

Annie couldn't help but be disappointed, yet when she saw the room they would share she was pleased. "It's much better than the third-class room I had before."

Maude plopped on the bed to the right of the porthole then removed hat pins securing her hat and tossed it on the low dresser in between. "Relax now. There will be plenty of commotion once we depart."

Annie couldn't remember any commotion from her trip over other than serving Miss Henrietta and her ladyship. "How do we spend our time on the voyage?"

"Eating, napping, reading, and strolling around the decks. Do you play cards?"

"No. The footmen used to play Whist, but I was never invited to join them."

"I'll teach you Pitch. But I warn you, I will win. I always win."

They stood at the railing and waved goodbye to those on the pier. Annie scanned the crowd for Edna and Iris but couldn't see them. The ship slowly moved away from the harbor.

Will my life be different when I return?

Passengers gradually left the rail and began their promenade of the decks. Annie turned her back on the sea. "Now what?"

Maude laughed. "You need to be entertained already?"

"I am used to having something to do. I am used to schedules."

Maude pointed to a long row of deck

chairs. "Sit."

Annie sat in one chair, and Maude sat next to her. They nodded at people walking by.

"You need to learn to put your feet up," Maude said, moving her feet to the chaise.

"It's not something I get to do very often."

"Suit yourself." Maude leaned her head back and closed her eyes.

Annie tried to do the same. The sun was warm and the sea breeze refreshing.

But then she sat upright with a startling realization. "I have never had leisure time! I have always worked."

"Everyone works, Annie. Even the wealthy have to work to make their money."

"But they have leisure time."

"More than us, that's for certain." Maude shielded her eyes from the sun. "You've never explained how you left servanthood behind."

"I ran away."

"Without telling them?"

"That's how running away works." Annie's past seemed like the skyline of the city, moving further and further away.

"You mentioned you'd run away but I didn't think you meant it so literally."

Annie told Maude about Lady Newley, the Friesens, Iris, and Danny.

At the mention of his name, a familiar lump formed in her throat. "Danny was killed by a footman named Grasston who worked at the Friesens'. He claimed I got him fired and was stalking me for months. He even attacked me."

"Meaning . . . ?"

"He tackled me to the ground and was on top of me, and . . ." She shuddered at the memory. "Some passersby saved me."

Maude hesitated. It seemed an odd reaction. But then she said, "How horrible for you."

"My pain was nothing compared to . . . Grasston killed Danny to hurt me. Danny died because of me."

Maude's feet found the deck, and she faced Annie. "Why don't I know any of this?"

"It's over now. Last December at Iris's wedding, the police were in the midst of arresting Grasston when he jumped off a roof and died rather than be arrested." She leaned back and closed her eyes.

"I'm so sorry you had to go through that."

"So am I." The stories she'd just shared about Iris and Danny came back to her, and with the stories came a conclusion. "Iris is where she should be — married and expecting a child. Perhaps I am where I should be."

Maude sat back in the lounger. "You're on a ship heading for Europe and the fashion shows in Paris. I'll take that over being married and having babies."

Annie glanced at her. "You don't want that?"

Maude shrugged. "Do you?"

The question loomed large, filling the expanse of sky and sea. "I like the idea of marriage, but the babies . . . I want to have a career. I just got started. I don't want it to end too soon."

"Then wait. Sean will wait for you."

"He hasn't asked yet." *I haven't let him ask.*

"Perhaps he doesn't want to ask until he knows you'll say yes."

"Perhaps." She thought back to her visit with Sean's mother. "His mother told me — almost warned me — to take my time in regard to marriage. She had dreams, too, but once she was married she had to give them up."

"I am determined not to give up my dreams for anyone." She put a hand on Annie's arm. "So . . . are you with me?"

It was a complicated issue. Annie loved Sean, but she also loved her work. All she could do was shrug.

Maude slapped the arm of her chair. "Enough of this serious talk. We're here to rest and relax. You are too tightly wound, Annie Wood."

She couldn't deny it.

They walked out of the second-class dining room, and Annie put a hand to her stomach. "That was delicious. But far too much."

"And we can have as much as we want."

"Ugh," Annie said, feeling overly full. "It was like putting butter on bacon."

Maude laughed. "Let's go into the game room and see if we can gather two more for a card game."

"I told you I don't play."

"And I told you I'd teach you."

The girls found a deck of cards in the game room where others were playing billiards, checkers, and chess. Maude began shuffling the deck.

"It appears you've done this before."

"A few times." Maude looked around the room and raised a hand. "We need two more for Pitch."

Annie was a bit embarrassed when two young men came over. She couldn't imagine hawking for partners like Maude had done.

"Pitch, you say?" said the man with a dark black mustache.

"Ten-point. Women against men."

"You're on," the blond man said.

"I . . . I don't know how to play," Annie said.

"All the better," the first man said. He held out his hand and made introductions. "I am William and this is Stanley."

"Maude and Annie," Maude said, as she began to deal the cards.

"Fifty-two!" Maude exclaimed. "We won!"

Stanley threw down his cards. "You two got the ace and the three nearly every time."

"You got the two a lot," Annie said.

"Small consolation," William said. "Let's play another."

Annie looked at the clock on the wall. It was nearly midnight. "I think not, gentlemen. I'm quite done in." As she pushed back her chair, Stanley rushed to pull it out for her.

"Until tomorrow, then?" he asked. "At two?"

"We'll see."

They bade the men good night and made their way back to their cabin. Only when they were inside, with the door shut and locked, did Annie feel the full measure of her weariness. "I had no idea it was so late."

"Time flies when you are having fun."

Annie sat on her bed and began to unlace her shoes. "It was fun. More fun than I've had in a long while."

"Stanley is interested in you."

"I know," Annie said, removing her shoes and enjoying the freedom. "I don't want him to be. I mentioned 'my beau.' I mentioned meeting Sean in Paris."

Once Maude's shoes were off she rolled down her stockings. "That doesn't matter to some men."

There was a slight edge to her voice. "William was nice to you."

"No, you don't," Maude said, setting her shoes near the wardrobe. "I do not want male attention. Ever."

Annie was shocked by this. "Whyever not? You're at ease with them, you're witty and pretty and —"

"I'm not saying I *can't* get their attention. I don't want their attention."

She stopped all movement and kept her back to Annie. Her voice became soft. "I can't have their attention."

Something was wrong. Annie went to her and touched her shoulder. "Will you explain what you mean?"

They stood together like that for a full ten seconds. Annie heard Maude's breathing hasten.

"Maude?"

Maude turned around, gave Annie a glance, and then pointed to the beds. "Let's sit."

Annie took a seat on her bed, while Maude sat on hers, her head down, her arms crossed like a protective shield. What had the power to quash the vivacious, unflappable Maude?

Annie waited, wanting yet not wanting to hear what Maude had to say.

Finally, Maude drew in a deep breath. "Two years ago I was assaulted." It took another breath to get out the rest: "I was raped."

Annie gasped and stood to go to her, but Maude waved her back. "I was walking alone at night, not paying attention to my surroundings, when a man grabbed me, pulled me into an alley, beat me, and . . ." She shrugged. "He left me for dead. I thought I was dead. I wanted to die."

"Oh, Maude." Annie found herself at a loss for meaningful words. "I'm so sorry."

Maude lifted her gaze to the porthole. "I remember lying there, my cheek against the dirt of the alley, with the pain so intense that I wished for death to give me release. I opened the eye that wasn't swollen shut and saw a rat coming toward me, sniffing at me.

Only the idea of him gnawing at my skin got me to move. Somehow I stood up and staggered to the street, where someone helped me."

Annie remembered Grasston's assault, and imagining what it *could* have been made her shudder. "I can see why that would put you off men."

Maude looked at her, shaking her head vehemently. "It's not that — though it certainly was at first. I was afraid of all men, but that eventually faded. It's not that I don't like men, or trust them, or even that I don't want one in my life, it's that . . . I can't ever marry."

"Why not?"

"I can't have children. I was . . . damaged."

Annie put the pieces together. "You don't want to encourage a man because he might want to marry you, and you don't want that because you can't give him children."

Maude touched the tip of her nose. "It wouldn't be fair."

Annie felt guilty for her previous talk about not wanting children at this point in her career. It was far different to face never having them.

"Not all men want children."

"Perhaps," Maude said. "But by the time

a beau and I would have such a conversation, we would have feelings for each other. His finding out I couldn't . . . I don't want to inflict that sort of pain on anyone — nor experience it myself."

"If a man really loved you, he wouldn't care."

"I would care." She began taking hairpins from her hair, setting them in a pile on the bed. "For a long while I tried to play the part of a shy and reclusive sort in public, hoping men would ignore me. But for some reason many of them took my reticence as a challenge, and they tried to bring me out of my shell."

"You, shy?"

She ran her hands through her now freed hair, raking her scalp. "Being who I was *not* was too much work. And so I decided to go the opposite route. I decided to overwhelm them with wit and sarcasm — trying to be too much for them."

"Has that worked?"

"You don't see a man around, do you?" She covered a yawn with her hand. "If I do spot interest, I quickly nip it in the bud." She collected her hairpins then began getting undressed. "I've accepted my lot. Please don't feel sorry for me. My career is rewarding and I have many friends — like you.

467

Those blessings save me from despair."

"You are the most courageous woman I know."

"It doesn't take courage to accept what is."

"But I think it does. You could resent it, fight it, and be bitter. You've chosen not to be any of those things."

"Don't make me a saint, Annie. I have plenty of bitter moments. Sometimes it's hard not to wallow in it." She stepped out of her skirt and moved to hang it up.

"Does my relationship with Sean make it more difficult? If it does, I won't talk about him and —"

Maude whipped around, making her petticoat swing. "Absolutely not," she said. "I am happy for the two of you. I want to hear the details of your courtship. I want you to be happy."

"Are you happy?"

Maude paused a moment then said, "I am. My mother always said, 'God is good, all the time.' I have to believe that. There's something good that will come out of my pain. It may be years down the road, but I truly believe that someday . . ."

Whether Maude wanted a hug or not, Annie embraced her.

CHAPTER TWENTY-SEVEN

Paris!

Madame LeFleur had so much luggage that she required her own carriage, leaving Maude and Annie on their own. Riding with Maude in the cab from the train station to the hotel reminded Annie of the same sort of ride she'd taken from the ship to the Friesens' home in New York City. "To think that a few months ago I was a maid at Crompton Hall, and had never traveled more than a few miles beyond Summerfield."

"Now you're a world traveler," Maude said. "And an expert Pitch player. We'll have to play on the ship going home."

"Sean will be with us then," Annie said. "I can't wait to —" She glanced at Maude. "Sorry."

"For what?"

"Being excited to see my beau."

Maude gave Annie a hard look. "There

will be none of that. Remember how I said I want to share your joy? Don't take that away from me, too." She pointed out the window. "Look. You can see the Eiffel Tower."

Annie and Maude stood at the check-in desk of Le Grand Hotel. Maude handled the paperwork, allowing Annie to fully take in the magnificent lobby. Fluted white columns, arches, and an enormous skylight in the center. A gorgeous spiral staircase made her want to climb it just to say she did. The entire area was bathed in the scent of fresh flowers, for a gigantic arrangement of white blooms graced a center table in the entrance, greeting the guests.

Annie could imagine Lady Newley staying in such a place, and Maude had told her that Napoleon's wife, Empress Eugenie, had inaugurated the hotel forty years earlier. Annie stepped beside a potted tree so she could watch the grand and the fashionable pass by.

Suddenly a man's voice sounded from behind her and asked, "What are you doing, mademoiselle?"

For a moment she feared she was in trouble. She turned around and saw . . . It was Sean! She flew into his arms.

"Now that's the kind of welcome I need."

They held each other until Annie noticed disapproving looks. She pulled away.

"I'm glad you've arrived," he said. "Was your voyage enjoyable?"

"I learned to play Pitch."

"Are you any good?"

"Maude thinks I am."

"Then you and I shall partner up on the trip home." He drew her to a duo of chairs, and they leaned forward so their knees touched. "I've missed you."

"I've missed you, too." She was glad to find it true. "How were the stores in Berlin, and London, and Vienna?"

"Thriving. I just have one more to visit here in Paris. I thought maybe you and Maude would like to join me."

"We'd love to." Maude strode forward holding two keys on large fobs. "Hello, Sean. Have you been here long?"

He stood to greet her. "Just a few hours. I thought I'd visit the Butterick shop this afternoon. Perhaps at three? That would give you ladies a chance to unpack and settle in."

It was a date.

"You need to rest, Annie," Maude said as she unpacked the last of their suitcases.

Annie shook her head, enjoying the view from their small balcony. Not all the floors provided such a luxury, but theirs, near the top of the building, within the roof itself . . . She felt heady with gratitude. "I can't come inside. Not with this view. The opera house is across the street. I can nearly touch it."

Maude joined her on the balcony.

"Look at the opulent detail of it," Annie said.

"The French are an opulent sort."

Annie gazed across the square where carriages and pedestrians intersected as they made their way from here to there. "These buildings have such odd roofs, not harsh and angled, but narrow and swooped upward."

"They're called Mansard roofs. Again, very French."

She nodded, taking in the information. "This is vastly different from New York."

"Which is different from London, and different from Vienna. Each is unique."

"You have traveled to those places, too?"

"In my youth."

The information added another layer to Annie's view of Maude. "Did you grow up wealthy? I only ask, because to travel so much . . ."

"Yes. Very. My father was a British diplo-

472

mat. We saw the world."

"You don't have an accent like I do."

"I've been in America a long while. Since I was twelve."

"What brought you there?"

"My father died, and Mother and I moved to New York to live with her sister."

"I didn't know you had family there."

Maude took in a deep breath. "We are estranged."

"May I ask why?"

Maude hesitated then sighed. "Mother wanted grandchildren. Since I am unable to give her what she wants . . ."

"Surely she didn't turn her back on you."

"I turned my back on her. She's suffered enough disappointment in her life." With a blink and a turn she changed the subject. "Come now. We have an hour to rest before we meet up with Sean."

The trio stood across the street from the Butterick Pattern store on the Avenue of L'Opera, just a ten-minute stroll from their hotel.

Annie was in awe. "I can't believe there is a store dedicated to our patterns. In Paris. France."

"I told you about it, and the ones in the

other cities. You knew I was making sales calls."

"I thought you were calling on sewing sections of department stores."

Maude adjusted a drawstring purse on her wrist. "The French love our patterns because we give them the essence of couture with simplified styles they can make at home." She swept a hand toward the storefront. "Shall we?"

They crossed the avenue, and Annie admired the mannequins in the windows wearing various dresses, blouses, and children's clothes, all made from Butterick patterns. Sean opened the door for the ladies. Inside was an elegant space — one room — with white fluted columns and tall wainscoting. Edging the room were tall tables and stools. Some women were perusing pattern catalogs as clerks helped them choose.

Another clerk approached. *"Puis-je vous aider, monsieur?"*

Annie was surprised when Sean answered in French. The two chatted back and forth, and then Sean turned to the girls. "Madame Seville, *Je peux vous présente* Mademoiselle Wood and Mademoiselle Nascato. Ladies, Madame Seville."

"Bonjour," the woman said.

Annie knew that much. "Bonjour, madame."

Madame proceeded to show them how the shop worked. The customers chose patterns from catalogs then purchased them from a supply in the back.

"It's similar to the system we had at Macy's, but larger."

"And more prestigious," Maude said, "because it's a stand-alone store, a destination."

Sean commenced with his business, talking with Madame, taking notes. Annie moved to a stool and looked through a catalog. The garment descriptions were in French. She assumed the ones in Berlin and Vienna were in German. "I'm so impressed. I had no idea I worked for such an international company."

"We sell more of our patterns here than anywhere in the world. We've even earned praise from European royalty."

Annie was dumbstruck. "To think that something we design could be worn all over Europe, and receive royal praise."

"We have to design it first. We see the fashion houses tomorrow."

Annie could hardly wait.

That evening Madame LeFleur gave each

of her workers an envelope. "Here is your stipend for ze meals during our visit." She glanced at a mirror in the hotel lobby, adjusting the plume on her hat. "I have reservations at ze Café de la Paix, here at ze hotel, but you may choose as you wish. Ta-ta."

And she was off again.

Annie looked in her envelope. "There is a lot of money here. Though, since it's French money, I may be wrong."

"You're not wrong," Maude said. "It's a lot. Restaurants in this part of Paris are expensive."

Sean slipped his envelope in an inner coat pocket. "I have an idea. A brilliant idea." He took Annie's hand and Maude followed as they exited the hotel and ran across the square. He led them to a street vendor who offered long loaves of crusty bread and glass bottles of what looked like lemonade.

"Let's save our money, get some bread, and go sit on a hotel balcony and watch all the fancy people come to the opera."

"That sounds smashing," Annie said.

It turned out they could get ham on the bread. They gathered their street wares, and Sean led them into a pastry store where they bought berry tarts for dessert.

They returned to Maude and Annie's

room. Their balcony was small, and not large enough for chairs, so they sat on its floor.

"It's a Parisian picnic," Maude said.

Annie took her first bite of the sandwich and moaned with delight. "The crust of the bread is perfect, and . . ." She opened the bread to see inside the sandwich. "There's so much butter."

"Of course there's so much butter," Maude said. "Parisians love their butter."

"As do I," Sean said, "love their butter. Love anyone's butter."

"Somehow it tastes better because it's Paris," Annie said. She looked across the street where the opera house was lit like a beacon for tonight's performance. She felt warm inside, as if *she* were glowing like a beacon from the inside out.

They had just finished their tarts when the carriages and automobiles began to arrive. Liveried footmen held the doors as beautiful people wearing beautiful clothing stepped out and made their way up the steps of the opera, disappearing inside.

Annie took hold of two rungs of the wrought-iron railing and peered through it, feeling very much like a child looking down on a parents' party. She'd seen Miss Henrietta do such a thing even as a young adult.

It was surreal: the sights, the sounds of gaiety and movement, the smells of the café wafting up from below, the crisp air of the spring evening. She closed her eyes. *Thank You for this experience, God. I will never forget it.*

"You seem lost in thought," Sean said.

She opened her eyes and nodded, returning her attention to the spectacle before her. "How can this be real? How can I be here?"

Sean ran a hand along her arm. "You *are* here. With me. With Maude. We all have a purpose here."

"We all appreciate being here," Maude added. "It will never get old."

Annie looked at them in all seriousness. "Even when I am old, I will remember this night."

"Ah," Sean said, with a mischievous look on his face. "But the night is not over. Come with me."

After getting their wraps, once again Sean led the girls out of the hotel. But this time he turned to the left. They walked past the grand entrance of the opera house, past the grand people going inside, and skimmed the side of the building, heading toward the back.

"Where are we going?"

They came upon a back entrance. Sean

looked both ways then opened the door. "Go! Inside."

The girls didn't have time to object. They came into a dark hallway but could hear voices calling to each other in French. Not genteel calls, but the calls of stagehands and actors backstage. They could hear the musicians warming up.

"Are we allowed in here?" Annie asked.

Even Maude looked apprehensive. "Sean, you go too far."

He stepped away as if scouting his next move. Apparently he found it, for he returned to them and said, "Not quite far enough. Not yet. Come with me."

He led them to a small space behind a curtain that was populated with extra music stands and stacked chairs. He freed three chairs. "Sit, mademoiselles."

The girls sat, and Sean sat with them. The space was small so they had to sit in a circle, with their knees touching. It was odd sitting in the dark, yet somehow the darkness heightened the experience. They could see a slit of light under the curtain.

Suddenly the cacophony of music stopped, and applause began. Some words were said, and then the orchestra began to play the most astonishing music Annie had ever heard. She'd never experienced any sort of orchestra. The sound was glorious, as if God Himself were directing His angels to play His own composition.

And then a new song began, and people began to sing with voices that soared and reached every corner of their hiding place, every corner of Annie's soul.

She began to cry.

Sean leaned toward her. "Are you all right?"

Since he couldn't see her nod, she answered by kissing him on his cheek and whispering, "Thank you. Thank you for letting me have a glimpse of heaven."

Chapter Twenty-Eight

The House of Paquin was a short walk from the hotel, on the Rue de la Paix. Sean explained that *paix* meant "peace," though he pointed out that the Column Vendôme at the apex of the street was originally erected by Napoleon to commemorate some war victory.

No matter. Peace followed Annie up the street and interwove its strands with happiness, contentment, and excitement. Yesterday spent with Maude and Sean, eating on the balcony, hearing the heavenly music of the opera . . . Her heart was full of thanksgiving.

And excitement.

"There it is," Sean said. "The building with the peach-colored entrance."

The entrance was set apart from the gray stone on either side and had PAQUIN in gold letters above it. Faux fluted columns marked the door. Above the windows to the right and left were planters of spring flowers. There was a queue of women in front of the shop. "Are these ladies potential customers?"

"Hardly," Maude whispered as Madame presented her invitation to allow them entrance. "These are the women we design the patterns for — the ones inspired by what we see inside. They are here to see the wealthy patrons."

"But we're not wealthy and we are going inside."

"If not for Madame LeFleur we'd be out here with the rest of them."

Annie noticed a few of the women whispering behind closed hands as their gaze lingered on Annie and Maude. She imagined they were assessing the girls' lack of fashion and probably discussing why *they* were allowed entrance.

Annie was glad when Madame motioned them inside.

The space was elegant with paintings on the wall, gilded trim, and ornate chairs and settees. They let Madame take the lead, and once again Annie was impressed with her contacts and her way of fitting in as if she was one of the rich patrons, not just a pattern designer from New York.

Suddenly Annie heard her name. "Annie!

Annie Wood!" She turned around and saw Mrs. Sampson coming forward to greet her.

"Mrs. Sampson," she said as the woman kissed her cheeks. "I didn't know you'd be here."

"Of course you did. You sent me a telegram saying you'd be in Paris in the spring. Harold and I always try to catch the fashion shows in Paris. The chance to see you again made it a must."

"*Galeries,*" Madame said, coming to make her own greeting. "Zey prefer ze term 'galeries' razer zan 'shows.' "

"How French of them." Mrs. Sampson extended her greeting to Maude and Sean. "So then. What other houses have you seen?"

"This is our first," Annie said.

"See as many as you can. I do hope there are no hobble skirts in the mix." Mrs. Sampson lowered her voice. "But now is the time to gain the knowledge of what's being done so you can do your own designing. You *are* designing, yes?"

"I am here to adapt the designs for Butterick, yes."

Mrs. Sampson let out a dramatic sigh then leaned even closer for Annie's ears alone. "My offer stands. Harold and I will back you toward the creation of your own fashion company. In your telegram during the holiday, you mentioned speaking when we were both in Paris. We are here. It is time to talk."

When Annie had replied to Mrs. Sampson's telegram, she'd assumed she would have an answer for her. Unfortunately all she could say was, "I do appreciate all you are offering. But I'm not ready."

Mrs. Sampson shook her head. "Doors that open can be closed, Annie. Perhaps Harold and I were wrong in believing you were the one for our project?"

She didn't want them to think that! "I didn't say I'd never . . . just that I wasn't ready."

The woman's left eyebrow rose, and Annie feared she had delayed too long.

Yet Mrs. Sampson simply sighed and said, "Someday you will be. I am confident there is a 'someday' in your answer."

More confident than I.

"When are you heading back to New York?" she asked Annie, including Sean and Maude in the conversation again.

"We take a train to Cherbourg April tenth to board the ship," Sean said.

Mrs. Sampson clapped her hands. "As are we! Which ship are you taking?"

Annie had to think a moment. "I believe

it's called the *Titanic.*"

Mrs. Sampson grabbed her arm. "As are we! How wonderful. We can enjoy the entire passage together. A few of our friends — John Jacob Astor, and Mrs. J. J. Brown — are also boarding in Cherbourg. I would love for you to meet them, especially Molly, for she is even more of a character than I am."

Annie had mixed feelings about sharing a ship with Mrs. Sampson. She enjoyed her company very much, yet she hoped the *Titanic* was as immense as its name so she would have some space. As she'd said, she wasn't ready to commit to the Sampsons' idea.

Then she thought of a way out. "Seeing each other on the *Titanic* might not be as easy as you hope, because I'm sure you are traveling first-class while the rest of us —" She stopped talking as she saw another woman she knew. Two women.

"What's wrong?" Mrs. Sampson asked, looking in the direction of Annie's gaze.

Annie glanced toward the door. Maybe she could avoid them if she slipped outside.

Maude took her arm. "Remove the look of panic if you please. And tell us what's wrong."

Annie turned her back on the women

she'd seen then answered, "It's Lady Newley and Miss Henrietta."

Unfortunately, Maude, Sean, and Mrs.
Sampson all looked in that direction.

"Don't look!"

"Too late," Sean whispered. "They're
coming over."

"Turn around," Maude added.

"Smile," Mrs. Sampson said.

Give me strength. Annie turned around
and braced herself for her mistress's anger.
She managed a smile and bobbed a curtsy
— feeling foolish for it in midbob. She was
not a servant anymore.

Which was the issue at hand.

"Annie," Lady Newley said.

"My lady. Miss Henrietta. How nice to
see you." *What a stupid thing to say!* The last
time she'd seen them she was a housemaid
— a housemaid who ran away with no
notice other than leaving Miss Henrietta a
note.

A few seconds passed and pulled on
Annie's nerves. Then Lady Newley said, "It
is nice to see you, too, Annie. How did you
get" — she motioned around the room —
"here?"

Annie looked at her friends. "Would you
please give us a few minutes?"

They stepped away. At least Annie could

endure her scolding in private. "I am so sorry for running out on you like I did."

"You mentioned 'no ladder to climb' in your note?" Henrietta said.

Annie didn't want to discredit the two lady's maids who'd betrayed her, for what did it matter now? "I have always loved fashion and . . ."

"You had a 'stirring,' I believe?" Lady Newley asked with a smile.

"You saw my note?"

"Henrietta shared it with me. There was much in it to remember," Lady Newley said. "Although it was perplexing at first, we soon discovered the reason for your departure."

Henrietta continued the explanation. "It seems Miss Dougard and Miss Miller have no talent for sewing without you doing the work for them."

Annie let out the breath she'd been saving for months. "You know."

"We found out quick enough. I do apologize for the two of them. If they'd given you the credit you deserved, you'd still be with us."

Annie's breath caught in her throat, and she took a fresh one. "But begging your ladyship's pardon, my place is not *there,* but here."

"You work for the House of Paquin?"

"No, no. I work for Butterick Pattern Company in New York. I help design patterns for home sewers. We are here to see the latest fashion and adapt it for the everyday woman."

Lady Newley's eyebrows rose. "My, my. Annie the housemaid is no more. Enter, Annie the pattern artist."

As if the words had the power of a strong wind, Annie felt knocked down with the truth of it. She was no longer the servant girl, Annie. She was the businesswoman, Annie Wood. "Thank you for saying that, my lady."

"I'm not your lady anymore. You have become an American entrepreneur."

Annie had to laugh. "I work for an American entrepreneur. I have much to learn."

"And you will learn it," Lady Newley said.

"I thank you for your encouragement. It means a lot to me."

"As your encouragement always meant a lot to me," Henrietta said.

With a nod, Lady Newley stepped away. "I'll leave you two to chat. Very nice seeing you doing so well, Annie. I wish you all the best."

"She's such a generous woman," Annie said.

"That she is. I am lucky to have her as a mother."

For the first time, Annie realized Miss Henrietta had lost quite a bit of weight. "I must say you are looking very fine, miss."

Miss Henrietta put her hands on her hips. "No more letting out seams for me. I've lost so much weight that we are here to order an entirely new wardrobe."

"How exciting."

"I plan on enjoying every moment. For I am not just ordering a wardrobe but a trousseau."

Annie gasped. "You are betrothed?"

"I am. He's an old family friend. He knew me when I was fat, and tells me he doesn't care how large or small I am. He loves me for me."

"He sounds like a true gentleman."

"Actually, now he says I'm too slim."

They shared a laugh.

"I have you to thank for my weight loss *and* my fiancé."

Annie was taken aback. "How did I . . . ?"

"When you ran away I was forced to stand on my own. Your courage to go after what you wanted made me think about what I wanted. I had been resigned to being a twenty-nine-year-old overweight spinster living with my parents. You gave me courage to think of what I *could* be. I finally gained the willpower to lose the weight, which gave me confidence enough to go after a man who truly loved me. Hank is that man. And I am a new woman."

"I'm so, so happy for you," Annie said. "Truly I am."

"As I am happy for you. Come. The show is beginning."

The three Butterick workers sat behind Madame for the fashion show. The models of the House of Paquin strolled by, pausing to pose and pirouette so the women could study the gowns and feel the fine fabrics and trims.

"I like that one," Annie whispered to Maude as a model approached. The girl wore a gown of ecru silk covered with delicate lace. The neckline crossed, forming a V, and the sleeves had no seam at the shoulder but were draped from the same piece of fabric as the bodice. The back bodice was the same as the front, but the back of the dress sported full-length pieces of blue silk embroidered at the bottom with mauve roses and green leaves. The blue was pulled around the sides at the empire waistline in the front and culminated in a pink rosette bow.

Annie quickly made a tiny sketch on the piece of paper they'd each been given to note the models and dresses they liked. Madame warned them to be discreet, and with just a few strokes, Annie simplified the dress into what could become a sewing pattern. The lace and silk were exquisite and out of the price range of home sewers, but the ensemble could be created in a cotton lace with a faille silk for evening. Or even a solid skirt with a contrasting color for the back piece, suitable for everyday use.

Model after model promenaded by, filling Annie's mind — and her card — to overflowing. She felt like a child in a candy store. She couldn't get enough.

But then it was over, and it was time to move on to the next galerie. The patrons who would order their own couture ensembles stayed behind to choose fabrics and have measurements taken. As her group was leaving, Annie caught the eye of Miss Henrietta, who pointed at a lovely dress of sage-green satin. Her nod asked a question, and Annie nodded back, giving her approval.

Annie walked a little taller as she left the House of Paquin.

The time in Paris flew by. Over the next

week the Butterick contingent visited the Houses of Louise Chéruit, Georges Doeuillet, Jacques Doucet, Paul Poiret, Redfern & Sons, and Worth.

Annie's stack of sketches grew. Back in their room, she arranged them, making changes and notes for each design. She held a sketch for Maude to see. "I think we can adapt this skirt easily if we —"

Maude snatched the page away. "Enough of this."

"Just a few more minutes."

With a sweep of her hands over the bed, Maude collected the pages and stuffed them in a drawer. "Tonight is our last night in Paris. We are *not* going to waste one more minute working."

"What did you have in mind?"

"It's not what I have in mind, but what Sean has in mind."

"Which is?"

"Dinner at Café de la Paix."

It was the restaurant in the hotel. "Isn't it expensive?"

Maude put her hands on her hips. "We've saved our meal money by eating simply. Don't we deserve one fabulous French meal?"

All hesitance left her. Work was done. Now was the time to celebrate.

■ ■ ■ ■

Annie perused the tray of desserts that was presented by the waiter. "Mademoiselle?"

Annie moaned as she sat back in her seat. "*Non merci.* I couldn't eat a bite."

"But you must," Sean said. "Just a bite." He looked to the waiter, held up one finger, and ordered, *"Crème brûlée à la vanilla, trois cuillères, s'il vous plaît."*

After enjoying an overabundance of exquisitely prepared French onion soup, *foie gras,* lamb, sole, and asparagus, Annie took one last look at the café, searing it into her mind forever. The ceilings and walls were detailed with ivory and gold embellishments; the chandeliers glistened in the deliberately dimmed light. Their table was set amid fluted columns with intricate scrolls like ram's horns at the tops. She ran a hand across the starched white tablecloth. The smells of food, both savory and sweet, combined with the perfumes of the fine ladies seated around them. It was like being in a palace — an eating palace.

"Annie? Are you still with us?" Maude asked.

She blinked and brought herself back to the moment. "Again I wonder at being here.

Has all this really happened to me?"

Sean reached across the table and took her hand. "It has. And the evening is not over."

"I'm not sure my senses can absorb any more. I'm quite done in. With us leaving tomorrow, don't you think we should pack and —"

"No," Sean said. "Not yet." He exchanged a look with Maude.

"No," she agreed. "Absolutely not. We can sleep on the train, or on the ship."

Sean nodded. "There is only one last night in Paris."

The dessert arrived and was set in the middle, between them. The waiter brought three spoons.

"You first," Sean said. "As it is your first crème brûlée."

"I don't even know what it is."

"It's a custard with caramelized sugar on top. Go ahead. Break into it."

The term *break* seemed odd but was immediately appropriate as Annie's spoon broke through the sugar shell and reached the rich custard below. They awaited her reaction.

"Mmm. I would deem it perfect, yet 'perfect' is too small a word."

They laughed and joined in the perfection.

Since she was tired, Annie was not keen on Sean's idea of a stroll along the Seine River. Yet not wanting to be a killjoy, she agreed to go.

The river flowed by them quietly, as befitted the late hour. The sky was deep navy, and the stars glittered and competed with the streetlamps.

"Worth the time?" Sean asked.

She squeezed his arm. "Mmm."

"That's what you said about the dessert."

"It still applies. This is delicious. And perfect."

"I think I'll sit here," Maude said as they passed a bench. You two go on. I will catch up."

As Annie and Sean continued talking, she glanced back. "Should we leave her alone? It's late, and it's a big city."

Sean stopped and suddenly faced her. "I needed to be alone with you, because . . ." He took both her hands in his. "I love you, Annie Wood. And more than that, I adore you."

Her heart flipped.

He knelt on one knee and took out a ring. "Annie, would you spend the rest of your life with me, as my wife?"

The knowledge that this was actually happening — and happening in Paris — collided with doubt and confusion.

Sean noticed the delay in her answer and stood. "You're supposed to gleefully answer yes and take me in your arms."

She felt horrible for causing him any sort of pain, yet there was no way around it. "I do say yes, but . . ."

He let out a sigh and rubbed the space between his eyes. "But?"

She looked to the river, to anywhere but the condemnation in his eyes. "But I am not sure I'm ready to be a wife."

"Is there training for it? If so, *I* am not ready to be a husband."

"There's more to it than that. With being a wife comes being . . . a mother."

He took her hands and smiled. "I would hope so. For part of my hopes for a future involve children. Don't you want children?"

"I do, but . . ."

His smile faded. "There is that awful word again."

"But I don't want to be a mother any time soon." She pointed back in the direction of the fashion houses. "I enjoy my job; I enjoy the challenge of it, the creativity of it, and the independence of it."

"You can do that and be a mother."

"Can I? None of our female coworkers have children. Few are married."

"But it's done. I know it is."

She thought of something else. "Mrs. Sampson is being persistent about their offer to back me. How could I ever start my own fashion design business *and* be a wife *and* be a proper mother?"

He dropped her hands. "You choose your career over me."

He made it sound dreadful and final. "I choose to get established in whatever path I'm supposed to be on, and then —"

He stepped back. "You assume I'll wait."

A wave of panic assailed her, nudging her to step close and take his hands once again. "I hope you will wait. I pray you will. For I do want to marry you, Sean. I love you, too. With all my heart."

She watched his clenched jaw relax. His eyes were plaintive. "You do?"

"I do. Immeasurably."

He began to lower himself once again to one knee, but she stopped him. "The next time you ask, I want to be able to gleefully answer yes and fall into your arms."

He nodded, but there was a mournfulness to his face. She slipped her hand around his arm and they turned toward the Seine flow-ing past them, in spite of them.

They joined Maude, and the trio walked back to the hotel. She looked at each of them expectantly. "So?"

"You knew?" Annie asked.

"Why do you think I hung back?" Not getting the answer from Annie, she turned to Sean. "So?"

"She answered, 'yes, but.' "

"That's no answer."

"That's what I thought," he said.

Annie stopped their walking. "It *is* an answer. It's all the answer I can give right now. I thought you understood."

"Understanding and liking are two different things," Sean said. "Come now. We have packing to do."

They walked back amid silence. And regret.

"I can't believe you didn't say yes to him," Maude said as she and Annie finished their packing.

"I explained it to you." Annie thought of another point in her favor. "His family is wonderful, and mine is . . . negligible. I don't deserve him."

"No, you don't. But you will not give him up using those lame excuses."

Maude was right. Annie was trying to rationalize what couldn't be rationalized. "I don't know what else to say."

"I think you've said enough. Just keep in mind that Sean is a remarkable, handsome man. Don't delay so long that you lose him."

Annie dropped a blouse she'd been folding. "You think there's a chance of that?"

"He wants to marry you now. You're putting him off because of what might happen in the future. One is a known, and one is an unknown. Just be careful you don't lose both."

Annie sat on the bed, the blouse hanging from a hand. "So you're saying I'm wrong in wanting to wait for marriage?"

Maude sat beside her. "I'm saying that none of us know the extent of our days."

"That's a pleasant thought."

Maude shrugged. "Just think about it."

Annie knew she would think of little else.

CHAPTER TWENTY-NINE

Annie enjoyed being a world traveler, yet the logistics were daunting. A carriage from the hotel to the Gare Saint Lazare train station, a train to Cherbourg, and then the *Titanic* to New York City. She was glad the fashion shows were behind them. Yet the promise of shipboard discussions with Mrs. Sampson remained. She appreciated the attention yet didn't look forward to being mollycoddled. Annie fondly remembered her other voyage, when she and Maude whiled away their time playing cards, reading books, and gazing at the sea from deck chairs.

A porter transferred their luggage from a taxi to a rolling cart to take inside the enormous train station, with instructions to hurry because they hadn't given themselves enough time. Madame had insisted on taking the first taxi with her enormous collection of luggage, so Annie, Maude, and Sean had no time to spare. Yet on a whim Annie intervened. "I can carry my own on board, thank you."

"Why don't you let him take care of it?" Maude asked.

"I just have this one case. It has all my sketches and notes in it. I don't know what I'd do if it got lost."

"Lost between here and there," Maude said, pointing toward the platform.

Annie shrugged.

Maude sighed dramatically. "I suppose now I'll have to do the same."

"Let me get yours and mine," Sean said.

Surprising them all, another carriage pulled up and Mr. and Mrs. Sampson emerged. They had no choice but to use a cart, for they had been in Europe all winter, with the luggage to prove it.

Mrs. Sampson swept toward them. "I wish I could get over the deplorable habit of being tardy, but here we are at the last minute." She took a breath. "I am ever so ready to go home. One can only be cosmopolitan so long. Let us proceed to the waiting hall."

Without meaning to, the young travelers were swept into her wake. They followed her through the arched doorways into the chaos that was the waiting area. Travelers of all sorts and sizes bumped against each other trying to get from here to there, all intent on the logistics of their journeys.

Sean checked the clock. "We only have five minutes until boarding."

"I despise cutting things so close," Maude said.

"You can thank Madame for —"

Annie cut off her sentence when she heard a child crying. She looked through the crowd and saw a boy of about six or seven, searching for someone. His cheeks were tear stained, his call of *"Maman? Maman!"* desperate. He looked like a younger Danny.

She rushed toward him. "What's wrong?"

The boy looked up at her, confused. Of course. He couldn't understand her. Since Sean could speak French, she called him over. "Shh. It will be all right, little one," she said, kneeling down to his level. To Sean she said, "Ask him what's wrong."

"Quel est le problème?" Sean asked.

The boy let out an agitated discourse, pointing this way and that.

Mrs. Sampson and Maude joined them. Mrs. Sampson listened intently. "His mother is missing? And she's expecting a baby?" she asked Sean.

"Seems so," Sean said. He put a hand on the boy's shoulder, trying to calm him. *"Il sera très bien. Ne vous inquiétez pas. Nous trouverons votre mère.*"

Suddenly there were shouts of, *"En voiture!"*

They all stood erect and looked toward the train. They were boarding.

"Go on ahead," Annie told the others. "I'll stay with the boy until he finds his mother."

"But you can't speak French," Sean said. "And I'm not leaving you alone."

"And I'm not going on the train without either of you," Maude said.

"Well, gracious sakes," Mrs. Sampson said. "You stay, we stay. Harold, go see if you can get our luggage off."

"What if I can't?"

"We'll catch up to it in Cherbourg."

Annie looked over the crowd and spotted Madame's face in the window of the train. She and Sean ran toward her. "Madame, we are staying behind to help a boy find his mother."

"What?"

Annie shook her head. "We need to help a boy."

"Zat is absurd. Let someone else help him."

Sean shook his head. "But no one else *was* helping him. He needs us — for a short while."

"Ze ship will not wait," Madame said.

Sean and Annie exchanged a look, and then Sean said, "Then we will board another ship."

Annie was ever so proud of him. "Go on, madame. We will see you in New York."

Madame looked past them. "Zis is ridiculous. You don't know ze boy. Let one of ze officials handle it."

That was an option, but Annie felt an intense nudge to stick with it to the end. "It will be all right. Let us do this. We must do this."

Madame rolled her eyes. "You are all ridiculous." The train began to move. She dismissed them with a flip of her hand.

Annie's heart beat wildly in her throat. What were they doing? It didn't make sense.

Sean took her arm. "We've made our choice. Let's see it through."

They returned to the boy, who was sitting next to Mrs. Sampson on a bench.

"Was Madame upset?" Maude asked.

"Confused," Annie said. "You realize we will probably miss the ship and have to take another."

"*C'est la vie,*" Mrs. Sampson said. "It won't be the first time. Two years ago we missed a ship that was taking us from Naples to Lisbon because I wasn't feeling well. When we boarded another ship a week later we met the nicest couple from Barcelona. We still correspond."

Annie felt an odd comfort in the story. Whatever her feelings, what was done was done.

Mr. Sampson returned from the platform. "It's too late. Our luggage is going on without us."

"So be it," Mrs. Sampson said.

Suddenly Annie looked down at the luggage that she, Sean, and Maude had taken from the trolley. "It's good we have ours."

"Us staying behind . . . it's like it was meant to be," Maude said.

It was. But enough about luggage. "Have you learned any more about the boy's mother and where she might be?"

"His name is André," Mrs. Sampson said. "He and his mother were waiting for his father to arrive from Calais. His mother said she wasn't feeling well, and told the boy to wait for her. But she didn't come back."

"I checked the ladies'," Maude said. "No expectant mothers in there."

Mr. Sampson glanced at his pocket watch. "The father's train should arrive within the half hour."

"Good," Maude said. "Then he will take care of it."

Annie shook her head. Oddly, she felt an

extreme sense of urgency. "But that may be too late."

"Too late for what?"

The baby? "We need to search for the mother. Get the porters to help. We stayed here for a reason. *She* needs us, too." They nodded in agreement, but just before they spread out, Annie felt a nudge to instigate something she'd never done before. "Stop a moment. We need to pray."

The contingent bowed their heads and each said a silent prayer. André crossed himself.

Mrs. Sampson stayed with the boy, and the rest of them fanned out over the enormous depot, gathering support from railway workers along the way. Even a gendarme became involved.

Annie looked again in the ladies', asking various women if they'd seen an expectant mother. Having no luck, she tried to imagine about how a very pregnant woman would react if she didn't feel well. Or if — even worse — she felt the baby coming.

She would seek a quiet place. A place to sit or lie down.

Annie walked the length of the waiting hall, peering through every archway. She was about to turn back when she heard a moan.

There she was! The woman was on the floor, her back to the wall, curled in pain, hidden from sight by a stack of crates. Annie knelt beside her. "Madame?"

The woman's eyes flashed with relief. She took hold of Annie's arm and pointed to her stomach. *"Le bébé s'en vient! Aide-moi!"*

"The baby. It's coming?"

"Le bébé!"

Annie stood. The woman grabbed at her, obviously afraid she would leave. Annie patted her hand. "I'll get help." She remembered a French word. *"Aide."*

The woman nodded. *"Merci."*

Annie stepped onto the platform and saw Sean talking to a couple in the crowd. "Sean! She's here! She's having the baby. Get help!"

Sean nodded and was off. Annie returned to the woman and sat beside her. She removed her jacket, rolled it up, and placed it under her head. She stroked her hair, which was matted with perspiration.

Suddenly the woman's eyes grew wide and panicked, and she looked out toward the platform. *"Où est mon fils? Mon fils!"*

Annie realized she must be asking about her son. "Your boy? *Garçon?*"

The woman nodded.

Annie pressed her hands down, trying to

507

portray calm. "He's safe. He's all right. Très bien."

The woman nodded then without warning grabbed her stomach and moaned loudly. Her face contorted and her entire body tensed. She held Annie's hand so tightly it caused pain.

"Hold on, hold on!"

Please God, help mother and baby be all right.

A doctor who'd been waiting to board a train came to the rescue and delivered the baby girl right there on the floor where Annie had found her — found Maria.

Annie witnessed the entire birth because Maria insisted she stay with her. She'd never even been around a woman who was expecting, much less be there at the birth, but Maria and the doctor did the work. Annie held her hand, mopped her brow, and offered reassuring words that needed no translation.

The baby was born and took her first breath then wailed at being forced out of her warm and dark cocoon into the cold and light. Annie cried happy tears with Maria.

Accompanying the miracle were waves of gratitude and praise to God, not just for the new life and the health of the mother, but for the sacred experience Annie had been allowed to share.

Annie left Maria's side and helped the doctor with the baby. A blanket, towels, and a bucket of water had been procured from somewhere, and once the cord was cut, Annie set the baby on a crate to wash her. The little girl squirmed, her fingers and arms spread wide as if she were testing her new limits. Once the baby was clean, Annie wrapped her in warmth and held her close, bouncing to calm her. For a brief moment, the baby opened her eyes. "Hello there," Annie whispered. "Welcome."

Maria held out her hands, needing to hold what she had nurtured for nine months. Annie placed the baby in her arms. Maria cuddled and cooed at her, and Annie witnessed an instant love between mother and child. An everlasting love.

Suddenly a man came around the stack of crates that had offered the only privacy to the moment and ran to his wife and daughter. The doctor was also finished and washed his hands in the bucket. "You did well to help me, miss."

Annie could only nod. Her part was over. She moved to leave, but the husband called to her. "Mademoiselle, *attendez!*"

Annie turned back to them.

"Comment vous appelez-vous?" he asked, pointing at her. *"Le nom?"*

She pointed at herself. "Annie."

He nodded and exchanged a look with his wife. She pointed at the baby then said, "Annie."

They were naming the baby after her? Annie put a hand to her mouth and nodded. *"Merci."*

He nodded his head and made a motion to include his whole family. *"Merci beaucoup."* Then he added, *"Que Dieu vous bénisse"* and crossed himself.

She guessed at his words. "May God bless you, too."

Behind her André approached tentatively. His father motioned him over, and the family was fully united. Annie slipped into the crowd.

"A girl?" Mrs. Sampson asked.

"Her name is Annie."

"They named her after you?" Maude asked.

Suddenly Annie's emotions got the better of her, and she began to sob. Sean pulled her into his arms.

While the baby was being born, Mr. Sampson made arrangements for passage on another ship and booked three rooms at a nearby hotel — at his expense. They enjoyed a light supper together, but Annie remembered little of it. She walked through the rest of the day and evening in a happy daze. The others respected her distance and talked around her, but their voices were vague, as though she were hearing them from the next room.

When it was time to retire, she went through the motions of her evening toilette by rote — and Maude had to help her out of her bodice when she forgot to unbutton the cuffs.

In her nightdress she sat upon the bed and found she could go no further without full release. "I witnessed a baby being born," she said.

Maude paused in the braiding of her hair. "I know."

"A new life, right there in the train station."

"Not ideal. Poor woman."

Annie blinked, bringing herself fully into the moment. "Fully ideal," she said with a shake of her head. "As if it was meant to be."

"The baby was meant to be born in a corner of a train station, on a dirty floor?"

Annie looked to the ceiling. It was hard to explain. "What if I hadn't heard André crying? What if we hadn't understood his mother was missing? What if we hadn't found her in time?"

"Someone else would have helped. Maybe."

"Maybe. But *they* didn't. We did."

"We missed our train and a chance to sail on the largest ship in the world. I was looking forward to being on the maiden voyage of the *Titanic.* It's been much talked about and is supposedly enormous and very lavish."

Maude was missing the point. Annie placed a fist at her stomach. "I feel very strongly that everything that happened today happened for a reason."

Maude got in her bed and pulled the covers up. "I guess we'll never know, will we?"

CHAPTER THIRTY

Finally!

The travelers stood at the rail as their ship left the dock at Cherbourg. They were only two days tardy from their previous schedule, but it seemed as though a lifetime had passed between April 10 — and the birth of little Annie — and today.

And though they weren't experiencing the excitement of being on the luxurious *Titanic,* their accommodations were first-class. Literally. For Mr. Sampson had booked the young people two first-class cabins. Being pampered started out as a bit of a lark, but it soon revealed its lesser merits.

Looking around at the exquisite attire of the other passengers, Annie felt horribly underdressed. "We don't belong here, with these toffs."

Mrs. Sampson shooed the thought away. "As I know these 'toffs,' I also know that a little frippery and finery is not a measure of

513

good character. You fit in with the best of them, Annie, and you overshadow the worst."

Annie laughed. "You do have a talent for making me feel right about myself."

Mrs. Sampson winked. "Ah, but I have ulterior motives, you know."

"I know."

"We'll talk at dinner." She turned to her husband. "Come, Harold. Let's take a stroll and leave these young people to wonder after us."

As soon as they left, Sean said, "She *is* eccentric."

"That she is," Maude said.

"But an eccentric woman of good character," Annie said. "They wouldn't have had to stay behind when we found André."

"I've thought about that," Maude said. "I do hope Madame is enjoying her voyage without us." There was sarcasm in her voice.

"We rarely saw her on the trip over," Annie pointed out. "She probably hasn't realized we're absent."

Maude faced away from the sea. "I for one don't miss her, either. What do you say we stir up some mischief in the game room?"

"Gaming parlor," Annie corrected. "We're first-class now."

Maude affected a haughty stance and

flipped her hand. "Come on, then. Let us dally and dawdle with the other upper crusts."

Their dinner in the first-class dining room rivaled their dinner at Café de la Paix. Six courses were served by white-gloved footmen. At first Annie thought it impossible that she would have the capacity to eat all the courses, but because of the refined pace of the service, she managed to enjoy each item — including Charlotte Russe for dessert. She'd seen the cook at Crompton Hall create the ladyfinger-and-fruit-cream delicacy but had never been allowed to taste it. Until now.

She savored every bite and tried not to close her eyes and moan at its scrumptiousness.

Tried and failed. "This is heavenly."

"Would you like another?" Mrs. Sampson asked. "It's fully within the concept of no limits stated in the first-class rule book."

"There's a rule book?" Mr. Sampson asked.

"Unwritten, dear one, but valid just the same."

"This one helping is plenty," Annie said. "It will more than suffice."

Mrs. Sampson laughed. "Well, then." She

515

waved to the waiter to remove her plate. "We have tippy-toed through conversations involving all things but the conversation I've been longing to have regarding your future."

Her husband shook his head. "Subtlety is not my wife's strong suit."

"I see no need," she said. "Annie knows the plans we have for her. We only need her yes and the world will fall at her feet."

"My," Maude said. "All that for a yes? But may I ask what the question is?"

Mrs. Sampson looked confused. "You haven't shared with your best friend?"

Annie shook her head, feeling guilty for it.

"Shared what?" Maude asked.

Mrs. Sampson did the honors. "Harold and I have offered financial backing and support for Annie to start her own fashion house, focusing on function over fad."

Maude blinked, and Annie could almost see her mind whirling. "I'll set aside my disappointment that you've kept me in the dark to advise you to say yes, Annie. If you don't, I will."

Mrs. Sampson got an odd look on her face then said, "Actually, I think that would be a fine idea. Why don't both you and Sean join Annie in her new venture?"

The notion beamed upon the table like a ray of sunlight sent from God. What had seemed gray and cloudy now glowed with promise. "You'd do that?" Annie asked. "You'd let all three of us work together and open a design shop?"

" 'Shop' is too meager a word, but yes," Mrs. Sampson said with a glance to her husband. "I think that would be a capital idea. Don't you, my dear?"

Mr. Sampson nodded and turned his coffee spoon over and over against the tablecloth. "I don't see why not. From what I've heard, you all have different talents to bring to the venture."

Sean raised a hand. "It's true that I have sales experience, and Maude —"

Maude interrupted. "I know dress construction better than anyone on the planet."

Mrs. Sampson laughed. "Confidence. I like that."

Mr. Sampson set the spoon aside and leaned forward. "So with the two of you we have sales and construction, and Annie brings design and illustration talent. With our financial backing and connections, it sounds like the makings of a strong and vibrant company."

"Hear, hear!" Mrs. Sampson said.

Sean looked at Annie. "Seeing the idea in this new light, as a larger whole . . . I never thought I'd say this, but it *would* be exciting to be a part of something totally new."

Annie couldn't believe what she was hearing. She'd never imagined the Sampsons would consider including Sean and Maude, but she now realized she couldn't imagine the venture without them. Yet to draw them into something that would pluck them out of the positions they'd held for years . . . "Are you sure?" she asked her friends. "It's an enormous risk. I am still new to this business. You two have far more experience, and your careers are well established. You'd be giving up much more than I." She looked directly at Sean. "When I previously mentioned this offer you seemed against it."

He bit his lip. "I wanted us to be together at Butterick. I didn't want to lose you."

Mrs. Sampson touched his arm. "And now you will be together." She turned her attention back to Annie. "You have intrinsic talent, my dear. It's a gift recently discovered, but a gift nonetheless."

Annie felt herself blush at the flattery and the opportunity. "This newest discussion has flipped the world on its axis."

"Because it's showing its full form, it's falling into place," Mrs. Sampson said. "Seeing you at the fashion show and having this special time on the ship together are blessings from God. I do not believe in coincidence."

"Nor do I," said her husband. "Things happen for a reason."

"That's what you said last night, Annie," Maude said. "All this is happening for a reason. Maybe this is the reason."

Mrs. Sampson extended her hands, palms up, presenting Annie the world. Her face was expectant.

Annie looked to Sean. "Are you truly for this?"

He let out a long sigh. "Oddly, I think I am. But it all hangs on you, Annie. The seed was planted with you."

"Indeed," Mrs. Sampson said. "You are the seed."

"Which makes you the sun?" she asked.

Mrs. Sampson chuckled. "I'll let Harold be the sun. I'll be the rain." She raised her right hand. "We promise to give you just enough sun and rain to thrive. No more, no less."

Annie was overwhelmed. She was in front of yet another door, being offered the chance to open it and step through, or back away. Had all the doors in her life been gifts from God, a series of chances to exercise the free will He championed?

"I've had so many doors," she said to herself.

"Doors?" Mrs. Sampson asked.

Annie pulled her thoughts together. "Since I've come to America I've been offered one door after another: leaving service, finding a job at Macy's, moving to Edna's, getting the job at Butterick, and traveling to Paris. And now this." Mrs. Sampson started to speak, but Annie stopped her with a hand. "It's not just a matter of the doors being opened for me, but the fact that every door that opened seemed to shut once I was through it."

"There's no going back," Sean said softly.

"I don't think there is — which is why this decision is so important, and why I haven't taken it lightly." *And why I'm waiting for Your direction, Lord.*

Everyone at the table nodded.

"It's your choice," Sean said. "I go where you go."

"Me, too," Maude said.

Annie looked into the eyes of her friends. It *was* up to her. Yet the stakes were far higher than they were when she was deciding only for herself. Her dearest friends were offering themselves to her, depending on her to take this leap together.

She drew in a long breath, and held it a moment. *Lord? Yes?*

As she exhaled she found herself saying,

"Yes. I say yes."

Not a single card game was played.

There was no time. After agreeing to start their own design company, the five partners put their heads together to make a plan. To start something from nothing was daunting. Where would they begin?

Mrs. Sampson offered an idea to gather regular women together and get their opinions as to how they would like their clothes to look and function. The idea was a good one, for if they were going to design for the masses, they needed to *ask* the masses.

The third day into their voyage they sat around a table in the ship's first-class lounge, and Maude took notes. "Who is our customer? Working women? The wives of merchants and middle-class families? Or your set?" She looked to the Sampsons.

Mrs. Sampson tapped her finger on the table. "We're not sure. We want to set women free of frivolous fashion, yet we need to make it affordable."

"But couture clothing is not affordable," Annie said. "Far from it."

Sean nodded. "To keep costs down it will have to be manufactured, not hand sewn."

Annie's mind swam. "Will stores like Macy's take it on?"

Mrs. Sampson nodded. "That's where Sean's expertise will come in as our salesman. Plus, we can sell to other department stores like Gimbel's, Henri Bendel, Bergdorf Goodman, Lord and Taylor —"

Suddenly the captain of the ship entered the room along with a large gathering of passengers, each noisily vying for his attention.

"What's going on?" Maude asked.

"Let's find out." Mrs. Sampson pushed back her chair.

"Please, ladies and gentlemen," the captain said from the middle of the lounge. "I assure you there is nothing to worry about."

Annie asked a woman nearby, "What are we not to worry about?"

"Last night another ship on the White Star line hit an iceberg and —"

"Which ship?"

"The *Titanic.*"

Annie's entire body gasped. "We were supposed to be on that ship!" She spread the news to the others in her party, and they all moved closer to the captain to get details.

"Is the ship being repaired?" Mr. Sampson asked.

"Her wireless installation enabled her to call for help. With this means of communication, the terrible isolation of her mid-ocean position was negated. Every ship within range hurried to her assistance, and all risk of graver loss of life was averted."

" 'Graver loss of life'?" someone asked.

"I assure you, all is well," he said.

"It doesn't sound well," Mrs. Sampson said.

The captain pressed his hands downward, trying to calm them. "A smaller ship than the *Titanic* might well have succumbed to the concussion caused by striking the iceberg. I believe this is proof that the increased size of our modern ships is a vital achievement."

"Big or not, it still struck an iceberg."

"But" — the captain said, raising a finger — "the *Titanic* is still afloat and has escaped without any loss of life."

This last didn't make sense. "You mentioned 'graver loss of life,' " Annie pointed out. "That means there were fatalities."

By now the crowd had grown to many dozen.

"Now, now. Do not jump to conclusions, ladies and gentlemen. I assure you the most violent collision means the crumpling of her bow and perhaps the filling of her forward compartments, at the worst. But with her gigantic size and the system of watertight doors in her bulkheads — that can be closed from the bridge — there is nothing to worry about. Modern methods of ship construction have been put to the most crucial test that can possibly be imagined, and they have triumphed. The *Titanic*'s situation is fresh proof of the safety of the modern steam vessel, a free illustration of the dominance that man has established over the most treacherous forces of nature. Now go back to your enjoyment of this fine vessel. I assure you we shall keep you informed of further news."

He left, but the crowd did not.

"I wonder how Madame is handling this," Maude asked.

"She would not appreciate any alteration to her entertainments," Annie said.

"Or meals," Maude added.

They laughed — though softly. For there *was* the chance their levity was misplaced. They returned to their table, but all thoughts of planning a new business were forgotten.

The moon shone brightly as Annie stood with Sean and Maude at the railing. They gazed out to sea. Somewhere to the west, the *Titanic* had hit an iceberg.

"We're all so quiet," Sean said.

"I can't get it out of my head," Annie said.

"I can't imagine such a terrifying event. There must have been utter chaos."

"And fear," Maude added. "I'm sure the passengers had no idea what was going on at first."

"Madame doesn't like not knowing what's going on," Annie said.

Her comment sparked another round of silence. Then Sean said, "I wonder if all the passengers have been taken to New York by now."

"Madame will have such a story to tell once we get back."

"But for a little boy in a train station, it could have been our story," Maude said.

Sean leaned his back against the railing. "Speaking of, how are we going to tell Butterick we're quitting? Do we do it all in one day?"

Annie looked down at the water below. "I feel dreadful quitting the job just months after I started."

"*Are* we quitting immediately?" Maude asked. "Or are we going to wait until our plans are more firmly set in place?"

"I choose the latter," Sean said.

Annie was a bit put off. "Don't you believe it will happen? Don't you trust the Sampsons?"

"Yes, to both questions," Sean said. "But

there are a lot of details to sort through."

Annie agreed. "I do want to finalize the sketches we're bringing back from Paris for Butterick. The company paid our way there. We need to make sure the work is completed well. We owe them that."

"I agree," Maude said. "One step at a time."

As if on cue, they all stepped away from the railing. "Good night, then," Maude said.

When Maude left them alone, Sean drew Annie into his arms, and she heard the beating of his heart. "I hope we're doing the right thing," she said against his chest.

She felt him nod. "We need to pray, to make sure we're doing what God wants us to do."

Annie pulled back to see his face in the moonlight. "I prayed during that dinner when we all agreed. I never imagined you would be a part of it, and then suddenly, you were. All that was left was for me to give the nod."

"I never expected any of it," Sean said. "And then the opportunity was suddenly set before me."

Annie suffered a moment of doubt. "Were we all drawn into the excitement of the idea? Is it the right thing to do, or are the Sampsons merely skilled in the art of persuasion?"

"That's what we need to figure out." He put his finger beneath her chin. "God will guide us if we ask."

"Ask for guidance and pray for the passengers on the *Titanic.*"

"Agreed. Now, let us try to get some sleep."

Annie guessed the latter would be the harder task.

CHAPTER THIRTY-ONE

"Annie, you must eat," Mrs. Sampson said at breakfast.

"If you don't like the eggs, request something else," Mr. Sampson said. "Toast? Porridge?"

To appease them, Annie ordered some toast. She simply wasn't hungry.

The toast was quickly brought, and Annie nibbled at a corner.

Mrs. Sampson put down her fork. "Really, Annie. What is the matter this morning?"

A list of possibilities streamed through her mind. She landed on one. "Logistics."

"Of the business?"

She nodded. "It's so complicated. Starting from nothing, resigning our positions . . . It's such a gamble."

"That it is," Mr. Sampson said. "But to gain much you must risk much. The Bible tells us that whoever is given much shall be asked to do much." He spread his hands, allowing the words to speak volumes.

"You're right. Forgive my doubt and my jumbled thoughts. What with the close call of us being on the *Titanic* —"

"Such a blessing we weren't," Mrs. Sampson pointed out.

"Such a blessing," Annie agreed.

"The captain said that everyone on the ship was rescued. All is well," Maude said.

Annie was being silly — and ungrateful. "I'm sorry to put a damper on the day. I promise to be all joy and anticipation from now —"

She was interrupted by a shriek coming from the hall.

Mr. Sampson and Sean rose. But before they could check on it, a man burst into the dining room and shouted for all to hear, "The *Titanic* sank! Hundreds are dead! They are compiling a list of the victims!"

Those in the dining room stood, and spatterings of disbelieving, panicked conversation intertwined.

"The *Titanic* was unsinkable. It can't sink."

"Victims! Hundreds?"

"I know people on that ship!"

"The captain said there were no fatalities!"

"Could this happen to us?"

The comments were universal, the questions frightening.

"Madame," Annie said.

"And our friends," Mrs. Sampson said. "Astor, Molly, the Strauses. Guggenheim."

"Mr. and Mrs. Straus?" Annie asked. "From Macy's?"

She nodded. "We ran into them in Nice and they said they were going back on our ship."

"Our ship," Sean said. "That was supposed to be our ship."

Maude put a hand to her mouth. Mrs. Sampson sat down. Annie couldn't move, frozen by the knowledge that their ship had gone down into the dark depths of the endless sea. "Would we have survived?" she asked aloud.

Mr. Sampson held Annie's chair for her to be seated. "Let's not jump to conclusions. The first news from the captain said everything was under control. This one says the opposite. One of them is wrong."

"But which one?" Maude asked.

"Let me see what I can find out. Return to your breakfast."

"Surely you jest, Harold," his wife said.

With a shrug he left them. All thoughts of food were forgotten.

Sean held out his hands. "Let us pray, ladies. Pray."

■ ■ ■ ■

The food was taken away, but the dining room was full. People stood in small groups, comparing fears, astonishment, and disbelief instead of their usual stories of villas, museums, and European soirees. There was a desperate need for facts yet an oppressive dread. Each minute that passed without Mr. Sampson's return added to the burden.

Finally he returned with a group of men who had left to gather news. Everyone stopped talking. All eyes fell on them.

Mr. Sampson stepped forward to speak for the group. His face was ashen, his forehead tight. Annie felt a wave of shivers course through her body.

"Yesterday's information was horribly false. The latest news is that the *Titanic* sank to the bottom of the ocean, and of the 2,358 souls on board over 1,500 people are missing."

There was a gasp, and many fell upon chairs for support. Some began to wail.

Another man stepped forward to add, "There were only enough lifeboats for 970 people, so even if . . ." He stepped back and muttered, "It's a travesty. The passengers were doomed from the start."

Mr. Sampson moved to their table, taking his wife in his arms.

"Our friends, Harold. Are they saved or not?" she asked.

"There are lists coming out, but none available over the wireless. We won't know until we land in New York."

"Poor Madame," Maude said.

"If she's alive," Sean said.

"Sean!" Maude said. "Don't say that."

"How can I not say that?"

Mr. Sampson had other news. "I sent a telegram to my office, asking after your Madame LeFleur, Mrs. Brown, Astor, Guggenheim, and the Strauses."

"Thank you, dear," his wife said. "I'm not sure I want to know the truth, yet not knowing is its own torture."

Annie heard the voices of the room rise and fade like the waves of the ocean around them. Their speculation was futile. There was no praying for the safety of those on board. Their fates were already decided.

As are yours.

She startled at the thought. "We were saved," she said softly.

"What?" Sean asked.

She looked at each one. "We were saved. If we had not missed our train we would be on that ship. We might have been among the missing. The dead."

Sean took her hand. "If you had not heard André's cries. If you had not helped him . . ."

"Helped his mother," Mrs. Sampson said.

"We owe our lives to you, Annie," Maude said.

Annie shook her head vehemently. "Don't place that on me."

"It's a compliment."

"But it doesn't belong to me. God did it. He gave us the opportunity to help the boy."

"But we wouldn't have had to accept it," Mr. Sampson said. "You could have ignored him. We could have felt sorry for him but left him to someone else because we had a train to catch."

"A ship to catch," Maude said.

The what-ifs assailed them. Then Annie remembered something else. "Madame LeFleur told Sean and me to leave the boy's problem to others."

"What if we'd followed her direction?" Sean said.

"What if I hadn't heard him in the first place? After all, it was a busy, noisy train station."

"What if we hadn't understood what he said about his mother?"

"What if we hadn't chosen to hunt for her?"

"What if we'd given up, and boarded that train?"

"What if Madame had gotten off the train with us?"

"What if little Annie hadn't been born right then, delaying us just long enough?"

This last comment stopped the questions. The timing of the events at the train station solidified the sobering conclusion that they had unknowingly been offered a way to be saved. Plus, they reached the equally sobering conclusion that if they hadn't said yes, they might all be dead in the cold, black water of the Atlantic.

The captain entered the dining room with a man wearing a clerical collar. "Reverend Benson would like to lead us in prayer before he visits the other areas of the ship to do the same."

The reverend nodded. "Let us pray."

What more could they do?

The friends moved onto the decks, strolling without seeing, simply needing to walk lest the news sink too deeply into their consciousness if they remained still. Perhaps the fresh air would awaken them from their awful nightmare.

A steward approached Mr. Sampson. "A telegram, sir."

Mrs. Sampson put her hands on her heart. "Oh dear. An answer to your query?"

Her husband rubbed a hand roughly over his mouth then expelled a breath. He opened the envelope, read the news, and then reread it out loud in a voice that quavered with emotion. "Astor, Guggenheim, LeFleur, and Strauses gone. Brown saved."

Annie grabbed the telegram away from him, needing to see the words. Unfortunately, they could not be denied.

Maude gripped Sean's arm. "Madame is dead? It can't be."

Annie's memories rushed back to the times she'd spoken with Mr. Straus during her time at Macy's. "Mr. Straus was the kindest of men. He took an interest in me. He showed compassion when Danny was killed. He can't be dead." She looked at the list. "His wife, too?"

Mrs. Sampson cried against her husband's chest. "A finer couple you could never know," Mr. Sampson said.

Annie couldn't take anymore. She ran away, along the promenade, bumping into people as she passed.

"Annie!" Sean ran after her.

She let him catch up to her and fell into his arms. "Why? Why?"

He stroked her head. "I don't know why they died. There is no sense to it."

She pulled away from him. "Not why did they die, but why did we live? If good people like Madame and Mr. Straus can die, and important people like Mr. Astor and Mr. Guggenheim, then why were we saved? Sean, tell me! Why were we saved when important people — and good people — died?"

He led her inside where it was warm and sat beside her on a settee. He kept his arm wrapped around her, and she leaned against him, feeling as if she would fully falter without his presence.

"I have no answers for you, Annie."

She sat erect to fully see him. "Why did God let this happen? What purpose could it serve?"

Sean didn't answer but shook his head back and forth, back and forth. Finally he said, "Only He knows."

Annie burst from her seat. "Why should we worship God if He causes such tragedy to so many people?"

"I'm not sure He caused it. Perhaps there were choices other people made that caused the accident. Not having enough lifeboats

536

was a choice someone made."

"He created the iceberg."

"But did the ship sail carelessly? There are a myriad of factors and choices that were made." Sean pulled her down beside him again. "Just as we made the choice to help André, so others made their own choices."

"You're making it too simple."

"The truth remains: it simply *is*. What happened to them, happened to them. What happened to us, happened to us. The biggest choice we have now is deciding what we do with our second chance."

Annie looked up and saw Maude and the Sampsons coming toward them. "Are you all right?" Mrs. Sampson asked.

"Silly question, my sweet," Mr. Sampson said. "None of us are all right. Lives were lost."

"And we were supposed to be on that ship," Maude said.

Annie's mind cleared. "Actually, no we weren't. Beyond our grief, *that* is what we must deal with."

Maude sat in a nearby chair. "Annie, do you remember what I said about not knowing the extent of our days?"

"I do remember."

"That is the gist of it, isn't it?" Maude said. "We don't know how long we have."

"We are alive now," Mrs. Sampson added.

Suddenly Annie heard Danny's voice inside her head. *"Make the most of today!"* She closed her eyes and could see him smiling at her with his impish grin. How wise he'd been for one so young. What a joy he'd been. What a gift.

She stood and faced the others. "My friend Danny had more life in him at the age of thirteen than people five times his age. He always told me to live for today. Don't waste a moment. *That* is why we were saved. To live. To grab hold of life and live it to its fullest each and every day."

"A commendable idea," Mrs. Sampson said.

"For what more can we do?" her husband said.

With a sudden clarity Annie knew exactly what could be done — what should be done. All that had happened since her arrival in America gathered together like a crowd of events and people and conversations. The murmurings of the others faded into a dull hum as her mind attended the gathering.

She remembered the Kidds who gave her a job and rescued her from a family where she was told she had no worth. They brought her to the United States — which was the start of everything. Without that trip, none of the rest would have happened. She thought about the lady's maids who'd been inept at sewing. If they hadn't been lacking that talent, Annie would never have been given the opportunity to step up and learn. And their betrayal, though hurtful, had been the impetus needed to move her out of a life as a servant into the streets of New York City. Into the American dream.

With a start she remembered how *her* dream had been to be a lady's maid. How meager that dream seemed now. And how thankful she was that God had closed that door and forced her out into the new and frightening world of New York City.

Without that door closing I would still be a housemaid. How cocky she'd been, thinking she knew best. How ignorant she'd been about life and God.

A wave of gratitude swept over her. *Thank You, Lord, for propelling me into the world and giving me a new dream — Your dream for my life. Thank You for getting my attention and showing me how Your way is the best way.*

She thought of Danny and Iris, her dear friends who'd had dreams of their own. And the kind Tuttles who had taken them in and eventually provided Iris the family and purpose she longed for and so desperately needed.

But what of Danny's dream? Annie thought of Danny's exuberance and love of adventure. His words would stay with her the rest of her life. She would always be thankful for his friendship and wisdom. There was no explaining his life being cut short, but she took comfort in knowing he was fully exploring the adventures of heaven.

Her thoughts clouded with dark memories of the torment, assault, and murder caused by Grasston. Where Danny elicited all things good, Grasston was the epitome of evil. There was satisfaction in his death in that he would not bother anyone ever again. She pushed all thoughts of him into a far corner of her mind. He didn't deserve her time. Yet even his presence had been important, for he had helped her leave her girlhood behind and become a woman.

She returned to the thoughts that stood at the forefront. Sunny memories of Mr. Straus and working at Macy's where she met friends she would have forever: Mrs. MacDonald, Edna, and even Mildred. She smiled when she thought of Edna, whom she loved as a mother. She would have so much to tell her about this trip *and* the business opportunity that was in the future.

Annie had a sudden thought. Surely there was a place for Edna in the new business. . . .

During Annie's time at Macy's she'd learned how to sew and had met Sean, who'd brought her to Butterick where she'd learned about fashion, design, and pattern making. There, she'd met Madame, Maude, and the Sampsons, and had been given the chance to go to Paris to see couture fashion in person. Her. Annie Wood. In Paris!

The details of the drama at the train station shot by in a flash: André, his mother, little Annie . . . And then the news of the *Titanic,* and the realization that they had been saved from death by the cry of a little boy.

"By Me. You were saved by Me, Annie."

Annie bowed her head in gratitude and humility. *You saved us. A thank-You is not enough.* A promise rose in her heart, and she voiced it to the One who deserved everything — her everything. *I give my life to You. Show me what to do.*

"You know what to do. Just do it."

With the blink of an eye, the moments and people that had sped through her thoughts stepped aside — but for one. And with the recognition of that one person, she knew what God wanted her to do.

During her mental discourse, the others had been talking, and she had no idea how long she had been caught in her reverie. But the nudge to "do it" was strong and could not be ignored a moment longer. She came back to the present and interrupted them. "Sean." She stood and held out her hand to him. "Come with me."

Annie led him down a corridor and out to the deck. She found a private place at the railing and faced him. Her heart pumped with a determined vigor. Her mind was clearer than it had been in months. "My darling Sean. We are alive."

"That we are," he said, leaning forward to kiss her.

She pulled back. "Let me finish."

He stood erect.

"We are alive. We are together when many couples on the *Titanic* have been ripped apart. No matter what happens with our careers, we are a pair, you and I." She glanced out over the sea. "What lasts beyond death is love. No matter what tragedy befalls us, love remains." She took his hands in hers. "I love you, Sean."

"I love you, too, Annie-girl. More than I can say."

"God brought us together. And saved us

to be together."

He nodded, and his voice caught in his throat. "I know it with my entire being."

Annie took a deep breath, recognizing this as the pivot point of her life, the point from which she would measure the before and the after. "Ask me."

"Ask you?"

"The question."

His face lit up, as if God's light shone down upon the moment. Then he knelt before her on one knee. "My darling, dear Annie. Would you marry me?"

She kissed him, saying yes to Sean, yes to God, and yes to their future together.

Dear Reader,

Thank you for entering Annie's world! It was a delight to write about her eventful life. Even though she didn't come to New York City to find the American dream, *it* found *her.* We probably all have such stories to tell regarding our ancestors first coming to America.

I have sewn all my life. I didn't have a store-bought dress until I was nearly in college. My mother made all my prom dresses and even the wedding dresses for me and my two sisters. My first job was in a fabric store where I saved up enough money to buy a Pfaff sewing machine. Just this year (after over forty years) it conked out on me! It was like saying good-bye to a friend.

I grew up making garments from multiple patterns and improvising. The true perk of home sewing is being able to create something unique. In many ways, all home seamstresses are pattern artists.

It was fun to incorporate moments of history into Annie's story. I hadn't planned on having her work at Macy's, but when I discovered an old book (1943) called *History of Macy's of New York* by Ralph M. Hower I was hooked. The book painstakingly details the store (including charts of operating data and photos). Discovering that the store she would have worked in on Thirty-Fourth Street was the store that still exists — and is the store in one of my favorite movies, *Miracle on 34th Street,* it was a done deal.

When I discovered that the New York Giants were playing in the World Series in 1911, and that crowds gathered across the street at the *Herald* offices to hear news of the games, it was an added bonus — and games four and five *were* delayed due to rain. I love when history falls at my feet and begs to be used in the story.

I hadn't planned on the *Titanic* being a part of the story, either, but when the dates worked out, and when I discovered that Mr. and Mrs. Straus (he was the owner of Macy's) lost their lives on the ship when she declined to get into a lifeboat, I had to share that bittersweet fact. There are memorials to the love of Isidor and Ida Straus. If you watch the James Cameron movie *Titanic,* they are portrayed as the older couple embracing each other in bed as the ship sinks. I urge you to do an Internet search for them, where you'll find many stories about their amazing love. Brett Gladstone, their great-great-grandson, says, "I have their letters. They spent only ten days apart from each other during their marriage, and then they wrote each other every day." The couple even gets a duet in the musical version of *Titanic* — which leaves the audience weeping. I tear up just thinking of them.

The initial words of the captain of Annie's ship, describing the *Titanic*'s accident, are taken from actual newspaper accounts — that obviously gave false information, and false hope.

The address of the Sampsons (451 Madison Avenue) still exists and is called the Villard House. In 1978 it was altered into Helmsley Palace (remember the notorious Leona Helmsley?).

I also slipped in a reference to some characters from my Manor House series. The love story of Lady Newley (Lila) is shown in *Love of the Summerfields* and *Bride of the Summerfields,* and Henrietta shows up in *Rise of the Summerfields.* I like to intertwine story lines when I can, as it makes the characters seem more real, as if life goes on after the last page. I hope you agree.

So if I didn't plan on Macy's, the World Series, or the *Titanic* being a part of the story, what *was* my story supposed to be about? In a single word: patterns. Ebenezer Butterick changed the world by developing sized patterns. Before his invention, women would have to buy a one-size-does-not-fit-all pattern and try to adapt it. What started out as a home-based business became one of the largest companies in the world. Again, the American dream triumphs! I wouldn't be a home seamstress if not for his invention. Butterick *did* have special pattern shops in Paris, London, Vienna, and Berlin. The Paris shop sold more Butterick patterns than anywhere in the world. There are a few old photos of this shop and the one in London on the Internet and on my Pinterest board for this book.

I stretched for the sake of story in having Annie and her contingent go to the fashion shows in Paris. From what I could determine, usually the fashion representatives from the couture houses came to New York to show their wares, which were then copied. Forgive me for my creative license. It *could* have happened the way I wrote it. It *might* have happened that way.

The Le Grand Hotel in Paris, across from the opera? My husband and I stayed there in the nineties (it's now InterContinental Paris Le Grand Hotel), and the Café de la Paix is still serving fabulous meals. It's interesting how life experiences can sometimes be resurrected and used. Actually, *all* life experiences are fair game to a writer.

I hope you enjoyed *The Pattern Artist.* Please let me hear from you!

Nancy Moser

www.nancymoser.com

553

DISCUSSION QUESTIONS FOR
THE PATTERN ARTIST

1. What do you think about Annie's decision to leave her job as a housemaid? What would have happened if she'd stayed?

2 Grasston becomes a threat to Annie and all who know her. Annie stealing his gloves does not seem to be enough to get him sacked. Why do you think he was sacked?

3. Danny's death in Chapter 12, defending Annie from a bully, is a blow to all who knew him. How does his death change Annie and Iris?

4. Chapter 13: Edna talks to Annie about her newly discovered gift to draw. "A talent uncovered is a talent recovered . . . it's always been there. You just didn't know it was there. It's a known fact that God's

555

gifts can't be returned." What talent have you recovered unexpectedly?

5. Chapter 13: God tries to get Annie's attention, flooding her mind with promises of love and care if only she will choose Him. But she does not. Why do you think Annie hesitates about surrendering to God?

6. Chapter 15: Annie talks about her parents being negative people, bringing everyone around them down. Do you know anyone like that? How do you deal with them?

7. Chapter 15: Sean suggests that Annie doesn't take compliments well, because, "To accept compliments means someone else has seen into your world and has judged it." How is this statement true?

8. Chapter 16: Before Annie calls Butterick to interview for the job she realizes if she *doesn't* call, the answer is automatically a no. She has to risk it. What time in your life did you accept a "no" rather than take a risk? If you could do it over again, would you handle it differently?

9. Chapter 16: Sean tells Annie: "The old

Annie is dead and a new Annie has risen in her place." Name a time in your life when you closed the door on the past and started fresh. Did the new life live up to your expectations? If you haven't done this yet, should you?

10. Chapter 17: Annie took a leap of faith in staying in NYC and not catching the ship back to England with the Kidds. Hebrews 11: 1 says that "faith is confidence in what we hope for and assurance about what we do not see." What leap of faith have you taken, a no-turning-back leap?

11. Should Annie have borrowed the dress? Do you think she got the punishment she deserved?

12. At her dinner party in Chapter 19, Mrs. Sampson tells Annie, "Just be who you are, Annie. Who you are is enough." Is that good advice, or bad? Explain.

13. In Chapter 20, Edna and Annie are stronger from forming a three-strand cord with God. Who in your life creates your cord of strength?

14. Chapter 24: On the Brooklyn Bridge Annie and Sean talk about their dreams. Sean explains his this way: "I dream of knowing I made a difference. I dream of knowing there is a definite reason I was born, a reason I exist now — not a hundred years from now. I dream of knowing that a portion of God's greater plan gets fulfilled through me." Do you have an inkling about why you were born — your purpose? Have you asked God to show you His purpose for you?

15. Chapter 24: Sean's mother encourages Annie to go after her dreams and her career goals. As we know, opportunities for women were lacking in 1911. What woman do you know who gave up their dreams or a career for the sake of getting married? What would you have done in a similar situation? Was it worth the sacrifice?

16. Chapter 25: Maude and Annie discuss their talents and how best to use them. Maude says, "Use your talent discreetly when necessary and boldly when possible." Share examples of people who have

done this — and those who have not. How did others react?

17. Chapter 29: Annie and her friends are saved from harm because God gave them a choice. They were not forced to help the little boy at the train station, but because of their kindness, they missed the horrors of the Titanic. Have you ever had such a "save" in your life? Share the details.

18. Chapter 30: Given the choice to take the job offer from the Sampsons, Annie realizes that her life has been full of doors — but more than that: "It's not just a matter of the doors being opened for me, but the fact that every door that opened seemed to shut once I was through it." What doors have you gone through, where the door was shut behind you?

19. Even though Annie didn't come to America to find the American Dream, *it* found *her*. Discuss some of your ancestors who immigrated here. Why did they leave their homes? Did they discover the American Dream?

20. Chapter 32: Annie realized that her old dream was to be a lady's maid. If the door

to that dream hadn't been closed, she never would have been propelled into New York City to find a better dream. Name a dream from your past that was exchanged for a larger, better dream.

ABOUT THE AUTHOR

Nancy Moser is an award-winning author of more than twenty-five novels that share a common message: we each have a unique purpose — the trick is to find out what it is. Her genres include contemporary and historical novels including *Love of the Summerfields, Mozart's Sister, The Invitation,* and the Christy Award–winning *Time Lottery.* She is a fan of anything antique — humans included. www.nancymoser.com.

The employees of Thorndike Press hope you have enjoyed this Large Print book. All our Thorndike, Wheeler, and Kennebec Large Print titles are designed for easy reading, and all our books are made to last. Other Thorndike Press Large Print books are available at your library, through selected bookstores, or directly from us.

For information about titles, please call:
  (800) 223-1244

or visit our Web site at:
  http://gale.cengage.com/thorndike

To share your comments, please write:
  Publisher
  Thorndike Press
  10 Water St., Suite 310
  Waterville, ME 04901